BUILDING DECKS, PATIOS & FENCES

BUILDING DECKS, PATIOS & FENCES

By Richard Day

Drawings by
Eugene Marino III

Published by
MEREDITH ® PRESS
New York

To the late Edward D. Dionne

Because of differing conditions, tools, and individual wood-working skills, Meredith® Press and the author assume no responsibility for any injuries suffered, damages or losses incurred during, or as a result of, the construction of projects in this book.

Before starting any project, study the plans carefully, read and observe all the safety precautions provided by any tool or equipment manufacturer, and follow all accepted safety procedures during construction.

Published by Meredith® Press
150 East 52nd Street
New York, NY 10022

For Meredith® Press
  Vice-President, Editorial Director: Elizabeth P. Rice
  Editorial Project Managers: Maryanne Bannon, Barbara Machtiger
  Proofreader: Guido Anderau
  Production Manager: Bill Rose

Produced by Soderstrom Publishing Group Inc.
  Book designer: Jeff Fitschen
  Compositor: Dix Type Inc.

ISBN: 0–696–11012–1
Library of Congress Card Number: 91-066935

10 9 8 7 6 5 4 3 2 1

CONTENTS

Preface   vi

1. **PLANNING YOUR DECK OR PATIO**   3

2. **BASIC CARPENTRY**   20

3. **CARPENTRY TOOLS**   71

4. **BUILDING A DECK**   107

5. **CONCRETE CONSTRUCTION TOOLS**   132

6. **DOING CONCRETE WORK**   147

7. **MAKING CONCRETE LOOK GREAT**   194

8. **BUILDING A PATIO**   226

9. **USING PAVERS**   238

10. **BUILDING DECK AND PATIO COVERS**   260

11. **FENCE DESIGN AND CONSTRUCTION**   272

    INDEX   292

PREFACE

This book presents design and construction concepts that will help you improve the utility and appearance of your home's outdoor areas. Here, you'll also learn how to do the work yourself.

Just about all outdoor home improvements are what I call "self-supporting." That is, they add about as much to the value of your house as they cost you. This is especially true of decks, patios, and fences. When purchasing materials, it's reassuring to know that the money spent is an investment rather than just an expense.

No matter how beneficial, no home improvement is worth an injury. An axiom of working safely is that if an accident *can* happen, it will. Though accidents can happen to anyone, you can take steps to prevent them. By wearing the proper safety gear, taking proper precautions, and working carefully, you can avoid the mishaps that plague the less careful. Safety should be your first concern.

Many after-project accidents, such as a slip on a too-smoothly finished concrete surface or the collapse of a deck, are prevented by proper design and construction. To help ensure that you are building safely, apply for a building permit and request each of the recommended inspections as the project progresses. Your local building inspector can bring his or her knowledge and experience to bear and alert you to any unsafe feature while it can still be corrected economically—and before anyone is injured.

If you are ever in doubt about how to do a task correctly, get qualified advice. Or else give the job to a professional.

Surveying your finished project is very satisfying. You can take pride in being the one who made it happen. This may be the best reason for doing a project yourself. It's a great feeling.

Acknowledgments

I wish to thank the following people and organizations for their generous help with this book.

Thanks above all to Charles R. Self, for his careful research and for his deck-building prowess, demonstrated in Chapter 4.

Up-front thanks to Neil Soderstrom, who oversaw every detail and then produced this book. Thanks also to Jeff Fitschen, the book's designer; Gene Marino, the illustrator; and Sandy Towers, who took my raw copy and made it more meaningful and useful.

Another person who made this book possible is John W. Sill. John conceived the idea way back, but retired from active participation before we could bring the book together.

Over the years, engineer William C. Panarese of the Portland Cement Association has provided much authoritative assistance on technical matters having to do with concrete. I've incorporated a great deal of Bill's expert advice.

Still others who helped make this book are: Ann M. Nostin, American Optical Corporation; Maryann Olson, American Plywood Association; Roger S. Smith, American Rental Association; Robert Drake, American Tool Company; Arthur C. Avril; Irwin Barr; Millard Beemer; Bomanite Corporation; Peter Cieslak, Brick Association of North Carolina; Charles N. Farley, Brick

Institute of America; Phyllis Bryan; Building Stone Institute; Pamela Allsebrook, Charlene Draheim, and Charles Jourdain, California Redwood Association; Andrew Stroud and M. J. Searle, Cement and Concrete Association; Jack and Tom Cofran; Cooper Tools; Sharon McNaughton, Council of Forest Industries of British Columbia; Ernie Cowan; Doug, Leanna, and Erica Day; Russ Day; Stuart W. Day; Dick Demske; Edward D. Dionne; John Dolstra; and Bruce Druliner.

David Easton, Earth Resources Technology; Frank Ramirez, Epmar Corporation; Lauren Dollmann, General Electric Company; Janet Folk, Georgia-Pacific Corporation; Tod and Norma Herring; Hickson Corp.; Aki Nozaki, Hitachi Power Tools U.S.A.; Bob Hunt; and Michael Isser and Thomas Crane, Isser & Associates.

Gail and Chris Kania; Charles Kearns; Larry Van Laar; Al Lees; Bill Rooney, Louisiana-Pacific Corporation; Tom and Sheila Miller; Debra Sajkowski, Milwaukee Electric Tool Corporation; Mine Safety Appliances Company; Leona M. Richards, Northwestern Steel and Wire Company; Jay C. Greenberg, Occupational Safety and Health Administration, U.S. Department of Labor; and Ted Schoeneman, Osmose Wood Preserving Division.

Janice N. Lee, Phifer Wire Products; Bob Hill, Photo Darkroom; Richard G. Schmidt, Porter-Cable Corporation; Walter C. Oram, Ralph Spears, and Bruce McIntosh, Portland Cement Association; Jack Rechnitzer; Dale Strnad, Rexnord Chemical Products; Carl Roth; Sakrete; Mark Weigel, Sandvik Saws & Tools Company; Leo Floros of Selz, Seabolt & Associates; Jim Sexton; Bill Abell, Simpson Strong-Tie Company; Sil Argentin, Skil Corporation; Stanley Tools; Don Allemand, Swanson Tool Company; David R. Norcross, TECO; United Gilsonite Laboratories; Ray Moholt, Western Wood Products Association; Willson Safety Products; Tom Wilson; James M. Moran, Wolmanized Wood; and Jerry Woods.

Useful Addresses

To locate hard-to-find tools, materials, and information, try contacting the following sources:

Brick publications, information. Brick Association of North Carolina, P.O. Box 6305, Greensboro, NC 27405; Brick Institute of America, 11490 Commerce Park Dr., Reston, VA 22091.

Brick forms. Argee Corp., 9550 Pathway St., Santee, CA 92071.

Concrete chemicals. The Burke Co., P.O. Box 5818, San Mateo, CA 94403; Empire Level Manufacturing Co., 2101 Broadway, Kansas City, MO 64108. Euclid Chemical Co., 19218 Redwood Rd., Cleveland, OH 44110; The Gibson-Homans Co., 1755 Enterprise Pkwy., Twinsburg, OH 44087; Construction Products Div., W. R. Grace and Co., 62 Whittemore Ave., Cambridge, MA 02140; Dewey and Almy Chemical Div., W. R. Grace and Co., 1114 Avenue of the Americas, New York, NY 10036; Hillyard Chemical Co., 302 North Fourth St., St. Joseph, MO 64501; Master Builders, 23700 Chagrin Blvd., Cleveland, OH 44122; W. R. Meadows, Inc., P.O. Box 543, Elgin, IL 60121; Preco, 55 Skyline Dr., Plainview, NY 11830; Sika Chemical Co., 201 Polito Ave., Lyndhurst, NJ 07071; Thompson's Water Seal, 825 Crossover La., Memphis, TN 38117; Thoro System Products Inc., 7800 N.W. 38th St., Miami, FL 33166; United Gilsonite Laboratories, P.O. Box 70, Scranton, PA 18501.

Concrete publications. Order Processing Department, Portland Cement Assn., 5420 Old Orchard Rd., Skokie, IL 60076.

Concrete tools, forms, accessories. Goldblatt Tool Co., 511 Osage, Kansas City, KS 66110; Marshalltown Trowel Co., P.O. Box 738, Marshalltown, IA 50158; (plastic and metal forms) R. L. Spillman Co., P.O. Box 07847, Columbus, OH 43207.

Deck adhesives. Rexford Chemical Products Inc., 7711 Computer Ave., Minneapolis, MN 55435–5494.

Personal protective gear. American Optical Corp., 14 Mechanic St., Southbridge, MA 01550; Direct Safety Co., 7815 South 46th St., Phoenix, AZ 85040; Mine Safety Appliances Co., 600 Penn Center Blvd., Pittsburgh, PA 15235; Willson Safety Products, Box 622, Reading, PA 19603.

Plywood publications. American Plywood Assn., P.O. Box 11700, Tacoma, WA 98411–0700.

Redwood publications. California Redwood Assn., 405 Enfrente Dr., Suite 200, Novato, CA 94949.

Western woods publications. Western Wood Products Assn., 1500 Yeon Bldg., Portland, OR 97204.

Separated from the ground only by inches, this low redwood platform deck is almost a patio. A slightly raised level at right serves a house door. (Jerry Fenby deck; California Redwood Association photo)

A side-yard patio with leave-in forms and pool is screened from the street by a masonry screen-block wall. Wood boards atop low brick walls provide seating. (Sakrete photo)

CHAPTER **1**

PLANNING YOUR DECK OR PATIO

Decks and patios provide outdoor living space for family activities—space open to gentle breezes, the sun, and the stars. A deck, in its simplest form, is a wooden platform on or above the ground. On the other hand, a patio is a hard-surfaced, on-ground living space. Both are usually attached to the house, but they need not be.

Decks and patios are highly suitable projects for do-it-yourselfers, and building your own is an eco-nomical option to contracting out. While improving the livability of your home, a well-designed and prop-erly constructed deck or patio also increases your home's value.

Planning a patio is similar in some ways to plan-ning a deck but has a few special aspects, particularly those involving grading. Decks are sometimes de-scribed as raised wooden patios, a generally valid de-scription that begs a few points, especially of

A large deck off a recreation room and kitchen features a firepit for outdoor cooking. (Photographer, Ed Dull; Western Wood Products Association photo)

Much planning went into this multilevel patio built around the swimming pool and between pool and home. Soft-set precast concrete rectangular pavers create levels and steps between. (Photographer, Trevor Jones; Cement and Concrete Association photo)

Smaller projects such as this deck can be made more interesting with patterned planking. Landscaping helps to provide privacy. (Photographer, George Lyons; designer, Bob Long; California Redwood Association photo)

materials, ground slope, and overall intent. For example, decks can be planned to suit widely varied terrain features, but you would normally plan a patio only for a ground surface that is fairly level with a house entrance or that slopes only gently away from it.

As with a house, the larger the deck or patio, the more features it can have. Patios tend to be larger than decks. Yet small patios can provide great enjoyment. And, like the familiar big wraparound deck, a big patio may wrap right around the house.

PRELIMINARY PLANNING

Look at your life-style in some detail. How much of the day would you enjoy spending outdoors when weather and schedules permitted? Do you simply want a place where you can cook a meal outdoors? Will you also be entertaining there? Will the children be using the deck or patio for parties? Or will it be just for general outdoor family relaxation, with occasional meals and snacks, some reading, and resting?

Much depends on how you expect to use the space. Yet keep in mind that changes in life-style may take place after the project is constructed. If you build a project that is too large for your needs, you're wasting money. But if you build one that is too small, you won't get the satisfaction you'd hoped for.

Decks and patios range from 8 feet square on up, with structural sophistication increasing with size and design complexity. A large deck or patio should probably have varied levels to keep it from becoming monotonous. To be honest, I think that any deck smaller than 10 × 12 feet should be called a stoop. Generally, decks should be larger than a house's average room size, and preferably no smaller than the largest room in the house. One rule of thumb advises that a deck or patio be one third the size of the house. Accordingly, a 1,500-square-foot house could use some 500 square feet of outdoor living space, say, a deck or patio 20 × 25 feet. Again, size must vary, depending on need and desire—and finances.

Deck size should be a function of anticipated uses. A large deck of pressure-treated lumber allows numerous areas for simultaneous use. (Wolmanized Wood Company, Inc. photo)

These three photos show that a simple wooden deck with plants can dramatically improve the appearance and utility of an outdoor living area. The bare house walls in the photo, above left, cry out for colorful plants. (California Redwood Association photo)

An outdoor living area that doesn't receive heavy traffic can be left unpaved. Here a border of concrete receives most of the traffic, helping spare the grassy patio. (Sakrete photo)

A general-purpose deck or patio for relaxing and entertaining should not give a cramped feeling. Probably the most basic benefit of outdoor living space is simply the feeling one gets from space. A too-small patio or deck reduces this benefit. When in doubt, you are wiser to build too large than too small. Your family is more likely to expand its activities to fit a large deck or patio than to contract them to fit a small one. A desire for distinct private areas can be satisfied by seating arrangements, screening, the use of split levels, and other devices.

While many people assume that a basic concrete-paved patio is cheaper than a deck of similar size, the cost difference will be relatively small if the patio is built properly. As size increases, the complexity of grading and extra drainage may even make patio construction more costly. For reasons of economy, then, patios are usually built on relatively level ground.

Styling Outdoor Living Space

The first step is to create the deck's or patio's basic overall shape. Start boldly, considering all the designs you have seen or dreamed of. At this point, you don't have to think of deck planking patterns or concrete textures, just the overall shape. Do you want a big square or rectangle? Maybe you'd prefer a hexagon or an octagon. Don't start by considering the disadvantages of the less-usual shapes. Think instead of how those shapes could harmonize with your home and yard, and your life-style.

Freestanding Vs. Attached Styles

Consider, too, whether you might like a freestanding deck or patio instead of one attached to the house. Each has advantages and disadvantages. The attached deck is generally easier to construct, because it re-

These photos show the value of varied geometric shapes. Such designs are especially good for steeply sloped and broken-up lots. The shapes may echo themes from the house itself. Wood-slat benches made of redwood 2 × 6s add focus and a sense of unity. (Photographer, Ernest Braun; designer, James Babcock; owner, Dr. James Greer; California Redwood Association photo)

quires fewer new supports from the ground up and no railing on the fourth side. Yet a freestanding deck or patio may offer more placement choices. Deck or patio accesses approaches—will differ, of course. Freestanding decks and patios may be level with the ground (as attached ones may be), in which case they can be approached by a walk constructed of the same material as the project. Or a freestanding deck may be elevated, with its approach over a walkway and staircase in the same style as the deck. Freestanding decks and patios can easily be placed so that house noises will not disturb people using them, and—probably more important—so that noises from the deck or patio do not disturb people in the house. The same placement principles can govern nighttime activities in either spot.

Whether freestanding or attached, your deck may be elevated close to ground level or elevated a great deal if the house has two stories and the deck is to be accessible from second-floor rooms. The deck or patio may also be set on a knoll near the house, with steps rising from the house to the deck. Terrain will dictate some of these decisions. And a patio may be combined with a deck for the best of both.

Patio materials are heavy and are not always as easy to move as those used for decks. Therefore, trucks delivering and unloading material should be able to approach close to the patio site. Bricks and other paving materials—*pavers*—are relatively easy to shift around in the bed of a pickup or in a wheelbarrow. But sand and gravel are not. Appreciable amounts of sand and gravel are usually lost in the moving. It's best to site these materials close to the project area and leave them there until needed. To avoid later problems, make sure heavy trucks don't roll across a septic seepage field or similarly sensitive area. You will need room for trucks to get in and out without tree or power line removal.

Now that you've been bold and imagined your six-level octagonal deck and patio combination some 100 yards from the house, start scaling back to what's practical. What can you build with available time and money? Now is the time to start thinking of the negatives of a huge deck or patio.

Tax Effects

Consider the immediate cost as well as how the project will affect your real-estate tax bill following a reassessment. That may sound like a minor concern, but

Left photo: Soft-set pavers of precast concrete grace the front of this English country home (Cement and Concrete Association photo). Right photo: Deck placement, a deck cover, and plantings provide privacy. The walkway is parquet-patterned pressure-treated wood, giving the deck the aura of a retreat (Wolmanized Wood Company, Inc. photo).

SITING FOR KITCHEN ACCESS

give it some thought. Even a small project adds to a house's value, and your tax assessor will know as soon as you apply for the building permit that your house's value is about to jump. Project done, the tax assessor will arrive to reassess your property. Your taxes are virtually guaranteed to rise. If possible, check with neighbors to see what their outdoor projects did to their tax bills. Or come right out and ask your tax assessor what to expect. Real-estate assessment prac-

tices vary widely around the United States and Canada, but a rough rule of thumb is that annual taxes equal 1 percent of assessed value. Where this is the case, a $3,500 deck or patio project would add $35 to your yearly real-estate taxes. This is a recurring cost. So do at least a little checking to find out how much the increase might be.

Remember, too, that in building a deck or patio yourself, you are saving a great deal of the money a contractor would charge—at least 50 percent and often 70 percent. So the cost of the materials and tools alone doesn't accurately reflect the value of the project. According to building-industry surveys, a deck or patio will return some 70 to 80 percent of its cost, if contracted out, when a house is sold. (This depends partly on climate: less return can be expected in a cold climate because outdoor space isn't used as much per year.) So if you build your deck or patio yourself and then sell your home, you should easily retrieve the cost of all materials and then some.

Locating a Project

Once your basic deck or patio size and pattern begins to take shape, focus again on location. Consider not only the size and shape of your house but also the size and shape of your lot, the size and shape of the project, and your needs, desires, and abilities. Also, there may be some limitations presented by local building codes, such as access and setback from property lines and streets.

Cost plays a part, too. How much do you want to pay for the whole project? You may wish to build a

This small patio for relaxing and sunbathing has ample privacy screening. The oval shape was formed with plywood. (Portland Cement Association photo)

large, single deck or patio with one or more levels. Or you may opt for two projects, or even more. As an example, a reasonably large deck or patio could serve for family activities and entertaining, while a small, well-fenced one might instead be placed off the master bedroom for private sunbathing and for reading and relaxing.

Patio costs increase if grading is needed to keep runoff rainwater from hitting the house foundation. These days, hiring for bulldozer work is far from cheap.

For most of us, proximity to the kitchen is important. The redwood deck project shown in Chapter 4 changed the owner's kitchen-remodeling plans. For now, access is from the rear of the dining room, but eventually the deck will determine a whole new dining room-and-kitchen floor plan.

The design of many houses strongly suggests the location of the outdoor living area. Some houses actually dictate the location, especially smaller houses. An L-shaped ranch house almost begs for a deck or patio in the angle formed by the L, unless it would too greatly invade bedroom or bathroom privacy. (On the other hand, a deck or patio designed for privacy off the bedroom or bathroom can expand the room delightfully.) A two-story house might make a multi-level deck seem attractive, while ruling out some other styles. The same is true for a split-level home.

Lot topography often dictates deck or patio options. A deck has one design advantage over a patio: it need not be on the ground. The deck shown being built in Chapter 4 is a case in point. The house has little space for a deck, and no grading that would permit a patio. Every living section of the house is at least a foot above grade. A front patio would therefore require a small retaining wall, adding much expense.

The back of the house extends from 7 feet above ground level down to 2 feet above, making a deck, not a patio, the logical addition.

Personal privacy has to be factored in. I don't know why, but visitors seem to have less of a sense of invading your privacy when they are standing on a ground-level patio than when standing on a raised deck.

At the same time, the lay of the ground may not favor a deck, and you may prefer to have a bedroom patio. Cures for the lack of privacy include privacy fencing and decorative fencing that is designed to pro-

Where a patio drains a large expanse, it must slope toward a good drainoff location, such as the hole in this low wall near the curbing.

HEIGHT AND TERRAIN FACTORS

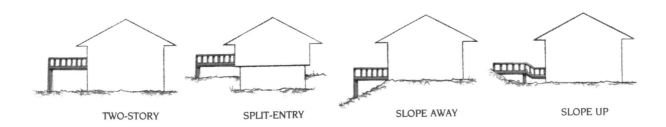

TWO-STORY   SPLIT-ENTRY   SLOPE AWAY   SLOPE UP

vide some privacy when pajama-clad wanderings reach the outdoors.

If you have an irregularly shaped lot, or lack a view, items that add visual interest may be desirable on and around the deck or patio. Whether you will be installing them immediately after the project is built or at a later date, it's a good idea to consider covers and screens. (These are discussed later in this book.) Also consider any screened fencing you might like. The two designs—for covers and fencing—should complement each other.

While considering views and screening, look around you. If your deck is to be elevated, use a steady stepladder to check out the view from the approximate deck height at different areas. At this point, you may become convinced that some kind of screen or barrier fencing is needed. A dead-on view of a local trash dump or your neighbor's garbage won't contribute to your enjoyment of your project. Patios, because they are not ordinarily elevated, are less likely to surprise you with a view problem.

When siting your outdoor-living project, you will be looking for the best possible view; the least possible traffic noise; protection from wind but access to light breezes; some shade for hot days, but some sun for warm and cool days; convenience to the house (especially the kitchen or dining room); and enough privacy for relaxation. Consider, too, that you are not limited to a deck or patio that's attached to the house, so positioning it right off the kitchen or dining room is not an absolute essential. It is best, of course, if proximity to one or both of those areas is still reasonable, because a lot of entertaining is done on decks and patios, and entertaining involves food and drink.

Regulations on Location

Like it or not, the local building code influences where your deck or patio project goes. Be sure to check with the local building department early on.

One ubiquitous code concern is setback. *Setback* is a zoning term that refers to a structure's proximity to a property line. Side setbacks tend to be more forgiving than front and rear setbacks. For example, a typical required setback might be 10 feet to the sides and 25 feet in front and back. Zoning as well as building codes determine setback, and you must investigate both before planning a project. Structures that do not meet building codes can be condemned. They will then have to be razed, moved, or drastically changed —all expensive options. It is far better to abide by the codes from the start, however irritating they may be. Remember that the code prevents your neighbors

from doing things that you might not like. So it protects you, as well.

Besides setback, building codes are concerned with what materials you use, how deep structural footings reach, and more. Building codes are regulations that enjoy the force of law. Anyone who violates them is sure to feel that force applied through the police powers of local government.

PRELIMINARY PLANS

If at all possible, take out pencil and paper and sketch a site plan. This need not be pretty or terribly accurate, but the plan should include essential features. Try to

A SITE PLAN

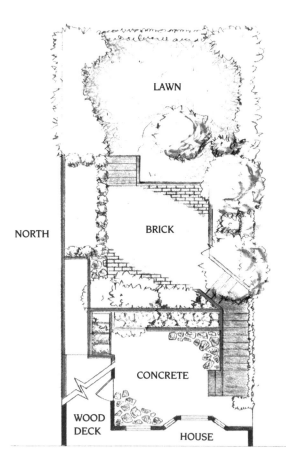

sketch in all traffic areas—public and private—such as roads, driveways, and walks. Also include trees and bushes, gardens, the house (of course), and other features that are important to you

In the process of drawing a site plan, you may wish to consider future outdoor improvements, perhaps some years down the road, and include those. Putting them on paper allows you to organize an overall, comprehensive plan for your home's outdoor living space. Consider fences, trellises, arbors, possible deck or patio additions, tree plantings, and other permanent outdoor structures such as gazebos, storage sheds, barns, and so on. If these are in your future, at least sketch representations of them on your site plan.

Immediate budgetary constraints force most of us to build our home projects in an incremental, step-by-step manner. (Some call this "muddling through.") But having an overall plan makes it easier to keep all the designs harmonious. It also helps in budgeting. Remove as much vagueness as possible from designs in the early stages.

It is impossible, here, to present a standard plan for an outdoor room. The options are far too many. Look at your neighbors' decks and patios, and at a number of deck plans—even plans supplied by lumber and building-materials dealers—and consider their features. Match them to your needs, desires, budget. Go over as many details of design as possible, as often as possible. Keep the family involved. Take sug-

gestions. Make suggestions. Change your mind. Let others change their minds.

Packaged Deck Plans

It's a good idea to look at the plans and packages supplied by dealers. Buying one might also be a good idea, but. . . . A number of considerations arise with deck packages. For example, such packages may include only the actual decking and the material for joists and beams. If the plan is for a multilevel project, the package may include material for stairs between levels—or it may not. In any case, you will have to figure on materials for supporting posts, post setting, rails, stairs to the ground, and any other necessary site-accommodating features. Thus—and this is the point—don't be fooled into assuming that the package price is the total price for the deck. The package price is likely a long way from it: quite probably not much more than half of the eventual overall deck cost.

Hiring for Plans

Good planning can prevent many mistakes, while lowering costs and even increasing the fun of building for yourself. And planning can be fun. But some do-it-yourselfers have difficulty transferring even their simplest conceptions into pencil sketches before putting them onto grid paper. Even if some people could cre-

A deck can also serve as a home entry. Here pressure-treated wood fences prevent anyone from falling over the edge. (Wolmanized Wood Company, Inc. photo)

ate building plans for a simple deck or patio, they may instead want something quite elaborate, with multiple levels and a professional designer's touch.

If lack of time or drafting experience gives you pause, consider hiring a moonlight drafter or a full-time professional building designer who draws plans for house contractors. Professional drafters are familiar with local codes and plan requirements, and usually charge far less than architects. If your concept is a relatively simple one, such a moonlighter may need to visit with you only once to discuss your concept, perhaps offer some suggestions, and then take some measurements. Try to anticipate the kinds of questions about the location of the project that I raise in the next section "Drawing Your Own Plans." Then, perhaps in less than an evening's work, the drafter may be able to draw a set of plans that local code officials will approve. (Of course, elaborate projects require more time, and those people who can afford more may benefit from the ideas of an architect.)

As in shopping for any service, ask around for names of good building designers or drafters and request a few references before commissioning the drawings. Many such professionals will quote a fee in writing that you need not pay until plans are approved by local building officials.

Drawing Your Own Plans

If you feel competent at basic sketching and the transferring of sketch concepts onto graph paper, you may enjoy drawing your own plans (and saving the cost of hiring a pro).

Before you attempt plans in much detail, visit your local building department to discuss your concept with the official who will be reviewing your final plans. The official may be able to give you printed guidelines and may be willing to provide copies of plans for projects similar to yours that received approval. The official may even rough out the kinds of views and materials data you'll need to show, as well as indicate special local concerns such as the frost line depths and recommended means of addressing them. After such a meeting, you'll have a better idea of whether or not you'll be able to draw your own plans.

Be forewarned: on elaborate decks and patios, even professionals may wind up making several trips to the code officials with revisions before obtaining approval.

If code officials seem rigid in their basic requirements and later nit-picky with your plans, they may just be trying to help you avoid an unsafe or otherwise impractical structure. That said, here are basics.

Scale. Once your sketched plan is ready to be redrawn on graph paper, decide on the scale in advance. Sticking to exact scale is important for construction detail, but less important for such items as trees and so on. For a plot plan, I suggest that you forget the usual ¼-inch-per-foot scale used by architects and building designers. The paper sizes can get unwieldy. Using ⅛-inch-per-foot scale (⅛ inch = 1 foot), a 100 × 80-foot plot plan will fit on a single sheet of large graph paper (about 10 × 13 inches). If your lot is larger, use a couple of sheets taped together from underneath, or make the drawing only of the parts of prime interest—the house, the project, and the immediately surrounding area.

Layout Tools. You will need: sharp pencils; an architect's plastic triangle (if you get only one, get a 30-60-90); and an architect's scale, a rule with a triangular cross-section with scales down to ³⁄₃₂ inch, saving you a lot of mathematics. It has a ⅛-inch = 1-foot scale on it. Your graph paper will probably have ¼-inch squares, but that is easily handled. Make each ¼-inch square stand for a 2 × 2-foot piece on your plan. Tracing paper may also prove handy for drawing possible variations.

Plotting on Graph Paper. You first need to show property lines and corners. Draw in the borders of your lot, using heavy lines that will show up clearly through tracing paper. Indicate compass directions on your graph-paper plot. Next, draw in the location and dimensions of your house, further indicating locations and dimensions of doors and windows. Pay particular attention to those on the side of the house on which the project is planned. While code officials won't require that you show the floor plan of the house, it's a good idea to show the rooms along the adjacent wall if the project will be attached to the house.

At this point, moving or changing the project is a simple matter of erasing a few lines and redrawing them. You'll want to know, for example, if the project will reach under a bathroom window—seldom a good idea. Again, the kitchen should be within a reasonable distance.

Show the outlines of any permanent features already existing—garage, storage shed, barn, gazebo, and so on. Indicate the location of a swimming pool or spa. Sketch in driveways, access walks, overhead or underground power and telephone lines, any other cables, fuel-oil tanks, sewer and water connections, septic system parts, water well, and so on. In some cases, you may have to guess at locations of underground utilities from the position of meters or terminals around the house. If the project will directly involve these locations, remember that adjustments, such as moving meter heads, could be costly. If you'll need to disturb the ground around an underground telephone cable, check with your telephone company for the exact location and depth of the incoming line. That is, unless you think you might enjoy being without phone service for a time.

Mark off any easements for power or water. Such easements are specified in your house deed and title policy.

Draw in trees, shrubbery, and garden areas as well. Include fences, whether along property borders or within your plot. Some of these may need to be transplanted or moved, but show them to help decide what to keep, what to build around, and what to remove. Stanley Tools offers planning kits to help you design decks and integrate deck design and landscaping.

Finally, show any locations for outdoor electrical outlets, water taps, and sprinklers for an underground system.

By the time you've noted all this on your plan, the plan may be cluttered, even messy. It will nevertheless be of great use during final planning and construction.

A number of building material and home-center dealers have computer-aided design experts who can custom-design a deck for you. This service allows you to view the deck as a three-dimensional structure, complete with furniture and so on. Meanwhile, several computer software programmers are developing deck-design programs for home computers.

Look over the plan, and immediately eliminate impossibilities and irrationalities, such as building beneath power lines, on easements, and into other permanent obstructions. It is usually smarter to build around a large tree than to uproot it or cut it down. The tree will continue to provide shade if built around. And it may enhance your property value as much as the deck or patio itself.

Now, out with the tracing paper. Use it to make overlays of the proposed design, lightly sketching in the project and its details (stairs and so on) in the area of your first choice. Adjustments at this point are a matter of changing the tracing paper and starting again, or erasing, gently, the lightly sketched lines and moving things around. As problems and obstructions crop up, trace around them.

Making changes at the planning stage can cause writer's cramp and irritation. But you'll find it far cheaper in time, energy, and money to make changes on paper than after you start digging and constructing.

Once you are satisfied with the appearance and location of your lightly drawn project, use the plastic triangle and architect's scale to draw in the lines on the tracing paper more heavily. A compass will draw

Project Planner kits by Stanley Tools provide deck and landscape designs. Using peel-and-stick ⅛-inch-scale cutouts makes planning and scaling far easier than trying to draw plans.

regular curves. Be sure to make a note of the radius as you lay out a curved area. Later you can scale this radius up and transfer it directly to the actual work site. For any irregularly curved areas, a French curve (with multiple curved shapes) will work well.

"Walking" the Project

At this point, you need to transfer dimensions from the tracing paper plan to the building site. Absolute accuracy isn't essential. Still, you want to get a feel for the space and a feel for the probable look of the project.

Use a stringline and 1 × 2 or 2 × 2 stakes to outline the project on the ground, right where it will go. If you want to avoid the bother of driving stakes and running out string, just use flour to outline the area. Lay out the square corners with a carpenter's framing square, and measure off the distances with a tape measure. A 50-foot tape measure is excellent for this. Start from one corner near the house and use the framing square to keep on line. This will give you sufficient accuracy for this preliminary check.

Once you've completed the outline, walk around in it, checking the feel of the area. As before, for view checks for a raised deck, place a stepladder at different spots.

Second thoughts: Is the project roomy enough? Is it close enough to kitchen and dining area? Will it create any noticeable traffic problems? That is, will it interfere with traffic to and from a swimming pool, a garden, or another area of the yard and house? Will small children or thoughtless adults be tracking over

WORKING PLANS FOR A DECK

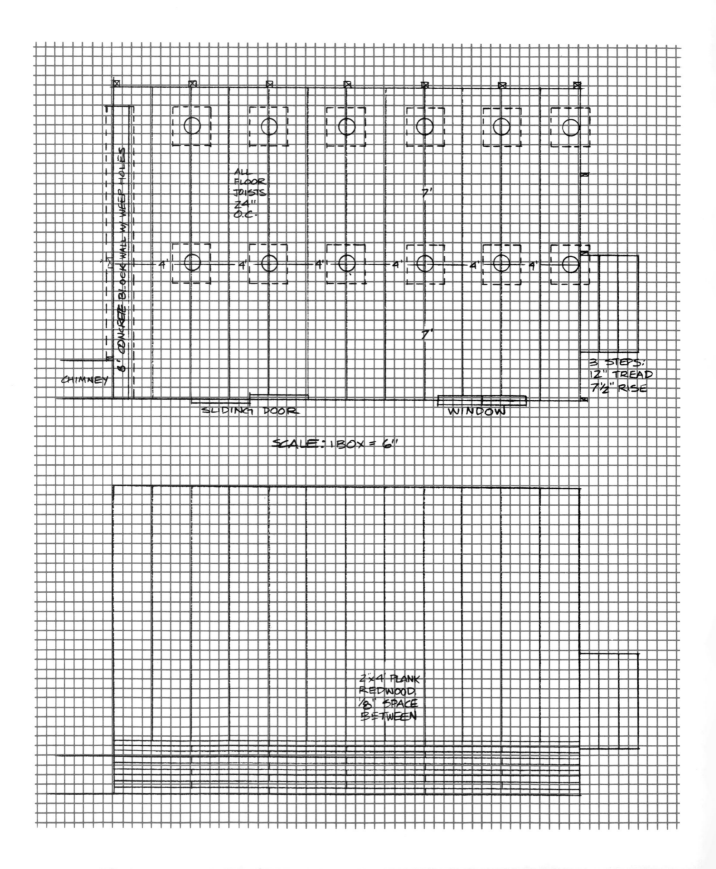

Drawn to ½-inch = 1-foot scale on graph paper by the owners, Tod and
Norma Herring, the plan's grid represents 6 inch squares. The plans were
approved by the Herrings' local building officials in New Jersey. Plans for
a second deck access stairway were scrapped, while the main one was
widened to 6 feet. A photo of this deck appears on page 108.

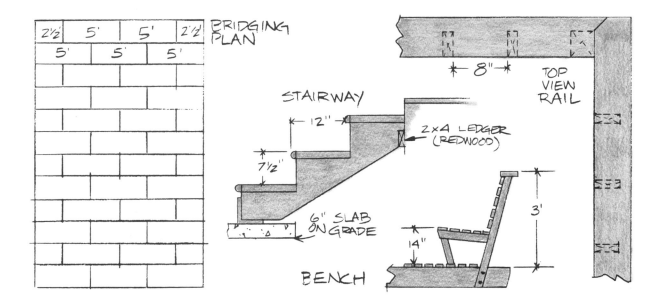

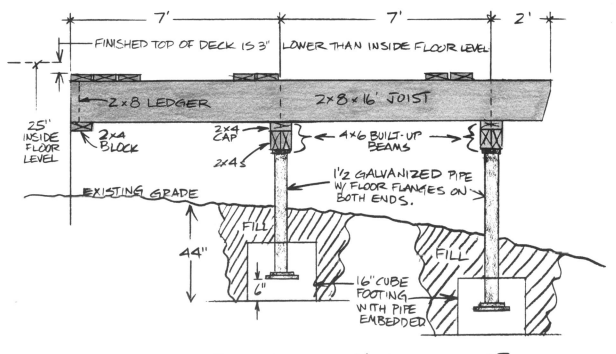

DECK FOUNDATION & UNDERSTRUCTURE

(LEDGER BOARD, BLOCKS, JOISTS & BEAMS
PRESSURE-TREATED SOUTHERN PINE
OR DOUGLAS FIR).

it and into the house with wet, muddy, or sandy feet?

Give some thought to street and driveway traffic. Is the project too close to a street, a neighbor's driveway, or your own driveway? How much traffic do these receive? Enough to be constraints on project location? If so, consider moving the project a bit. Distances look a bit different when laid out full size than when done in ⅛-inch scale. If altering the plan isn't possible, give some thought to erecting barrier fencing between the project and high-traffic areas.

Appearance Planning

Once you've decided on the best possible location, it's time to consider how the overall design will look in relation to your house. Unless you are a skilled artist or drafter, the easiest and simplest way to do this job is to take snapshots. Instant-developing photos or one-hour prints will do fine. Take snapshots of the house on the side, or sides, where the project will be and maybe enlarge them on a photocopier. Tape tracing paper over the photographs and sketch in the proposed project, showing supports, posts, railings, steps, and any other important features, including screening. There's still time for cosmetic alterations.

As the appearance planning goes on, and while the staked or floured outlines remain outside, check the view from inside the house. Will the project or its screening block an especially attractive view? Will the project obstruct views of children at play?

THE WORKING PLAN

Once you have made all the changes you expect to make, your rough plan should be approaching the ideal. Transfer the plan from the tracing paper to the original plot plan, providing a larger-scale drawing, and consider this the start of your working plans. You will need a top-view plan and, in the case of a deck, views (*elevations*) from all four sides, unless connected to the house. In that case, you'll need only top view and three sides.

Changes and additions will be needed in the drawing, of course. To meet codes, and get a building permit, you will almost certainly need some construction details labeled in the drawing, along with a specifications list. That's why it's smart to request some guidance from code officials before you begin drawing.

Details such as slab thickness, subbase (if any), posts, and connections may need to be drawn to larger scale for clarity. You may wish to raise the scale for such detail drawings to 1 inch per foot so that you can more easily estimate materials and provide requisite detail to code officials.

The overall drawing of the project itself should, in fact, be larger in scale than the plot plan. If you originally worked in a ⅛-inch scale, you will want to increase to ¼-inch scale, with details enlarged as noted above. An ordinary 8½ × 11-inch sheet of paper allows

Deck screening, plus pre-existing trees for shade, give protection and interest even to low-level, simple projects. (Wolmanized Wood Company, Inc. photo)

for drawing a project 24 feet tall and 36 feet long. For larger dimensions, you will need larger sheets, or more sheets pieced together, as before.

Your plot plan can remain as is at ⅛-inch scale. You need only redraw building details at any wall or walls meeting the project and the project details themselves at the larger ¼-inch scale. Only special design details such as those mentioned above need to be drawn to the 1-inch scale. It is best to use separate sheets for detail drawings.

At this point, you may wish to get an idea of the scale of some furnishings before finally committing yourself to building. Make small-scale cutouts of chaise longues, tables, chairs, planters, benches, barbecues, serving carts, or other items you expect to use on the deck or patio. Make the cutouts to the same scale you used for the larger overall plan. Position the cutouts on the plan to see how they fit. You may wish to change the project in some way to suit the furniture.

In the end, it's important to avoid overcrowding. Outdoor living space shouldn't be crowded. If necessary, try to find a way to add a few more square feet rather than remove furnishings you want.

DETAIL PLANS

In concept, detailing a project plan is simple: you must supply details of materials needed. For a deck, this includes not only the overlay of decking, rails, and similar materials, but also the underlying joists, beams, girders, posts, and so on.

The details of detailing are not so simple, though. You must be, or become, familiar with lumber sizes, permissible spans, the distance between supports, fastener types, waste allowances, and other aspects of general carpentry. You also need to know the characteristics of various kinds of wood, the prices of wood in different sizes and of different species, local frost depths, and a fair list of skills and bits of lore. (Much of this is covered in the next chapter.)

This may be the time to show your rough plans to a building designer or moonlight drafter (check the yellow pages) and pay for a set of detailed working plans to use in applying for a building permit and later in building the project. Or draw your own detailed working plans. Again, it is imperative that whoever does the drawing has a working knowledge of standard building codes.

When all drawings are completed, it's time to double-check your finances. If they can stand the bite, then make a couple photocopies of the drawings. Save the originals for yourself. Deliver a copy to the local building department and apply for your building permit. Once you receive approval, you can break out the tools and begin construction with your plans as guidance.

You may find all of this preliminary work a chore, but it familiarizes you with what goes where and hence eventually reduces cost and time wasted. Next comes the sweat-equity part, which is where the real fun comes in.

CHAPTER 2

BASIC CARPENTRY

Using basic carpentry, you can transform piles of lumber and other materials into structures that are useful, attractive, and safe. Although I provide basic carpentry concepts throughout this book, the skills themselves come only with practice.

single out the project's key requirements; then check the properties of the various species of wood to see which ones meet them. For example, deck beams and joists require a wood species that is stiff and strong. (The accompanying "Lumber Selection" table shows the best uses for a number of woods.)

MEASUREMENT

Basically, carpentry involves cutting of wood to size and then fastening it in place. This first calls for accurate measurement.

Lumber Defects
Since woods vary in quality, you must take variation into consideration. Recognized defects in wood—such as knots, splits, warps, and rot—may affect only

How to Measure
To measure accurately, first confirm the measurement on the plan. Then envision dimensions in your head. Finally, transfer the measurement to wood. Measure twice. And if your second measurement doesn't match the first, make two more measurements.

When marking, allow for the kerf of the saw on the waste side of the measurement. To remind yourself which side is waste, mark a big X or series of X's using a sharp No. 2 pencil. If you need high accuracy, mark the cut with an awl or a knife.

WOODS

Woods are either softwoods or hardwoods (see the table "Wood Species For Outdoor Projects" beginning on pages 22–23). In selecting a wood for a project,

When sawing wood, keep in mind which side of the line the sawcut should be on. A penciled "X" on the discard end can help remind you.

LUMBER SELECTION

Lumber	Joists	Deck Planks	Fence Boards	Fence Posts	Exterior Paintability
Western red cedar	3		2	1	1
Cypress	2		1	1	1
Douglas fir	1	2	1	1	1
White fir	2		3	3	2
Hemlock	2		3	3	2
Western larch	1		1	2	3
Ponderosa pine	3		2	3	2
Southern pine	1	1	1	2	3
White, sugar pine	3		2	3	2
Redwood	2	1	1	1	2
Western spruce	2		3	3	1
Poplar	2	1	2	3	2

1 = best; 2 = good; 3 = usable

S4S LUMBER SIZES

Nominal Size (in.)	Green Size (in.)	Dry Size (in.)
1	25/32	3/4
2	1 9/16	1 1/2
4	3 9/16	3 1/2
6	5 5/8	5 1/2
8	7 1/2	7 1/4
10	9 1/2	9 1/4
12	11 1/2	11 1/4

An S4S ("surfaced on 4 sides") 2 × 4 actually measures about half an inch less than its nominal size. This is typical of most dried and surfaced lumber.

strength, only appearance, or both. You must decide what is important. So long as you choose lumber with only minor defects and blemishes, you can usually save money by being selective as you search through the lumber pile.

Nominal Size Vs. Actual Size

Almost all lumber you buy will be *surfaced* (or *dressed*), that is, planed on all four sides before leaving the sawmill. Lumber that is surfaced on all four sides is called S4S. Unsurfaced lumber is called *rough* lumber.

The S4S boards will not measure their full labeled dimension. For example, a 2 × 4 is not actually 2 inches thick and 4 inches wide. Instead, the 2 × 4 designation is its *nominal* size. Nominal lumber sizes translate to about ½ inch more than actual sizes, both in thickness and in width (see the table "S4S Lumber Sizes"). On the other hand, specified lumber lengths are actual lengths.

Board Foot Vs. Lineal Foot

Lumber is sold in one of two ways: by the board foot or by the lineal (running) foot. For example, if you buy a 2 × 12 that is 8 feet long, you pay for 8 lineal feet. A board foot is calculated on the basis of a board that is 1 inch thick, 1 foot wide, and 1 foot long. To find the number of board feet in a piece of lumber, multiply its nominal thickness *in inches* by its width *in feet* by its length *in feet*. Convert the width dimension given in inches to feet by writing it as a fraction with the inches

WOOD SPECIES FOR OUTDOOR PROJECTS

SOFTWOODS Wood Species	Locale	Characteristics	Outdoor Uses
Cypress	Maryland to Texas	Easy to work; insect-resistant; decay-resistant; holds nails and paint well; may be costly and difficult to find	Decks, posts, fencing, furniture
Douglas fir Western larch	Pacific Coast, British Columbia	Strong; light; clear-grained; tends toward brittleness; decay-resistant; widely available; moderately priced; easily worked; holds nails well; available pressure-treated	Decks, fencing, posts
Hemlock White fir	Pacific Northwest from Oregon to Alaska	Light-colored; attractive straight grain; stiff; pitch-free; tough, long fibers; lightweight	Deck planks, fences
Norway pine	States along the Great Lakes	Light-colored; moderately hard for a softwood; easy to work; not durable	Decks, fences
Red cedar	East of Colorado, north of Florida, Pacific Northwest	Very light and soft; weak and brittle; works easily; warp-free; may be hard to find in wide boards; decay-resistant; holds paint well	Decks, fences, posts, furniture, walks
Redwood	California	Ideal construction and durability characteristics; tends to higher cost; heartwood is rot resistant; shrinks and splits little; straight-grained; exceptionally durable with no finish at all; warp-free; holds paint well	Decks, fences, posts, furniture, trim, leave-in concrete forms
Spruce	New York, New England, West Virginia, Great Lakes states, Idaho, Washington, Oregon, much of central Canada	Light; soft; warp-resistant; close to ideal for outdoor projects, except not rot-resistant	Deck planking, fencing
White cedar	Eastern coastal U. S., around Great Lakes	Soft; light; durable; close-grained; excellent for outdoor uses, except that strength and stiffness require larger members	Decks, fences, posts, furniture

figure over 12. Then multiply. The 8-foot 2 × 12 in the example would thus be calculated 2 × $^{12}/_{12}$ × 8 = 16 board feet. A 10-foot 2 × 6 would be figured 2 × $^{6}/_{12}$ × 10 = 10 board feet. And a 12-foot 2 × 4 would be figured 2 × $^{4}/_{12}$ × 12 = 8 board feet. Both 1 × 12s and 2 × 6s contain the same number of board feet as lineal feet.

Lumber Grading

Grading standards are government set. Lumber comes as boards, dimension lumber, or timbers.

Boards are less than 2 inches thick and 1 inch wide or wider. Boards less than 6 inches wide may be called *strips*. Board lumber grades refer to appearance. Boards are used for fencing, furniture, and trim.

Dimension lumber is generally 2 inches to 4 inches thick and 2 or more inches wide. Its grading refers to strength and stiffness rather than to good looks. Dimension lumber is used in deck construction and for forming concrete.

Timbers are 5 inches thick or more. They are used in heavy construction, not usually around the home.

Lumber grades are especially important when you are choosing lumber for structural purposes, such as for deck joists or posts. Grade has a lot to do with the

SOFTWOODS

Wood Species	Locale	Characteristics	Outdoor Uses
White pine	Maine, Lake Michigan states, Idaho, Montana, some stands in eastern states other than Maine	Fine-grained; easily worked; sometimes found with few knots; durable; soft; not exceptionally strong; economical; excellent outdoor use	Decks, fences, posts, furniture
Yellow pine	Virginia to Texas, some species classed as Southern Pine	Hard, tough, strong softwood; heartwood fairly durable; hard to nail; saws and generally works easily; inexpensive; excellent for outdoor uses; pressure-treats exceptionally well	Decks, fences, posts, furniture

HARDWOODS

Wood Species	Locale	Characteristics	Outdoor Uses
Ash	East of Rockies	Strong, hard, tough, straight grain; holds nails well	Furniture
Birch	East of Mississippi, southeastern	Hard; strong; does not weather well	Furniture
Live oak	Coasts of Oregon, California, southern Atlantic and Gulf states	Heavy; hard; strong; durable; hard to work; otherwise, superb for small projects	Furniture
Maple	All states east of Colorado, southern Canada	Heavy; tough; strong; easy to work; not durable; may be costly; rock (sugar) maple is the hardest	Furniture
Poplar	The Virginias, Kentucky, Mississippi Valley states	Soft, cheap hardwood; good for getting wide boards; warp-free; rots quickly if not protected; works easily; holds paint well	Furniture
Red oak	The Virginias, Kentucky, Tennessee, Arkansas, Ohio, Missouri, Maryland, parts of New York	Coarse-grained; easily warped; not durable. Not for outdoor uses	Furniture
White oak	The Virginias, Tennessee, Arkansas, Kentucky, Missouri, Maryland, Indiana	Heavy, hard, strong, moderately coarse grain; tough; dense; most durable of all native American hardwoods; reasonably easy to work (using sharp tools); tendency to shrink or crack	Furniture

LINEAL FOOT VS. BOARD FOOT

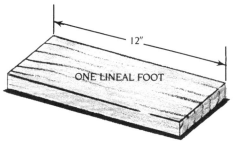

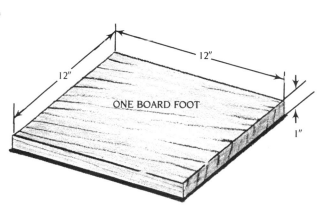

The grade stamp on each board tells a great deal about it. "S-GRN," as shown, indicates that the board has more than 19 percent moisture content and so is considered "green" lumber. Dry lumber would be marked "S-DRY."

wood's strength and stiffness and its resistance to bending and breaking.

Hardwood lumber grades are typically Firsts, Seconds, Selects, No. 1 Common, and No. 2 Common. The top two grades are often combined into Firsts & Seconds, or FAS.

Graded softwood lumber for construction purposes is classed as *Light Framing*, *Structural Light Framing*, *Studs*, and *Structural Joists and Planks* (see the table "Classes of Softwood Lumber"). The Structural Light Framing class is of prime concern in deck-building. The class contains Select Structural, No. 1, No. 2, and No. 3 lumber. These designations apply to 2- to 4-inch-thick, 2- to 4-inch-wide dimension lumber for use where higher bending strength is needed for light-

framing purposes, such as in posts, beams, joists, and other horizontal loadbearing members. For most outdoor-building purposes, Softwood No. 2 lumber is as good as you need. Local building codes may have something to say about what grade you use.

Appearance is another factor to consider. In decks and similar outdoor structures, virtually all framing is visible, and though No. 2 lumber is strong, the appearance of No. 2 lumber is nothing to brag about. The table "Construction Lumber Grades" shows the widely accepted Western Wood Products Association grade standards for lumber.

As to loadbearing uses of lumber, the simplest rule is to follow the span tables listing spans and grades of lumber, and to pick out your own lumber

CLASSES OF SOFTWOOD LUMBER

Category	Size	Classes
Dimension	2" thick, 2"–4" wide	Light Framing, Structural Light Framing, Studs, Structural Joists and Planks
Board	1" thick or less, to 12" wide	Select, Finish, Common, Alternate

CONSTRUCTION LUMBER GRADES
GRADE (best to least)

Grade	Use
Select Structural	Best, strongest (but most costly)
No. 1	Best grade for deck-building
No. 2	Excellent grade for deck-building
No. 3	Marginal for deck-building
Construction	Minimum recommended for deck-building
Standard	Not recommended
Utility	Lowest grade, not recommended
Stud	Not for outdoor structures

BOARD APPEARANCE GRADES
Grade (best to least)

Select	B & Better, C Select, D Select
Finish	Superior, Prime, E Finish
Common	No. 1 Common, 2 Common, 3 Common, 4 Common, 5 Common
Alternate Board	Select, Merchantable, Construction, Standard, Utility, Economy

The best way to buy lumber is to shop where you can sort through the piles yourself. Framing lumber should be chosen for strength. You'll want the visible boards in your project to look better and be straighter than those that are hidden from view.

whenever possible. The stronger species, such as Douglas fir, Southern pine, and Western larch, will handle greater spans for the same-sized member than the weaker species. For this reason, try to choose beams and joists from these three species. The lumber should be pressure-treated unless you plan to give it a wood-preservative treatment yourself (described later). Posts, too, should be of one of these stronger species, and should be pressure-treated because of their proximity to the ground. Deck planking may be made from any species, but no wood beats redwood for decking.

Board Grades. Board lumber, defined as less than 1 inch thick, is appearance-graded. It is used for such things as outdoor furniture, fence panels, and rails. Boards may or may not be grade-stamped but should be kept separated by the dealer, with all those of a single grading kept together. The table "Board Appearance Grades" shows grading for boards. No. 1 Common and No. 2 Common are usually combined into a 2 & Better Common grade when offered for sale.

Moisture Content. It's hard to tell the moisture content of lumber by looking at it. Yet moisture content affects performance. Green boards shrink a great deal, so you should make allowances for this. If lumber is dry, the grade stamp S-DRY should be apparent; if green, S-GRN.

PLYWOOD

Plywood is a wooden sandwich with a lot going for it. Because it comes in a wide variety of thicknesses, plywood can be used economically for many purposes. Fencing and paneling a deck railing are two important uses for plywood. All home centers carry plywood in at least a few types. Plywood is available in structural,

APA 303 Siding exterior plywood makes great one-sided fence panels. This pattern is rough-sawn Texture 1-11. (American Plywood Association photo)

nonstructural, and decorative panels.

End-use is a term to remember in plywood selection. Always buy plywood suited to its end-use. Strength and use information on plywood panels is readily available.

Softwood plywood, the kind used most often for outdoor projects, is usually made of Douglas fir or Southern pine, but may be made of any of 30 other species, depending on locale. Plywood is made of thin sheets of wood called *veneers* held together by glue layers. Grain direction of each veneer layer is at right angles to the ones above and below in the plywood sandwich to give strength in two directions. Each species of wood in softwood plywood has different strength characteristics. But all follow one voluntary industry standard, U.S. Product Standard PS 1–83. This standard has been adopted by the U.S. Department of Commerce. Before buying plywood, look for the American Plywood Association (APA) trademark.

Plywood Type

The word *type* when applied to plywood refers to its indoor-outdoor utility. Although you can get plywood panels for both indoor and outdoor applications, we're interested only in outdoor, which is called *exterior-type* (and sometimes *Exterior* or just *Ext*). Interior-type and exterior-type plywood are made with different glues and veneers. Only completely waterproof glues and better-grade veneers are permitted in exterior-type plywood. As you might expect, exterior-type costs more. In interior-type plywood, the glues are highly moisture-resistant but not waterproof, and interior-type plywood therefore should not be used outdoors, even if painted or stained.

Plywood Grades

Construction and industrial grades of plywood are generally identified in terms of the veneer grade used on the faces and backs of the panels. Those for outdoor building are identified according to veneer quality and have the following grades.

A-Grade has a smooth, paintable face with neatly made repair patches permissible—though not more than 18 patches per 4 × 8-foot panel face. A-Grade normally comes well sanded, and it is the highest grade generally available. While A-Grade is mostly a painting-grade panel, it may also be used with a natural finish for less finicky applications.

Left photo: Exterior siding plywood panels can be staggered to create a two-sided fence that looks good from inside and outside the yard (American Plywood Association photo). Right photo: Every plywood panel you use should bear a stamp indicating that it meets U.S. Product Standard PS 1–83. "APA" is the American Plywood Association grading. "A-C" indicates the panel has an A-Grade face and a C-Grade back. *Group 1*" refers to the species of wood used—Douglas fir in this panel. "*Exterior*" should appear on every panel used for outdoor projects. Here "182" is the mill identification.

C-Grade has openings in the face and tight knots up to 1½ inches. Limited splits are also allowed. C-Grade is the minimum veneer permitted in exterior-type plywood under PS 1–83 and the APA trademark stamp. Sometimes C-Grade has open defects such as knotholes removed and plugged to give an almost-smooth face. This is called C-*Plugged*.

The grades of veneer on the face and back of a plywood panel may vary. For example, a panel with an A-Grade face and a C-Grade back is termed A-C. If this panel is rated for exterior use, it would also contain C-Grade inner plies.

All these veneer grades are minimums; the actual veneers vary from the minimum up to nearly perfect.

Panel Grades. Additionally, plywood is divided into sanded and unsanded grades. Sanded, or *appearance*, grades are chosen for their good looks.

Appearance-grade plywoods made for special purposes include APA 303 *Siding*, which comes in a variety of textures highly suited to fence paneling.

Improved sidings are offered by a number of manufacturers. These are prefinished and stained or primed, making them good for fences. Consult your dealer for what's available locally.

APA Performance-Rated panels include composites that are not veneered plywood. They're called *oriented-strand board* or OSB. OSB has become widely accepted in the construction industry. A few of these are exterior-type panels.

Thicknesses

Plywood is available in a whole range of thicknesses from ¼ inch to 1⅛ inch. Most plywood comes in 4 × 8-foot panels, though 4 × 10 and larger sizes are sometimes available. Mini-panels are recut from full-sized panels and offered in separate racks by dealers.

APA improved sidings make excellent fence panels. (American Plywood Association photo)

OUTDOOR USES FOR SOFTWOOD PLYWOOD *

Project	Usual Thickness (in.)	Ideal Grade	Alternate Grade	Usable Grade
Solid decking	¹⁵⁄₃₂, ½, ¹⁹⁄₃₂, ⅝, ²³⁄₃₂, ¾, ⅞, 1⅛	Sturd-I-Floor Ext	Sheathing Ext **	Sheathing Structural I Ext **
Deck-rail panels	¹¹⁄₃₂, ⅜, ¹⁵⁄₃₂, ½	MDO Ext (one-side)	A-C Ext	C-C Ext plugged and touchsanded (gives poor appearance)
Fence Panels	¹¹⁄₃₂, ⅜, ¹⁵⁄₃₂, ½, ¹⁹⁄₃₂, ⅝, ²³⁄₃₂, ¾	303 Siding Ext or MDO Ext (two-side)	C-C Ext or A-A Ext	Any Exterior grade
Outdoor furniture Picnic tables	¹⁹⁄₃₂, ⅝, ²³⁄₃₂, ¾	MDO Ext (two-side, seven-ply)	A-C Ext	
Outdoor storage units	¹⁹⁄₃₂, ⅝, ²³⁄₃₂, ¾	MDO Ext (two side) or 30 Siding Ext	A-A Ext	A-B Ext, B-B Ext, or A-C Ext
Concrete forms	¹⁹⁄₃₂, ⅝, ²³⁄₃₂, ¾	Plyform B-B Class I and II Ext	A-C Ext or B-C Ext	Any grade

* APA-rated grades
** Sharp heels may punch through knotholes in unplugged inner plies

Working with Plywood

Plan your plywood-cutting to avoid waste. You can even sketch the required pieces on paper, allowing for the width of the saw kerfs (cuts between pieces). The face grain should run lengthwise on each piece. Plan the first cuts to reduce the panel to a workable size.

Plywood expands and contracts with moisture changes, so be sure to allow space between panels for this. Most authorities recommend ⅛-inch spacing between panel ends and ¼ inch between sides. Follow the specifications for the panels you are using. The face·grain direction should be perpendicular to the supports.

A good way to attack a panel is with a circular saw or saber saw with a fine-toothed plywood-cutting blade. For sawing, lay the panel facedown over sawhorses or with a pair of 2 × 4s flanking the cut. Lay out the pieces and use a chalkline to snap your cutting line.

Appearance grades of plywood are already sanded. It's best not to sand anything but the plywood edges before sealing or priming the panel. Sand plywood in the direction of the face grain only.

Like lumber, plywood can take many finishes. But whatever finish is applied to one side of a plywood

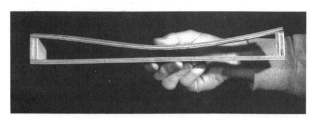

This demonstration shows that plywood is stiffest in the direction of its face grain. Two strips of ⅜-inch plywood were cut 1½ inches wide and nailed to spacers. The strip on top was cut across its face grain; the one on the bottom was cut parallel to its face grain. The bottom one is stiffer.

panel should also be applied to the other. Otherwise the panel is likely to take on moisture differently on one side than the other and so curl. Thus, if you seal the face, be sure to seal the back. If you paint the face, at least prime the back. To prevent face-checking on plywood used outside, prime the back and seal it along the edges with a heavy coat of exterior primer or aluminum paint intended for wood. This is true for all edges, whether exposed, lapped, butted, or hidden.

 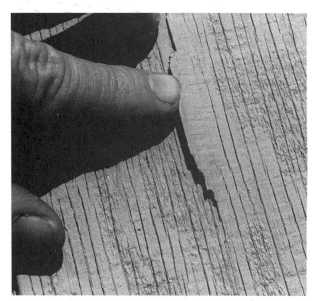

Left: Face-checking in plywood is so common that it is not considered a plywood defect for grading purposes. To minimize face-checking, keep panels dry before, during, and after use, and keep them well protected with a good finish. Right: Defects called *ring shakes* cause the wood to peel up between its growth rings. Boards, too, can develop ring shakes. Ring shakes are ignored by the plywood grading system.

DECAY RESISTANCE

Decay in wood is caused by fungi. Outdoor wood close to or in contact with the ground is especially susceptible to rotting. To control decay, you must deprive the fungi of one of their three essentials—warmth, moisture, or air. Wood must be damp to rot. (There is no such thing as "dry rot.") If kept dry (that is, with a moisture content under 20 percent), wood will not rot.

Wood is often treated with chemical preservatives to increase its rot resistance. Outdoor projects usually call either for treated wood, preferably pressure-treated, or for one of the three naturally rot-resistant woods—heart cedar, cypress, or heart redwood. In these species, the darker-colored wood from the middle of the tree, called the *heartwood*, is what is decay resistant. The lighter-colored wood from the outer layer, called the *sapwood*, is not.

Outdoor wood needs to be selected and installed with a thought to decay resistance. A pencil can be stuck into wood of a rotted fence post. Left: The pressure-treated fence post of equal age has not rotted.

Naturally rot-resistant heart redwood may be installed in or near the ground, and will last for many years. (Photographer, Ernest Braun; California Redwood Association photo)

Redwood

Redwood is probably the premier wood choice for most deck-building projects. The heartwood color of redwood ranges from a pinkish brown to a cinnamon brown; sapwood portions are cream-colored. Redwood, which grows on the West Coast of the United States, has a uniform fine texture and straight grain. It also has a low density, making it light yet strong for its weight. It is easily worked with hand or power tools, and fine joints are easy to achieve. Left untreated, its natural color changes to a soft gray when the wood weathers. Other colors are obtained by staining. Redwood lumber comes either rough or surfaced.

Redwood Grades. Redwood grading follows a somewhat different pattern than grading for other lumber, with reference more to the amount of heartwood contained. Heartwood redwood contains natural chemicals that resist decay and insects. The California Redwood Association recommends the use of heart redwood for loadbearing structural members, in and close to the ground (any closer than 6 inches). No preservative treatment needs to be applied to the surface of all-heart redwood. In any case, the redwood grade should be chosen on the basis of appearance, strength, or durability.

One method of avoiding the higher cost of redwood, and still getting its benefits, is to use what are called *garden grades*. There are four garden grades of redwood: *Construction Heart, Construction Common, Merchantable Heart,* and *Merchantable.* See the table "Garden Grades of Redwood on the next page."

Red Cedar

Less expensive than redwood, red cedar (or Western red cedar) is often difficult to locate in useful sizes for anything other than siding, fence posts, and rails. Also, red cedar is not a particularly strong wood. Its color varies more than redwood's does, and cedar is likely to contain more knots. Left untreated, red cedar, like redwood, weathers to a silvery gray. Industry sales figures indicate its popularity is increasing.

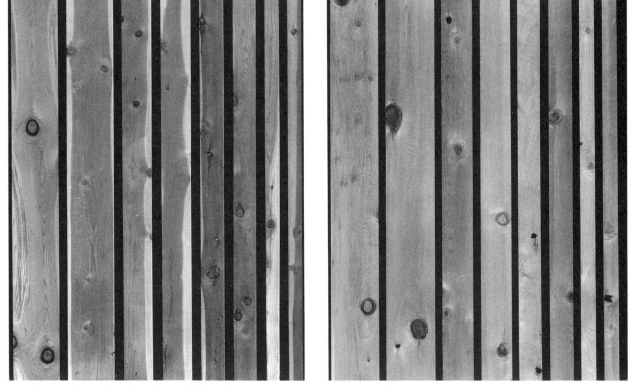

Garden grades of redwood make for economical outdoor building. The grades shown here are Construction Common and Merchantable Heart. (California Redwood Association photos)

GARDEN GRADES OF REDWOOD

Grade	Characteristics	Uses
Construction Heart	Heartwood with some knots, blemishes, and manufacturing imperfections; resistant to insects and decay	Posts; beams; joists in, on, or near the ground; deck planks; patio covers; rails; fencing; benches; furniture; planters; trellises; leave-in concrete forms
Construction Common	Contains some sapwood; attractive grade with a combination of sapwood's lighter color, heartwood, and knots	Deck planks, rails, fencing, benches, furniture, trellises, patio covers (all aboveground)
Merchantable Heart	All heartwood with a few larger loose knots and knotholes; most economical grade	Fencing, benches, planters, trellises, patio covers, retaining walls; not for structural members
Merchantable	Lowest grade; can be recut economically for many uses	Fencing, benches, trellises, furniture, aboveground garden and utility applications; small pieces in which knots can be eliminated

Cypress

Low availability has limited the use of cypress. It can be found in the Deep South, but even there it is now rare enough to be extremely costly.

Pressure-treated Wood

Outdoors, near or in contact with the ground, if you don't use a naturally rot-resistant wood, then use one that is pressure-treated. Far more effective than soaking boards in a wood preservative, pressure treatment forces chemical preservatives into the wood cells under pressure. Sometimes, especially in posts meant for in-ground use, closely spaced knifelike cuts are made into the boards to aid chemical penetration. While you wouldn't want these cuts showing on deck planks or rails, they won't be seen in below-deck post lumber.

Pressure-treated wood may be labeled as outdoor wood or all-weather wood. In either case, the wood should carry the stamp of the American Wood Preserver's Bureau, along with other marks of identification.

The major reason for using pressure-treated wood instead of naturally rot-resistant wood is economic: pressure-treated wood is less costly than any of the naturally rot-resistant woods.

Another reason for using pressure-treated wood is long life. The lifespan of properly pressure-treated lumber is 50 years. Naturally rot-resistant woods, on the other hand, will last about 10 years in contact with the ground. To get the maximum lifespan from pressure-treated wood, soak a do-it-yourself wood preserv-

Some pressure-treated wood is given closely spaced knife-like cuts to improve chemical penetration. Since these cuts make a board unsightly, use such wood where it will be least noticeable.

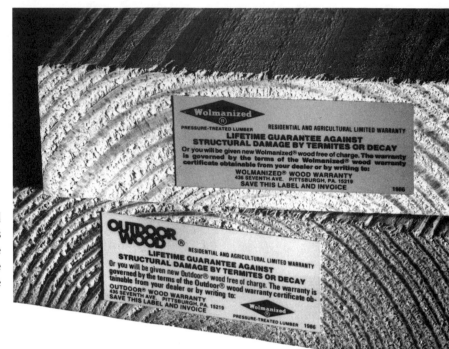

Some pressure-treated wood bears brand identification, such as this. Unlike the wood shown on the previous page, these boards have no knife cuts and so could well be used where they will show.

ative into the sawed-off ends of the boards and into drilled holes before assembly. These are the places where pressure-treated lumber first becomes vulnerable. Be sure to wear eye protection and rubber gloves, work outdoors or in a well-ventilated area, and follow the preservative manufacturer's instructions.

Pressure-treated lumber comes in two degrees of waterborne preservative treatment, Weather Exposure (sometimes marked LP-2) and Ground-Contact (sometimes marked LP-22). Weather Exposure lumber is pressure-treated to a 0.25 pound of preservative per cubic foot of wood. This is suitable for all outdoor uses except in-ground or ground-contact. Ground-Contact pressure-treated lumber, which has been treated to a 0.40 rate, should be used for posts, beams, and the joists underneath a very low deck (anything within 6 inches of the ground), and for leave-in wood forms in a concrete patio. (It serves all the uses that Weather Exposure does.) But for in-ground deck support posts, knife cuts and heavier pressure treatment are necessary. The stronger the treatment, the better the wood resists decay.

Modern pressure-treated woods are generally safer to use than older ones. Nevertheless, you should take a few precautions. Wear gloves whenever handling pressure-treated lumber. Also, to keep sawdust and sanding dust off your skin and out of your lungs, wear

tight-fitting safety goggles and a good dust mask when sawing and sanding. Wash up immediately after work and before eating. Wash all work clothing separately from other laundry. Properly dispose of wood scraps and sawdust from pressure-treated lumber. *That means not burning them.* Instead, take the debris to a qualified landfill or other recommended disposal site for hazardous wastes.

Retailers who sell pressure-treated wood are required to offer information sheets to consumers listing precautions to take.

Finishing Pressure-Treated Wood. Sunlight will degrade pressure-treated wood, so it needs to be finished. It's best, however, to leave pressure-treated wood unfinished for two to four weeks to acclimate. Some preservatives used in pressure-treating form an excellent base for stain or paint.

Wood Preservatives
As I've already noted, ensure that all wood in contact with the ground is naturally rot-resistant or, better yet, pressure-treated. Wood used 6 inches above the ground may be home-treated with a wood preservative to make it more rot resistant. If pressure-treated wood isn't available locally, you may have no choice other than home treatment with a wood preservative. A

Brushing on a water-repellent preservative gets only a little preservative into the wood. Dipping is better. The surface should be flooded with preservative, helping as much soak in as possible.

good do-it-yourself treatment can add five to ten years to the life of outdoor aboveground wood.

Successful wood-preserving depends on how much of the preservative soaks into the wood. Brushing the preservative on is easy, but not very effective. The brush-applied preservative achieves only slight surface penetration. The more effective method is to soak wood overnight. A 24-hour soak is better still. Typical penetration by soaking is four times that of a brush-on application: $\frac{1}{10}$- to $\frac{1}{8}$-inch preservative penetration.

Some wood preservatives are clear and some colored; some are paintable and some not. Check the label for coverage information. Moreover, be sure to follow the manufacturer's instructions.

Especially for benches and similar items, to prevent a person's direct skin contact with wood preservatives, apply at least a light coat of exterior finish over the soaked-in preservative.

ORDERING WOOD

Once you have your building permit and your project dimensions are definite, you can purchase materials. As I've noted, always use the appropriate grade of materials for a project. For instance, do not use No. 3 Common lumber for any horizontal loadbearing member, no matter how attractive the savings may seem.

Minimizing Waste

Planning ahead can save both cutting time and materials cost. For example, if you have a 14-foot measurement, then a 14-foot board will fit; but if the measurement is 14 feet 6 inches, give some thought in your plan to reducing or increasing that dimension. Cutting off a whole row of 16-foot planks to make them 18 inches shorter is very uneconomical. Avoid such waste wherever you can. For almost the same cost, you could have 18 inches more project.

Many professionals allow 10 to 15 percent for job waste. We do-it-yourselfers had better allow 15 to 20 percent. Careful planning and meticulous work, however, can reduce waste.

DECK STRUCTURE

Before you build a deck, a fundamental understanding of structures is helpful. Any structure is a load-supporting combination of members. In a deck, the members are wood and are called *framing* members. The load being supported is the combined weights of the framing and decking members themselves. This is termed *dead load*. The usual dead load on a deck is 10 pounds per square foot (*psf*). Added to it are the weights of the people, furnishings, and accessories on the deck, called the *live load*. The usual live load on a deck is 40 psf. The live load includes forces of wind and snow that may affect the structure. As you can see, while the dead load is constant, the live load varies. Dead load plus live load equals the total load: 50 psf for a typical deck.

Loads are supported by horizontal members—the planks, joists, and beams. These transmit loads to vertical framing members: the posts, which are supported by concrete footings. Ultimately, all deck loads are transferred to the ground or to the house wall.

The *loadbearing capacity* of a soil is also measured in

pounds per square foot. Soils vary in their loadbearing capacity. (See the table "Loadbearing Values of Foundation Materials" on page 42.)

Two types of loads may be applied to framing members. They are *concentrated loads* and *uniformly distributed loads*. A water-filled hot tub resting over a horizontal beam represents a concentrated load. A group of people chatting on the deck usually is a fairly uniformly distributed load.

Size and Strength Vs. Span

The strength of a framing member is its ability to accept loading without breaking. A fixed relationship exists between the distance it can safely span and its strength. Its thickness and depth also have an effect, especially its depth. For example, if a 2×4 and a 2×8 are laid on edge between supports, the 2×8 is twice as deep a member as the 2×4, yet it has, not twice, but *four* times the load-carrying ability of the 2×4.

To get a member that has more load-carrying abil-ity, you can: (1) increase its strength and stiffness by using a stronger species or grade of lumber; (2) decrease its span; (3) increase its thickness; or (4) increase its depth. In the case of deck joists—the members that support the deck planking—you can place them closer together, making more members share the load.

The joints between framing members are called *connections*. Connections, too, must be able to transfer loads from one member to another.

Because a deck must be strong enough to support all the loads applied to it, building codes set standards for design and construction. Normally, a deck must be designed to support a total load of 50 psf. An unroofed deck in a heavy-snow climate must be designed even stronger in order to support snow without collapsing. These values are reflected in the span tables that are approved by the local building codes. The span tables apply to horizontal members. Vertical members—posts—have tables of their own, maximum-length tables. You need to comply with all of these tables as you design your deck.

EFFECTS OF SPAN ON FRAMING MEMBERS

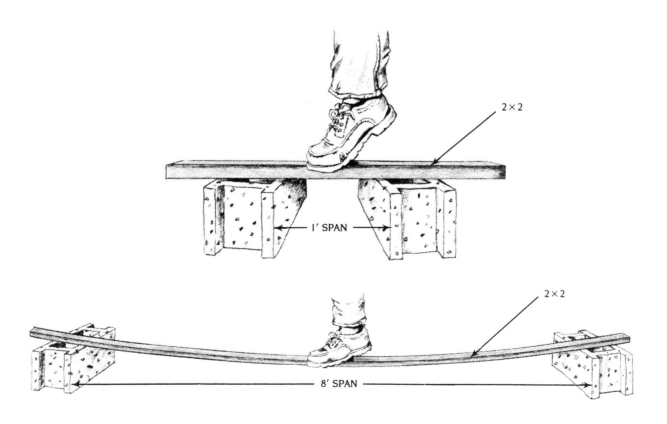

DECK FOOTINGS

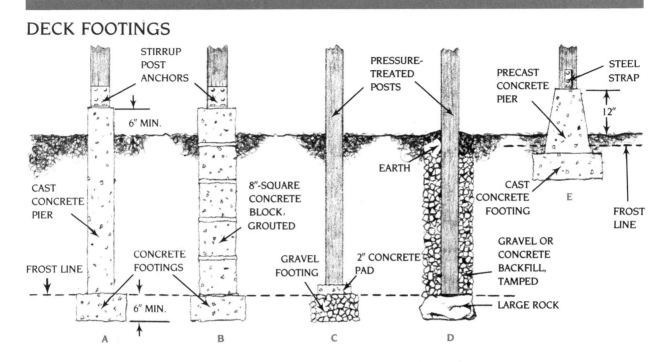

Shown are (**A**) concrete footing and cast-in-place concrete pier; (**B**) concrete footing and concrete-block pier; (**C**) gravel footing with thin precast concrete pad supporting pressure-treated wood post; (**D**) large rock supporting pressure-treated wood post in tamped-gravel-backfilled hole; (**E**) cast concrete footing supporting precast concrete pier. Note that all footings are below frost line.

Deck Parts

Footings.   The usual deck structure starts below the ground, at least 6 inches beneath the frost line, with concrete pads called *footings*.

Footings are usually 8 to 12 inches or more square and at least 6 inches thick. They distribute the deck's load to the earth according to the soil's loadbearing capacity. The footings may be extended above the ground with concrete blocks or cast concrete piers, normally reaching a minimum of 6 inches above grade. These hold steel straps that are fastened to the wood members. Every succeeding framing member is tied to the one below and thus into the ground so the deck cannot be pushed or lifted off its supports.

Posts and Beams.   Deck posts—often decay-resistant 4 × 4s—either extend into the earth and rest on the footings or on tamped gravel in a concrete-filled hole, or they may rest on concrete piers 6 inches or more above the ground. At the upper ends, the posts support beams. Beams usually run parallel to the house wall, and are often 4 inches thick, or else made of doubled 2-inch lumber. If one side of the deck is supported by the house, as is often the case, a

3 × 6 or 3 × 8 *ledger board* (horizontal support board) is bolted to the house wall in place of a post-supported beam there. Laid atop the beams, or sometimes hanging from them, are joists, often of 2-inch lumber. Joists normally run perpendicular to the house wall.

Planks.   The planking runs across the joists, either perpendicular to them or diagonally. (Diagonal styling looks attractive but is more work and produces more lumber waste.)

Railings.   If the deck is more than 18 inches above the ground, it must also have a safety railing that is 36 to 42 inches high (local codes vary) and capable of keeping a baby from crawling through. Usually, this means that its vertical members must be spaced no farther apart than 6 to 9 inches. The railing is often a 2 × 4 or 2 × 6. Deck accessories may include steps, seating, and planters.

Sometimes, on a small deck, the joists can be eliminated and the planks laid directly across the beams. The no-joists method requires that the beams be close together, necessitating more posts with more footings. It's a matter of economics. If the deck is small and low (that is, with short posts), simpler beams-as-

STRUCTURE OF A SIMPLE DECK

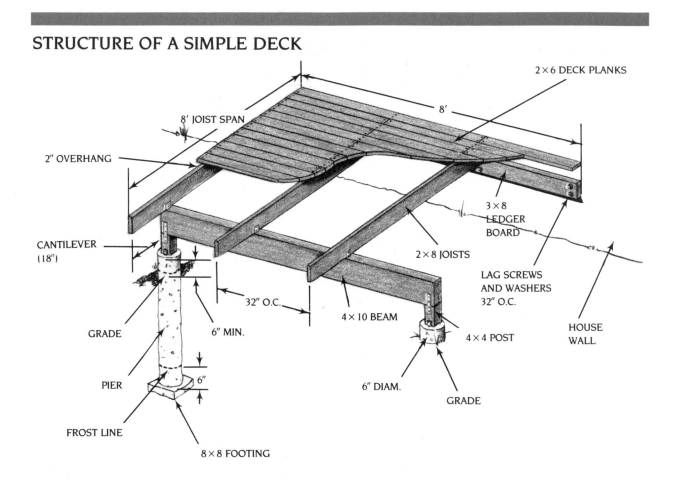

8' JOIST SPAN

2" OVERHANG

CANTILEVER (18")

GRADE

PIER

FROST LINE

8 × 8 FOOTING

32" O.C.

6" MIN.

6"

4 × 10 BEAM

6" DIAM.

2 × 8 JOISTS

4 × 4 POST

GRADE

2 × 6 DECK PLANKS

8'

3 × 8 LEDGER BOARD

LAG SCREWS AND WASHERS 32" O.C.

HOUSE WALL

joists construction may be favored. Some on-ground decks have no posts at all and are built with their pressure-treated beams resting directly on the footings. Remember that any wood member within 6 inches of the ground should be decay-resistant.

STRUCTURAL DESIGN

You can start deck-designing at the top with the planks—the usual approach—or start at the bottom with the footings. I prefer to start at the top. This way, you begin by choosing the planks, which is the part of the deck you'll see most.

Planks. Deck planks are often 2 × 3s or 2 × 4s laid flat. If you want a pattern of narrow lines, 2 × 3s or 2 × 4s may be laid on edge (though this is a less efficient use of the lumber).

Choose planking lumber from one of the species listed in the table "Wood Species Groups," shown.

Next, check the "Maximum Deck Plank Spans" table, which is arranged according to species group, size of plank, and whether planks are to be laid flat or on edge. The table assumes that more than one plank carries the load. With concentrated loads, maximum plank spans should be reduced accordingly.

WOOD SPECIES GROUPS

Species Group	Wood Species Included
1	Douglas fir, larch, Southern pine, ash
2	Hemlock, white fir, Douglas fir-south
3	Western pines, cedars, redwood, spruces, soft pines

Deck planks can be laid on edge. Although letting some planks extend on a low-to-the-ground deck adds interest, first check local code requirements as to deck heights and need for railings. (Photographer, Ed Dull; Western Wood Products Association photo)

MAXIMUM DECK PLANK SPANS *

| Species Group | BOARD SIZE | | | | | | |
	1 × 4	2 × 2	2 × 3	2 × 4	2 × 6	2 × 3 on edge	2 × 4 on edge
1	16″	60″	60″	60″	60″	90″	144″
2	14″	48″	48″	48″	48″	78″	120″
3	12″	42″	42″	42″	42″	66″	108″

* Construction grade or better (Select Structural, Appearance, No. 1, or No. 2). Boards spaced slightly apart. Not for concentrated loads.

Joists. Now look opposite the species group under the size and method of laying of the planks you've chosen. Suppose you've selected 2 × 6 Western red cedar planks laid flat. According to the span table, these will span up to 42 inches. That is, your deck's joists must be spaced no farther apart than 42 inches on centers (that is, 42 inches between the midpoints of the top edges of the joists). If you prefer a stiffer-feeling deck, you may reduce this maximum dimension, but in no case should you increase it.

PLANK SPANS VS. DECK STRENGTH

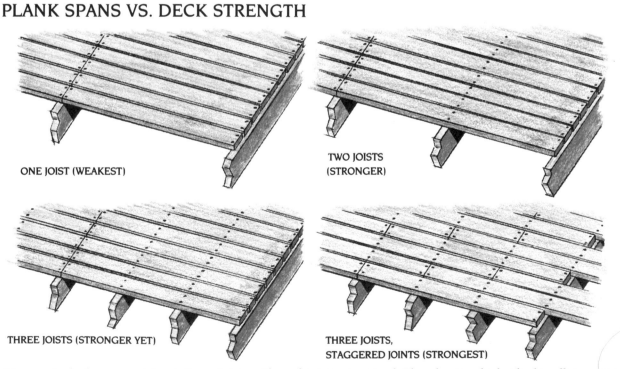

ONE JOIST (WEAKEST)

TWO JOISTS (STRONGER)

THREE JOISTS (STRONGER YET)

THREE JOISTS, STAGGERED JOINTS (STRONGEST)

Strongest planks span at least three joists with end joints staggered. Thus longer deck planks offer greater strength, usually requiring purchase of no additional lumber.

MAXIMUM DECK JOIST SPANS*

Species Group	Joist Size	MAXIMUM JOIST SPACING		
		16"	24"	32"
1	2 × 6	9' 9"	7' 11"	6' 2"
	2 × 8	12' 10"	10' 6"	8' 1"
	2 × 10	16' 5"	13' 4"	10' 4"
2	2 × 6	8' 7"	7' 0"	5' 8"
	2 × 8	11' 4"	9' 3"	7' 6"
	2 × 10	14' 6"	11' 10"	9' 6"
3	2 × 6	7' 9"	6' 2"	5' 0"
	2 × 8	10' 2"	8' 1"	6' 8"
	2 × 10	13' 0"	10' 4"	8' 6"

* No. 2 or Better, No. 2 medium-grain Southern pine. Spans are center-to-center distance between supports. Joists on edge. Based on 40 psf live load and 10 psf dead load.

REDWOOD BEAM SPANS*

Beam Size	BEAM SPACING (ON CENTERS)			
	6'	8'	10'	12'
4 × 6	4' 0"	3' 3"	3' 0"	2' 9"
4 × 8	5' 0"	4' 3"	3' 9"	3' 6"
4 × 10	7' 3"	6' 3"	5' 6"	5' 0"

* Non-stress-graded Construction Heart and Construction Common redwood lumber with 40 psf live load and 10 psf dead load. Deflection limited to 1/240th of span.

—Figures from California Redwood Association

Next, use the table "Maximum Deck Joist Spans" by species group, nominal joist size, and joist spacing. (Though redwood appears in Species Group 3 and follows that group in some respects, separate tables give more precise joist and beam spans just for redwood. For joists, see the table "Redwood Joist Spans.")

At this point, it helps to make a few assumptions. It's safe to assume that digging footings and casting them is going to be hard work. Therefore, footings are best minimized. So, unless the deck is very wide, try for a single footing-supported beam at the outer edge of the deck. At the house edge, use a ledger board bolted to the house wall or the foundation with ½-inch lag screws or carriage bolts spaced 16 inches apart and staggered 2 inches from the top and bottom edges. (If you live in a frost-free climate where footings can be shallow and you think that installing an intermediate beam is more economical than installing fewer footings and fewer posts, your assumptions may differ from these.)

REDWOOD JOIST SPANS*

Joist Size	JOIST SPACING (ON CENTERS)	
	16"	24"
2 × 6	7' 3"	6' 0"
2 × 8	10' 9"	8' 9"
2 × 10	13' 6"	11' 0"

* Non-stress-graded Construction Heart and Construction Common redwood lumber with 40 psf live load. Deflection limited to 1/240th of span.

—Figures from California Redwood Association

First you must know the width of your deck from house to outer edge. Let's say it is 12 feet. The joists must reach that distance in one or more spans across beams. Remember that joists can cantilever (that is, extend out beyond the outer support) by as much as one fourth their span. Cantilevering is a way of making a larger deck without adding another row of beams. If the joists are cantilevered, however, they must be well fastened at their house ends with framing anchors so they do not see-saw when loaded at the outer end. Don't just toenail (angle-nail) them. (In fact, it is a good idea to use framing anchors at *all* connections between framing members.)

You'll see in the "Maximum Deck Joist Spans" table that Douglas fir 2 × 10s on 32-inch centers will span 10 feet 4 inches. A cantilever of less than 2 feet would allow them to support the entire width of a 12-foot deck with only one beam and a ledger board.

Be sure to check joist specs against the maximum plank spans. The 32-inch spacing for the Douglas fir joists in our example doesn't exceed what the 2 × 6 Western red cedar planks will span (from the "Maximum Deck Plank Spans" table on page 37). Everything is fine so far.

Beams. Next comes beam design. Beams of 3- and 4-inch thickness are often used. Beams may be built up using 2-inch lumber nailed or bolted together. For example, two 2 × 10s can be fastened together to qualify as a 4 × 10. Sometimes, instead of the beams being sandwiched right together, they are bolted on either side of the supporting posts. This allows the posts to extend upward above the beams and support the deck railing.

The table "Maximum Deck Beam Spans" takes into account species group, beam nominal size, and spacing between beams to give maximum deck beam spans. Spacing between beams will be based on the joist span you selected, so use that figure. In the ex-

CANTILEVERED JOISTS

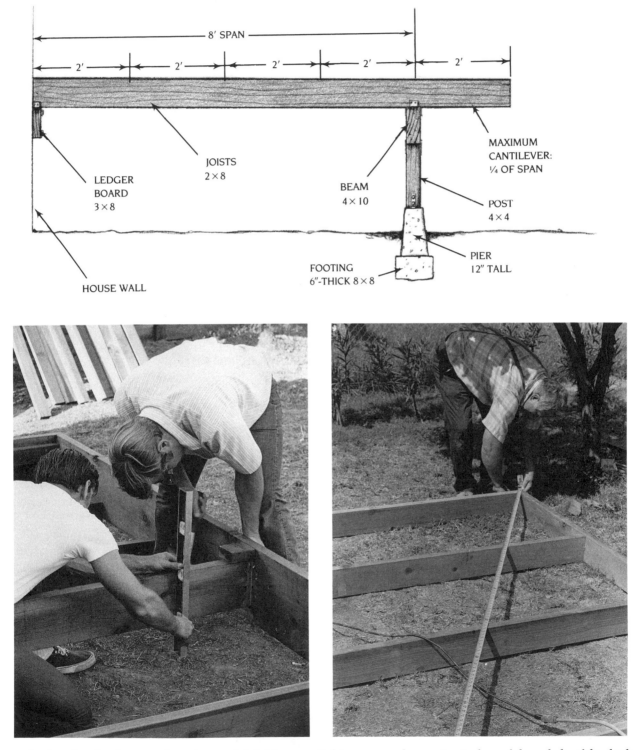

8' SPAN

2'   2'   2'   2'   2'

JOISTS
2 × 8

MAXIMUM
CANTILEVER:
¼ OF SPAN

LEDGER
BOARD
3 × 8

BEAM
4 × 10

POST
4 × 4

PIER
12" TALL

FOOTING
6"-THICK 8 × 8

HOUSE WALL

Left: Care in plumbing and setting each joist is essential to a properly constructed, useful, and durable deck (photographer, Larry McCoy III; California Redwood Association photo). **Right:** After framing a deck's joists, be sure to measure both diagonals. If the deck is square, the diagonals will be equal.

MAXIMUM DECK BEAM SPANS*

Species Group	Beam Size	Beam Spacing (Feet)								
		4	5	6	7	8	9	10	11	12
1	4×6	to 6'	to 6'	to 6'						
	3×8	to 8'	to 8'	to 7'	to 6'	to 6'	to 6'			
	4×8	to 10'	to 9'	to 8'	to 7'	to 7'	to 6'	to 6'	to 6'	
	3×10	to 11'	to 10'	to 9'	to 8'	to 8'	to 7'	to 7'	to 6'	to 6'
	4×10	to 12'	to 11'	to 10'	to 9'	to 9'	to 8'	to 8'	to 7'	to 7'
	3×12		to 12'	to 11'	to 10'	to 9'	to 9'	to 8'	to 8'	to 8'
	4×12			to 12'	to 12'	to 11'	to 10'	to 10'	to 9'	to 9'
	6×10					to 12'	to 11'	to 10'	to 10'	to 10'
	6×12							to 12'	to 12'	to 12'
2	4×6	to 6'	to 6'							
	3×8	to 7'	to 7'	‧to 6'	to 6'					
	4×8	to 9'	to 8'	to 7'	to 7'	to 6'	to 6'			
	3×10	to 10'	to 9'	to 8'	to 7'	to 7'	to 6'	to 6'	to 6'	
	4×10	to 11'	to 10'	to 9'	to 8'	to 8'	to 7'	to 7'	to 7'	to 6'
	3×12	to 12'	to 11'	to 10'	to 9'	to 8'	to 8'	to 7'	to 7'	to 7'
	4×12		to 12'	to 11'	to 10'	to 10'	to 9'	to 9'	to 8'	to 8'
	6×10			to 12'	to 11'	to 10'	to 10'	to 9'	to 9'	to 9'
	6×12				to 12'	to 12'	to 12'	to 11'	to 11'	to 10'
3	4×6	to 6'								
	3×8	to 7'	to 6'							
	4×8	to 8'	to 7'	to 6'	to 6'					
	3×10	to 9'	to 8'	to 7'	to 6'	to 6'	to 6'			
	4×10	to 10'	to 9'	to 8'	to 8'	to 7'	to 7'	to 6'	to 6'	to 6'
	3×12	to 11'	to 10'	to 9'	to 8'	to 7'	to 7'	to 7'	to 6'	to 6'
	4×12	to 12'	to 11'	to 10'	to 9'	to 9'	to 8'	to 8'	to 7'	to 7'
	6×10		to 12'	to 11'	to 10'	to 9'	to 9'	to 8'	to 8'	to 8'
	6×12			to 12'	to 12'	to 11'	to 11'	to 10'	to 10'	to 8'

* Spans are center-to-center distance between supports. Beams on edge. Based on 40 psf live load and 10 psf dead load. Grade: No. 2 or Better; No. 2, medium-grain southern pine.

ample, I chose joists with a maximum span of 10 feet 4 inches. This becomes the beam spacing. The table lists many beams that permit a 10-feet 4-inch beam spacing—all those in the 11-foot column. The beams that could be used vary from beams that are able to span from 6 feet to 12 feet. (Use the "Redwood Beam Spans" table on page 38 for redwood.)

Deciding to use a Douglas fir beam (Species Group 1) narrows the selection to seven beams in the example. Which one to choose? Easy. Consider your deck's length. Which beam span works best with it? Our deck is to be 16 feet long, let's say. If we choose a beam giving a 6-foot span, a post would be necessary at least every 6 feet, or four posts for the 16-foot-long deck. If we choose 8-foot spans, allowed by 3×12s, one post can be eliminated.

Moreover, beams, like joists, can be cantilevered up to one fourth their span, thus offering further possibilities for economizing on lumber. For our example, cantilevering would allow a beam spanning 7 feet: 7 feet between posts, plus 1-foot cantilevers at each end. Cantilevering has esthetic advantages, too. It lets the two end posts be set in somewhat, getting them farther out of view. (But the posts should not be set in more than one fourth of the beam's span. With the 7-foot span, slightly less than a 2-foot cantilever could be used at each end.)

For our example, we chose a 4×10-inch Douglas fir beam. Normally you'll want to use as large a beam as is practical to minimize the number of posts and footings. (Beams are easy to deal with; posts and especially footings represent a lot of manual labor.)

The "Maximum Deck Beam Spans" table shows that lower-quality lumber from other species groups would also work for beams with our example. A quick call to your building materials/home center dealer will tell which species are available and most economical.

Posts. The last thing to figure is the size of the

CANTILEVERED BEAMS

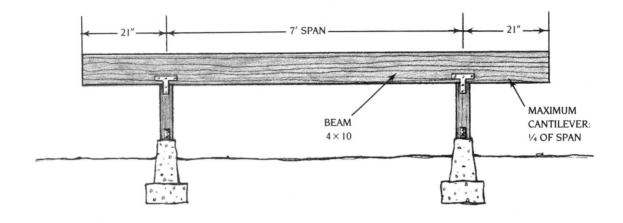

21" | 7' SPAN | 21"

BEAM
4 × 10

MAXIMUM
CANTILEVER:
¼ OF SPAN

A doubled 2 × 8 beam acts as a single 4 × 8 beam would. Ends are cantilevered beyond supporting posts. This beam is supported on one post and leveled; then center and other end posts are measured, cut, and installed.

supporting posts. These hold up the beams, often continuing up to support a railing and perhaps seating. In most cases, 4 × 4 posts will work. If the beam is to rest on the post tops, post size should relate to beam width so that the two line up for simple connection. For example, a 4 × 10 beam could fit over a 4 × 4 or 4 × 6 post flush on both sides.

Post figuring is done by calculating the deck area supported by each post. For posts underneath a deck on the inside, simply multiply the beam spacing by the post spacing in feet. That's it. In our example, this is 10 feet 4 inches times the post spacing of 8 feet (with cantilever) for a total of approximately 83 square feet, the maximum area supported by any post. Actually, in the example, it is less than this, which can be established by sketching a plan of the posts and the deck areas supported by them. But, for our example, no difference in post size would result, anyway. (See next page drawing "Deck Area Supported by a Post.") A post supports halfway to the next post or the ledger board, plus all of the cantilevered deck.

With that area in mind, see the next page table "Maximum Post Heights." It gives maximum heights by species group, nominal post size, and area of deck supported. For Douglas fir posts (Species Group 1), look under 84 square feet, which is the next-higher figure, and see that 4 × 4 posts will support 84 square feet of deck up to a 10-foot maximum height. That accommodates the height of our low deck just fine.

Footings. It is a rare soil that won't support all the loads coming down 4 × 4, 4 × 6, or 6 × 6 posts on 8 × 8- or 12 × 12-inch, cast-concrete footings (see the table "Loadbearing Values of Foundation Materials"). Your

POST SUPPORT OF DECK AREA

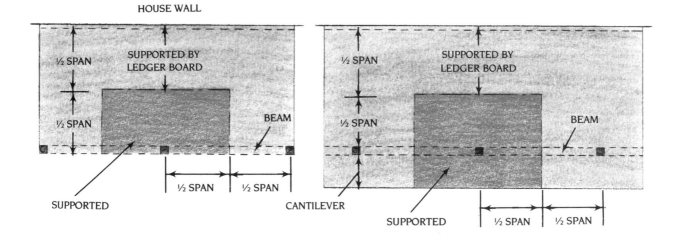

MAXIMUM POST HEIGHTS*

Species Group	Post Size	36	48	60	72	84	96	108	120	132	144
					DECK AREA SUPPORTED BY POST (SQ. FT.)						
1	4 × 4	to 12′	to 12′	to 12′	to 12′	to 10′	to 10′	to 10′	to 8′	to 8′	to 8′
	4 × 6					to 12′	to 12′	to 12′	to 12′	to 10′	to 10′
	6 × 6									to 12′	to 12′
2	4 × 4	to 12′	to 12′	to 10′	to 10′	to 10′	to 8′	to 8′	to 8′	to 8′	
	4 × 6			to 12′	to 12′	to 12′	to 10′	to 10′	to 10′	to 10′	
	6 × 6						to 12′	to 12′	to 12′	to 12′	to 12′
3	4 × 4	to 12′	to 10′	to 10′	to 8′	to 8′	to 8′	to 6′	to 6′	to 6′	to 6′
	4 × 6		to 12′	to 12′	to 10′	to 10′	to 10′	to 8′	to 8′	to 8′	to 8′
	6 × 6				to 12′	to 12′	to 12′	to 12′	to 12′	to 12′	to 12′

* Based on 40 psf live load and 10 psf dead load. Grade: 4 × 4 posts—Standard & Better; 4 × 6, 6 × 6 posts—No. 1 & Better.

LOADBEARING VALUES OF FOUNDATION MATERIALS

Material	Support Provided (psf)	8″ × 8″	12″ × 12″	24″ × 24″
		MAXIMUM SQ. FT. OF DECK ON A FOOTING		
Solid bedrock	50,000 +	640 +		
Soft or broken bedrock	20,000	256		
Gravel and sand-gravel	12,000	107	240	
Sandy and gravelly soils	6,000	53	120	
Loose sand (confined)	4,000	36	80	320
Stiff clay	4,000	36	80	320
Soft broken shale	3,000	27	60	240
Soft clay	3,000	27	60	240
Peat and other organic soils	Not suitable			

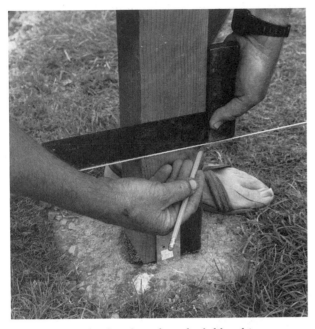

Deck posts, whether for a low deck like this one or a high deck, can be measured for length by stringing a taut line between two end posts that have been cut to the correct elevation. Use a square to make squared cutting marks.

local building department can advise you more specifically for your soil.

That completes your deck design—planks, joists, beams, posts, and footings: all must be structurally sound. Once you study the span tables a bit, you'll quickly see leeway for working economy of materials into your deck design. For example, by spacing your joists a little closer together, you may be able to safely take advantage of a current lumber yard extravaganza sale of poorer-grade lumber. It's a good idea to figure things all ways and see what is most economical. On the other hand, when it comes to appearance, you may not want to stint at all.

Redwood Deck Calculations

Calculate a redwood deck the same way, but use the redwood tables, which were were developed by the California Redwood Association for around-the-house uses. For other uses or uses with engineer-designed plans, structural grades of redwood lumber (not covered here) are recommended. Follow the design values set up for those grades.

For choosing redwood posts, use the table "Maximum Post Heights," just as for the other Group 3 species. In our example, redwood 4 × 4s work out to be capable of handling post heights to 8 feet.

On any deck, a concentrated load, such as an in-deck spa or hot tub, may require alternate figuring, possibly engineering. Often, for this reason as well as others, spas and hot tubs are placed on their own foundations, separate from the deck. Then the deck supports can be calculated in the usual way.

Note: Be sure to consult your local building department for the span tables approved by them. These are the tables you'll ultimately be required to follow. Though local tables may vary from those given here, the procedure for using them is similar.

DESIGN DETAILS

Outdoors, wide members tend to shrink, swell, and cup more than narrow ones. So when you need wide members, such as 2 × 6 deck planks, try to use edge-grain boards. Edge-grain boards (that is, boards with their annual rings running across the thickness rather than across the width) tend to distort less than flat-grain ones.

In the same vein, install flat horizontal members so they drain water off rather than collect it. Use outward sloping railings rather than dead-level ones. A slope of about 5 degrees is ample for drainage. If there's a choice, use rectangular members with thickness and width as nearly equal as possible—for example, 2 × 4s rather than 2 × 6s.

Headers (made of 2-inch lumber), fascias (made of 1-inch lumber), or skirts (often of lattice) can be added to a deck to hide the joist ends and help conceal the underdeck area. Also, a low deck needs careful animal-proofing. You don't want a skunk setting up housekeeping under a low deck.

Ledger Boards. While the ledger board can measure 2-by one size deeper than the joists, it should ideally measure 3-by, and be the same depth as the joists. This gives a little more space for the joist ends to bear on (that is, if they rest on top of it instead of being hung from it by joist hangers).

To keep it from rotting, the ledger board must be attached to the house wall in such a way as to allow air circulation behind it. One way is to slip stacks of plated washers over the lag screws or carriage bolts between the ledger board and the house. Use enough washers to space the ledger out from the wall from ½ to ¾ inch. It's smart to install metal flashing above the ledger to lead water over the top of the ledger rather than letting it flow behind, where it could cause decay. Another method is to caulk the joints between the house and ledger board with silicone rubber sealant.

For good deck drainage, locate the ledger board so that the top of the deck planks will be 1 inch or more below the house floor level. If solid decking rather than planking will be installed, the deck should slope

about an inch in 8 feet (⅛ inch per foot) away from the house, to allow rain runoff.

Joists.   To keep joists from tipping, install blocking at the midspan of all joists with more than an 8-foot span. For joists deeper than 2 × 8s, use metal or wood cross-bridging.

Setting the two joists at both ends of a deck slightly in from their normal positions will create a plank overhang at the ends.

Joists may be spliced above beams by overlapping them and nailing them together or by butting them with nailed-on wood or metal splices at those locations. Beams may be spliced, too, but the splice must always be centered over a post. The two pieces must be well tied together with a T-strap or wood cleats attached by nailing.

Joist-to-beam connections are illustrated in the accompanying drawing. All of these methods ensure rigidity.

Beams.   Post-to-beam connections need to be secure, as well. First of all, if the beams rest atop posts, all posts should be trimmed square and to the proper height so the beam can bear across the full

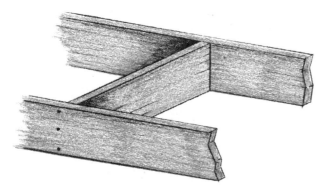

METHODS OF TYING JOISTS INTO LEDGER BOARDS

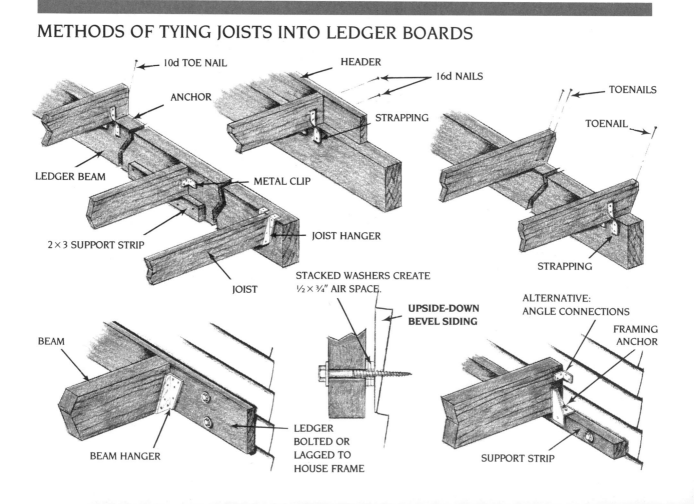

POST-AND-BEAM CONNECTIONS

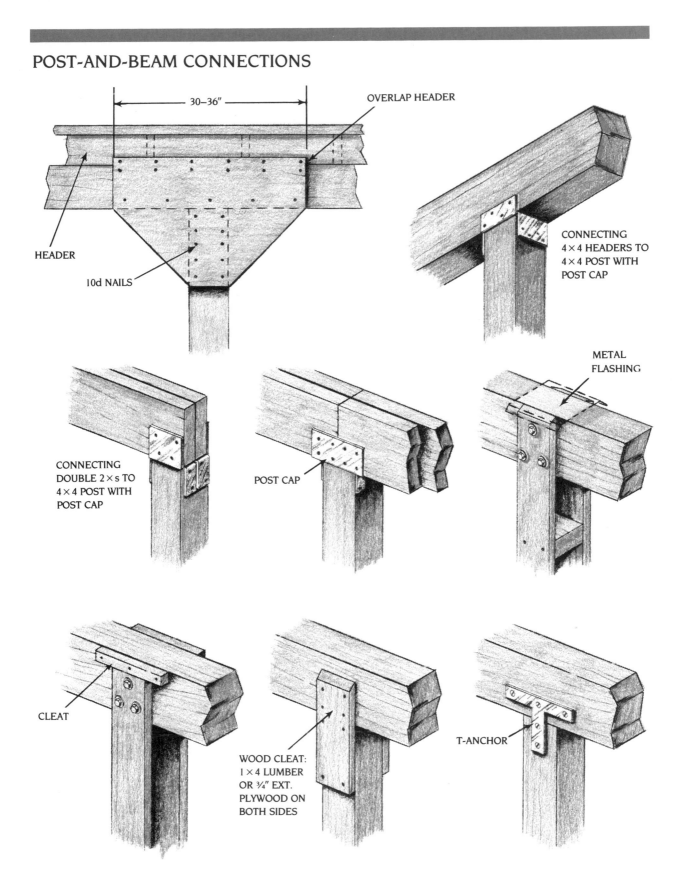

30–36″

OVERLAP HEADER

HEADER

10d NAILS

CONNECTING
4 × 4 HEADERS TO
4 × 4 POST WITH
POST CAP

CONNECTING
DOUBLE 2 × s TO
4 × 4 POST WITH
POST CAP

POST CAP

METAL
FLASHING

CLEAT

WOOD CLEAT:
1 × 4 LUMBER
OR ¾″ EXT.
PLYWOOD ON
BOTH SIDES

T-ANCHOR

area of the post top. Of course, the posts should be *plumbed* (made perfectly vertical) with a carpenter's level on two adjacent sides.

Then the beams should be fastened tightly to the posts to prevent push-off or lift-off. Toenailing is the poorest method of doing this—unacceptable, really. A better method is to use 1 × 4 lumber or ¾-inch exterior-type plywood as cleats on both sides of the post. The cleats are nailed to post and beam with 2½-inch-long weatherproof deformed-shank nails. The tops of the cleats should be cut at an angle to drain water from the end grain. Better still, use nail-on or bolt-on galvanized metal T-anchors or straight metal straps. Nail-on sheet-metal flanges are also available.

Piers.   Good pier construction helps ensure that your posts are well anchored. The post anchorages must be able to resist lateral movement as well as lift-off from high winds.

The best post anchors are designed to prevent

To prevent rot-inducing concrete contact, place a 3½ × 3½-inch "washer" cut from an asphalt shingle beneath every wood post. The metal tie-anchor, shown, is cast into the concrete footing.

METHODS OF LATERAL BRACING

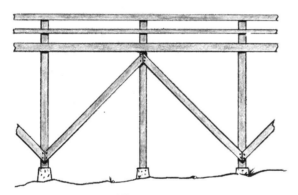

W-BRACING

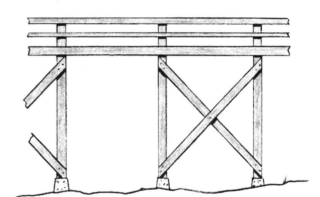

X-BRACING

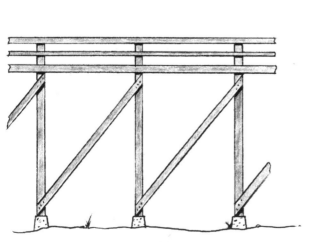

ANGLE-BRACING

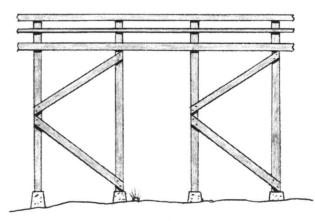

K-BRACING

PREVENTING ROT IN BRACING

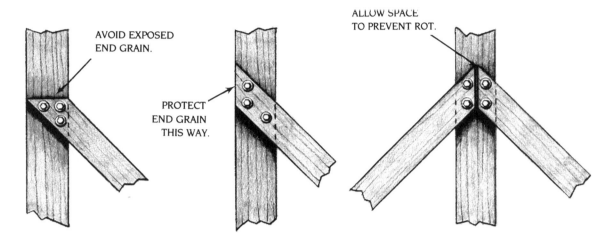

AVOID EXPOSED
END GRAIN.

PROTECT
END GRAIN
THIS WAY.

ALLOW SPACE
TO PREVENT ROT.

wood-to-concrete contact and thus to help prevent decay of the post bottoms. Metal post anchors do this well and are widely available. The best post anchors create a space between the posts and the concrete.

Lateral Bracing. To keep it from swaying, any deck with posts taller than 5 feet needs some sort of lateral bracing. You can use angle-, **X**-, **K**-, **W**-, or **Y**-bracing. For single bracing consisting of one member per bay (the space between adjacent posts), use 2 × 4s. For braces more than 8 feet long, use 2 × 6s. Secure braces to their posts with ⅜-inch lag screws or carriage bolts and flat washers. Angle-braces run from the bottom of one post to the top of the next. Angle-braces on adjacent sides should run in opposite directions. If spans and post heights are great, install **X**-bracing at every bay; otherwise, at every other.

A ¾-inch exterior-type plywood gusset at each post location will sometimes work as a partial brace for decks of moderate height—5 to 7 feet. The gussets also serve as connections between posts and beams. Fasten the gussets with 10d nails spaced about as shown in the accompanying drawing. The top edge of the plywood needs to be protected from moisture by a member extending over it.

Another type of partial brace may be made of 2 × 4s lag-screwed or carriage-bolted as shown.

Some deck members, such as the planks, can extend over the ends of the braces to protect their exposed end grain from moisture. If such a member is not in place, and you have space, make the 2 × 4 cut-offs vertically so that the end grain won't collect water. The accompanying drawings show how to avoid decay

damage from moisture trapped at end grains.

Planking. Deck planks should be fastened by nails or screws. Use deformed-shank nails or screws (see pages 54–55) in the lengths shown in the table "Fastening Deck Planks." On 2 × 3 planks, the fasteners should be located ¾ inch in from the edges, and on 2 × 4s, 1 inch in. Fasteners on planks laid on edge should be centered on them, or the planks should be toenailed. To tie adjacent planks together, spacers are needed for on-edge planks with nails driven horizontally through them. You need such lateral support at least every 4 feet along planks. If the joists are farther apart than that, you'll need an extra row of spacers between joists. To prevent water from penetrating between planks and spacers, use construction adhesive on the spacer faces.

Railings. Every deck more than about 18 inches off the ground (check your local code for the exact figure) needs a childproof protective railing around it. If a deck railing is required, the principal members are its posts. They must be large enough and well enough fastened to provide strong support for the horizontal rails. The deck railing may be supported by posts that are extended up in one piece from below the deck. Or you may attach posts to the sides of joists or beams. Full-size wood blocking installed between end joists and the joists next to them at post locations will increase post support. The ends of beams or joists can also support deck rail posts.

Caution: don't mount railing posts to deck planks, even with post anchors. The planks cannot provide enough lateral support to create a sturdy railing.

ON-EDGE DECK PLANKING

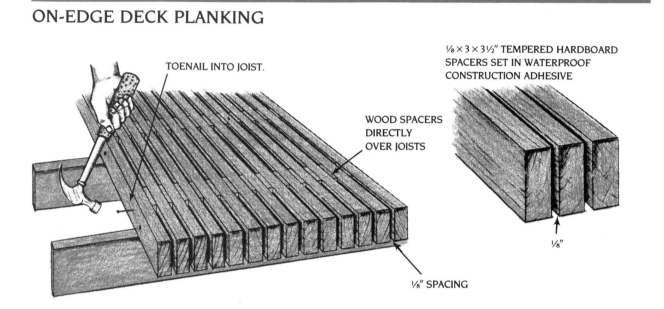

TOENAIL INTO JOIST.

⅛ × 3 × 3½" TEMPERED HARDBOARD SPACERS SET IN WATERPROOF CONSTRUCTION ADHESIVE

WOOD SPACERS DIRECTLY OVER JOISTS

⅛"

⅛" SPACING

PLANK OVERHANG

PLANKS MAY BE FASTENED BY NAILS OR SCREWS. FOR GUIDELINES, SEE PREVIOUS PAGE.

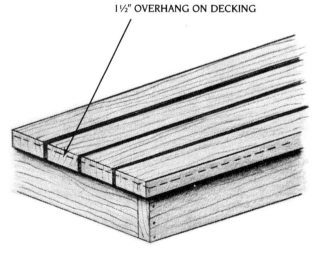

1½" OVERHANG ON DECKING

Photo above: Decking nails can be used as temporary spacers between planks as you nail. A nail's thickness is the minimum recommended spacing between planks. It anticipates expansion of wetted wood. Drawing above: Recommended plank overhangs are discussed on the previous page.

PLANK PATTERNS

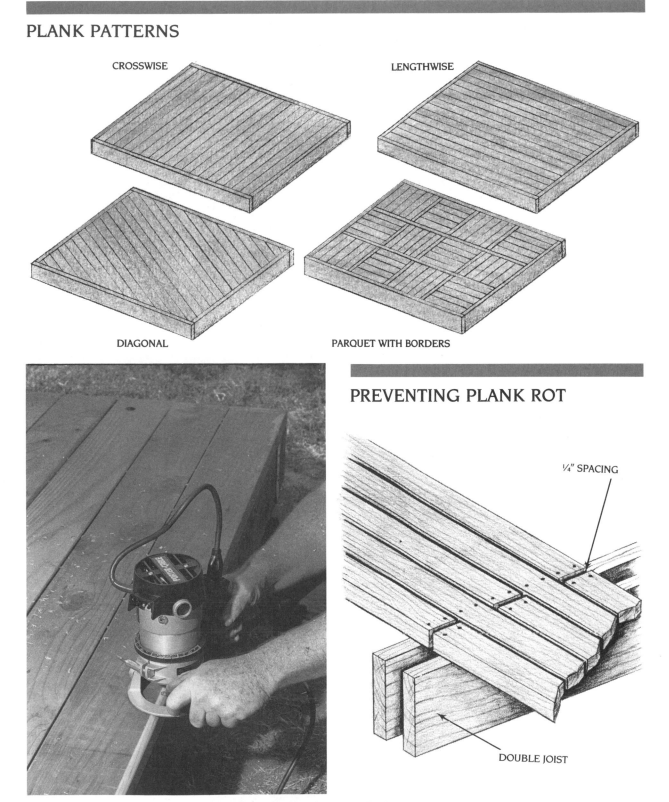

CROSSWISE

LENGTHWISE

DIAGONAL

PARQUET WITH BORDERS

PREVENTING PLANK ROT

¼" SPACING

DOUBLE JOIST

Photo: For a handsome touch, round the outside edges of a deck by means of a router with self-guiding bit. On a router that spins clockwise, as most do, cut from left to right so the bit pulls itself into the work. This ½-inch Porter-Cable router did the heavy cutting. Drawing: Spacing between ends of deck planks helps prevent rot.

CALCULATING PLANK SPACING

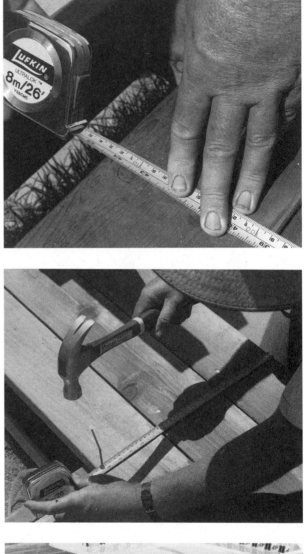

It's possible to make deck planks work out evenly at far edges without need to rip a narrow edge plank. But this takes planning. As shown in the top two photos, take a careful metric-tape measurement of the outside edges of joists, adding 150mm for the plank overhang at both edges. Using a calculator, figure the number of planks *with desired spaces* needed to fit evenly across the deck. Adjust spacing to make the planks come out even. (Remember, there is one more plank than there are spaces.) When installing the planks, use the calculator to figure what millimeter mark the edge of each plank must reach and fasten them that way. The finished job looks better than if a narrow plank is ripped at one edge.

RAILING SUPPORT

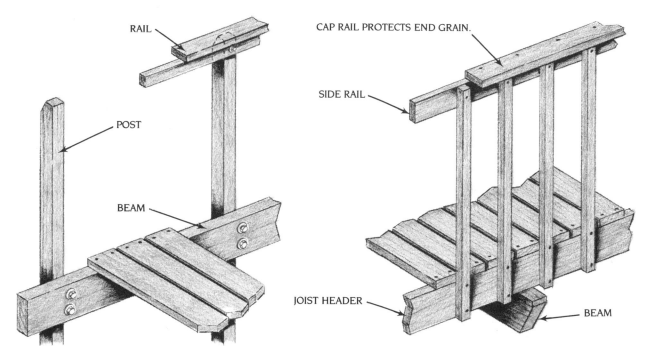

RAIL

POST

BEAM

CAP RAIL PROTECTS END GRAIN.

SIDE RAIL

JOIST HEADER

BEAM

BALUSTER SUPPORT

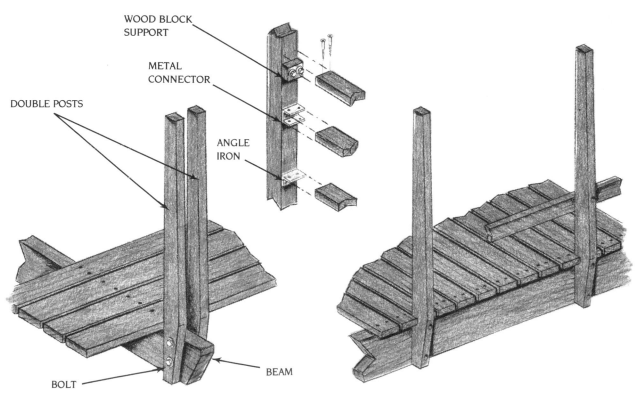

WOOD BLOCK SUPPORT

METAL CONNECTOR

DOUBLE POSTS

ANGLE IRON

BOLT

BEAM

Here a cross-lapped 2 × 4 railing sits atop a 4 × 4 supporting post. As childproofing, 2 × 4-inch galvanized steel wire mesh is stapled around the railing.

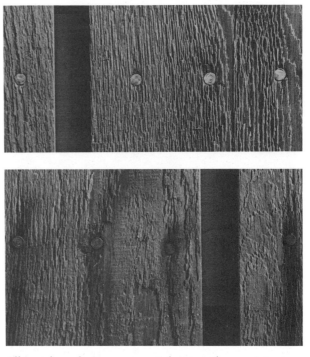

All outdoor fasteners must be weather-resistant or else they will stain the wood. Top photo: These aluminum nails have weathered without staining. Bottom photo: Corroding steel nails leave ugly marks. (Aluminum Association photo)

FASTENERS

In carpentry, the most common fasteners are nails. Screws place second in popularity. Nails and screws come in many kinds and sizes, and they are now supplemented with outdoor-type construction adhesives and framing anchors.

Nails

Nails come in many varieties. Wire nails, so-called because they are made from wire, are most often used and are usually sold by the pound. Aluminum, copper, brass, bronze, and stainless steel nails are also available but are not commonly used for decks. The table "Common Nail Lengths and Quantities" shows the quantity of nails in a pound for each size. Nails are useful for almost all butted-up joints.

For outdoor projects, corrosion resistance is a major factor in nail selection. Corrosion of fasteners makes surface streaks that give a tacky look to the project. Worse, fastener corrosion all too soon causes loss of structural integrity. Mild (soft) steel nails are not recommended for outdoor construction—especially in pressure-treated wood—because they rust too easily. Galvanized nails are suitable, as long as the galvanizing stays on the head during hammering. Galvanized nails are coated by tumbling with zinc chips.

The resulting finish is not as weather-resistant as that obtained by hot-dipping in molten zinc. Rougher and better gripping, and thus preferable, are double-hot-dipped, zinc-coated nails.

Aluminum nails, especially hardened aluminum ones, may be used for outdoor woodworking and carpentry. These have one large drawback: if not struck squarely, they bend more easily than steel nails.

Nails useful in outdoor carpentry come in several types: common, box, finishing, casing, masonry, and brad. The kind of nail is determined by its head, the shape of its shank, and its purpose. Common and box nails are similar, except that common nails are thicker and are more generally used for heavy construction, whereas box nails are thinner and are used more for lighter holding jobs. Finishing nails are thin so they won't split fine trim woods, and have heads small enough to be driven below the surface without leaving a large hole. Casing nails resemble finishing nails but are a bit thicker for better holding. Their heads are driven flush, but are not set. Casing nails are more

NAIL SIZES (NAILS SHOWN ACTUAL SIZE)

6d   8d   10d   12d   16d   20d

COMMON NAIL LENGTHS AND QUANTITIES

Size	Length (in.)	Number per Pound*
6d	2	167
8d	2½	101
10d	3	66
12d	3¼	62
16d	3½	47
20d	4	30

* Approximate

The "d" symbol in accompanying tables stands for "penny," which originally related to the price per hundred but today signifies only length. When ordering nails, ask for "8 penny," "10 penny," etc. The "o.c." abbreviation in the table below stands for "on centers," meaning distance apart.

NAILING OUTDOOR CONSTRUCTION*

Location	Method	Nail Size	Nail Quantity
Joist resting on beam or ledger	Toenail	10d or 8d	2 3
Header to joist	End-nail	16d	3
Built-up beams with two members	Face-nail, clinched or Face-nail, staggered	16d 10d	16" o.c. 16" o.c.
Built-up beams with three or more members	Face-nail	20d	32" o.c. each side
Bridging to joist	Toenail	8d	2
Bracing to posts, 2"	Face-nail	16d	3
Bracing to posts, 1"	Face-nail	8d	4

* Weather-resistant nails   o.c. = on centers

likely to be used than finishing nails in trimming out a deck.

Double-headed nails (also known as *form nails* or *duplex nails*) come in common-nail shank diameter. They are useful for temporary nailing, such as in making concrete forms, where the nails can easily be pulled out after the concrete form has served its purpose.

Common nails have flat, round heads that stick out beyond the shank. The thick shafts of common nails tend to split wood, especially when driven close to the end of a board. Nevertheless, I prefer common nails for deck-building and box nails for making boxes.

Nail Length.   Nails are available in many lengths and shank sizes. Nail sizing is stated in "pennies," a word abbreviated *d*, as in 8*d*, 12*d*. Nail sizes run from 2d—1 inch long—up to 80d—8 inches long. Anything under 2d is a brad (as are many 1-inch nails with slender shanks), while nails over 60d (6 inches long) are considered spikes. The sizes required most frequently will be 8d, or 2½ inch; 10d, or 3 inch; 12d, or 3¼ inch; 16d, or 3½ inch; and 20d, or 4 inch.

A good rule of thumb for any construction job is to use nails two-and-one-half times as long as the thickness of the board being attached to another member. This, of course, applies where the boards being attached are thick enough to accept such nails. For example, when nailing a 1½-inch-thick brace to a 4×4 post, you'd use a nail 4 inches long (2½ × 1½ = 3¾—the next size is a 4-inch, 20d nail). If the nails are clinched (that is, if their protruding points are bent over after driving them), they may be longer.

Despite the rule of thumb, 16d nails are generally used to nail 2-inch nominal boards together. A deck-building project uses many nails this size.

A nail's holding power varies with the species of wood it is driven into. As you might expect, the stronger the wood, the better the nail holds. Smooth-shank nails have the least holding power. As a rough rule of thumb, a 16d nail will hold about 100 pounds in shear (where the force is across the nail's shank, trying to slice it in two). Enough nails must be used to total more than the shear load being placed on the member. (Better yet, use framing anchors to take these loads.)

Shanks.   The shrinking and swelling of wood when dried and wetted tends to make smooth-shank nails loosen. Therefore, some form of deformed-shank nail is essential for virtually all outdoor uses. Deformed-shanks have much greater pull-out resistance than smooth-shanks, often two or three times as much. Ring-shank, barbed, or annular-ring nails, as

NAIL SHANKS

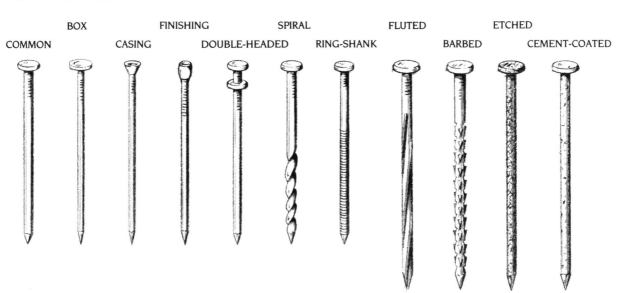

COMMON   BOX   CASING   FINISHING   DOUBLE-HEADED   SPIRAL   RING-SHANK   FLUTED   BARBED   ETCHED   CEMENT-COATED

FASTENING DECK PLANKS
(at each joist)

Plank	Nails*	Screws**
2 × 3, 2 × 4 flat	Two 12d	Two 3"
2 × 6 flat	One 12d alternated sides and two at plank ends. Construction adhesive used	One 3" alternated sides and two at plank ends. Construction adhesive used
2 × 3 on edge	One 40d	One 4½"
2 × 4 on edge	Not recommended	One 5"

* Deformed-shank, weatherproof
** Weatherproof

they are called, are among the best in pull-out resistance. Spiral-threaded nails, also called *screw nails* or *drive nails*, also have good pull-out resistance. They rotate as they are driven into wood and are especially useful for hardwoods. The drawing on page 52 shows types of nails available.

The table "Nailing Outdoor Construction" on page 53 indicates nail sizes and number of nails to use for most outdoor carpentry tasks.

Reducing Splitting. Nails, especially ones driven near the ends and edges of boards, tend to split wood. To reduce splitting when hammering nails, try various tricks. Blunt the nail by placing it head-down on a hard surface and hitting the nail point lightly once or twice with the hammer. Predrill for nails, using a bit about three fourths the nail's diameter. Use a greater number of slightly thinner nails in place of fewer large ones. Allow greater spacing between nails. Stagger the nails in each row so that they don't fall in the same annular rings. Or, for boards 8 inches and wider, avoid placing any nails near edges. The rule of thumb on nailing close to edges and ends is this: place nails no closer than half the board's thickness to an edge and no closer than the board's thickness to an end. Use a minimum of two nails per board, two nails for 4- and 6-inch widths and three nails for 8- and 10-inch widths.

Another nailing tip: avoid nailing into end-grain. If you must fasten into end grain, use screws instead.

Screws

Screws do a better job of holding than nails do, so smaller sizes may be used. Screws are also highly resistant to pull-out. Moreover, screws can be removed to disassemble a project; nails can, too, but not so easily or neatly.

Screws come in two categories: wood screws and metal screws. Here the terms *wood* and *metal* refer to application, not makeup. All screws are made of metal.

Heads. Screws have threads, shanks, and heads. Types of screw heads include flat-head, round-head, oval-head, and pan head. The most commonly used wood screws are the flat-head type. Screw heads include slotted, Phillips, hexagonal-recessed, Robertson (square-recessed), and hexagonal-head.

Sizes. Wood screw diameter is measured in gauge numbers from 2 to 24, the larger numbers representing the larger sizes. Gauge sizes practical for outdoor carpentry run from No. 6 to No. 14.

Length. Screws should be long enough to penetrate the receiving member at least to the thickness of the thinner (outside) member, but with not less than a 1-inch penetration. For example, fastening a ¾-inch member to a 2 × 4 calls for the use of 1¾-inch-long screws. Screw size is always stated as a combination of gauge number and length, for example No. 10, 1½-inch.

Corrosion Resistance. All screws for outdoor work should be corrosion-resistant. Avoid unplated steel screws; most screws today have at least a thin plating to forestall corrosion. While zinc-, cadmium-, or chrome-plated screws are best for outdoor use, and use in pressure-treated wood, the rough coating on some plated screws can make them hard to drive. Aluminum screws are corrosion-resistant but not very strong. Still, they're fine for light holding purposes.

Pilot holes. To avoid splitting the wood, drill a small *pilot* hole for the threaded portion and a larger *clearance* or *shank* hole for the screw shank. A third tapered *countersink* hole allows a flush or recessed head placement. Since deck woods are usually soft, the screwdriver can usually turn down screw heads flush without noticeable wood damage and without preliminary countersinking.

SCREW TYPES AND SIZES

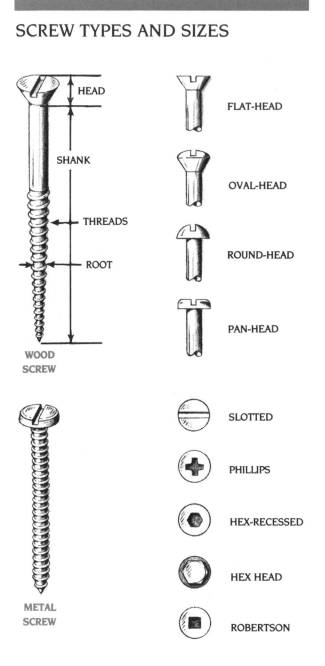

HEAD

SHANK

THREADS

ROOT

WOOD SCREW

FLAT-HEAD

OVAL-HEAD

ROUND-HEAD

PAN-HEAD

SLOTTED

PHILLIPS

HEX-RECESSED

HEX HEAD

ROBERTSON

METAL SCREW

To prevent splitting, especially at the ends of boards, you need both clearance and pilot holes for screws, and you need clearance holes for nails.

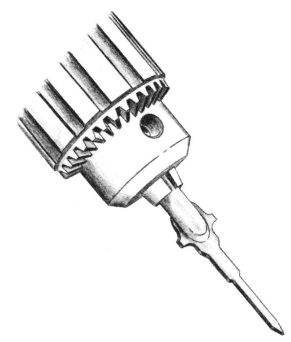

This specialized bit drills the pilot hole, clearance hole, and countersink hole in one operation. The bit must be matched to the gauge and length of screw.

DRILL SIZES FOR WOOD SCREWS

Screw Size (No.)	PILOT HOLE Softwoods	Hardwoods	CLEARANCE HOLE
6	1/16"	5/64"	9/64"
8	5/64"	3/32"	11/64"
10	3/32"	7/64"	3/16"
12	7/64"	1/8"	7/32"
14	1/8"	9/64"	1/4"

The correct drill size for pilot and clearance holes for some common wood screw sizes is given in the table "Drill Sizes for Wood Screws." But it's easy to select the correct size of pilot- and clearance-hole drills for any screw, working by eye as shown in the accompanying drawing.

If the pilot hole is too large, the screw's holding power will be reduced, allowing the screw to strip when tightened or loaded; too small, it can make for hard driving. To hold well, screws should be snugly driven.

Power Screwdriving. Before the advent of the electric drill, driving screws took longer than driving nails. For this reason, screws were seldom used.

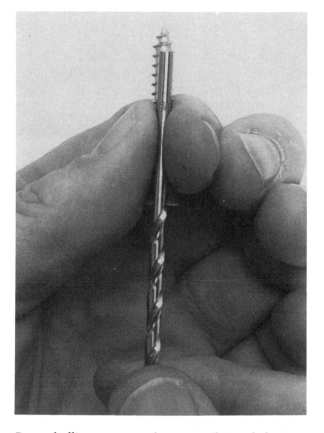

By eyeballing, you can choose a pilot and clearance drill for any screw. Hold the screw and selected drill up to light and compare their sizes. A pilot drill should be two-thirds the size of the screw's root (solid area between threads) for softwood. The clearance hole should be the same size as the screw's shank.

Today, the trend is to power-drive screws, usually screws with Phillips or Robertson heads. Canadian-developed Robertson heads are becoming increasingly popular because the driver will not cam-out (that is, slip out of the screw head). Screws are driven with a hardened-steel bit attached to a variable-speed electric drill designed for double duty as a power screwdriver. This is called a *driver/drill.*

In general, it's sensible to use screws wherever you can drill and install screws with modern methods. And it's possible to use fewer screws than nails and still get better holding, for example, in deck planking. If neither a cordless driver/drill nor a spiral-ratcheting screwdriver is available, a screwdriver bit for a bit brace can take much of the wrist-tiring work out of driving screws.

You can ease the driving of nails and screws and help prevent their splitting of wood by lubricating them with paste wax, candle wax, beeswax, or paraffin. To prevent splitting, screws that are run in near the edges and ends of boards will require pilot holes.

Drywall Screws. If you'd like something that does the same job as nails, but holds a whole lot better, try zinc-plated drywall screws. Drywall screws are designed for easy, trouble-free driving. They make their own pilot holes in most softwoods. If run in with a driver/drill (wearing safety goggles), there's almost zero effort. Most have Phillips or Robertson flat bugle heads.

Zinc-plated drywall screws are useful substitutes for outdoor nails and for wood screws. If 3-inch zinc-plated drywall screws are used for deck planking, they should eliminate popping. One manufacturer markets drywall screws as "multi-use" screws. Another calls them "deck screws." CAUTION: The ordinary black-looking phosphate-coated drywall screws aren't corrosion-resistant enough for use outdoors. Drywall screws for the outdoors should be zinc-plated.

ANOTHER CAUTION: Since the centers of drywall screws are soft, they should not be used where lateral loads would place them in shear. Therefore, do not use drywall screws as substitutes for framing-anchor nails. Framing-anchor nails are engineered to withstand considerable shear. Drywall screws are not.

Get an assortment of weather-resistant drywall screws in No. 6, No. 8, and No. 10 sizes from ½ to 4 inches long. Once you've tried drywall screws, you may have little use for nails or wood screws thereafter.

Sheet-metal Screws. Another great power-driven fastener that may replace nails and wood screws is the sheet-metal screw. Sheet-metal screws have greater holding power, even in wood, than wood screws. While they ordinarily come with slotted pan

DRILLING CLEARANCE AND PILOT HOLES

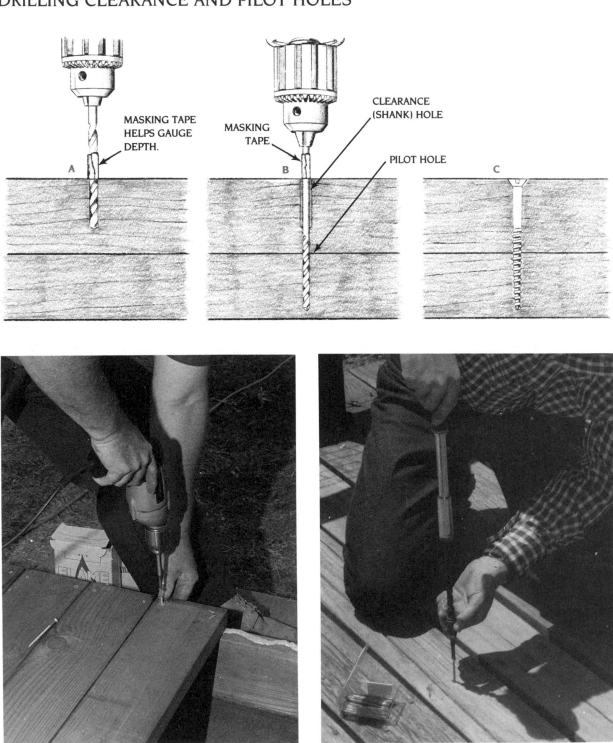

Left: One type of drywall screw is called a *deck screw*. Weather-resistant and made with a self-tapping head in 3½- and 4-inch lengths, it drives easily without pilot-drilling. Right: A spiral-ratcheting Yankee screwdriver makes driving screws almost as easy as driving with a power drill and much easier than driving with an ordinary screwdriver. This large model accepts various bits.

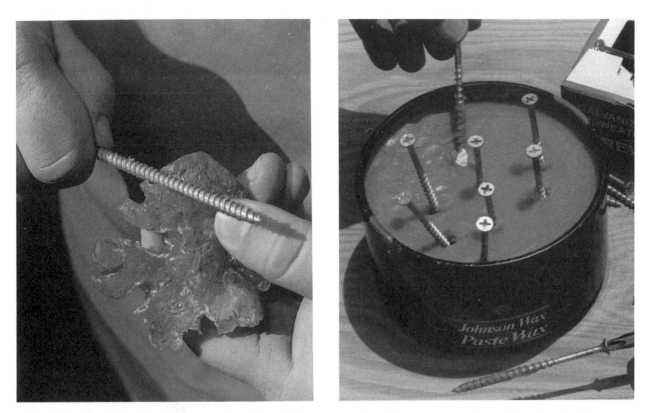

Lubricating the threads of screws makes them drive more easily. Apply wax or paraffin by rubbing the screw through the lubricant or by inserting the screws into paste wax before use.

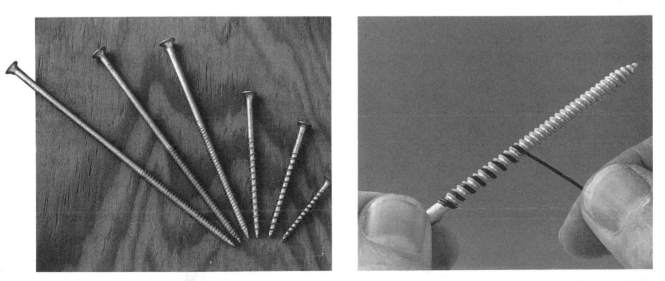

Left: Drywall screws have flat bugle heads, most with Phillips (X-shaped) drive recesses, but are also available with Robertson (square) and hex recesses. While this screw head was designed for plasterboard, it also works well with wood. Right: Drywall screws are often twin-threaded, as following a screw thread with black string here shows. This makes them drive faster and grip better. The sharp point makes the screw easier to drive, and helps eliminate the need for pilot-drilling.

heads, you can also get them with tapered or oval Phillips heads. They're case-hardened, toughened around the exterior surface, zinc-plated, and threaded their full length. If you have a selection of No. 6 and No. 8 weather-resistant sheet-metal screws in lengths from ½ to 2½ inches, you'll be in good shape for most outdoor woodworking projects.

Construction Adhesives

If you combine screws with modern construction adhesives, you can use half the fasteners and have a more secure hold. When installing deck planking, lay

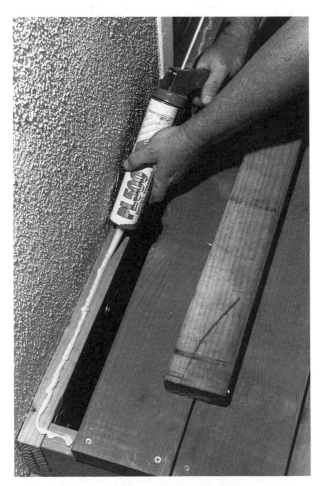

The use of deck adhesive is said to reduce by half the number of fasteners ordinarily needed, as well as to reduce warping and nail-popping. Run a bead of outdoor adhesive onto the framing before laying each deck plank. As shown, the ripped plank that will go over the ledger board also needs a bead of adhesive.

the deck planks over a wiggly strip of adhesive atop the joists (and place the screws to one side of the plank or the other at alternate joists). Instead of two 16d or 12d nails in 2 × 6 deck planks at every joist, you can use an exterior-rated construction adhesive and a single screw. Before proceeding, though, check with local building officials: this alternative may not meet codes everywhere.

Large Fasteners

Other larger fasteners are needed when constructing certain projects. For example, holding a deck's ledger board to the house almost always calls for the use of either lag screws or carriage bolts. Here, you'll also need plated flat washers to prevent cave-in damage to the wood. If they're being attached into a masonry wall, lag screws and carriage bolts will require lag-screw shields, as shown.

Lag Screws. Lag screws or lag bolts are large, coarse-threaded wood screws with a square or hex-head. They may be threaded into wood or lag screw shields in masonry. In general, lag screws should extend 1½ inches into solid material for every inch of material *thickness* they're supporting. So, to hold a 1½-inch-thick ledger board, a lag screw should be 3¾ inches long (call it 4 inches). Of this, at least 2¼ inches enters the solid material behind the ledger board. Lag screws in masonry need lead lag-screw shields lightly tapped into holes that are drilled for them. The two halves of the shields expand as the lag screws are driven, gripping tightly to the walls of the hole.

You'll find lag screws in diameters from ¼ inch up to 1 inch. Most-used for outdoor construction around the home are the ⅜- and ½-inch diameters.

Before purchasing lag screws, check job requirements. Most ledger boards can be hung with lag screws every 2 feet, but some long and heavy decks might require lag screws every 16 inches. It's always good to be on the safe side and use more than you need rather than too few. In a wood wall, drill a same-size shank clearance hole in the ledger board and a hole two thirds the root size of the lag screw into the wall framing. Do not countersink lag screws, because that would reduce the wood's sectional strength. When working in wood, use large, flat-plated washers under lag screw heads. This provides a large bearing surface that allows secure fastening without caving-in the wood's surface. And it keeps normal wood movement from tearing up the wood beneath the head. A wrench will run the lag screws in fully. Don't over-tighten. It helps to wax the lag screws first.

Carriage Bolts. Carriage bolts have rounded

ATTACHING THE LEDGER BOARD

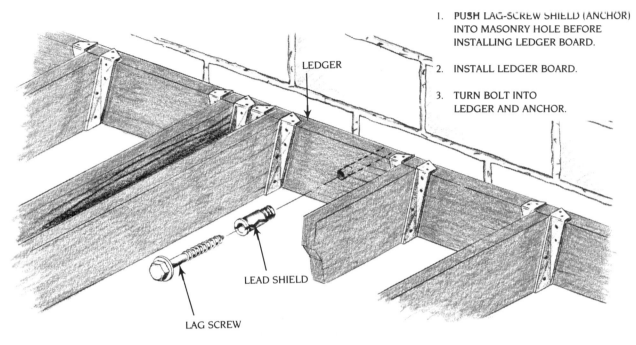

1. PUSH LAG-SCREW SHIELD (ANCHOR) INTO MASONRY HOLE BEFORE INSTALLING LEDGER BOARD.

2. INSTALL LEDGER BOARD.

3. TURN BOLT INTO LEDGER AND ANCHOR.

LEDGER

LEAD SHIELD

LAG SCREW

LARGE FASTENERS

CARRIAGE BOLT

MACHINE BOLT

LAG SCREW

TWO-PIECE LEAD SHIELD FOR MASONRY

heads with squared-off shoulders on the undersides. These have machine-screw threads and blunt shafts designed for metal nuts and so are used only when you have access to the back of the bolt. A carriage bolt fits a hole and the squared portion is pulled into the wood to grip the side of the hole so the nut can be tightened on the bolt without needing another wrench to prevent the bolt from turning. For softer woods, use a flat washer under the head of a carriage bolt. Always use a washer under the nut. The clearance hole for a carriage bolt is bored to the same diameter as the bolt shank—½-inch carriage bolt, ½-inch hole—and the bolt is tapped in.

Framing Anchors

Stamped-metal framing anchors are highly recommended whenever installing posts, beams, joists, or other deck-framing members. These galvanized anchors are formed from sheet steel and are used with specially hardened framing-anchor nails. Framing-anchor nails are short and thick, designed to hold the metal anchors to the wood. They are designed to take the concentrated shear loads produced by framing anchors, to resist corrosion, and not to penetrate through 2-inch lumber. If the special nails don't come

Left photo: To fasten deck posts with carriage bolts, first clamp the posts in place and drill clearance holes, two holes per post. Right photo: Then slip $1/4 \times 8$-inch weatherproof carriage bolts into the holes, fitted with large, flat washers and nuts. Tighten with a wrench.

Left photo: Railing posts can be lag-screwed or carriage-bolted to the sides of beams. For best lateral support, place the bolt holes as far apart as practical. Right photo: Framing anchors range from simple flat, perforated straps to complex hangers. To prevent separation of the members, nail the straps across connections using short, high-strength framing-anchor nails.

Left photo: All-purpose framing anchors may be used plain as angles between joists and beam, to take the shear loads, or bent in different shapes and used in numerous other modes. Right: You should cast metal nailing straps integrally with precast concrete piers and tie deck posts to them by anchor-nailing.

FRAMING HANGERS

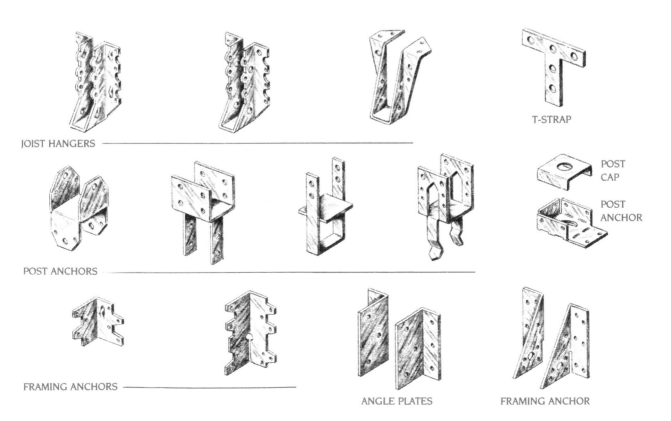

JOIST HANGERS

T-STRAP

POST CAP

POST ANCHOR

POST ANCHORS

FRAMING ANCHORS

ANGLE PLATES   FRAMING ANCHOR

Left photo: Framing anchors for stair treads are bolted to the uncut stringers with three ¼ × 2-inch machine bolts. Then the stair treads are set onto the hangers and screw-fastened from beneath. Right photo: For a full discussion of stair installation, please refer to page 123.

with the anchors, buy them separately by the pound. Avoid using ordinary nails with framing anchors.

The most common framing anchors in deck-building are *joist hangers* with a square-bottomed **U** shape and flanges that rest atop the ledger board. *Universal framing anchors* have a right-angled fold of galvanized metal with stamped holes and flaps that can be bent to fit the application. *Tie-down anchors* help keep members from being lifted off by a strong wind. *Post anchors* or *post caps* are also available to secure loadbearing connections. One framing-anchor manufacturer produces a line of anchors designed specifically for deck construction.

Although framing anchors add slightly to the cost of a deck, they reduce labor and greatly increase the strength and safety of the deck's connections.

OUTDOOR FINISHES

The weathering process makes dark woods lighter and light woods darker. Once weathered to gray, the wood will stay that way for a long time. Many coatings are available to decrease or completely stop weathering. These include paints, varnishes, and water-repellent penetrating finishes. Consult the table "Suitable Outdoor Finishes" on the next page.

Water-repellent Preservatives

It's a good idea to apply a water-repellent preservative treatment to a deck. The California Redwood Association recommends this for all exterior redwood, especially for the grades containing sapwood. If you use no other finish, use this as a minimum. Ideally, the preservative will contain a mildewcide. Apply two coats. The preservative serves as a finish as well as an undercoat for any other finish you apply.

If the surface begins to show blotchy discoloration after a year, clean it by scrubbing with a strong detergent. Let that dry, then re-treat the wood with a liberal brush application of water-repellent preservative. See the can label for coverage information.

Log Oil. You can make your own water-repellent preservative, called "log oil." Mix equal parts boiled linseed oil, silicone-containing masonry water repellent, and spar varnish. Apply one or more coats. The more you use, the glossier the finish and greater the protection provided. The linseed oil is good for the wood; the water repellent keeps the wood dry; and the varnish gives a hard coating.

Stains

Stains beat paint for protecting and coloring a deck. Give the wood a couple of months to dry out before staining it, even when applying stain over a water-

SUITABLE OUTDOOR FINISHES

Type of Finish	Choices	Application	Benefits
Water repellents (with mildewcide)	Alone or combined with a stain	Brush or roller, two coats. Let soak in	Good as a preliminary to another finish or as a natural finish
Penetrating finishes	Commercial finish or home-mixed log oil	Brush or roller in one or two coats to new and old wood	Oil- or water-based, contains mildewcides, protects against ultraviolet radiation and moisture damage to give wood a natural look
Stains	Semi-transparent oil-base	Brush is better than roller. Two coats	Ideal for new wood, to let the texture and grain show through. Lets wood breathe. Oil-base recommended
	Semi-transparent latex	Brush or roller in two coats	Easy to use, nonpolluting, lets texture and grain show through
	Solid-color oil-base	Brush is better than roller. One or two coats	Ideal for recoating of darkened wood. Restores bright appearance, letting texture show through. Lets wood breathe. Oil-base recommended
	Solid-color latex	Brush or roller in two coats	Easy to use for recoating of darkened wood. Restores bright appearance, letting texture show through. Nonpolluting
	Deck stain	Brush or roller to new or bleached wood	For high-traffic areas, resists abrasion
Bleaching oils		Brush or roller, one or two coats	Gives light gray-toned finish. Low maintenance
Brighteners	Household bleach	Brush on one or two coats periodically, rinse and let dry	Lightens aging wood
	Oxalic acid	Mix in water and apply, scrubbing in and rinsing	Bleaches out stains, removes mildew, lightens wood
	Wood brightener	Mix in hot water, apply and scrub in, then rinse	Rejuvenates gray and weathered wood to look like new. Removes mildew, algae, dirt stains
Paints	Alkyd	Apply alkyd primer and two finish coats. Brushing is best. Roller okay	Quick-drying
	Oil-base	Apply zinc-free oil-base primer and two finish coats	Zinc-free primer provides blister-resistance
	Latex	Apply zinc-free oil-base primer and two finish coats. Best as top coats	Easy to use; works best over oil-base primer. Durable and nonpolluting
	Floor-and-deck paint	Brush, roller, or spray over zinc-free oil-base primer	Alkyd or latex for heavily traveled areas
Clear finishes (not recommended for outdoors)	Polyurethane	Thin first coat, follow with others as directed or sand between	For outdoor furniture and small projects, to protect yet show off the wood
	Clear varnish	Brush, roller, or spray in two or more coats	Richens wood-stained effect while protecting
	Clear exterior latex	Brush or roller in two coats over new wood	Retains unweathered look of new wood. Easy to use and nonpolluting

Left photo: A 5-gallon pail and a clipped-in hardware-cloth screen offers the easiest way to put paint on a roller. Dip the roller into the paint and roll out excess paint on the screen. Right photo: If you prefinish all framing members before putting them up, all that's needed after assembly is a touch-up of board ends. Once you try prefinishing, you'll become a strong proponent.

repellent preservative. Stains come in two types: semitransparent and solid.

Semitransparent stains soak in, letting the wood grain show through while adding some color. They will not flake or peel, and they let the wood breathe. They should be used only on new wood and for recoating of clean, previously stained wood in good condition. The oil-based semitransparent stains protect the wood better, though the latexes are easier to use.

Solid-color stains are highly pigmented to color much as paints do but still show wood textures. They are more durable than semitransparent stains and are best for older wood that has discolored and needs rejuvenating. Use a stain-blocking primer to avoid bleed-through with redwood, cedar, and Douglas fir. Either oil-based or latex solid-color stain may be used. Oil-based does the better job, but latex is considerably easier to use.

Tint bases are available in three grades of solid stains (light, medium, and dark) and two of semitransparent stains (light and dark). The oil-based ones are preferable, though harder to use.

Deck stains, unlike ordinary stains, are tough enough for use under foot traffic. Deck planking should be stained with an oil-based deck stain. Once you stain

ZAR Wood Brightener by UGL comes as a concentrated white powder. Mixed with water, it lightens age-darkened wood, making it look newer.

or paint deck planks, however, you're committed to periodic recoating with stain.

Bleaches

Bleach wood darkened by weathering using a *wood brightener*. Mixed with hot water and scrubbed into the weathered wood, it restores a fresh, clean wood tone.

Clear Finishes

Film-forming clear finishes are not recommended for the outdoors because they quickly begin to flake. If you must, choose an exterior polyurethane.

Most finishes contain additives to protect against mildew, but in a mildew-prone region you may want to add additional mildewcide to your finish. It should be mixed in thoroughly, preferably by the paint dealer using a mechanical paint shaker.

Deck Paint

Exterior paints and other coatings may also be applied. An oil-base primer is best for raw wood. For a top coat, use a floor-and-deck paint, either oil-based or latex. The latexes are good, and are both much easier to work with and long-lasting.

Local and state environmental restrictions have affected the chemical formulations of various paints and stains. The new low-volatile formulations may or may not be inferior to the original products. Therefore,

it may pay you to ask your dealer about the changes and how they affect your use of the finish.

Solvents are used in thinning and cleaning up after oil-based paints. Volatile and flammable, these should be handled properly. Avoid excessive skin contact and do not breathe the fumes. Instead, use solvents outdoors or in a well-ventilated area (such as a garage with all the doors open). If you spray solvent-thinned paint, wear a tight-fitting respirator with organic-solvents cartridges. Keep flammable solvents away from sparks, heat, and open flames; *do not smoke around them.* Close the solvent container after each use. Store paints and their toxic and flammable solvents in closed, unbreakable cans in a locked cabinet or up high where children cannot get at them. Do not transfer any solvent to an unlabeled container.

One of the safest solvents for paint is turpentine, though it will burn. Pure gum spirits of turpentine is the grade to get for use with oil-base paints, though mineral spirits, sold as paint thinner, are less costly.

Paints and their solvents are considered hazardous materials in many locales, so don't simply throw the leftover paints and solvents away. The best way to dispose of old paint is to use it up—paint something with it. Once you leave empty paint cans open to dry, you can dispose of them normally.

Don't simply pour leftover paints down a drain. Watch for the next hazardous-waste pickup day in your area. If in doubt about how to get rid of something that might affect the environment, call your local environmental protection office.

COATED ABRASIVES (discussed on next page)

Designation	Old Grit No.	Ind. Grit No.	Use on Softwood (with closed-coat paper)	Use on Hardwood (with closed-coat paper)	Use on Paint (with open-coat paper)
Extra coarse	3½	20			
	3	24			Heavy removal
	2½	30			
Coarse	2	36			
	1½	40			
	1	50	Rough, heavy sanding	Moderate to light sanding	
Medium	½	60			
	1/0	80	Soft shaping, leveling	Light sanding	Prior to recoating
	2/0	100			
Fine	3/0	120			
	4/0	150	Smooth, paintable finish	Smoothing	Prior to priming
	5/0	180			
	6/0	220	Satin-smooth polish	Prior to staining	Hand-rubbing
Extra fine	8/0	280		Prior to clear finish	
	10/0	400			Rubbing clear coatings

Abrasives

Abrasives are needed to smooth wood and to roughen finishes so that successive coats of finish will adhere properly. Abrasives, you'll find, come as closed-coat and open-coat. Closed-coat abrasive papers contain more grit and cut quickly. Open-coat abrasives have particles spread farther apart to resist loading. They last longer than closed-coat abrasives when working on soft materials such as paints. You can use abrasives by hand or with power equipment. See the table "Coated Abrasives" on the previous page for information on the types and uses of abrasives.

Avoid flint paper (commonly known as "sandpaper"), except for removing heavy paint, which loads up any kind of grit quickly. Aluminum oxide paper is best for power-sanding on wood, plastic, and metal and is an excellent choice for all sorts of outdoor-building purposes. Silicon carbide paper is good for wet-or-dry sanding of finishes and metal. On bare wood it should be used dry.

Any sanding goes easiest with a sanding block. Get one with a rubber backing. And always sand wood with the grain. Norton Abrasives and other companies make a handy sponge-backed sanding pad containing two different grits.

Extra-fine steel wool may be useful for hand rubbing a clear finish between coats. It can also be used effectively after the final coat.

CARPENTRY TIPS

Building anything outdoors can hold risks. Make up your mind to work safely.

One of the most dangerous things you can do is to try to lift too much. The safe lifting limit for most workers seems to be about 50 pounds. Be sure to lift properly: lift heavy loads with your legs, not your back, keeping your back relatively vertical.

Jobsite Safety

Safety depends on attitude and attention. Pay attention to the site layout, keeping obstructions to a minimum. That means picking up tools and wood scraps before anyone can trip over them. Keep slippery areas well fixed in your mind and either avoid them or cross them with extra care. Most important, keep visitors—especially children—well out of the work area. If children are too young to understand, make sure that someone *else* keeps an eye on them. It is not possible to combine carpentry with babysitting. Both are full-time jobs. A high deck under construction has no railing and so is totally unsafe for children. Arrange things to prevent anyone from coming onto such a deck—day or night—until it is completed.

Be your own judge of safety. If a procedure seems dangerous to you, don't risk it. And remember that the safe worker proceeds at a steady, careful pace.

Using Ladders.   Ladders—both stepladders and extension ladders—can be one of the more dangerous accessories on any job. Improper ladder use can lead to a serious fall. If you use a ladder, follow a few simple rules. (On newer ladders, a safety decal is affixed to one rail. Heed those rules.) Also, inspect the ladder every time you use it, looking for such things as loose bolts, insecure rungs, and cracked rails. (The need for inspection is why wooden ladders should

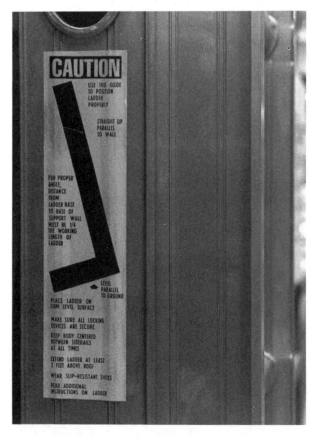

Up-to-date extension ladders bear a level-plumb indicator that shows when the ladder is being used at a safe angle. When the long bar on the backward L is vertical and the short bar is horizontal, the ladder is leaning at the correct angle.

never be painted; instead, use a wood preservative that allows visual inspection. *Never* climb a damaged or broken ladder.

Use a ladder of a size and weight appropriate for the job. Generally, you are safe on a consumer's-grade ladder, provided that your total load doesn't exceed 200 pounds. Otherwise, use a commercial-grade ladder. A commercial-grade ladder is recommended for around-the-house use. It costs more but is safer and should last longer.

When setting up an extension ladder, make sure the ground underneath isn't slippery or spongy. Set the ladder feet on level ground, or apply commercial leg-levelers. Never use a rock or chunk of wood to level an extension ladder's feet. Don't use temporary supports to increase the working height or adjust for uneven working surfaces. Keep an extension ladder's angle right around 75 degrees (current ladder models all have the correct angle marked on the side.) To achieve this angle, position the bottom of the ladder one-fourth as far out from the wall as the height of the ladder against the wall. An extension ladder used to climb up on a high deck should have three rungs above deck level to give you something to hang onto while stepping onto the deck or off the deck and onto the ladder.

Make sure that a stepladder is fully open, with its spreaders fully locked and its pail shelf in down-and-locked position. Don't climb on the backside of a stepladder. It is not made for that.

Wear shoes with a pronounced heel that will prevent your slipping through the steps. Avoid carrying work and tools in your hands while climbing. Either carry tools in a tool pouch or haul them up later with a rope and pail. Materials should be hauled or handed up after you are situated. When climbing a ladder, always face it and grasp the steps—never the side rails—firmly with both hands. Face the ladder while using it.

Do not climb *above* the second step from the top of a ladder. In other words, at least two unused steps should be above the step you are standing on.

Do not lean out from any ladder. The rule of thumb is that your belt buckle should stay between the ladder rails. If you can't reach, get down and move the ladder. Restrict from-the-ladder movements to arm's-length only, without stretching.

Work gloves can help minimize splinters and cuts, though for some jobs they tend to cut down on sensitivity. Any job that requires carrying lumber is probably best done wearing well-fitting gloves.

Whenever using tools, have the good sense to quit before you're so tired that a serious mistake becomes

DANGEROUS STEPS

DON'T STEP!

DON'T STEP!

You can help reduce potential for falls from ladders by keeping your weight centered between the side rails and by not standing on the top two steps.

inevitable. It's risky to push beyond your capacity, whatever the temptation.

Clean-ups

Don't put off all jobsite clean-up until the end of the day. A good broom, a rake, and a large dustpan are major helps at any jobsite. So is a trash can. Have one place to put unused lumber and another place for cut-offs and debris. Keep the two sites apart, but not so far that it makes a long walk between them.

If you are taking any medicine, including aspirin, check with your doctor or pharmacist to be sure it won't undermine your working safety.

CARPENTRY SAFETY TIPS

- Lift properly, using your legs rather than your back.
- Use the proper tool for the job, and use it correctly.
- Maintain your tools well and store them safely.
- Keep a safety-conscious attitude at all times.
- Stay alert for potential dangers and take necessary steps to avoid them.

- Stop working when you feel tired.
- Never work when you are taking drugs, even cold medicines, and don't drink alcohol while you work.
- Don't smoke when making cuts, drilling, and so on. The smoke can obscure vision.
- Wear work gloves when needed, but not, preferably, when using power tools.
- Store flammable liquids only in small quantities and in approved containers, *never* in glass bottles.
- Make sure oily rags and similar wastes are kept in a tightly sealed metal container, and properly dispose of them. Spontaneous combustion in such materials can start a fire without any other cause

CHAPTER 3

CARPENTRY TOOLS

Good tools—especially power tools—add to the enjoyment and ease of doing home improvements. In purchasing tools, look for a reputable brand. You'll find quite a few. Test a tool's fit in your hand and check out its balance. Read the warranty.

Cheap tools are almost never a good buy. Cheap handsaws, for example, will not cut a straight line and are sure to dull quickly.

SAFETY GEAR

Vital to protecting you from accidents on the job is *personal protective equipment*. This includes safety glasses or safety goggles and face shields; hearing protectors; safety helmets (also called "hard hats"); dust masks; respirators; work gloves; neoprene rubber or vinyl gloves, and fire extinguishers.

Eye and Face Protection
Always wear eye protection while working, whether safety glasses, safety goggles, or a face shield. Safety glasses have toughened, impact-resistant lenses— prescription or uncorrected—and often specially coated polycarbonate lenses that resist shattering if hit by a flying object. The safety glasses providing the best protection have side shields to prevent debris from entering from the sides.

Safety goggles with side shields help keep dust out of the eyes. When working where you could bump your head or where something could fall on you, you should also wear a hard hat.

Still more protective are soft plastic safety goggles, which protect against flying objects as well as against splashes coming from either the front or sides. The goggles provide ventilation and a snug fit and can be worn along with prescription glasses. Wear them for dusty work and when using chemicals that could splash in your eyes.

A face shield fits over your head on an adjustable, swing-up harness. It provides complete face protection, needed, for example, when sawing concrete or sharpening tools on a grinding wheel. For dust and flying-debris protection, wear both safety goggles and a face shield.

Safety glasses, and goggles and face shields must fit well and conform to ANSI (American National Standards Institute) Z87.1 or CSA (Canadian Standards Association) requirements. They should be specifically recommended for protection against the hazard you wish to avoid.

Protective Headgear

Most broken bones and cuts are not life-threatening, but head injuries can be deadly. If, while working, your head could come into contact with anything sharp or hard, or if anything might fall on you, wear a hard hat (safety helmet). Wear one where headroom is limited or dangerous. As the saying goes, if you don't have a hard head, then you need a hard hat.

A safety helmet is a one-piece, molded, impact-resistant plastic or stamped-metal shell with an adjustable harness to fit over the head. To minimize any impact, the harness leaves lots of space between the helmet and the head. The helmet should conform to ANSI Z89.1 or CSA requirements as a Class A, B, or C helmet, depending on the job requirements. (A Class A helmet is metal; a Class B helmet is non-conductive to protect against electrical hazards, as well; Class C helmets are lightweight protective caps.) Check for damage each time you wear the helmet and wear it with the protective shell resting squarely over your head, not tipped to one side or back. Adjust the harness for a snug fit.

Hearing Protection

For extended, noisy jobs, wear hearing protectors. Hearing protectors keep high-volume, high-frequency sounds from the eardrums. Long exposure to such noises can cause hearing loss, though short exposure may not be as harmful. Once hearing has been impaired, it cannot be restored.

Both insert (ear-plug) type and muff-type protec-

tors are available. Insert-type protectors are purchased in disposable form or in reusable molded sizes to fit the ear canal. Muff-type hearing protectors consist of plastic cups filled with foam or liquid to help block certain sounds (a process called *attenuation*). The two types may be worn separately, or worn together for combined effect. Some muff-type hearing protectors are designed for wear underneath a safety helmet.

The package a hearing protector comes in should bear an Environmental Protection Agency noise reduction rating (NRR) indicating the effectiveness of the protector, which should be at least 20 decibels (db). This means that the hearing protectors reduce the sound reaching your ears by 20 db, enough to help a great deal. For example, if a power saw emits a 110-db noise while you are wearing hearing protectors with a 25 NRR, your ears will be exposed to 85 db, a much less damaging noise level.

The U.S. Occupational Safety and Health Administration (OSHA) recommends that hearing protection be worn when the noise level exceeds 85 db for an 8-hour workday. For comparison, a train moving at high speed generates about 110 db, while an average busy street generates about 60 db.

The best policy is to wear hearing protectors when using noisy power tools, no matter how short the time of use.

Respiratory Protection

For dust- or fume-producing projects, especially those involving pressure-treated lumber, you will need respiratory protection. Two types of respiratory protection are available: the simple disposable or reusable dust mask and the dual-cartridge respirator. A disposable dust mask is good for keeping dust and fine particles from being inhaled during a single procedure. It consists of a filter pad and holder with elastic strap that fits around the back of the head to hold the mask tightly over the nose and mouth. The reusable type has a replaceable cotton fiber or gauze filter. Dust masks are available for protection against nontoxic dusts and mists as well as toxic ones. The best ones are NIOSH/MSHA-certified (National Institute for Occupational Safety & Health/Mine Safety & Health Administration). When you can taste or smell the contaminant, it's time to replace the dust mask.

If solvents are involved—for example, when spray painting—a chemical-cartridge respirator should be worn instead of a dust mask. The cartridges chemically counteract or remove toxic fumes. With an installed filter, the respirator also removes particulates the same way a dust mask does. Various chemical cartridges are available, and your respirator should be fitted with the right cartridge for the kind of material you are working with. One type is suited for use with organic vapors and another for paint, lacquer, and enamel mists. As with dust masks, chemical-cartridge respirators should be NIOSH/MSHA-certified.

Like a dust mask, the respirator is held over the nose and mouth by an elastic band. Be sure to check the fit and inspect the mask or respirator before using it. It should fit well so that all inhaling is done through the filter or cartridge canisters, not around a loose-fitting mask. Dust masks and respirators should be used only for protection against the contaminants they are approved for. Be sure to follow the manufacturer's instructions.

Hand and Foot Protection

Projects involving risks to the hands—such as those involving glass, rough or splintery lumber, concrete, concrete blocks, brick, or stone—call for heavy work gloves. The best, in my opinion, are fitted buckskin gloves. These may be tight enough to wear while operating power tools. Cotton work gloves are for light-duty work; leather or the more comfortable and less costly leather-palm work gloves are for heavier, rougher work.

Other hand risks are posed by chemicals. For handling glues, adhesives, paints, solvents, and toxic chemicals, wear neoprene-rubber work gloves. In the case of chemicals, check to see that the gloves are suitable for the material you are working with. Vinyl, instead of rubber, may be called for. You can get super-handy, low-cost, throwaway vinyl gloves for working with paints and solvents.

Safety work shoes containing flexible steel sole inserts are designed to keep nails from penetrating. It is a good idea to wear them while working around wood containing nails.

Good sources for personal protective equipment not available at local building materials dealers are American Optical Corporation, Direct Safety Company, Mine Safety Appliances Company, and Willson Safety Products—addresses listed in this book's "Preface."

Fire Extinguishers

A multipurpose Class ABC dry-chemical fire extinguisher should be standard equipment around the workshop. It effectively fights fires in combustibles, liquids, and electrical equipment. How large a blaze you can battle depends on the size of the extinguisher. While the minimum is a 5-pounder, I recommend a

10-pound extinguisher for the shop. Any extinguisher you purchase should bear the familiar UL listing (CSA in Canada).

Mount the extinguisher on the wall in your workshop, next to an exit. The extinguisher should be located away from potential fire hazards, such as a paint storage area. Be sure to inspect the extinguisher monthly to see that the pressure-gauge arrow indicates an adequate charge. If the arrow points to *recharge*, or if you ever have to use the extinguisher, have it professionally recharged or get a new one.

If a fire breaks out, have someone call the fire department while you remove the lock pin from the extinguisher. To use the fire extinguisher, aim the nozzle at the base of the flames. Squeeze the handle and spray dry chemical quickly in a short side-to-side pattern, continuing until the fire goes out. In case of a flashback, be ready to spray again. If the chemical runs out before the flames are extinguished, evacuate the house and wait for the fire department. If the fire was electrically caused, turn off power at the main service panel. Later, have the firefighters inspect the site, even if you put the fire out yourself.

HAND TOOLS

The basic hand tools needed for almost any construction work include the following:

BASIC TOOL INVENTORY
- Safety glasses or safety goggles
- Face shield
- Hearing protectors
- Safety helmet
- Dust mask
- Chemical cartridge respirator
- Work gloves
- Rubber or vinyl gloves
- Safety work shoes
- Fire extinguisher, type ABC
- Utility knife
- Measuring tape, 25-foot or 30-foot
- 3-foot metal rule
- Chalkline
- Crosscut saw, 8-point
- Hacksaw
- Curved-claw hammer, 16-ounce
- Ball-peen hammer, 16-ounce
- Mason's line
- Slip-joint pliers, 8-inch

- Toggle-locking pliers, 6-inch or 8-inch
- Set of flat-blade and Phillips screwdrivers (covered by most five- to seven-piece sets)
- Open-end adjustable wrench, 8-inch or 10-inch
- Carpenter's level, 2-foot
- Torpedo level
- Line level
- Try square or combination square
- Framing square
- Spiral-ratchet screwdriver
- Smoothing plane
- Center punch
- Wood chisel, ¾-inch
- Woodworking vise
- Sawhorses
- Electric drill, variable-speed, reversing, ⅜-inch
- Set of twist bits (⅛-inch through ⅜-inch)
- Set of spade-type wood-boring bits
- Set of screwdriver bits for electric drill
- Circular saw
- Assortment of circular saw blades

RECOMMENDED TOOLS
- Framing hammer, 20-, 24-, or 28-ounce
- Small sledgehammer, 3-pound, or sledgehammer, 8-pound
- Measuring tape, 50-foot or 100-foot
- Work apron, belted-style with pockets
- Water-tube level
- Carpenter's tool box
- Miter box
- Backsaw
- Countersink
- Keyhole (compass) saw
- Wood rasp
- Mill file, 8-inch or 10-inch
- Triangular file
- Socket wrench set
- Bevel square
- Saber saw
- Reciprocating saw
- Saw guide
- Stair-gauge markers for framing square
- Crosscut and miter gauge for circular saw
- Metalworking vise
- Holding table
- Bench grinder
- Driver/drill, cordless, clutched, ⅜-inch

LUXURY TOOLS
- Router and assorted bits
- Hammer-drill, ⅜-inch
- Table saw or radial saw

Hammers

Nailing hammers are either curved-claw hammers or ripping hammers with straight claws. Curved-claw hammers grip nails more easily for pulling and give slightly better control when driving nails, and so are preferred for general work. Ripping hammers are most often used for heavier framing work. For nail driving, they are less well balanced than curved-claw hammers.

When you shop for a hammer, look for a very slightly crowned face to allow directional control in driving nails, with a clean chamfer all around the face. The entire head should be cleanly finished, and the claws cleanly and sharply beveled.

Hammer handles may be made of wood, fiberglass, or steel. Each has its advantages. Whatever the handle material, the head should be securely attached to it. Head weight varies from 13 ounces (light) to 28 ounces (heavy); a 16-ounce head is ideal for most outdoor carpentry.

PULLING A NAIL

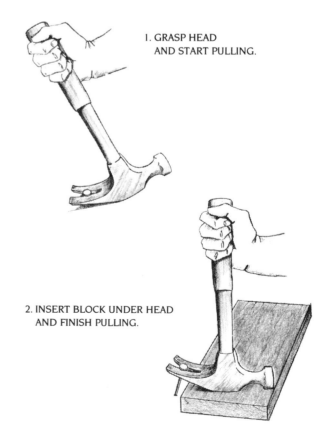

1. GRASP HEAD AND START PULLING.

2. INSERT BLOCK UNDER HEAD AND FINISH PULLING.

Small sledgehammers serve better than carpenter's hammers for heavier pounding, such as stake driving. This 3-pounder can also be used on cold chisels and for hand-powered drilling in masonry.

Handsaws

A wide variety of handsaws is available, with handles of wood or plastic and blades of tough, springy steel. For most general outdoor carpentry, only three handsaws will prove of any use: the crosscut saw, the keyhole (compass) saw, and the backsaw.

The crosscut saw once was the handsaw of choice for cutting boards at a right angle to (that is, across) the grain. Today, things are different. The circular (power) saw is used far more often for cross-cutting. The venerable crosscut saw has been relegated to neaten-up chores, except in situations in which electric power isn't available.

A good general-purpose crosscut saw is about 26 inches long. It should have an 8-point blade. (*points* relates approximately to teeth per inch). For thinner woods and for fine work, a 10- or 12-point crosscut saw works better. Crosscut saws come in sizes from 7- to 12-point. The finer the teeth, the slower but smoother the sawcuts.

For ripping boards, that is, for making with-the-grain cuts, the circular saw is used almost exclusively. You can do a bit of ripsawing with a crosscut saw, but you can't crosscut very well with a ripsaw. Most ripsaws have about 5½ points per inch.

Hammer faces are available plain or milled. Milled faces are useful only for rough framing.

You need to keep a ball-peen hammer on hand, if only to avoid improperly using a claw hammer to hit tools designed to be struck. A claw hammer is solely for nailing. It should never be used to drive a chisel: use the ball-peen hammer for that. A 16-ounce ball-peen is right for most purposes.

Sledgehammers—8-pound is generally best—are used for driving stakes into the ground in concrete formwork and for fence and deck layout work. A small, or baby, sledge—also called a *hand-drilling hammer* or *mash hammer*—weighs from 2½ to 4 pounds and may be substituted for the larger sledge. It is smaller and easier to handle. Both sledges come with double-faced heads.

Never use a hammer with a loose, or cracked, or slippery handle. The head could fly off and injure you or someone nearby, or the hammer itself could slip from your grip, with similar consequences. Either throw such a hammer away or have it repaired before using it again.

This handy tool-box saw from Sandvik doubles as a square. Angled edges on the handle give 90-degree crosscut and 45-degree miter readings.

This crosscut saw has seven teeth per inch but is designated an 8-point saw, since the first and last teeth are counted when calculating points.

Miter Boxes

A miter box, which is designed for accurate cutting of angles, can be as simple as a channel of wood with saw kerfs at 90 degrees and at 45 degrees each way. A backsaw is usually used with a miter box, though any crosscut saw will work. The best miter boxes have swivel heads with a degree scale, plus indexing locks at 90 and 45 degrees.

This low-cost miter box has preset 45-degree and 90-degree angles. Bottom holes allow your fastening it to support planking.

Hacksaws

Hacksaws cut metal. They consist of an adjustable frame and a metal-cutting blade. Hacksaw blades come with 14 to 32 teeth per inch. The coarser the blade, the faster it cuts. Nevertheless, the blade should be fine enough that at least three teeth are in contact with the work. For thin work a fine-toothed 32-tooth-per-inch blade should be used. Blade lengths are 8, 10, and 12 inches, with most hacksaw frames adjustable to fit all. Hacksaw blades are designed to be disposable. So a dull hacksaw blade is replaced rather than sharpened. Hacksaw blades are installed with the teeth pointing forward.

A minihacksaw holds a hacksaw blade without any frame. This is useful for cutting where the frame would be in the way. For frameless hacksawing, you can hold a blade with a gloved hand or wrap it with tape.

The tubular frame on this Stanley hacksaw holds extra blades. The saw can be adjusted to receive blades ranging from 10 to 12 inches.

Screwdrivers

You can never have too many kinds of screwdrivers. The screwdriver used to drive or remove a screw must be designed for the screw's head and be correctly sized for it, as well. For example, when driving a screw with a slotted head, use a flat-blade screwdriver. The blade should be as wide, or almost as wide, as the screw head, so that it fully fills the slot. Using a flat-blade screwdriver that's too small is likely to bend the driver tip and damage the screw slot. If the screwdriver slips out of the slot, it may damage the work, as well.

The old flat-blade hand-turned screwdriver has value but is less visible these days as power-driving becomes popular. (See the table "Flat-blade Screwdriver Selector.") The flat-blade screwdriver is being replaced for most construction work by Phillips and other screwdrivers such as the Robertson (square-drive), both illustrated in the previous chapter. These allow the application of more torque to the screw without worrying about the tip slipping and marring the work (or the worker).

It's wise to choose screwdrivers with an average-

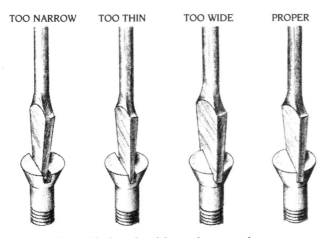

TOO NARROW   TOO THIN   TOO WIDE   PROPER

Screwdriver blades should match screw slots.

This Yankee Handyman Spiral Ratchet Screwdriver made by Stanley stores screwdriver bits and drill points inside the handle.

FLAT-BLADE SCREWDRIVER SELECTOR

Screw Size	Blade Size
No. 6	¼"
No. 8	⁵⁄₁₆"
No. 10	⁵⁄₁₆"
No. 12	⅜"

length shank, say 6 to 8 inches, whenever possible, because they are easiest to control. Very short lengths ("stubbies") or very long lengths should be used only when there's no other way to do the work.

Phillips screwdrivers are needed for the cross-slotted Phillips screws used in many around-the-house jobs. Phillips screwdrivers come in five sizes, No. 0 through No. 4. No. 1 is small, No. 3 is large, and No. 4 is larger still. The most common and useful size is the No. 2 Phillips.

Both the Robertson and the hexagonal-drive screwdrivers minimize what is called *cam-out*. Screws with heads recessed to accept these drivers are too often available only in boxes of 1,000, although they are becoming much easier to find in smaller quantities. If you are working on a large deck with the planks to be held with screws, the Robertson drive may be the way to go. Robertson screwdrivers come in sizes No. 1 to No. 4, smallest to largest.

The next-best thing to an electric driver/drill for installing and removing screws is a spiral-ratchet screwdriver, shown in the previous chapter. Also called a Yankee (a brand name for Stanley's model), this tool allows you to push down on the handle to drive

screws, thus without tiring the wrist. In the locked position the screwdriver works like an ordinary one. The screwdriver can be set to spiral for loosening or tightening. The spiral-ratchet screwdriver tip is designed to take an assortment of bits, which are stored in the handle.

Measuring Tapes

The standard retractable steel-blade measuring tape costs little and does much. Every homeowner needs at least one. The end of the tape has a sliding hook designed to fasten over an edge of a board or panel or hook onto a nailhead. For taking inside measurements, the hook slides in flush with the end of the tape. For taking outside measurements, the hook slides out, allowing you to make the edge being measured even with the end of the tape. If you have something to hook over, you can take measurements out to the maximum tape length unassisted. Tapes are often plastic-coated for friction-free retraction and long life. They are replaceable.

For carpentry and building construction, a wide (1-inch) and long (25- to 30-foot) tape measure is desirable. The wider tapes, being less flexible, can be held straight out for some distance in taking readings. Inch-wide tapes also contain more information. Nevertheless, a ¾-inch-wide, 10-foot tape will also serve.

Average 16-inch centers for framing are noted on most tape measures to facilitate the laying out of framing.

Inside measurements are made with the hook pushed against one edge and the tape's case held against the other edge. On some tape measures, an indicator at the point where the tape emerges from the case gives a reading, to which the length of the case must be added. The case's measurement (usually 2, 2½, or 3½ inches) will be marked on it. On a few

MEASURING-TAPE SAVVY

Left photo: Better measuring tapes have a bumper to cushion the stopping jolt at the end of spring-powered reel-in. Even so, it's best to ease up before the tape hits the bumper because repeated hits could break off the tip. Right photo: The scales on wider tapes show total inches as well as feet and inches.

Left photo: For accuracy in transferring dimensions from a measuring tape, tilt the blade to one side, placing the scale's edge against the work. The tape's hook end is designed to give an accurate starting point whether pushed against a surface or hooked over an edge and pulled. Right photo: Steel measuring tapes also take inside measurements, as between two deck-rail posts. Set the end of the tape snugly against one post (*out of picture at right*) and the tape's case against the other, as shown. Read at the edge of the case and add case width, for this tape, 2½ inches.

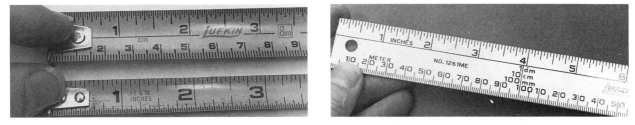

Left photo: Steel measuring tapes are available in inch-foot (*lower tape*) or in metric scales. The upper tape has both inch-foot and metric. For extra-close measurements, most tapes have the first foot on one side scaled in 32ds of an inch—thereafter, in 16ths. Right photo: A steel or aluminum rule is handy for making layouts, especially on plywood panels. This aluminum rule by Lufkin includes both inch-foot and metric scales. It is 1 meter long, which is a little over 39 inches.

tapes, a window through the case provides direct inside readings making addition unnecessary.

A good supplement to the retracting tape measure is the 3-foot steel or aluminum rule, the woodworker's yardstick. No shop should be without one. The handiest rules are 1 meter long (a bit more than 3 feet) and have one side marked in inches, the other in metric measure. Because the rule is rigid, it beats a tape measure for making layouts on panels and for drawing straight lines.

Squares

Squares come in many forms. At least two types are needed for most carpentry, indoor or outdoor. Most useful is the simple, basic try square. An all-metal or wood-and-metal try square is ideal for marking cutoffs on boards. All try squares give a 90-degree angle, and some also have a 45-degree cut across the stock for marking 45-degree miters. Blade length may be 6 to 12 inches, and the blade may mark in inches or in metric measurements.

A slightly different version of the standard try square is the combination square. It has an 8- to 12-inch blade that slides into the square head and

A combination square can double in service as a marking gauge. Just slide the blade out to the desired measurement and lock it. Then hold a pencil against the blade end as you slide the square along an edge to mark a line parallel to the edge.

Useful squares (*left to right*): bevel square for transferring odd angles; try square; combination square; and framing square. The combination square is the only efficient square for 45-degree angles.

HOW TO CHECK A SQUARE'S ACCURACY

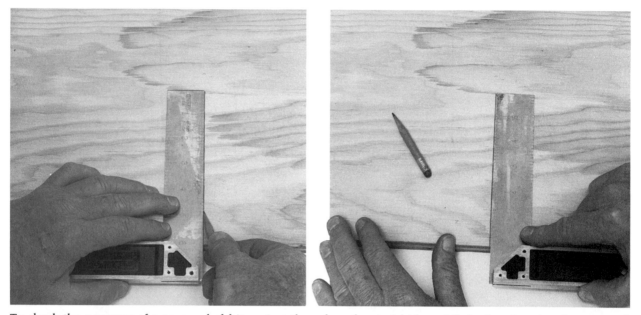

To check the accuracy of a square, hold it against the edge of a straight board (left photo) and make a pencil mark along the blade. Then (right photo) flop the blade over and check it against the mark you've made. Any misalignment represents twice the square's error.

For the accuracy test to be valid, as shown at left, the board edge must be straight. Check the board for straightness first.

To mark square cutting lines with a framing square before making saw cuts, hold the blade tightly down one side of the board and mark along the tongue.

can be locked in any location. The cast-iron head also has a 45-degree face for marking 45-degree angles. The combination square is slightly less accurate than a good try square but can take its place for most purposes. The sliding blade permits using a combination square where a try square cannot fit, such as for measuring the depth of a groove. The sliding blade also allows a combination square to serve as a marking gauge.

The framing square (also called a *carpenter's*, *roofer's*, or *steel* square) is a stamped metal **L** with 2-inch-wide blade (the longer member) and 1½-inch-wide tongue (the shorter member). It has considerably longer arms than either a try square or combination square for better squaring of framing members and for marking cuts in panels where greater accuracy is needed. The framing square also contains charts useful for laying out stair stringers. The blade is lengthy enough to make a good straightedge.

All squares are designed for use on both outside and inside angles.

Levels

Bubble or spirit levels are essential to any construction work. Three kinds of bubble levels will cover almost every job required by outdoor projects.

Left photo: You can use a carpenter's level and a straight board to check whether the tops of two adjacent deck posts are level with each other. Right photo: When the bubble in a level is centered, the level rests on a level surface. Most levels have one vial for level (horizontal test) and two for plumb (vertical test). Some also offer a 45-degree vial, useful for aligning angle-bracing on a deck.

Carpenter's Level. The standard carpenter's level, usually 2 feet long, is made of aluminum or wood. It has three vials with bubbles used for leveling and plumbing everything from posts and piers to fence posts. All carpenter's levels have vials for taking horizontal and vertical readings, and some have a 45-degree vial, as well. To protect the vials and general accuracy, a level should be handled with care. Hang it up when not in use.

Torpedo Level. About 9 inches long, the torpedo level is shorter than a carpenter's level and will fit where a longer level cannot.

Line Level. A line level is very short, having only one bubble vial. It's made with hooks, to be hung from a taut mason's line for leveling over longer distances than other levels can. It also works resting on a flat surface and has the advantage of fitting in your pocket.

Water Tube Level. A water-tube level consists of a pair of graduated vials at each end of a long vinyl tube. When the tube is filled with water, the water levels in the two vials are level with each other, allowing highly accurate leveling over long distances. This can prove very useful in patio and deck work.

When suspended under taut mason's line, this line level indicates relative heights of distant points.

A chalkline is indispensable. As shown in the main photo, hook the line end over the edge of a workpiece or a nail, stretch the line tight, lift, and snap. The line leaves a straight line of colored chalk powder on the work as your guide for cutting or leveling. After extended use, when the chalkline starts making pale marks, you can refill the case (inset photo) with the chalk powder.

Chalklines

The carpenter's chalkline has many home-improvement uses. It beats a pencil and straightedge for making long, *very straight* level or sloped lines. The chalkline consists of a reel of 50 to 100 feet of string inside a hollow case containing chalk powder, white or colored. On the end of the string is an angled hook and ring for fastening the string over an edge or to a nail. A rewind crank allows the string to be wound back up after use. During rewinding, the string gets rechalked.

Hand Planes

Sooner or later in all woodworking projects, you'll need a hand plane. It removes wood, one shaving at a time, to smooth a surface, reduce size, or round off sharp edges. The most useful plane is a smoothing plane about 2½ inches wide and 9½ inches long.

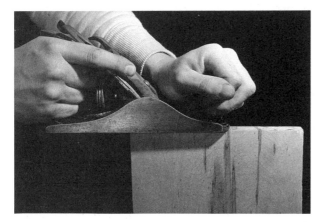

Hand planes, such as this bench plane, tackle end grain, whether to reduce board length slightly, smooth rough edges, or make bevels. They can also trim board edges. But for straightest results on long board edges, longer planes serve better.

Holding Tools

Besides hand tools, you need a few items to help hold what you're working on.

Sawhorses. One essential is a pair of sawhorses. Sawhorses, whether made at home or purchased, should be 3 to 4 feet long and 28 to 30 inches high to support panels and boards at a good height for marking and cutting. They must be sturdy. While metal brackets are widely sold for making sawhorses out of short 2 × 4s, my experience has been that bracket-held sawhorses wobble badly.

Clamps. All home carpenters need an assortment of clamps. The most useful of all are C-clamps, which come in opening sizes from 1½ inches to 12 inches and more. Especially useful, in my opinion, are the sliding-bar clamps by Jorgensen and Sandvik that adjust in an instant to grip work from paper-thin to a couple of feet thick. There's also a similarly useful clamp on the market by Vise-Grip called the Quick-Grip Bar Clamp. Pipe clamps, bar clamps, self-closing alligator clamps, and woodworker's parallel screw clamps are more useful for in-shop projects than for outdoor uses. Still, you can never have too many clamps.

Vises. Vises hold pieces securely while you work on them. It would be tough to get along without a woodworking vise.

The bench or woodworking vise mounts to the side or end of the workbench, either permanently (which is best) or temporarily (held with clamps), to secure boards while you saw, sand, or plane them.

The metalworking vise, which is marginally useful

This bar clamp, the Quick-Grip by Vise-Grip, locks with a squeeze of the trigger and comes in several lengths. It lets go when you squeeze the release lever. The clamping surfaces are vinyl-padded to prevent their marring the work.

for outdoor projects, bolts (best) or clamps to the top of the workbench to hold metal objects while you are sawing, filing, bending, cutting, or otherwise working on them. Smooth-faced jaws should be available for holding things that you don't want marred in a metal-working vise.

A good utility vise, which resembles a metalworking vise, can do double duty as a woodworking and metalworking vise, if you cannot have a dedicated woodworking vise.

While the preceding doesn't cover all the hand tools you'll need for jobs in this book, it does provide the most important.

Unless you're a kangaroo, a tool belt is handy. This belt has a holster for a cordless drill; a small pouch for a measuring tape; and a multicompartment pouch for pencil, try square, hammer, and fasteners.

A hang-up tool board helps keep the home workshop organized. Perforated board, spaced out from the wall, accepts hooks of various configurations for storage of just about any hand tool.

PORTABLE POWER TOOLS

Power tools make hard work easy. While power tools are fun to own, you can easily get by with only two of them, the electric drill and the circular saw. Frankly, neither an electric drill nor a circular saw is absolutely essential. But estimates indicate that portable power tools make carpentry five to seven times faster—and five to seven times easier—than with hand tools alone. This is reason enough to get a power tool or two.

Portable power tools greatly facilitate operations, such as drilling and sawing, that would otherwise be done by hand. Moreover, they generally do a better job than hand tools. They should be used only under dry conditions and within reach of a suitable extension cord.

This shows how a ground fault energizes metal parts of a tool and endangers the operator. Contact with the ground or a grounded object lets the worker complete the circuit to ground, giving a dangerous shock.

Ground-fault Protection

When dealing with electric-powered tools, having some kind of backup electrical protection is mandatory for your safety. If other safety systems fail, backup electrical protection can save your life. A faulty electrical power tool may have its metal parts energized by a ground fault within the tool. Anyone who is grounded and comes into contact with the tool forms an electrical pathway for those wayward electrons. And it takes very little electricity to kill—just the little power that lights a Christmas tree bulb can be deadly.

Tool Grounding. As one method of ground-fault protection, a metal-bodied plug-in power tool is grounded through a third green-insulated grounding wire and a round grounding prong on its plug. This causes so much current to flow during a ground fault that the house branch circuit fuse or circuit breaker cuts off power to the circuit and thus to the defective tool. Grounded plug-in tools have three-prong grounding-type plugs. *Never cut off the grounding pin to make the plug fit an older two-slot ungrounded outlet.*

Grounding Adapters. Because three-to-two grounding adapters allow you to use an electric tool that should be grounded without actually grounding it, in my opinion, they should be thrown away. (They're not permitted in Canada.)

Double-Insulated Tools. Many portable electric tools now use double-insulated design. Both primary and secondary levels of electrical insulation built into the tool protect the user from electric shock. One level of protection is the plastic body or handle. It puts a nonconductor of electricity right where it counts—in your hand. Double-insulated tools have two-prong electrical plugs. They are either labeled "double-insulated" or are marked with the square-within-a-square

Look for these designations on electric tools. The "UL" indicates that a tool has been tested and listed by Underwriter's Laboratories. The "CSA" indicates certification by the Canadian Standards Association.

Left photo: Plug-in power tools with three-prong plugs must be used only with three-wire grounding-type extension receptacles like this one. Do not use two-prong, nongrounding adapters with such tools. Right photo: Double-insulated power tools *with two-prong plugs* may be used with either two-wire nongrounding extension receptacles or three-wire receptacles. In any case, the cord should be heavy enough to supply the tool's motor without excessive voltage drop.

double-insulated symbol. A double-insulated tool is not grounded. It may be used either in a three-slot or an older two-slot outlet.

Ground-fault Circuit-interrupters. The ground-fault circuit-interrupter (GFCI) gives excellent backup electrical protection against ground-fault shocks. Placed in the current-carrying circuit to a tool, the GFCI monitors incoming and outgoing electron flow. If a ground fault occurs, the GFCI immediately detects an imbalance of in/out current, and instantly turns off the incoming power to remove the ground-fault shock danger.

GFCI protection should be used with all power tools, even double-insulated ones. The GFCI may be located in (1) the circuit breaker for the branch electrical circuit, (2) in the receptacle or another feed-through receptacle GFCI located upstream in the branch circuit, (3) as a portable plug-in GFCI, or (4) in a GFCI extension cord. Do not use a portable plug-in power tool without providing GFCI protection for it.

Electric Shock

If you should encounter anyone receiving an electrical shock from a power tool, do not touch the victim—or you may be shocked, too. Very often, an electric shock

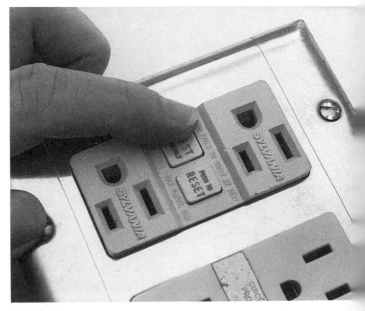

Boxes, like this, for GFCI extension cord shown more clearly on the next page, contain ground-fault-protected outlets. Each time it is plugged in for use, the GFCI should be checked by pressing the test button. Power should immediately trip off, indicating that the GFCI is working. After testing, you can restore power by pressing the reset button.

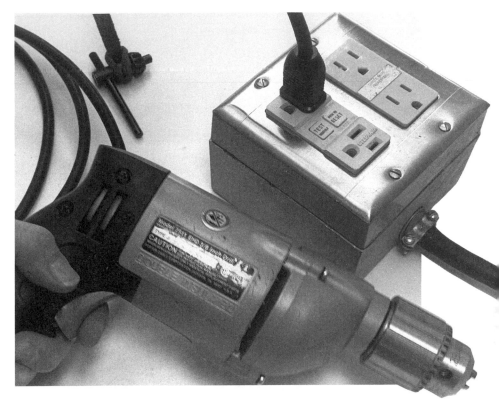

Give each of your plug-in power tools a periodic ground-fault test by plugging each one into a GFCI outlet and running it in all modes, such as fast, slow, forward, and reverse. If the GFCI trips off at any time, "red tag" the tool; that is, do not use it until repaired.

knocks the victim free, but it may cause the victim's hand to tightly clutch the tool. If you cannot quickly and safely unplug the tool, try to knock the tool out of the victim's hand with a dry broomstick. Or turn off the power at the house service panel. If the victim is unconscious afterward, call for medical help. While waiting for help to arrive, give all the assistance you can, administering CPR if the victim has stopped breathing and if his heart has stopped, and if you are qualified. Front pages of most telephone books give emergency phone and first aid information.

Extension Cords

Voltage drop is created by resistance to the flow of electrons. It's like the reduced water pressure at the end of a too-long, too-narrow garden hose: when current flows through an extension cord that has wires too small to carry enough current to the far end, the voltage drop that results causes a power tool to run slower than it should and to overheat. Running a portable power tool with an excessive voltage drop can damage a tool's motor. So an extension cord used with power tools must be capable of delivering each tool's rated power without excessive voltage drop.

Since extension cord length creates electrical re-

sistance, which results in voltage drop, always use the shortest cord that will reach. The table "Extension Cord Wire Gauge (AWG) for 115V Portable Electric Tools" shows the size of extension cord needed for various tool power ratings and cord lengths. (For the

EXTENSION CORD WIRE GAUGE FOR 115V PORTABLE ELECTRIC TOOLS **

Ampere Rating*	Volt-Ampere Rating (Watts)	LENGTH OF CORD (FEET)				
		25	50	100	150	200
2	230	18	18	18	16	16
3	345	18	18	16	14	14
4	460	18	18	16	14	12
5	575	18	18	14	12	12
6	690	18	16	14	12	10
8	920	18	16	12	10	10
10	1150	18	14	12	10	8
12	1380	16	14	10	8	8
14	1610	16	12	10	8	6
16	1840	16	12	10	8	6
18	2070	14	12	8	8	6
20	2300	14	12	8	6	6

* Line voltage drop limited to 5V at 150% of rated amperes.

** American Wire Gauge (AWG).

Extension cords used outdoors must be marked with the suffix "W-A" as shown ("W" in Canada), following the cord-type designation.

good of the tool, these figures limit voltage drop to 5 percent at 150 percent of the tool's rated power draw.)

Never use a power tool with an ordinary zip-cord extension, which is for light-duty uses, not for power tools or outdoor use. Outdoor extension cords should contain a W-A or W as part of the cord's designation, for example, SJTW-A. If an extension cord is damaged or worn, don't use it. And never cut off the grounding prong of a power tool's or extension cord's plug, since that would destroy the grounding protection.

Portable Power Tool Safety Rules

Keep safe tool use foremost in your mind. Don't try to defeat the tool's built-in safeguards. Learn what damage a tool can do to you and your materials; then avoid situations in which such damage might occur. Work gloves recommended for handling rough wood are not recommended for working with power tools. If gloves are worn, they must fit well.

To reduce the risk of injury, electric shock, and fire when using electric tools, read and heed the specific instructions in the tool owner's manual. Save the manual and read it from time to time to refresh your memory. Here are pointers on electrical power tool safety.

- Have the work area clean and well lighted.
- Use the right tool for the job.
- Before you use a power tool, make sure that all of its fasteners are tight and that all its parts—especially guards and other safety devices—are in place and undamaged. Any damaged part should be repaired or replaced. Check for alignment and binding

of moving parts. Check the tool to make sure it will operate as it should and will perform as intended. Do not use the tool if its switch will not turn it on and turn it off. A defective switch should be replaced.

- Make sure you have a clear cutting line, and that tool cords are out of the way so they will not snag as you cut.
- Check the direction of force of the tool, and check for the direction of any kickback that may occur.
- Use only sharp, clean cutters, and avoid forcing dull or dirty ones through the work. Keep tool handles dry, clean, and free from grease and oil.
- Treat the tool's power cord with respect. Pull it from the receptacle by its plug, not by the cord, and never dangle a tool by its cord. Keep the cord away from oil, heat, and sharp edges. Inspect the cord regularly, and replace a damaged or worn cord right away.
- Use your tool in an outlet with the correct voltage.
- Do not work where it is wet or damp. Power tools are designed for use in dry conditions only.
- Even when using a double-insulated tool, avoid body contact with any grounded surfaces, such as plumbing and heating fixtures, appliances, and metal pipes.
- Be sure the tool's power supply is ground-fault-protected.
- Keep children and visitors out of the work area.
- Don't force the tool into the work.
- Have the work secured with a vise or clamps, freeing both hands to operate the tool.
- Maintain a secure balance and footing at all times.

A tool's nameplate should give the information you need to decide if the tool is adequate for the situation: function (drill), chuck size (3/8-inch), electricity (115 AC 60Hz), power draw (3.3 ampere and 360 watts), speed (0–1,100 rpm), whether double-insulated, and whether UL-listed.

Don't overreach. Wear nonskid footwear.

- Don't cut into any electrical cables behind a wall; know what you are cutting.
- Make a habit of removing adjusting keys and wrenches before using a tool. Otherwise, they may fly off at great velocity and injure someone.
- Always turn off a tool before unplugging it. Unplug the tool before working on it, making adjustments, or changing accessories, such as bits or blades.
- To avoid accidental startup, never carry a power tool with your finger on the switch. Also, make sure the switch is off before plugging the tool in.
- Store electric tools high and dry, and where children cannot get at them.
- Wear sensible, well-fitting clothing. Avoid loose cuffs, ties, jewelry, and watches. Tie back long hair.
- Wear proper eye protection when using power tools —safety glasses or goggles and possibly a face shield. If the operation is noisy, use hearing protectors. If the operation produces dust, wear a dust mask. Moreover, anyone else in the area should have the same protection.
- Be alert and watch what you are doing.

Electric Drills

Electric drills have many home-repair uses. They are used chiefly for boring holes, both large and small, in wood and metal. They may be fitted with attachments that enable them to wire-brush, grind, disc-sand, mix paint, and more.

In an electric drill, the chuck's maximum opening gives the drill its size designation. For example, a 3/8-inch drill will accept bits to 3/8 inch in diameter. A drill can accept a bit as tiny as 1/64 inch up to its maximum designated size. Chuck speed relates to drill size, the larger drills turning more slowly than the smaller ones but having more torque (twisting force). Drill speed, more than anything else, determines what jobs a drill will do (see the table "Recommended Spindle Speeds for Twist Drills").

On most plug-in drills, a locking button may be depressed to lock the trigger in the ON position. Using the lock button, however, poses the distinct danger of torque-windup injury, which occurs when the bit stops in the hole and the drill body begins turning in the reverse direction. Do not use a drill's trigger lock unless you are absolutely certain the bit will not catch in

RECOMMENDED SPINDLE SPEEDS FOR TWIST DRILLS (RPM)

Drill Size	MATERIAL	
	Soft	Hard
1/16"	4,700	4,700
1/8"	4,700	4,700
3/16"	4,700	2,400
1/4"	2,400	2,400
5/16"	2,400	1,250
3/8"	2,400	1,250
7/16"	2,400	1,250
1/2"	2,400	1,250

the work. Some drills have a side handle to help you handle reverse torque. If your drill has provision for a side handle—a threaded hole in its side—put the handle in place and use it.

Better drills may be rated as to their work capacity: check the owner's manual. If so, do not attempt to exceed the drill's capacity (see the table "Typical Maximum-size Holes").

The ⅜-inch drill is most useful to the average homeowner. As for pluses, the variable-speed feature is well worthwhile. So is a reversing switch, which allows you to back a stuck bit out of a hole.

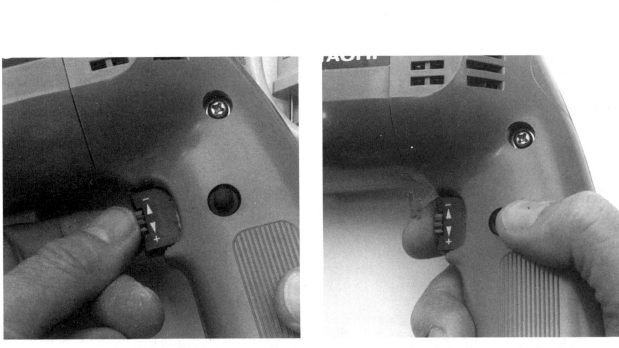

You are looking down the barrels of three high-caliber electric drills —¼-inch, ⅜-inch, and ½-inch. The ¼-inch drill (*left*) spins fastest but has the least torque. The ½-inch drill (*right*) is slowest but has the greatest torque. The ⅜-inch drill in the center is a good all-round size for the outdoor builder.

The variable-speed trigger on this Hitachi drill can be adjusted to limit top speed. Turning the knob increases or decreases speed. Right photo: Squeezing the trigger and pressing the trigger-lock button keeps the drill running without continued pressure on the trigger. But it's safer not to use this feature much.

TYPICAL MAXIMUM-SIZE HOLES
TYPE OF BIT

Size Drill	Twist Drill *	Spade Bit	Self-feed Bit
¼"	¼"	½"	⅜"
⅜"	⅜"	1"	¾"
½"	½"	1⅜"	1¼"

* In wood or metal; others wood only.

Costlier hammer-drills are most useful for boring holes in concrete and masonry. Only a percussion-type masonry-boring bit should be used in a hammer-drill (noted on the bit's packaging). You can disengage the hammering action on many hammer-drills for simple drilling with regular bits.

To get off to a good start, mark holes in wood or metal with a center punch. Remember that the work should be secured, never held in the hand. When drilling sheet metal, back up the intended hole with a scrap of wood.

Drill Accessories

Due to their popularity, electric drills have numerous accessories. The collection begins with bits, including twist drill bits and spade-type bits (sometimes called *flat bits*). Every homeowner needs a set of high-speed (steel-drilling capability) twist drill bits from 1/16 to ⅜ inch in 1/32-inch increments and a set of spade-type bits from ⅜ to 1 inch, ⅛ inch apart. Drill bits should be organized in a case and kept sharp. An extension bit is available for deep boring, such as making holes through a house wall from inside to outside. There are also screwdriver bits (flat-blade, Phillips, and Robertson). Note, however, that some electric drills not designated as "driver/drills" are not intended for driving screws: check the owner's manual before you use a drill this way. A set of masonry bits in popular sizes ranges from 3/16 to ½ inch, all with ¼-inch or smaller shanks. Larger sizes are also available with ¼-inch shanks.

Other accessories include sanding pads, several kinds of wire-brush wheels, flap-sanders, and even paint-mixers.

Read your drill owner's manual and follow the specific safety rules it contains.

Left photo: For drilling holes in masonry, a hammer-drill cannot be topped. The Skil variable-speed reversing ⅜-inch hammer-drill delivers from 0–40,000 blows a minute, depending on how hard it is pushed. For hammer-drills, you need percussion-type masonry-boring bits. Right photo: Always turn off and unplug a drill (or remove the battery pack on a cordless drill and lock its trigger off) before changing bits. Install the bit until it bottoms in the chuck (or up to the flutes on a small bit), then insert the chuck key in each of the three holes in succession and tighten. Be sure you remove the key before using the drill.

DRILL BITS

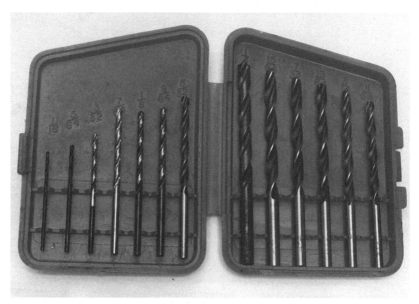

The best way to purchase twist drills is in a complete set. This one holds sizes from 1/16-inch to 1/4-inch in 1/64-inch increments in a handy case, with each size labeled.

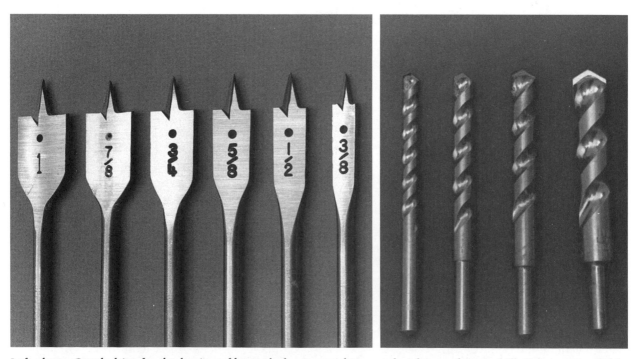

Left photo: Spade bits, for the boring of larger holes in wood, are perfect for an electric drill. Sizes are available to 1½ inches, though this set of Irwin Speedbor bits ranges only to 1 inch. Right photo: Masonry boring bits are carbide tipped. They tackle concrete, concrete block, and brick. This set of Nicholson masonry bits comes with ¼-inch shanks to fit even a small "homeowner" electric drill.

This stripping wheel, for an electric drill, is used at high speed for removal of paint and rough rust. Its wide-open surface resists clogging.

CORDLESS TOOLS

Cordless portable power tools—especially electric drills—are rapidly gaining in popularity. But while they free you from the extension cord, they lack the brute power of plug-in tools. Cordless tools also lack the battery capacity to do a large amount of work. The better, more professional cordless tools partially solve this problem with removable battery packs. The battery or battery pack is the critical part of a cordless tool. A group of wired-together rechargeable nickel-cadmium cells provide the power. A "nicad" tool battery is capable of some 300 to 800 charge-use cycles.

Cordless tools offer shock safety. Running on 12 volts or less of direct current (DC) when not on charge, they cannot shock you (unless, of course, you cut into a live wire).

Some cordless drills have gear shift buttons. Best

TWO WAYS TO AVOID SPLINTERING WHEN DRILLING

1. FIRST DRILL UNTIL POINT SHOWS ON OTHER SIDE.

2. THEN DRILL FROM OTHER SIDE.

OPTION A

OPTION B

CLAMP BACKUP PIECE TO WORK BEFORE DRILLING.

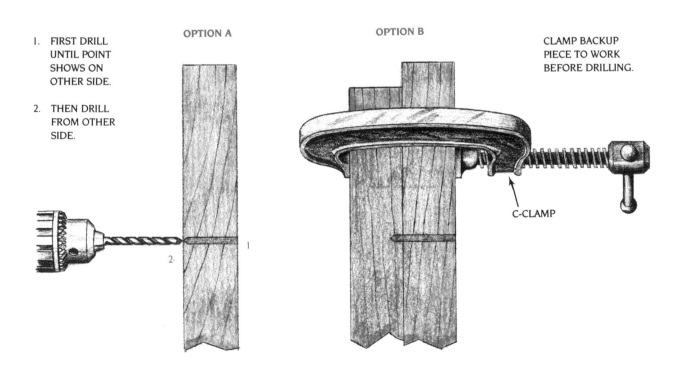

C-CLAMP

Left photo: A plug-in ⅜-inch drill is a real workhorse, but it needs a connection to electricity, with consequent cord trailing you. Right photo: A cordless ⅜-inch drill/screwdriver works anywhere. If you will purchase just one drill for bigger projects, a plug-in will outwork the cordless.

Left photo: Users of cordless driver/drills wonder how they ever did without one. This Milwaukee variable-speed-gear-shift model is reversible; to prevent overtorquing of screws, you turn the collar (*as shown*). Right photo: Most combination driver/drills have gear shifts, such as this slide button.

of all are the variable-speed reversible cordless drills, the high-end models with gear shift and adjustable-torque clutch as well. These driver/drills are high-tech and may be quite expensive. But if you will be using one much to drive screws, it can be well worth the money. Modern, professional lines of cordless driver/drills will drive large numbers of screws before running out of battery charge. Then they recharge in an hour.

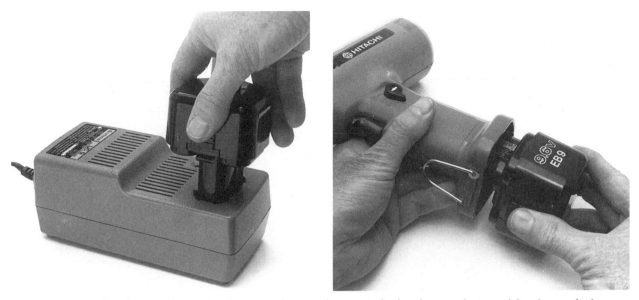

This battery pack is being plugged in for a one-hour recharge. Only the charger designed for the tool's battery should be used. If a battery feels hot from use, let it cool before charging.

An extra battery pack can keep you moving without needing to stop to recharge.

It's helpful to have a holster for your cordless drill. Widely available, such holsters keep the drill ready for a fast draw when needed.

Charging Cordless Tools

The cordless tool's battery charger is designed specifically for the manufacturer's own tools. It converts household 120-volt alternating current (AC) to the tool's specific direct-current (DC) charging voltage. Charge cordless tools only with the charger designed for them. In many, a sensing switch turns off the charger before the nicad cells can be damaged by overcharging. The pilot lamp will go out, indicating no charging. With this kind of charger, it's okay to leave batteries on charge for long periods. Otherwise, overcharging is to be avoided.

If possible, avoid using the charger on an extension cord. If you must, the cord should be adequately sized for the charger's input.

While cordless drills offer ample power for most household jobs, the cordless saws and sanders offered thus far are too limiting.

Cordless-tool Safety Rules

Cordless tools have a few safety precautions all their own. Be sure to read and refer to the owner's manual.

- Charge cordless tool batteries only with the charger intended for use with them.
- Charge indoors; do not expose the charger to rain or snow. Don't charge when the temperature is below 50 degrees F (10 degrees C) or above 95 degrees F (35 degrees C). Don't store the tool or battery where temperatures could exceed 104 degrees F (40 degrees C).
- Avoid operating the charger if it has been dropped or otherwise damaged.
- Unplug the charger before cleaning or otherwise working on it.
- Consecutive charging is hard on the charger; give it a 15-minute rest between charges.
- Never take apart a nicad battery.
- Do not incinerate a battery: it could explode. Instead, take it to the tool manufacturer's authorized service center for proper disposal.
- Lock the tool's trigger in the *off* position and remove the battery (if removable) before changing cutters or otherwise working on the tool.

This photo compares circular saw configurations. At left is a 7¼-inch gear-drive Skilsaw. At right is worm-drive saw. Many users prefer the worm-drive saw because its blade is on the side nearer a right-handed operator where cutting action can be seen conveniently. Gear-drive saws with blades on the right side tempt users to lean over the top to see the cut, a less-safe practice.

Circular Saws

The circular saw, also called a *portable power saw*, takes the place of the carpenter's handsaw in just about all situations: cross-cutting, ripping, and beveling boards and panels. It also makes dadoes and pocket cuts.

A combination blade is great for both cross-cutting and ripping. Other blades are suitable for just cross-cutting or just ripping, or for fine-cutting or sawing through wood containing nails. For ripping, a rip guide can be installed to follow along one edge of a board. A clamped-on straight board can do the same job in places where an edge is not close at hand, such as in the middle of a sheet of plywood. (See the table "Basic Circular Saw Blades.")

A lower, movable blade guard is spring-loaded to close over the otherwise exposed bottom of the blade when the saw is not cutting. During a cut, this guard gets pushed back out of the way by contact with the work. On completion of the cut, the guard snaps back to cover the blade safely. A circular saw is often rested on the lower guard when not in use. A lever fitted to the lower guard allows it to be swung backward by hand for making pocket cuts (that is, by lowering the blade into the wood surface, rather than by cutting from the edge of the wood).

This small but nifty 6-inch Porter-Cable Saw Boss will cut through dressed 2-by lumber at both 90-degree and 45-degree angles. Unlike most other gear-drive circ saws, this saw has its blade on the left side for a better view of the cutting action (for a right-handed user). Caution: All circular saw cuts should be made with the saw's shoe resting on supported wood, not the wood that will fall away.

CIRCULAR-SAW BLADES

If you use a circular saw for various woods and tasks, you'll need an assortment of blades. Clockwise, starting with the dark blade: tungsten carbide-tipped cut-off blade for smooth cuts and plywood-cutting; rough-cutting carbide-tipped blade; general-purpose carbide-tipped blade; decking blade with tungsten carbide teeth; and thin-kerf chisel-tooth blade for ripping and for cross-cutting. All blades shown here have ⅝-inch round arbor holes.

BASIC CIRCULAR-SAW BLADES

Blade Type	Description	Best Uses
General-purpose	24-tooth	Cross-cutting, mitering, and ripping; used mainly where smoothness of edge does not count
Crosscut	Fine, outward-looking teeth	Cross-cutting and mitering
Ripping	Coarse, forward-looking teeth with long, sloped top angles	Ripping boards to narrower widths
Plywood-cutting	Very fine teeth (200), usually hollow-ground	Sawing plywood panels without splintering
Carbide-tipped	Few or many teeth with tungsten carbide blocks brazed on	Smooth, fast, durable sawing of wood and composition materials
Nail-cutting	Fine teeth, cheaply made, throwaway blade	Sawing flooring or wood with nails
Abrasive	Looks like a thin grinding wheel	Sawing concrete, concrete block, brick, tile, and nonferrous metals
Dado	Sandwich of blades or a wobbling blade with adjustable collars	Sawing wide grooves in wood

During cutting, the saw rests on a broad base plate, or *shoe*, which is either hinged or mounted on a vertical rail so that the blade can be raised and lowered. A locknut secures the setting. Normally, you should set the blade depth so that one tooth-length penetrates through the backside of the wood. The shoe can be tilted as much as 45 degrees to one side for making bevel cuts. Tilting, of course, reduces the maximum thickness of the material that can be cut through.

Look for the following features in a circular saw: a thick base plate, an 8- to 10-foot-long cord, a top handle or a worm-drive saw, and at least a 10-amp motor. Even the smallest circular saw will cut through common 1½-inch-thick framing lumber (with the blade perpendicular to the work), with plenty of blade to spare. Begin shopping in the lower cost levels of professional-grade circular saw lines.

Circular Saw Blades. Circular saw blades come in many forms. Most circular saws come with a general-purpose blade. If you have this blade plus a cross-cut blade and a plywood-cutting blade, you're off to a good start.

Circular-saw blades must be installed so they rotate in the correct direction. Many have arrows showing the direction. Since the blade cuts from the bottom to the top of a board or panel, the circular saw is used with the work facedown—especially plywood.

It doesn't pay to resharpen circular-saw blades yourself. Take them to a professional. Or, if the blade is not expensive, throw it away and get a new one. The more teeth the saw blade has, the higher the cost, but the smoother the cut and the better suited the blade is to sawing thin materials such as plywood.

Handy circular saw accessories include carrying cases, cutting guides, adjustable ripping guides, protractors, and cutoff gauges. (The ripping guide may well come with the saw.)

Some circular saws have a blade-clutch arrangement that permits the blade to slip when the saw is overloaded, reducing kickback and chances of consequent motor burnout. Kickback occurs when the saw

blade jams in the work. This makes the saw jump backward in your right hand, and can happen at any time. Therefore, stand to the left side of the blade and be prepared for kickback. Make sure, as well, that no one could walk through the saw's kickback path while you're cutting.

Read the owner's manual and follow the specific safety rules contained in it.

Saber Saws

The saber saw, sometimes spelled *sabre saw* (olde friend), is a versatile hand-held portable power tool with a ⅙- to ½-hp universal motor. It is also sometimes called a *jigsaw* (a name better reserved for the larger bench-mounted workshop tool). The saber saw is good at cross-cutting, ripping, sawing bevels, and beginning a cut in the middle of a board or panel. Saber saws can cut straight or in tight, intricate curves. Some saber saws have an air blast directed onto the work ahead of the blade to blow sawdust away from the cutting line. This helps in following cutting marks.

A handle with an on-off or variable-speed trigger switch permits guidance. Some saber saws have a second handle in front. These should be guided with both hands. A flat base plate or shoe rests on the work.

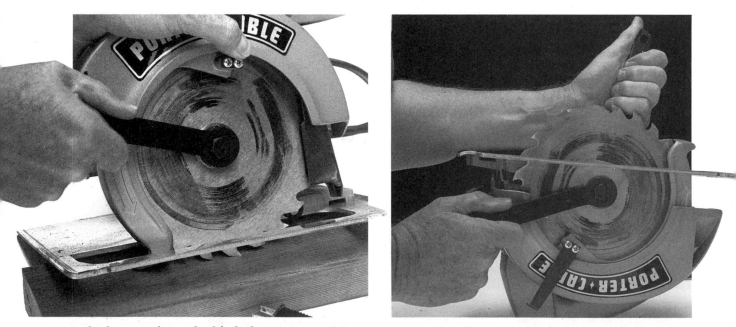

Left photo: To keep the blade from turning while removing and installing the arbor bolt, dig teeth into wood scrap. For removal, turn the arbor bolt the same way the blade turns, opposite to tighten. Right photo: Some circular saws have arbor flats or arbor-lock pins to keep the blade from turning while you turn the arbor.

A rip guide can be fitted to the saber saw's shoe for making long, straight cuts near an edge. Or a straight board can be clamped to the work and used as a guide for the shoe while making a straight cut. To get truly straight cuts, one or the other guidance system must be used.

Saber saws are handy substitutes for handsaws in cutting boards and panels from ⅛ inch to 2 inches thick or so.

Saber saws have interchangeable blades. Blade length, naturally, limits the thickness of the material that a saber saw can slice through. The standard

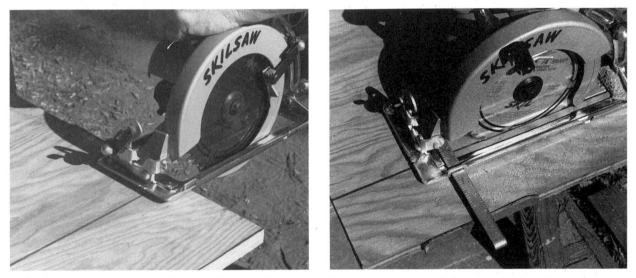

Left photo: To start a cut with a circular saw, first secure the work so you don't have to hold it. Then place the front edge of the saw's shoe on the workpiece with the shoe's cut-indicator mark aligned with the cutting line. Trigger the saw to full speed before starting the cut. Right photo: A ripping guide helps ensure straight cuts when the cut is close to a straight edge. Even if you use a guide, it's smart to mark the cut beforehand, so you can check progress. Another guide method employs a straight board clamped to the work surface, as shown for the saber saw on the next page.

To make a pocket cut (an inside cut) with a circular saw, first mark the cut on all sides, as shown. Set the blade to proper cutting depth. Then, as shown, rest the front edge of the saw's shoe firmly on the work with the blade clear of the wood and just above the intended first cut. Swing the lower blade guard's manual retracting lever up and forward to expose the blade above the work. Start the saw and lower the spinning blade into the work on the waste side of the line, as shown. Be ready for a possible kickback as the blade contacts wood. After the blade has sawed through the wood and the saw's shoe rests flat on the work, follow the line forward; never pull a spinning saw backward. Saw the other three sides of the pocket cut the same way. Finally, using a manual keyhole saw, finish the cuts into all corners.

SABER-SAW SAVVY

A straight guide, such as a straight board clamped to the work and off-set from the cutting line enough to match the blade-to-shoe distance, enables straight-line cutting with a saber saw or a circular saw.

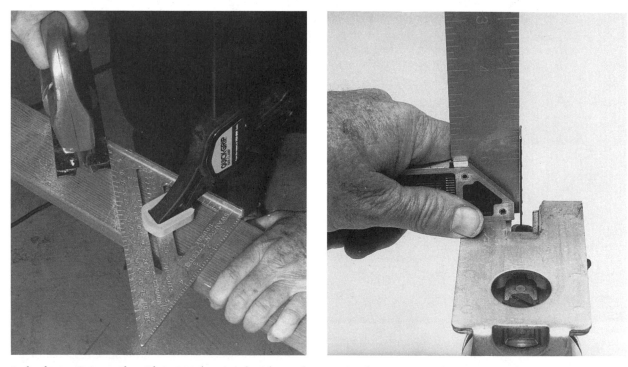

Left photo: Patented guides may be used with a saber or circular saw in making square cuts, 45-degree cuts, and other angle cuts. Like the Swanson Speed Square here, most guides may be hand-held but work better when clamped to the work. Right photo: Determine the squareness of a saw's shoe with the blade by means of a try square. If the shoe and blade are not true, the bevel indicator can be adjusted or remarked.

SABER-SAW BLADES

Saber saw blades are available for all kinds of cutting. Those with coarser teeth cut faster but make rougher cuts.

BASIC SABER-SAW BLADES

Blade Type	Description	Best Uses
General-purpose fine-toothed	14 teeth per inch	Fine-cutting of hardwoods
General-purpose medium-toothed	8–10 teeth per inch	Sawing plywood
Heavy duty	6–10 teeth per inch, bimetal	Cutting wood with embedded nails
General-purpose coarse-toothed	4–6 teeth per inch	Rough, fast sawing in softwood
Hollow-ground	Teeth not set; blade tapers	Smooth-finished cuts, sawing plywood
Carbide-tipped	Teeth tipped with tungsten carbide; outlasts steel blades	Sawing hard materials
Abrasive-chip	"Sandpaper" edge of tungsten carbide chips	Sawing hard materials, ultrasmooth cuts in hardwood
Metal-cutting	Fine-toothed, 12–32 teeth per inch	Sawing of metals and plastics; thinner materials call for finer teeth
Flush-cutting	Teeth stick out in front of saw	Sawing up to obstructions
Scrolling	Narrow	Sawing sharp curves

3-inch saber saw blade will cut through materials up to about 2 inches thick. A 4-inch blade allows cutting to about 2½ inches. With a relatively coarse 4-inch, 5-teeth-per-inch blade, a quality saber saw can actually substitute for a circular saw for some outdoor carpentry.

Standard saber-saw blade teeth are designed to cut on the upstroke. This holds the saw's shoe in firm contact with the work. For this reason, the finished side of the work should be placed down so that any splintering of the wood grain shows up on the back of the work, not on the finished side. Also, the use of a hollow-ground blade with no set or a wavy-set blade tends to reduce splintering. For a sampling of avail-

Left photo: A saber saw can create its own starting hole if you haven't first drilled one. Begin with the front of the saw's shoe in contact with the work and the saw tipped forward enough to keep the blade clear of the work, as above. Start the saw and tip the reciprocating blade toward the work, maintaining pressure as the blade penetrates the work and the saw's shoe rests flat on the wood. Right photo: Once the saw's shoe is flat on the wood, proceed with cutting along the marks.

Left photo: A reciprocating saw slices completely through a 4 × 4 or 4 × 6 deck or fence post in one cut. Rest the saw's shoe against the work with the blade clear. Trigger the saw and cut. Right photo: For safety, recip-sawing is a two-handed operation. Mark the work on all sides and saw carefully on the waste side of the marks. Using a reciprocating saw with adjustable speeds, such as this Hitachi, you use faster speeds for the cutting of wood and slower speeds for metal.

able saber-saw blades, see the table "Basic Saber Saw Blades" on page 101.

To make bevel cuts, most saber-saw shoes can be adjusted from square to a 45-degree tilt to one side. As with a circular saw, the saber saw can handle less depth for a bevel cut than for a straight cut. How much less depends on the degree of the bevel. In most uses, the shoe is set square with the work.

When using a saber saw, follow the safety rules contained in the owner's manual. For example, you should never change blades or work on the saw without unplugging it first.

Reciprocating Saw

Reciprocating saws are the overlooked tools of carpentry. Functioning as though they are heavy-duty in-line saber saws, reciprocating saws are used primarily in remodeling work, which frequently requires that you cut through walls. Fitted with the right blade, the reciprocating saw is great for trimming deck and fence posts and other structural members that are too thick for a circular saw to slice through in one pass.

Blade speed is 1,600 to 3,000 strokes a minute. Two-speed and variable-speed models are available. Some recip saws have a speed adjustment and offer

RECIPROCATING-SAW BLADES

One of the best reciprocating saw-blade selections is Milwaukee's bi-metal assortment. It includes blades for fast-cutting, smooth-cutting, cutting nail-embedded wood, sawing tight curves in wood or metal, and cutting various metals, composition boards, and plastics. Bi-metal construction combines softer, flexible steel at the rear of the blade with hard high-speed steel in the teeth area. Bi-metal blades cut faster than ordinary high-speed steel blades.

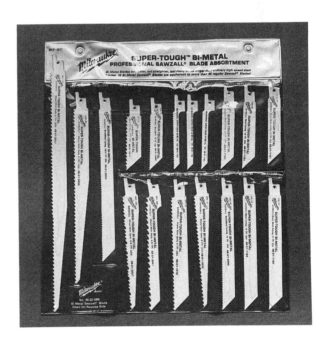

BASIC RECIPROCATING-SAW BLADES

Blade Type	Description	Best Uses
General-purpose wood-cutting	3–10 teeth per inch	Sawing nail-free wood
Fast wood-cutting	6 teeth per inch	Rapid sawing in wood and nail-embedded wood
Wood-cutting/nail-embedded	6–10 teeth per inch	Sawing wood and nail-embedded wood
Metal-cutting	10–32 teeth per inch	Sawing metal
Tungsten-carbide grit	Coarse- or medium-grit coating	Ultrasmooth cuts in brick, tile, fiberglass (coarse blade), hardwood, and plywood
Pruning	6 teeth per inch; tapered back; 12" long	Trimming trees, sawing green wood

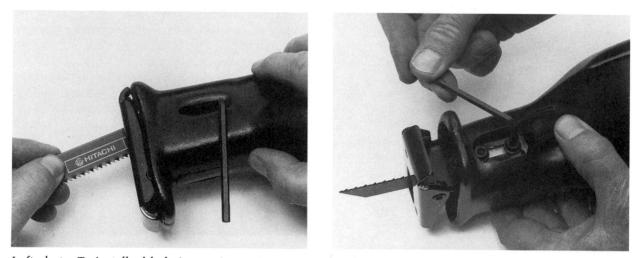

Left photo: To install a blade in a reciprocating saw, unplug the saw and loosen the blade-lock screw with the furnished wrench. Slip the blade in, making sure its opening fits over the lock pin inside the blade lock. Then tighten the screw. Right photo: Most recip saws have a foot-positioning adjustment. You can loosen the adjusting screws in order to slide the foot in or out and then tighten them to hold the foot in the desired position.

orbital action. Orbital action gives faster, more aggressive cutting.

Reciprocating Saw Blades. Recip saw blades come in lengths up to a foot. As with a saber saw blade, always select the proper blade for the job. Per the table "Basic Reciprocating Saw Blades" on page 103, blades are available for cutting wood, metal, brick, plywood, hardboard, plastic, fiberglass, nail-embedded wood, plaster, and other materials. An offset blade adapter often is available for outfitting the saw to cut flush, as for cutting off deck planks right up to the house wall. A recip saw will also make plunge cuts, those done without drilling a starter hole for the blade.

Follow the manufacturer's instructions.

TOOL CARE

Tool care is largely a matter of common sense.
- Use tools only for the jobs for which they were intended.
- When you finish using a tool—hand or power, portable or stationary—clean, lubricate, and sharpen it (or have a professional sharpen it). If necessary, pro-

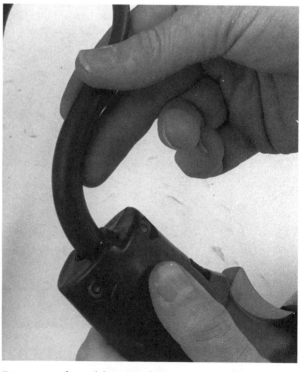

To ensure the rubber insulation is not cracked, bend the strain-relief on each of your power-tool cords. If you see any faults in the strain relief, the power cord, or the plug, replace the entire power cord.

HOW TO CLEAN POWER TOOLS

To clean a power tool, turn it off and unplug it. Then don safety goggles and, as shown in the top photo, blow compressed air into the tool's cooling passages to clear them of sawdust. If you don't have access to compressed air, use a round-bristled soft brush, as shown below left. Finally, wipe down the unprotected steel parts with a lightly oiled cloth to keep them from rusting.

tect any exposed surfaces from corrosion, make necessary repairs, and store the sharpened tool in its proper place. As my retired Navy friend Vic Butler has been known to say, the job isn't done until all the tools are put away, Buster.
- Hang tools up instead of dumping them into a box or drawer to jostle or be jostled.
- Keep all tools as clean and rust-free as possible.

Lightly oil or otherwise lubricate or protect those that need it. Fine steel wool and multipurpose lubricant are great for removing corrosion from tools.
- See that power-tool cords, plugs, and strain-reliefs are in safe condition. Wipe down and loosely coil cords. Protect them from oils and solvents.
- Unplug electric tools before cleaning them. Never apply any solvent to plastic, because it could dis-

solve or otherwise damage the plastic. Avoid immersing an electric tool in liquid or allowing a liquid to flow into it. Cleaning may be followed with a coat of light machine oil or a multipurpose lubricant on the steel parts.

- Use a damp cloth and household detergent to remove slight traces of gum buildup or grease and other dirt buildup that cannot easily be removed by wiping with a dry cloth. Dry thoroughly and then liberally coat any exposed steel or iron parts with light machine oil or multipurpose lubricant.

- Saw blades that get heavy use, and thus build up heavy coatings of gum, need more severe measures. Several commercial gum-and-pitch removers work well with circular saw and other blades. An overnight soak in kerosene or paint remover does wonders. Once the last bit of gum is off, use a good coating of multipurpose lubricant to protect the blade from rust. You can keep saw blades cleaner by spraying them with a nonstick pan coating, such as PAM. Just be sure to make a cut or two in scrap wood to remove excess coating before using the blade on finished work.

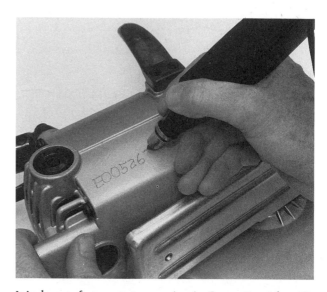

Join law enforcement agencies in Operation Identification by permanently marking your valuable tools with an engraving tool. Imprint your driver's license number and state designation—or other number recommended by local authorities. The number discourages thieves and helps police return stolen tools.

To clean dirty blades, spray on oven cleaner, let it soak, and wipe it off with a damp cloth or sponge. Wear rubber gloves (although not shown) and safety goggles.

CHAPTER **4**

BUILDING A DECK

Most photos by Charles R. Self

A deck needs to be sturdy and it should be cleanly built. If not freestanding, it should be solidly attached to the house.

DECK LAYOUT

However complex the design of any deck, the basic principles of construction remain the same.

All deck construction starts with siting and layout. A deck may be sited in a number of ways. For an attached deck, the simplest is to start with the ledger board, a board fastened to the side of the house that takes the place of posts and a beam on that side. Figure out its height and length, marking off its exact lengthwise position on the house. Of course, be sure to site the deck so that house doors don't open into deck railings, and to keep any changes in house trim minimal.

Another early step is to determine the deck's floor height. Normally, this should be at least 1 inch below the house floor level, to prevent problems with blown-in rain and with snow buildup. Slightly lower is acceptable, but higher is not.

Friend and fellow do-it-yourself author Charlie Self and his family built the garden-grade redwood deck, frequently illustrated in this chapter. The Selfs' deck was set in from the house corner to avoid a downspout and to keep deck stairs from interfering with passage of Charlie's pickup truck.

Because the Selfs' windows were located above the deck, determining deck elevation was fairly simple. Charlie planned to replace the windows with a Stanley door. If a window or door will open to your deck, you can follow the same procedure Charlie used: measuring through it. Take the inside house floor measurement from the opening down to the inside floor. Then just repeat the process outdoors. Mark the measurement on the house. Then mark down 2½ inches from that point to position the top of the ledger board. This allows for the 1-inch elevation difference you want, plus the 1½ inches that typical deck planks rise above the ledger board. If your joists are to rest atop the ledger board, allow that much more for their depth before marking the desired top of the ledger board. Plan for actual wood dimensions, not nominal dimensions.

Other circumstances may require other solutions. For example, to establish deck elevation, you may need to measure up under the house between floor joists to find the distance to the bottom of the subfloor. Then add for the thickness of subfloor plus the finished floor. You'll need access to the house sill to repeat this measurement outdoors. For this you may have to remove the lowest piece of siding, or part of it. (It's much simpler to work through a door or window, as Charlie did.)

At this point, you have one end mark for the ledger board, plus a single height mark. Use a level to extend the height mark along the side of the house, or use a line level to mark off several points along the ledger-board line. Snap a chalkline through those marks.

Whether a deck is low-to-the-ground, like this deck designed by John Matthias, or raised high off the ground, deck construction is a matter of cutting the pieces to fit and installing them. (Photographer, Ernest Braun; California Redwood Association photo)

This 15 × 24-foot redwood deck built by Tod Herring is planked with flat-laid 2 × 4 boards held with 16d weatherproof nails. Six-foot-wide redwood steps allow entry. The deck has a slanted-out railing. An experienced do-it-yourselfer, Herring placed 2 × 8 joists (2 feet on centers) across doubled 2 × 6s used as beams (positioned 7 feet on centers). Bridging was installed between joists at 5-foot maximum intervals, staggered from joist to joist. Herring's posts spotted every 4 feet are his own design, using 1½-inch galvanized pipes with floor flanges screwed to both ends. The lower ends are cast into large concrete footings placed on undisturbed soil 44 inches below existing grade, beneath the local frost line. The 16-foot beams have a 2-foot cantilever at the outer ends. House access is through a sliding door. To view Herring's building plans, see pages 16–17. (Tod Herring photo)

HIGH-LEVEL DECK

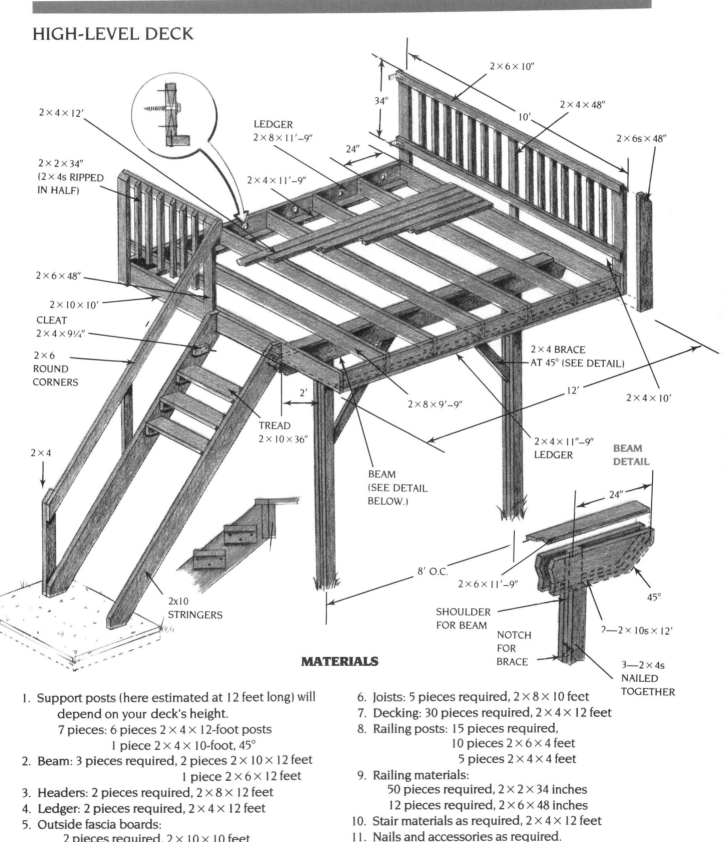

2×4×12′

2×2×34″
(2×4s RIPPED
IN HALF)

2×6×48″

2×10×10′

CLEAT
2×4×9¼″

2×6
ROUND
CORNERS

2×4

LEDGER
2×8×11′–9″

2×4×11′–9″

2×6×10″

34″

24″

10′

2×4×48″

2×6s×48″

2×4 BRACE
AT 45° (SEE DETAIL)

12′

2×4×10′

2×8×9′–9″

2′

2×4×11″–9″
LEDGER

TREAD
2×10×36″

BEAM
(SEE DETAIL
BELOW.)

8′ O.C.

2×6×11′–9″

SHOULDER
FOR BEAM

NOTCH
FOR
BRACE

2×10
STRINGERS

BEAM
DETAIL

24″

45°

2—2×10s×12′

3—2×4s
NAILED
TOGETHER

MATERIALS

1. Support posts (here estimated at 12 feet long) will
   depend on your deck's height.
   7 pieces: 6 pieces 2×4×12-foot posts
   1 piece 2×4×10-foot, 45°
2. Beam: 3 pieces required, 2 pieces 2×10×12 feet
   1 piece 2×6×12 feet
3. Headers: 2 pieces required, 2×8×12 feet
4. Ledger: 2 pieces required, 2×4×12 feet
5. Outside fascia boards:
   2 pieces required, 2×10×10 feet
6. Joists: 5 pieces required, 2×8×10 feet
7. Decking: 30 pieces required, 2×4×12 feet
8. Railing posts: 15 pieces required,
   10 pieces 2×6×4 feet
   5 pieces 2×4×4 feet
9. Railing materials:
   50 pieces required, 2×2×34 inches
   12 pieces required, 2×6×48 inches
10. Stair materials as required, 2×4×12 feet
11. Nails and accessories as required.

Adapted with permission from Wolmanized Wood drawing

CHARLIE SELF'S REDWOOD DECK

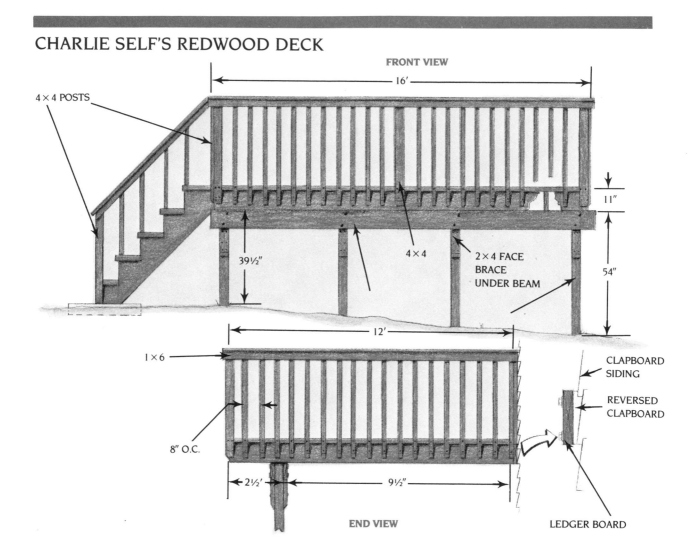

FRONT VIEW

16'

4 × 4 POSTS

11"

39½"

4 × 4

2 × 4 FACE
BRACE
UNDER BEAM

54"

12'

1 × 6

CLAPBOARD
SIDING

REVERSED
CLAPBOARD

8" O.C.

2½'   9½'

END VIEW   LEDGER BOARD

This all-redwood 12 × 16-foot deck was designed, built, and photographed by do-it-yourself author Charles R. Self. It features 2 × 6 planking, 2 × 10 ledger board, doubled 2 × 10 beams on each side of 4 × 4 posts, 2 × 10 joists, 2 × 4 balusters between the 4 × 4 supporting posts, and a swing-out Stanley Courtyard Door. Many of the step-by-step photos in this chapter, as on the next page, show construction details. Many drawings in this chapter are based on Charlie's concepts.

ESTABLISHING DECK ELEVATION

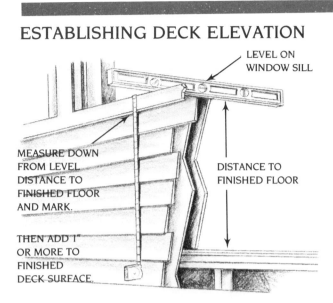

LEVEL ON
WINDOW SILL

MEASURE DOWN
FROM LEVEL
DISTANCE TO
FINISHED FLOOR
AND MARK.

DISTANCE TO
FINISHED FLOOR

THEN ADD 1"
OR MORE TO
FINISHED
DECK SURFACE.

Charlie Self determines desired deck floor height, based on floor height inside the house, using rationale described in the above drawing.

Before the ledger board can be mounted onto clapboard siding, the clapboard must be shimmed (wedged) so that the ledger board doesn't tilt. To do this, fit-in pieces of clapboard the same (or similar) size, upside down, and nail with aluminum nails.

Fastening the Ledger Board

The ledger board goes up easier with a helper, especially if the board is more than 10 feet long. With or without a helper, though, the following procedure is useful. Measure down 9⁹⁄₁₆ inches from the ledger-board height mark and drive 12d nails in at a slight angle. (You will have to use masonry anchors and lag bolts for masonry walls.) Use a nail every 3 to 5 feet. A 2 × 10 ledger board is rested on these to help keep it steady at the correct elevation.

A ledger board is held by ½-inch-diameter fasteners placed on 12-inch centers, staggered between top and bottom edges of the board. But before placing any fasteners for the ledger board, mark it for all of your joist centers, including an allowance on both sides of the centers where the joist edges or joist hangers will fall. Space the ledger-board fasteners so that none are needed in those critical areas.

The ledger board should be spaced out from the house wall for air circulation behind it. Plan for this by having stacks of flat washers or spacer blocks ready to install at each fastener.

If the house exterior is brick or other masonry, drill holes for the fasteners into the masonry units, not into the mortar joints. Lead shield anchors will go into the holes, followed by ½-inch lag screws. Start with the

Lag screws are turned into the ledger board with a ratchet-handled socket wrench. The zigzag top-and-bottom pattern, with at least one fastener per foot of ledger, ensures a strong installation.

ledger board held in place and marked for its joist locations. The nail system is a real help here, even though you will have to use hardened steel masonry nails to hold up the ledger board. Use an old but sharp spade bit to drill ½-inch clearance holes through the ledger board, and either let the drill bit mark the masonry to indicate hole position, or use a center punch to mark the holes once the drill is removed. Take the ledger board down. Drill for the lead shield anchors with a masonry-boring bit. Insert the anchors, put the ledger board back in place, and run in the lag screws and flat washers through their already-drilled clearance holes.

This process works best if you mark both the ledger board and the wall to make sure the ledger board goes back in exactly the same place. Even small deviations here can cause trouble.

For a masonry wall, you can save work by using Tapcon concrete anchors. These come with their own masonry drill bits and are available in a wide variety of sizes and lengths. Use the largest shank available, and use more fasteners than you normally would. Simply place the ledger board as described above, and drill through board and into the masonry with the supplied drill bit. Install the Tapcon anchor with a wrench. No extra lifting or insertion of lead anchors is required, because the special screw threads cut their way into the masonry and form the ledger board anchoring system.

In all cases, large, flat, plated washers should be used under the heads of lag screws and Tapcon anchors wherever there is contact with wood. Carriage bolts need washers under the nuts.

MARKING LEDGER BOARD FOR END JOIST

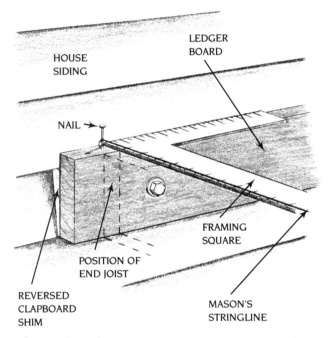

After marking the ledger board for desired position of the end joist, use taut stringline and a carpenter's square to determine the approximate perpendicular to the corner post. This can be adjusted in final layout.

Laying Out Sides and Ends

With the ledger board in place, you already have end marks for the insides of the joists on the ledger board. Extend these downward with a square, the full width of the ledger board.

Use a mason's stringline and a framing square to extend the inner line of the two end joists out from the wall at a right angle. Go at least 4 feet beyond the final deck length, placing a stake, or a batter board across two stakes, at the outer point. Batter boards work more easily because the line can be moved across them, but if you're careful coming out, single stakes will also work. Stakes more than 3 feet high or driven into soft ground need to be braced against the pull of the line.

Measure out your deck's end distance, tie a cord to one stake or batter board, and carry the cord parallel to the house wall and across the joist lines. Charlie

Self's deck has a cantilever of slightly more than 2 feet, so he placed this cord well inside the end lines. (That cantilever distance also led Charlie to a couple of minor goofs. His line was too short. Leave yourself plenty of working distance.) Place all stakes and batter boards well away from the digging areas for footing holes for posts.

Check all corners with a framing square, and then use the "3–4–5 method" to square up more accurately, as follows. Measure out one way from the corner 3 feet and make a mark. Measure the other way 4 feet and make another mark. Then measure diagonally between the two marks. Your diagonal measurement should be exactly 5 feet. Adjust the angle if necessary to make the final dimension work out right. For a final check of squareness, measure the deck layout diagonally from the corners. If the two corner measurements agree, it's square.

LAYING OUT A DECK

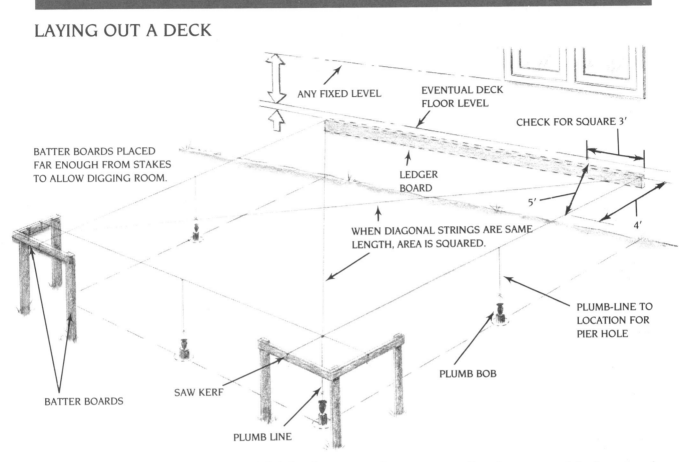

ANY FIXED LEVEL

EVENTUAL DECK FLOOR LEVEL

CHECK FOR SQUARE 3'

BATTER BOARDS PLACED FAR ENOUGH FROM STAKES TO ALLOW DIGGING ROOM.

LEDGER BOARD

5'

4'

WHEN DIAGONAL STRINGS ARE SAME LENGTH, AREA IS SQUARED.

PLUMB-LINE TO LOCATION FOR PIER HOLE

PLUMB BOB

BATTER BOARDS

SAW KERF

PLUMB LINE

Drawing above: Batter boards help establish levels at various locations, as well as the square of the layout and the plumb to post holes. Extend batter boards at least 1 foot beyond corner post locations to allow room for digging. Below left: A flat-topped support, such as a 5-gallon can, makes a serviceable builder's level. Just level its top in two perpendicular directions and use it as a platform for making level sightings. Sight along a carpenter's level to a helper with tape measure to ground. Below right: Plumb corner layout posts using a carpenter's level on two adjacent sides. Posts this tall will need good bracing.

SITING AND SETTING POSTS

Getting deck posts sited so that they'll properly support your beams can be finicky business. The easiest way—not permitted by some code officials—to set posts is to bury them in the ground, in oversized postholes. To site them, a plumb bob is used. The posts themselves can be wiggled into plumb with little hassle, and then braced. Then concrete is placed in the holes to hold the posts solidly. Use pressure-treated wood posts made for in-ground use, not just for Ground-contact. (Look for a treatment level of 0.60 pounds per cubic foot.)

Measure the post distances in from the lines used for joist positioning and use a plumb bob to find the center location.

Stake the center of the posthole site. Dig out at least three times the post size, and preferably four times. Of course, make certain that your postholes reach at least 6 inches below frost depth and end in undisturbed soil.

Now, pour in 6 to 8 inches of gravel, followed by a flat rock or piece of concrete—about double the size of the post—to serve as a footing.

Check post lengths to the line. If the beam runs under and the posts are centered on the beam, the post height should be the burial depth plus ground height to the joist line, minus the depth of your joists. (It pays to leave the posts a few inches long and trim them after the beams are in place. Do this with a handsaw or reciprocating saw. To aid in sawing post tops off squarely, mark the posts all the way around with a pencil and square.)

Drop the plumb line again, and see that the center of the hole is as close as possible to being directly under the center of the post. Set the post in place, plumbing it to the line above. Brace it well, and check the plumb one more time, making any necessary adjustments. When checking plumb, always check on two adjacent sides; for example, north and east. (Empire Level Company makes a strap-on level that fits one corner of a post to level it in two directions at once. The address is in this book's "Preface.")

Use at least one 60-pound bag of ready-packaged concrete mix around the base of each post. You can use it dry, tamping it down hard and letting the damp soil around it cause it to harden, or you can mix it with water as the manufacturer directs and then place the mix around the post.

Pier Method

While burying posts is the fastest and easiest way to settle things in, the method fails to meet code in many areas, where *all* wood, whatever the type, must be at least 6 inches aboveground. Because Charlie Self used heart redwood for his deck posts, he chose to use concrete footings and anchor bolts, with post anchors that support the posts an inch or so above the concrete, and adequately above the ground. This is not the easiest way to do things, but Charlie wisely preferred it to having to replace rotted deck posts a decade or two down the road.

For this method of post siting, a plumb bob or carpenter's level may be used, but you need to be more careful to keep the footings from drifting too far out of line. Some drift is acceptable if the footings are large enough. As soon as the concrete is cast for each footing form, a 12-inch anchor bolt should be set into the form's center, thread and nut protruding enough to hold the eventual anchor under the nut without leaving thread exposed on top. Leave the nut on now, because it will clean bolt threads as it is run off.

After 48 hours, come back and set each post anchor. The post anchor is a three-piece unit, with large U-shaped lower sections, with the bottom of the U fitting on the concrete. The bottom has a large hole in its center and an eccentric washer to fill that hole. The anchor bolt runs up through the washer, and the nut is installed finger-tight (according to the directions on the package—but read on). The second U section is then placed on the base, flat side up. The post is placed on that flat side, and the two sides of the lower plate are nailed to the post, using eight nails supplied with the anchor.

This works fine, except for tightening the anchor bolt nut only finger-tight at the outset. Instead, tighten the nut down firmly with a ¾-inch open-end wrench. This keeps the anchor from dancing around as it is nailed to the post. If you later need to loosen the nut to make any changes for plumb, the task is easy.

SETTING THE BEAMS

Techniques for setting beams vary, but you should never simply toenail them. In many cases, beams go right on top of posts. The best procedure is to set beams properly into framing anchors. However, to do this you must first have carefully cut post tops level from post to post.

To prevent post rot, it's best to set tops of piers at least 6 inches above grade (ground level). Pier footings should reach below frost line; check with local building authorities. Left photo: Make forms for piers by slicing the bottoms from tapered plastic containers, such as this plant container. Right photo: After digging out for footings and partially filling the holes with concrete, lay the plastic containers upside down on top of the footings and fill with concrete; make sure the pier concrete bonds well to the footing concrete. After the pier has set, lift or cut the plastic away.

Nail the sides of each anchor to the 4 × 4 wood post using framing-anchor nails. Post anchors support 4 × 4 redwood posts slightly off the concrete piers, anchored by a bolt embedded in the top of the pier.

In many cases, beams are hung from the posts using lag screws or carriage bolts, with the posts either trimmed off at the tops of the beams or else extended upward to serve as deck rail supports. Joists then ride on the beams and are held in place with joist tie-downs (not toenailing).

Beams may be cut to length and fitted right in, or they may be placed full-length (as Charlie placed them) with an overhang at one or both ends to be cut off before the deck is finished.

According to Charlie, one of the best benefits of constructing his deck from redwood was the lack of splinters. Any major wood construction project is usually accompanied by a daily splinter or two, but over the time required to get his deck in place, the only splinter he picked up was from a piece of plywood. (Nevertheless, a redwood splinter can be painful, because the natural preservative in redwood makes it burn.) Other admirable working qualities of redwood that tend to redeem its extra cost include ease of cutting, ease of nailing, and ease of driving screws, Charlie found. He also noticed that redwood warps and cups less than other woods. Redwood does, though, warp and cup somewhat. Like other woods, it should be protected from the elements until it is measured, cut, and fastened into place.

Two ways of setting beams: Photo above shows beams being placed atop 4 × 4 posts, as Carmen Cabral is doing for an aboveground pool deck. For this method, post tops must be cut square and twisted tie-downs added for adequate hold-down. Photo at right shows three staggered 5/16 × 3 lag screws being fastened into a 4 × 10 redwood beam and its 4 × 4 post. A second 2 × 10 beam will be mounted on the post's other side.

PLACING JOISTS

Joist placement is simple if everything is square. Charlie got the beam square with the ledger board and simply cut the 2 × 10 joists to length, laid one end on the beam, and went along the ledger board marking the positions for the joist hangers. The outside joist hangers go on first, using the proper size for the joists. (Some suppliers may try to tell you it doesn't matter which size hanger you use, after 2 × 8. Don't listen.)

Set the first joist hanger on its outside line, making sure the base of the hanger will allow the joist to fall level with the lower edge of the ledger board. This is important. If you allow the hanger itself to be level with the lower edge of the joist, you will end up with a slightly raised set of joists.

Sight on the inner part of the bottom of the **U**, the part that will be level with the bottom of the joist. Nail one side of the joist hanger, then set the joist into it carefully. Hold the joist in place and drive one nail

through the ledger-board side of the loose hanger. Then nail the joist to the hanger. Finally, finish nailing the hanger to the ledger board. As with all framing anchors, use framing-anchor nails.

When you've hung the outside joists, adjust for square, using a framing square to make a rough check. Do this by moving the joist's outer edge, on the beam, until the joist is square. Next, check diagonal measurements. The measurement from one inside corner diagonally to the outside corner should closely match the measurement of the corresponding diagonal. If this is so, mark the beam where the joists sit, and apply the tie-down strips to hold the joists to the beams. Charlie used small angle-nailers (1½ inches) to make sure the joists stayed properly sited, but used twisted tie-downs to provide more wind-lift resistance.

Check diagonal measurements again after nailing. Correction is far easier now than later, when you might find all the joists out of line.

With a square, draw a line offset ¾ inch to one side of each on-center joist mark on the ledger board. (This assumes the use of 2-inch-nominal joist lumber,

Left photo: Set the outside joist hanger so that its bottom edge is even with the bottom edge of the ledger board, then nail the inner flange with framing-anchor nails. Install the rest of the joist hangers the same way, waiting to nail one flange until after placing the joists into the hangers. Right photo: For a low deck, instead of using beams and joists, a simple gridwork of 2 × 8s may be screwed together, with the framing members spaced so the deck planks will span properly. The gridwork is set on piers and may be attached at the house to a ledger board or more piers.

which will be 1½-inches thick. If you use a different thickness for your joists, adjust this measurement accordingly to half the member's thickness.) Line up the inside edge of the corresponding side of the joist hanger with this offset mark and nail in place.

When one end joist is set and lightly secured in its hanger, go to the other end and get your on-center measurement and ¾-inch offset mark on the far beam. Position the joist and apply angle ties and tie-downs as you wish (and as codes in your area require). Even if code does not require tie-downs in your locality, I recommend them; any area is likely to get high winds

Now the joists can be laid in their hangers and rested on the single outer beam. These will cantilever beyond the beam. Nail twisted tie-downs, shown next page, to prevent liftoff in a strong wind.

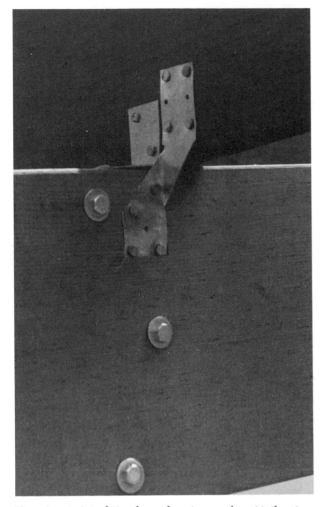

Here is a twisted tie-down framing anchor. Nail a tie-down to each joist on both sides of the beam.

at some time. The added cost per deck is low, and the extra construction time probably adds up to less than an hour.

Install the rest of the joists. Once they are in place, check the measurements one more time. Go back over joist hangers and tie-downs to make sure all are securely nailed. This part of the job is the base for all that follows and so must be square, plumb, level across, and securely built.

Once the joists are ready, add a fascia board to the open front of the joists. Some builders also use fascia boards along the edges, but with good-looking joist stock, this isn't essential.

LAYING DECK PLANKS

Deck planks may be laid in practically any pattern. Simplest is a running pattern at a right angle to the joists. With complex deck patterns, you need more of the longer pieces. To keep planking patterns such as a herringbone looking neat, it is essential to use a single length of board for each element in the pattern. You can break up the herringbone sections with straight sections to reduce the number of long boards needed, but that, again, requires more figuring and cutting. Central boards on herringbone patterns can be quite long, especially if the entire deck is laid in herringbone instead of in parquet-style.

With the deck structure complete, the 1 × 12 redwood fascia board and the first plank can be attached. The first plank starts even with the outside of the fascia.

DECK PLANK PATTERNS

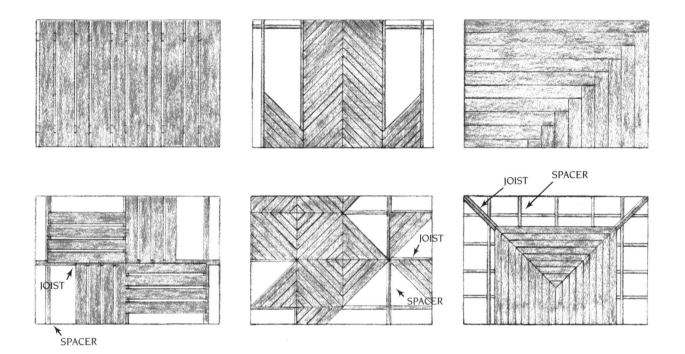

Break out the tape measure. Check cross-joist measurements to make sure all is well. Line up the tools and materials to be used.

Generally, deck planks are not cut to exact lengths when being fitted and fastened into place. Some overhang is left at the outside edges—usually at least 2 inches—and the excess is cut off afterwards to get a straight trimline at the edges.

Depending on plank layout, it is usual to start at the outer edge of the deck, leaving any width adjustments to be made on the last plank to go down against the house wall. This plank can be fastened directly to the ledger board, making its finished size less important than that of the other planks. The other planks must be used full-width for strength and for comfort under foot. Begin herringbone and parquet patterns at an outside corner or in the exact center.

Align the first deck plank with the top of the fascia board to give a smooth appearance to the outer edge of the deck. If a full-length plank is not available, lay down the longest one you have and add a shorter

plank to fill out the length. The planks must butt on the center of a supporting joist. Leave at least three joists for the additional plank to span. (In other words, on a 2-foot on-center distance, the short plank should not be less than 4 feet long. Ideally the short plank will be 6 feet long, but this isn't always possible.) Planks should be long enough to span more than one between-joist space. Two is the minimum, three better. The more continuous spans the planks make, the stronger the deck will be.

Most of Charlie's 2 × 6s were 10 feet long, so he could alternate joist breaks with fair ease. That is, he'd lay down a 10-foot deck plank from one side, and then lay a 6-foot plank from the other side. On the next row of planks, he'd lay a 6-foot plank alongside the earlier 10-foot plank. This system breaks the pattern of fastening two adjoining planks into a single joist and adds to overall deck strength.

At several points, Charlie placed two 8-foot planks to break the joist pattern further, and then added a couple of 16-foot full-deck-length planks to break it up further still. Esthetically it's better not to break all deck planks on the same joist.

As deck planks are laid, do your best to get the bark side up. Because of wood conditions, this isn't always possible, but cupping (curling up of board edges) is reduced when the bark sides are placed up. The bark side is on the convex side of the growth rings, which you can see by looking at the end grain of each board.

You may note as you start that the deck framing tends to shake a bit if you step too hard from one joist to the next. This slight shake disappears once enough of the deck planks are fastened, drawing the structure into an integral whole and making it quite rigid.

To hold his deck planks in place, Charlie used 3-inch coarse- or twin-thread, Phillips-head deck screws. For greatest security with deck planks, he used three of these screws at each junction—that is, if two plank ends met at a joist, he put three screws into the joist from each plank end. At middle points, he used two screws. In many areas, you will find the building code allows two screws at the joist junctions, and one, on alternating sides of the deck plank, at intermediate points. I especially like the California Redwood Association recommendation of using one deformed-shank nail (or screw) on alternate sides at each support, including plank ends. The goal, of course, is to avoid loosening of the planks later on.

Weather-resistant deck screws are driven to fasten a curved plank after it was first drawn into line by means of the long pipe clamp, shown. The powerful ½-inch variable-speed reversing drill drove screws all the way in, making initial pilot holes unnecessary. Not all electric drill manufacturers approve such use.

Left photo: Stuart Day, the author's brother, applies deck adhesive to gridwork prior to plank placement. A ledger board with joist hangers for the beams secures the deck to the house. No joists are used in this mini-deck. Right photo: Charlie Self brings two cordless driver/drills to bear on deck planks. One cordless drill makes ⅛-inch pilot holes for the deck screws. The other drives them in.

Pilot holes are recommended for deck screws, especially at plank ends and anywhere you are driving nails or screws within an inch of an end or side of a plank, where a plank is more likely to split. Because Charlie kept near the outside edges of the planks, he drilled an ⅛-inch pilot hole for each screw. This cost him a bit of time, but the result was that not a single board split from screw-driving. The time saved by not having to replace any boards probably made up for most of the time spent drilling the pilot holes.

The simplest way for one person to work is to drill pilot holes and fasten deck planks at the ends and at one or two intermediate points, with spacers in place. After several planks are in place, the rest of the pilot holes on those planks are drilled. And then the screws are run in.

Power-driven screws are the way to go. But it can be irritating to need to change your drill chuck over from pilot bit to screwdriver bit and back again numerous times. A good way to handle the bit exchange is to purchase a combination driver tool with matching hex-shank screwdriver bits and hex-shank pilot bits. With the driver tool chucked into your cordless

driver/drill, you simply slide out one bit, slide in the next bit you need, and go. Such an accessory may be purchased in most places where quality power tools are sold. The tool may also be magnetic so that screws won't fall off when the tool is pointed downward.

Charlie chose to leave ¼-inch spaces between his deck planks. He cut plywood strips to help maintain even spacing. Such spacers can readily be lifted out or tapped on through. Nails or deck screws often work well as spacers, too. One deck builder I know uses a wide mason's chisel as a spacer.

If more than one person is working, the job is much simpler. The plank is set and its pilot holes are drilled with one person holding it in place. The first worker drills and the second runs in screws later. If you don't use the driver/drill, you will need two tools. Whenever three or four planks are in place, their screws, or nails, are driven in. This makes keeping track of proper screw application easier. No pilot holes are missed, and no spot where a screw or nail is needed is left vacant.

When you reach the house wall, you may need to rip one plank narrower to fit against the wall. As your

PARQUET DECK (SEE PHOTO NEXT PAGE.)

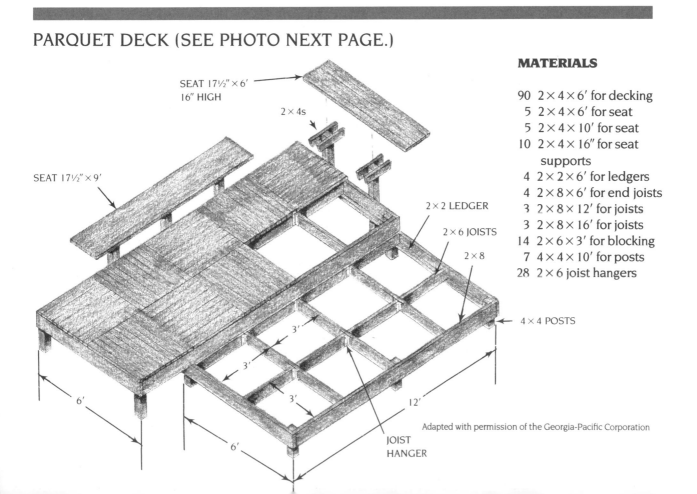

SEAT 17½" × 6'
16" HIGH

2 × 4s

SEAT 17½" × 9'

2 × 2 LEDGER

2 × 6 JOISTS

2 × 8

4 × 4 POSTS

3'

3'

3'

6'

6'

12'

JOIST
HANGER

MATERIALS

90 2 × 4 × 6' for decking
 5 2 × 4 × 6' for seat
 5 2 × 4 × 10' for seat
10 2 × 4 × 16" for seat
     supports
 4 2 × 2 × 6' for ledgers
 4 2 × 8 × 6' for end joists
 3 2 × 8 × 12' for joists
 3 2 × 8 × 16' for joists
14 2 × 6 × 3' for blocking
 7 4 × 4 × 10' for posts
28 2 × 6 joist hangers

Adapted with permission of the Georgia-Pacific Corporation

You can build a low-to-the-ground deck using 4 × 4-foot "parquet" squares of decking assembled from 2 × 4s. The layout uses 2 × 6 joists and 2 × 8 headers. See drawing on previous page for plans and materials. (Georgia-Pacific Corporation photo)

To zip off overhanging deck planks with a circular saw, place the saw in the desired cutting position at each end and mark where its shoe rests (left photo). Then tack-nail a straight board between the marks and saw (right photo). Although the normal plank overhang is 2 inches, Charlie Self chose not to have any overhang. The planks nearest the wall needed sawing by hand.

Color Portfolio of
DECKS, PATIOS & FENCES

Above photo: Deck planks can be arranged to radiate from a center square in ever-larger squares. Here, blocking is needed between joists at the center to support both ends of the short planks. Mitering and plank-matching needs to be meticulous. The railing consists of 4 × 4 posts and 2 × 2 balusters held by 2 × 6 horizontal and vertical rails. Stair rail style should match the deck's (Photographer, Ernest Braun; California Redwood Association photo). Right photo: A herringbone pattern adds a handsome touch. But it requires special arrangement of framing members and careful measurements and miter marks before sawing (Georgia-Pacific Corporation photo).

This low deck features a wrap-around step, a corner food center, a lattice screen, and ample benches. Stair risers have recessed downlights. The 4×4 posts at the corners provide area lighting. A gravel edge eliminates grass-trimming problems next to the deck. (Photographer, Tom Rider; designer/builder, John Hamingway; California Redwood Association photo)

Photo left: If your deck fancies lean toward the elaborate, they might call for the services of an architect with design flair. Archadeck is a national network of design and construction specialists that also restores decks ravaged by time (Archadeck photo, U.S. Structures Inc., 2112 W. Laburnum Avenue, Richmond, VA 23220). Photo below: This plank pattern is divided into quarters—planks on diagonal quarters aligned. Here, there are two options for support: (1) Solid 2-inch blocking for two grids where planks run parallel to underlying joists. (2) Additional beams that allow the joists to accommodate the quartered plank pattern (Photographer, Maris Semel; California Redwood Association photo).

Above left: The author's eldest son Russ soft-set this patio with brick. The patio doubles as a walkway, wrapping around to a utility area in back. The painted-concrete curb holds the bricks, which are laid tightly on a 2-inch sand subbase. Edge bricks were carefully trimmed to fit. Fine silica sand was broom-swept between joints. Above right: Pattern stamping on this surface-colored concrete makes it look like tile hard-set into concrete, especially since the joints are grouted. Other stamping patterns can create the illusion of brick, flagstone, and cobblestone. The result costs a fraction of a patio made with hard-set tile or stone (Bomanite Corporation photo, courtesy Portland Cement Association). Below: This "deck-stretcher" patio is made of precast concrete pavers (Portland Cement Association photo).

Above: Less than 18 inches above ground level, this deck needs no railing and features slatted benches and a house-wall counter. Planking runs perpendicular to the house, requiring that joists run parallel to the house. Four hollow columns built from 1×6 boards support beams for the deck cover, constructed of 2×6 rafters and 2×2 slats (Photographers, Hursley/Lark; designer, Milton L. Sandy; California Redwood Association photo). Photo below: To please owner and neighbor, this "good-neighbor" fence is identical on both sides. It has 4×4 posts and 1×4 rails, and was built and paid for jointly by Doug and Leanna Day and their neighbors.

This main deck's plank walkway leads to a satellited deck. The 2 × 4 skirts around the bench/planter configuration cover plank ends while contributing a sense of substance. The 2 × 6 planking requires careful mitering. Beams for such low decks often rest directly on concrete footings, with no underlying posts (Georgia-Pacific Corporation photo).

Above: The decorative top of 2 × 4s was built in place. The Xs, which make up a goodly portion of the upper fence, require double 45-degree miters and are notched for half-lapping (Photographer, Mark Becker; designer, Scott E. Smith; California Redwood Association photo). Photo right: This plant-accented fencing consists of 4 × 4 posts and rails paneled with horizontal 1-bys in random widths. Decorative 2 × 4s along the top also improve security. The patio is soft-set brick, the surface sloping to a drain grate (Photographer, Karl Riek; architect, Robert Engman; California Redwood Association photo).

The bottom portion of this Victorian redwood fence employs standard post-and-rail construction. Installed after the bottom section, the top frames lattice panels between nailed-on 1 × 2s. Dowels and weatherproof glue attach the finials to the extension posts. The gate arches into an overhead lattice panel, echoing the shape of the finials. (Photographer, Andrew McKinney; California Redwood Association photo)

planking approaches the wall, keep a running check on the remaining space from at least 6 feet out. To look good, that last plank needs to be at least 1½ inches wide, and it could do with a bit more width. Make small adjustments in spacing between planks for any required added width. If you start making the adjustments far enough out, the change in spacing will not be obvious. (Better yet, use the spacing method illustrated in the previous chapter. Then the last plank should end up being full-width.)

You may have to tilt and tap the final plank into place under the door sill, so make sure you have an accurate fit before going ahead. Those last planks under door sills can be terrors to remove if further trimming should be needed.

Once the deck planks are down, check to see that all nails or screws are set flush with the surface (or a bit below); that all pilot holes have screws in them; and that all the other spots you want fastened down have screws or nails in them.

STAIRS

The test of a good carpenter is stair-building. Indoor stairs *usually* have treads and risers: *treads* are the horizontals and *risers* are the verticals. Deck stairs consist of stringers with treads mounted across them. Outdoor deck stairs are usually built without risers, leaving open spaces between the treads. These spaces are best held to between 6 and 8 inches. For a good stairway, tread width multiplied by riser space should equal 75, or close to it. In other words, a 7-inch riser requires a 10- or 11-inch tread. Slightly wider treads are acceptable, and even useful, in outdoor construction. All of a stair's treads and risers must be the same depth and height, and final cutting and construction must be accurate enough to keep the riser heights to within a total variation of ¼ inch. (Some building inspectors insist on ⅛-inch maximum variation, and the

STAIR-BUILDING MEASUREMENTS

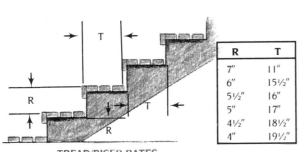

R	T
7"	11"
6"	15½"
5½"	16"
5"	17"
4½"	18½"
4"	19½"

TREAD/RISER RATES

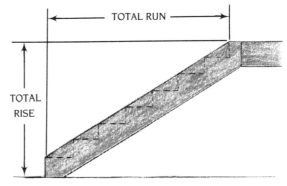

MEASURING RISE AND RUN

STEPS PLACED ON CLEATS

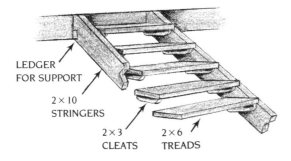

LEDGER FOR SUPPORT

2 × 10 STRINGERS

2 × 3 CLEATS   2 × 6 TREADS

STEP SUPPORTS CUT OUT FROM STRINGERS

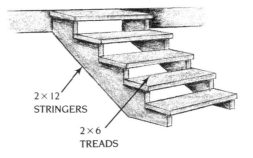

2 × 12 STRINGERS

2 × 6 TREADS

true craftsman should aim for that.) Any more than a ¼-inch variation invites tripping.

One riser height is called the riser or *unit rise*; one tread width is called the tread or *unit run*. All of the risers added together must equal the total rise, the amount of elevation from ground (or other level) to deck. All the treads added together must equal the total run, the horizontal distance the stairway takes up from ground to deck. If a riser must differ from the standard, make this allowance at the bottom stair, keeping any variation as slight as possible. Coming off a short last step when going downstairs tends to make you feel as if brakes have been jammed on, even if the difference is only an inch. On the other hand, the effect of coming off a too-high last step resembles that of an elevator losing its cables. Dig out or build up around the bottom stair as needed. But proper figuring should help you avoid compensating at the end.

Stair Planning

Three types of staircase construction are in general use: the housed stairway; the cleated-stringer stair; and the cutout-stringer type. The housed stair, with its water-trapping areas, is not useful outdoors. But both cleated-stringer and cutout-stringer stairs are well suited to outside use. These are shown in accompanying drawings and can be built fairly quickly if you take measurements carefully and transfer them properly. Cutout stair stringers must have at least 4 inches of solid wood diagonally from notch to opposite edge remaining after the tread and riser cutouts are made.

When it comes to stairs, don't use your plan dimensions to lay out and cut wood. Instead, measure the actual total rise and do your final figuring with that measurement in hand.

To help keep stairs from collecting puddles outdoors, make treads from two 2×6s spaced ¼ inch apart to give an apparent tread width of 11¼ inches. This is not an actual tread width, though, because at least an inch of this will be what is called a *nosing* sticking out beyond the stringer cutout. This nosing is not counted as part of the tread width. One 2×6 is placed against the back of the riser cutout, resting in the tread cutout on the stringer, and screwed or nailed into place. Then a spacer is placed. The second tread goes against the spacer, and the overhang beyond the stringer cutout is the nose.

Stair width is another factor to consider. A minimum is 32 inches for main interior stairs. That is quite narrow. Space restrictions are seldom a problem in outdoor construction, so consider a width of 42 inches as a starting point and go wider from there.

A stairway four or more treads high should have a handrail at least on one side. Stairs more than 88 inches wide need two side rails and possibly a center rail as well. Handrail height should be from 30 to 34 inches from the stair nosing, and handrails should extend 6 inches past the bottom riser, and, if possible, beyond the top riser (or into the deck railing).

Stair Layout

Select a straight, clear-grained 2×12 for your first stringer layout. If you doubt your capabilities, buy a cheap 1×12 board to use as a pattern. This can be cut, test-fitted, and the final successful pattern transferred to the more costly redwood or pressure-treated 2×12s (used because they rest on concrete).

Start with careful deck-to-ground measurement of the total rise, done by two people if the stairs will be more than four treads high. One person holds the tape in contact with the ground while the other holds the tape at the top of the overall rise and reads and writes down the measurement.

There's a kicker. The ground may slope toward or away from the top of the deck. Here, measuring directly to the ground under the point where the top of the stairs will connect to the deck gives a false reading. The problem is resolved by tack-nailing a level length of 1×3 or 1×4 to the deck, extending out to the point where the stairs should reach ground. (This may be hard to judge exactly, but can be guesstimated.) From the underside of this level board, measure to the ground.

Figure the approximate height of each riser. Let's say the total rise is 75 inches, and you initially hoped to make risers 7 inches. If you divide 75 by 7 inches, you get 10 risers with 5 inches left over. So, to get 10 equal risers, you would use 7½ inches instead. But because such a high riser would make the stairs steep, you might wish to use more risers but lower ones, such as, for our example, 11 risers of 6¹³/₁₆-inches each. In any case, simply divide the number of risers desired into the total rise to get the final result for each riser. The stairs can meet the deck at deck level, as Charlie's did, or the top step can be exactly one riser below deck level, as you choose.

Charlie's stairs were 50½ inches high (total rise). The 7-inch riser standard suggested using seven of them. The result of dividing the total rise by 7 was a riser just a hair under 7¼ inches. With the possibility of digging out or adding soil at the bottom, Charlie cut all stair risers to 7¼ inches. Though the figures are based on seven treads, the bottom "tread" is the ground, leaving a total of six treads to cut. (One more riser than tread had to be made.)

Ramps—which may be used instead of or in addition to stairs—should have a gentle slope of not more than 1 in 5, that is, one foot of rise for each five feet horizontally. Instead of being notched out for steps, the stringers for a ramp are left straight on top. Only the top and bottom of the stringer are cut.

Marking Stair Stringers with Framing Square. Working with a framing square is the only sensible way to lay out stairs. It speeds the work to attach a pair of stair gauges to the framing square, but you can work just as accurately, though more slowly, without them. Use the inch measurements along the two outer edges of the square's arms, and do all marking along those edges. With the top of a stair stringer lying on the worktable or across sawhorses to one side, say your left, lay the framing square down on the stringer with its 90-degree angle away from you and its blade (longer arm) on the left. Bring the tread dimension on the blade even with the edge of the stringer and hold it there while moving the riser dimension on the tongue (short arm) even with the same edge of the stringer. In this position, the square denotes tread on the left and riser on the right. If you have stair gauges, install and tighten them to hold the framing square against the edge of the stringer precisely in this desired position.

In Charlie's case, the blade of the square met the edge of the stringer at 10 inches and the tongue met it at 7¼ inches.

First mark the top end of the stringer. From this point, step off the correct number of treads and risers along the stringer. The riser of one step's cutout points to the start of the tread of the next. The last (bottom) step gets cut off at the same tread angle to position the bottom tread off the ground or landing by the right amount. To accomplish this, normally, the thickness of the stair-tread material (1½ inches) is cut from the bottom of the first riser (the part that rests on

HOW TO MARK A STRINGER

Here's how to mark a stringer or stringer pattern for stair cutouts: (**1**) Set a framing square at the upper end with the desired tread and riser dimensions positioned and (with stair gauges in place) mark for both. (**2**) Remove the stair gauges, if used, and slide the square along the just-made tread mark until it reaches across. Mark across for stringer cutoff. (**3**) Position and mark all stair cutouts, top to bottom. One cutout leads the framing square into the next. (Sequence continues on next page.)

the support block), making it come out the same as the others.

Recheck your marking. For strength, be sure you've left at least 4 inches of solid wood—no knots—from the point of each cutout diagonally across the width to the opposite edge. Once you're satisfied, make the stringer cutouts.

Once the final corner cuts are made, you have your first stringer (or your stringer pattern). Check it for fit against the deck. If the fit is good and the tread cuts are level, use this first stringer (or pattern) to mark all the other stringers. Cut them in the same manner. Stringers are spaced about the same distance apart as joists, with no more than a 24-inch on-center distance for redwood treads and up to 30 inches on-center distance for some species of fir and pine. Charlie used three stringers on a 42-inch-wide set of redwood-planked stairs.

If cleated stringers are used, do the layout just as

Continuing from previous page, make all the stair cutouts in the stringer or the pattern. This is best done with a circular saw along the marked lines. Saw each way, almost to the inside corner, and then stop. Finish into the corners with a hand or saber saw.

above, but cut just the bottom and top edges of the stringer. A stringer for cleated stairs may be a 2 × 8 or 2 × 10. Then screw on the cleats, using stainless steel No. 12 × 2½-inch wood screws, at the tread marks. Use top-grade 2 × 3 or similar wood for cleats, or get special stair-tread anchors.

Stringer Support

Next, determine exact placement for the stringers. Stringers may be supported at the top and bottom. At the top, the most common, and the worst, method is simply to toenail or screw the stringers directly to the header or deck joist. You can do better. Make up a 2 × 2 or larger cleat the entire width of the staircase. It should extend from the outside edge of one outside stringer to the outside edge of the other outside stringer. Notch out the tops of the stringers to fit around it, being careful to get a square corner at the top of the cut. Place the stringer, using angle braces as fasteners, and then place the cleat, securing it *temporarily* with two 3-inch drywall screws. (Do *not* use these as final fasteners, no matter how many you use. These drywall screws do not have the shear strength needed for permanent fastening here.) Instead, drill pilot holes and run in four (on a 42-inch-wide staircase) ¼ × 3-inch lag screws, with flat-plated washers under the heads.

The stairway must be anchored at the bottom edge of the stringers to keep it from moving from side to side. You can sink a concrete block into a hole. (If codes require 6 inches between wood and ground, you'll need two such blocks to achieve the proper height.) The hole should be deep enough that the top of the block meets the bottom of the stringer at the proper elevation. Fill the block cavities with concrete. Set the stringer bottoms on the blocks, and use angle-fasteners to hold them in place. Drill and drive Tapcon

Once the stringer is finished, use it to mark cutouts for the next stringer.

SUPPORT FOR A STAIR STRINGER

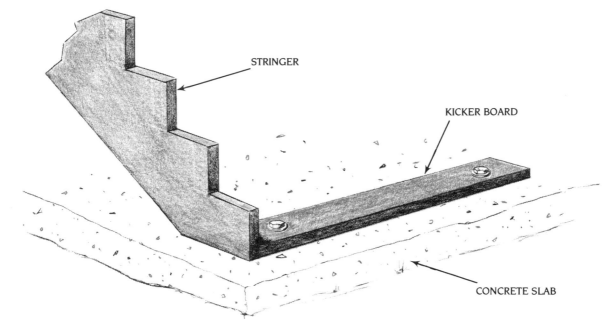

STRINGER

KICKER BOARD

CONCRETE SLAB

Charlie Self's finished stairway, with railings added for safety, is as solid as his deck. Gravel at the bottom covers dug-in concrete-block stairway supports.

screws through the angle-fasteners. Or cast a concrete slab for the stringers to rest on. A kicker board may be used to secure the connection. In any case, stringers should *not* rest on the ground.

Finally, nail or screw the stair treads on, starting at the bottom. Work up the stringers from there. You will soon have a fine-looking stairway.

RAILINGS

Deck railings are quite similar to fences. Dozens of fence designs are adaptable to deck railings.

Though time-consuming, constructing a deck railing can be one of the simplest jobs involved in building a deck. Intermediate posts should be 2×4s or 4×4s. Use 2×4s when intermediate distances are 6 feet or less and 4×4s when distances are 8 feet or more. Add upper and lower rails, of 2×4 or 2×6 material, with the upper rail fastened on top of the uprights and the lower rail fastened about 8 inches above the deck surface, between the upright members. Use angle-brackets or fence-rail brackets for easiest fastening. Or you can dado the posts. For the railings on his deck, Charlie Self chose a simple design he had used before: a series of uprights, based on 4×4s at the outside corners, with a center 4 × 4 support, and intermediate 2 × 4s notched to fit over the deck floor. Some other railing styles are illustrated in Chapter 2.

To build Charlie's railing style, start by shaping the corner 4 × 4s. Cut a 45-degree bevel on the bottom corner edge that will face the outside. Measure up 9½ inches from the bottom edge (for 2 × 10 deck joists). Mark inward 2 inches from that back edge, and rip the 4 × 4s to the 9½-inch mark. Cross-cut at the 9½-inch mark. You now have your basic form for all the deck posts. Charlie constructed his to place the top of the railing 36 inches above the deck surface, an acceptable minimum height under many building codes. (Before settling on a height, check your local building code.)

Once the corners are placed, find your on-center measurement for the center 4 × 4 post and put it in place, checking with a level on two adjacent sides to be sure it is plumb. Then add house-end posts of 2 × 4 stock. Because Charlie had added 1½-inch wings to the ledger board to allow flat nailing of the joist anchors, these did not need notching at the lower edge but were cut to a length of 34½ inches and screwed to the house walls.

The structural members for the top rail and bottom rail, if any, should be made from at least 2 × 4 material for sturdiness unless closely spaced uprights —24 inches on-center or less—are used.

Charlie used 1 × 6 redwood tops and edging for the railing, the tops horizontally (but sloped enough to drain) and the edging vertically. First install the edging flush with the tops of the posts. Charlie used 2-inch weather-resistant drywall screws to hold his deck railing members. Use three screws at each 4 × 4, and two at the 2 × 4s. Next, add the top rail, again a 1 × 6, screwing it into the tops of the 4 × 4s and the 2 × 4s.

The deck still lacks intermediate 2 × 4 balusters (fillers on Charlie's deck), which are cut the same way as the 4 × 4 posts. The fillers may be any style you choose. Often, **X**-members are used. These are fairly simple to make. With 2 × 4 or 2 × 2 material, form angles at the ends by holding a slightly over-length member in place, accurately (either with a helper or by tack-nailing). Mark the cutoff angles. Then hold the member that will form the other part of the **X** in place on the other side of the uprights. Mark its cutoff angles, and mark the centers of both boards where they cross. Cut the angles, and cut angled notches in each board to half the overall board depth so that the centers fit over each other. Then screw or nail the boards in place.

For a different style, position top and bottom rails and use 2 × 2 or 2 × 4 material to make balusters be-

RAILING DETAILS

Erecting the railing begins with installation of corner posts—here 4 × 4s notched to fit over the deck.

To cut notches, 2 × 4 balusters can be clamped together so ganged cuts can be made with a circular saw. Be sure to set the saw's depth precisely to the desired depth. Rip cuts for notches can be started in a similar way and finished individually by hand or saber saw. Beveled end cuts can be ganged, too.

Left photo: This is a 2 × 4 baluster bottom fitted to deck framing. The 3-inch drywall screw was first driven to position the baluster. Then came two ¼ × 3-inch weather-resistant lag screws—pilot-drilled and cranked in. Right photo: The 1 × 6 redwood railing was attached with two 2-inch weather-resistant drywall screws.

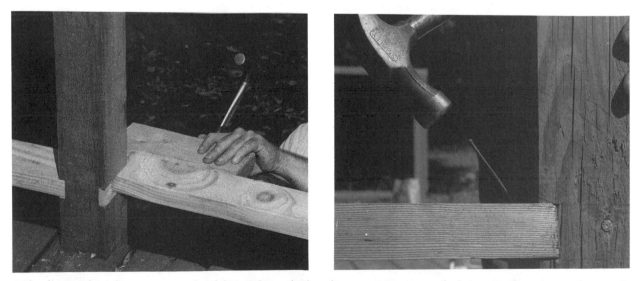

Left photo: This alternative method for making deck railings requires post dadoing. Dado cuts can be made with a circular saw, handsaw, or router. Then tap the cut-to-length 2 × 4 rails into the dadoes in opposing posts. Right photo: Angled galvanized casing nails prevent the rail from sliding out.

Standard for deck construction, Charlie Self's deck is 1 inch lower than the house interior floor. He staggered ends of deck planks for best strength—none aligned next to each other on joists. And he finished his deck with clear wood sealer and a brush. Sealers can also be sprayed or rolled on.

Charlie played it safe by spacing balusters close together, though local code did not require it. This prevents small children from falling through. A sheet of 6-mil plastic under the crushed rock would prevent weed growth.

tween the rails. This is most easily done *before* the bottom rail is attached, with the short uprights cut to length in the uprights.

Though his local code did not require it, Charlie ultimately opted to place balusters 8 inches apart, for the safety of small children. Most codes require close spacing, typically a maximum of 8 inches. (Even then, children should not play on an elevated deck unless an adult is not only in attendance but also paying attention to the children.)

The necessary notch cut in balusters is difficult if each board is done singly, but easy when all the boards are done together, as shown on page 128. Make the rip cuts to complete the notches, either with a circular saw or with a bayonet blade in a saber saw. To keep things neat yet easy, Charlie used a circular saw for each and finished the cuts with a saber saw.

These 2 × 4s are placed using a 3-inch weather-resistant drywall screw as a siting anchor. Make certain they are plumb.

Before the post bottoms are firmly attached, come back on the deck and, first rechecking plumb, attach the rail and edging board to the balusters using 2-inch drywall screws, two to a baluster per board. Even with the lightweight 1 × 6 material as railings, this makes a sturdy rail system.

FINAL TOUCHES

For a final check, go over the deck and make sure that all fasteners are secured and all nails or screws driven flush with wood surfaces. Round over any rough edges, using either a belt sander or a Stanley Surform tool. Then give your deck the preservative treatment or finish you want it to have.

When the carpentry is finished, you can install lighting, as needed.

CHAPTER 5

CONCRETE CONSTRUCTION TOOLS

Many of the tools essential for concrete construction cost little and are useful for other kinds of work as well.

Concrete mixers are an exception. A concrete mixer is costly and is designed to do only one thing —mix concrete. You must have a concrete mixer if you are to do much concrete-making. Nevertheless, you may find it practical to rent rather than own it.

As with carpentry tools, buy only top-quality concrete tools. If you already own carpentry and garden tools, some will serve as concrete construction tools.

Concrete construction tools fall into three groups: basic tools, concrete mixers, and concrete placement and finishing tools.

To do any concrete placement or finishing, you will need, at the very least, safety goggles; safety hat; flat-ended shovel; stringline; pail and batch-cans; pneumatic-tired wheelbarrow; bullfloat or darby; edger; grooving tool; hand-float; and kneeboards. That's a bare-bones shopping list.

BASIC CONCRETING TOOLS

Here is a brief rundown on the basic construction tools plus others that are useful (though not specific to concrete-making).

Safety Goggles
Safety glasses with side shields to protect against wind-blown dust or wraparound safety goggles are mandatory for concrete work. Provide a fresh pair of safety goggles for yourself and for every helper. The flexible plastic safety goggles cost little.

Safety Hats
Should you bump your head on something solid— say, a concrete chute—it's preferable to be wearing a safety hat. Also, something could fall on your head. A safety hat can be replaced.

Rubber Work Gloves
Rubber or heavy vinyl work gloves are recommended for the range of concrete jobs from handling the fresh mix to curing. Waterproof work gloves may not be very comfortable, especially on a hot day, but they will keep your hands from being dried out by the alkali in the concrete.

Before mixing and after curing, ordinary cloth or leather work gloves work well and are more comfortable than the waterproof gloves. But because they don't protect against the wet concrete mix, these gloves have only limited uses for concrete projects.

Rubber Boots
While doing any large concrete project, it's hard to avoid wading out into the fresh mix. For this, you need

Here is a collection of concrete-finishing tools (clockwise from top): magnesium hand-float, waterproof kneepads, one kneeboard, texturing broom, homemade bullfloat, flat-end short-handled shovel, contractor-type wheelbarrow, another kneeboard, deep-bitted groover, edger, darby, and margin trowel. With these tools and safety goggles, you can handle most concrete construction projects.

to wear rubber boots high enough to prevent mix from running over them. If you wade in plastic concrete wearing running shoes or street shoes, the alkaline concrete will eat away at any tender skin it reaches.

Hand-Tampers

Your homemade hand-tamper should have a "footprint" area of 9 to 15 square inches, the ideal size for compacting earth subgrades, according to soils engineers. Larger-footed tampers, though common, do not develop enough pressure to compact the soil properly. Though they work well enough on sand and stone subbases, on soil they merely smooth the surface. Concrete doesn't require a uniformly smooth surface; it requires a uniformly *dense* one.

You can easily make a good tamper from a 5-foot length of 2×10 or 4×4. These cross sections are

HOME-BUILT TAMPER

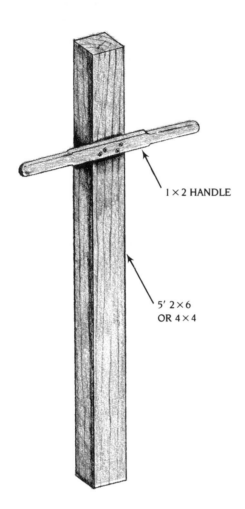

1 × 2 HANDLE

5′ 2 × 6
OR 4 × 4

just the right size. Nailing and gluing a smoothed 1 × 2-inch crosspiece near the top as a handle makes the tamper even easier to work.

Garden Hoses and Nozzles

You'll also need a garden hose to dampen the forms and subgrade just before placing concrete. If you mix your own concrete, you'll also use a hose for supplying mixing water. Moreover, a garden hose is indispensable for cleaning a concrete mixer drum and concrete-finishing equipment at the end of a project. Fit the hose end with a handy trigger nozzle.

If you're working on a hot day, have a garden hose with a separate fog nozzle handy to keep the piles of aggregates properly cool and damp, as well as to fog-spray the stiffening concrete surface in order to stretch out its setting time.

Flat-ended Shovels

A concrete shovel has a flat and square end about 8 inches across, and a short handle with a **D**-shaped handgrip. Use this shovel for pushing concrete down the ready-mix chute and into place on the subgrade. This shovel is never used for shoveling concrete. You'll need one flat-ended shovel for each helper. Either rent or borrow them.

Every concrete worker needs to be equipped with a flat-end short-handled shovel. It's especially useful in encouraging ready mix along the chute and then pushing it into place on the subgrade. (Roth/Woods project photo)

Small Sledgehammers

A small sledgehammer weighing about 3 pounds is ideal for driving form stakes. A full-size 8-pound sledgehammer or a wood-splitting maul may be substituted if you don't have a smaller sledge, or if you don't wish to buy one.

Framing Squares

If you want your projects to look professionally done, lay out the forms or at least check them with a framing square. A square is also useful for starting control joints squared with the side forms.

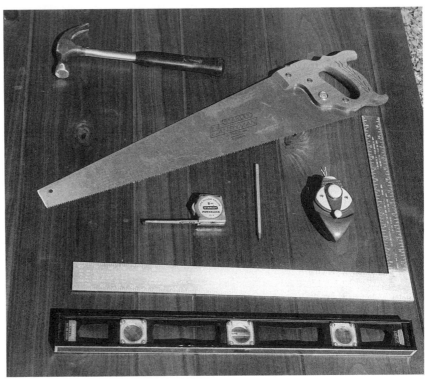

Carpentry tools helpful in making forms for concrete include hammer, crosscut saw, measuring tape, pencil, chalkline (or mason's stringline), framing square, and carpenter's bubble level.

Claw Hammers, Measuring Tapes, and Crosscut Saws

A few carpentry tools, such as a claw hammer, measuring tape, and crosscut saw, are needed to set up the forms for a slab. For laying out a large patio, you'll certainly need a 25-, 30-, or 50-foot tape measure—one long enough to allow you to measure the project's diagonals to be sure they're equal.

Circular Saws

Use a circular saw to cut form lumber. A circ saw quickly cross-cuts form boards to length and rips the 15-degree tapered moldings used in making a construction joint. About the only form-building job that a circular saw won't do well is lopping off the tops of form stakes. For that, a manual crosscut or an electric reciprocating saw works better.

Stringlines and Chalklines

The mason's stringline is invaluable in laying out a concrete project, though a carpenter's chalkline will suffice. The chalkline is also used in snapping colored-chalk guidelines for control joints across a slab.

Ideally, a stringline should be nylon or polypropylene so it won't collect concrete and can be stretched tightly without breaking.

Levels

To be sure your project is properly sloped for drainage, set it up with a good level. The 2-foot-long carpenter's bubble level is standard, though a 9-inch torpedo level is a good substitute.

A line level is a handy tool in combination with a tightly stretched stringline. The line level hooks over a taut stringline in the center of the span.

A tube or water level has a long tube containing fluid to indicate whether things a considerable distance apart are level. Be sure that no air bubbles are in the tube—they will affect the reading. In place of a tube level, you can get by with a bubble level.

Pails

For any concrete work, you need pails—for carrying concrete, carrying water, measuring water into a mixer, and for the cleaning of tools. Pails also serve as batch-cans for cement, water, and aggregates. A 5-gallon plastic or metal pail and a 10-quart (or 10-liter) bucket are handy sizes. At least two are needed. Better yet, have several on hand.

Bathroom Scales

For weight-batching concrete ingredients yourself, a bathroom scale is ideal. If you will be using ready-mixed, ready-packaged, or haul-it-yourself concrete, however, the scale can remain in the bathroom. Remember to cover the scale with clear plastic to protect it from water and the dry mix.

Utility Knives

From slicing open sacks of cement and ready-packaged concrete mix to cutting plastic curing blankets to size, the utility knife has plenty of uses around a concrete project. When not in use, its blade can be retracted safely into the handle. A kitchen knife could substitute but lacks the safety feature.

Concrete Mixers

To make your own concrete, you'll need a concrete mixer (try not to call it a "cement mixer"). It has an electric motor or gasoline engine belted and geared to a rotating drum. Blades inside turn with the drum, slicing through and turning over the concrete ingredients until they are blended and uniform throughout. A tilting mechanism on the drum permits discharging the mix.

Mixers are available in drum sizes from ½ cubic foot to as much as 7 cubic feet. (A cubic yard contains 27 cubic feet.) A concrete mixer's capacity should be stamped on its identification plate. Avoid exceeding the stated capacity because overloading the drum hampers the mixing action. A mixer's capacity is 60 percent of its actual drum volume. For example, a 3-cubic-foot mixer drum will handle batches of about 1¾ cubic feet; an 8-cubic-foot drum, 4½ cubic feet. The handiest concrete mixers are mounted on wheels so that they can be moved easily wherever needed. The larger ones can be towed behind vehicles. Level the mixer in a location where it will remain stable and not roll. If you place it on an old sheet of plywood,

Left photo: A gasoline-powered concrete mixer can be used anywhere, an advantage over an electric-powered mixer. Mixers can be rented. Such a mixer turns out fresh concrete at least 10 times faster than you can by hand-mixing (not to mention the work it saves). Right photo: A concrete mixer with a 5-cubic foot drum that accepts 3 cubic feet of mix is a convenient size. Called a "half-bag" mixer, it handles half a sack of portland cement along with the other ingredients.

you'll have an easier time cleaning up with a shovel.

Most mixers require periodic maintenance. Follow the manufacturer's maintenance instructions. For instance, the drum axles of some mixers should be greased. To do this properly, you'll need a grease gun filled with a multipurpose grease.

Electric-powered Mixers and Tools. An electric-powered mixer is easier to use than a gas-powered mixer. But to avoid shock hazard, be sure you use a GFCI-protected outlet. A concrete mixer needs a three-wire grounding-type extension cord plugged into a three-slot grounding receptacle. The mixer should be fitted with a three-pronged grounding plug. To minimize the start-up load on the motor, either start the mixer drum empty or tilted and looking up when first plugged in.

To minimize shock hazard, never use an electric concrete mixer outdoors in damp or wet weather. Move the mixing operation into the garage, if need be. Cover the mixer with a waterproof tarpaulin when not in use, or park it inside.

As for other electrical tools, be sure that any extension cord you use with them is rated for outdoor use. This will be indicated by a "W-A" or "W" suffix following the cord-type designation—for example, SJTW-A. A 14-gauge or heavier extension cord can handle the typical ½-hp mixer motor's load as far as 100 feet of cord without excessive voltage drop.

Gasoline-powered Mixers. If the project is some distance from an electric outlet, a gasoline-powered concrete mixer allows you to minimize concrete hauling distance. Chief drawbacks of gasoline-powered mixers are that the engine must be started each time you mix and that its fuel and lubricating oil must be checked and replenished periodically. As you might expect, gasoline-powered mixers also cost more to rent or buy.

With a gasoline-powered mixer, you need not worry about electric shock or tripping over an extension cord. But this mixer has a hazard of its own: flammable fuel. You will need a proper can for storing and pouring gasoline into the engine's fuel tank, a supply of gasoline, and motor oil suited to the engine. Don't refuel the engine while the mixer is running or while the engine is hot. Stop the mixer and let the engine cool before adding fuel. To pour the fuel into the tank, you may need a flexible-spout funnel. Wipe up any spills *immediately* with rags. And don't start the engine with spilled gasoline around.

Never run a gasoline engine in an enclosed space. The carbon monoxide fumes that are produced can cause dizziness, nausea, disorientation, and even death. Run a gasoline-powered mixer outdoors only.

PLACING AND FINISHING TOOLS

The following tools handle concrete: that is, to place it, finish it, and cure it.

Pneumatic-tired Wheelbarrows

Wheelbarrows with air-filled rubber tires are available in three sizes. The very largest size is best left to contractors, since it holds too much concrete for do-it-yourselfers to carry comfortably. What we need is the intermediate size, a do-it-yourself-size, contractor-type wheelbarrow, the kind found in DIY outlets. It generally comes knocked down for owner assembly. The third size available is a small, rubber-tired garden wheelbarrow, useful for small projects. It isn't as stable as the two larger, heavier wheelbarrows. In any case, a pneumatic tire is essential for transporting concrete without the jiggling that produces segregation in concrete. For this reason, avoid steel-wheeled or hard-rubber-tired wheelbarrows.

A garden wheelbarrow is okay for mixing and transporting small batches of concrete, if it has a smooth-riding pneumatic tire and thus prevents segregation. (Sakrete photo)

CONCRETE-FINISHING TOOLS

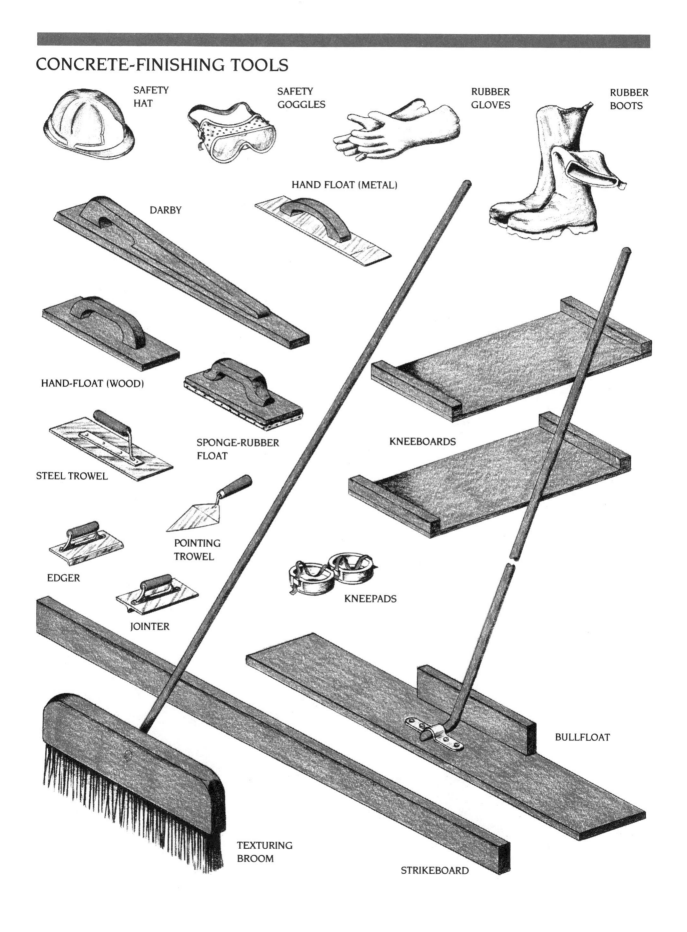

SAFETY HAT

SAFETY GOGGLES

RUBBER GLOVES

RUBBER BOOTS

HAND FLOAT (METAL)

DARBY

HAND-FLOAT (WOOD)

SPONGE-RUBBER FLOAT

STEEL TROWEL

KNEEBOARDS

POINTING TROWEL

EDGER

KNEEPADS

JOINTER

BULLFLOAT

TEXTURING BROOM

STRIKEBOARD

Strikeboards

The strikeboard, also called a *straightedge* or *strike-off tool*, is a long, straight board for striking off the concrete surface. You can get one by ordering more 2 × 4 form lumber than is needed so that one arrow-straight length may be set aside ahead of time to be used as a strikeboard. It should measure 2 feet or so longer than the distance between forms. Strikeboard lengths can run from 3 feet to 16 feet.

Bullfloats

For initial finishing, you'll have to choose between a bullfloat and a darby. You won't need both. The bullfloat's long handle allows you to reach across large patio slabs to give them an initial finish, working solely from outside the forms. For any project large enough or with space enough to work comfortably, the bullfloat does a better job than a darby. It brings a little cement paste to the surface.

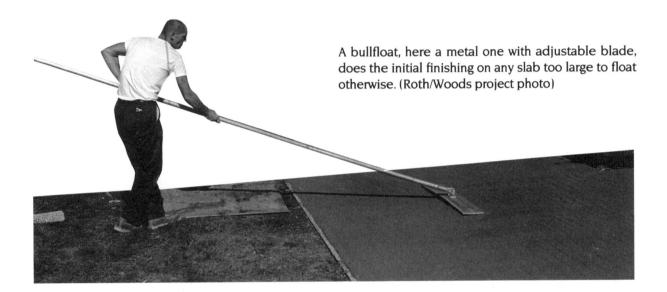

A bullfloat, here a metal one with adjustable blade, does the initial finishing on any slab too large to float otherwise. (Roth/Woods project photo)

HOME-BUILT BULLFLOAT

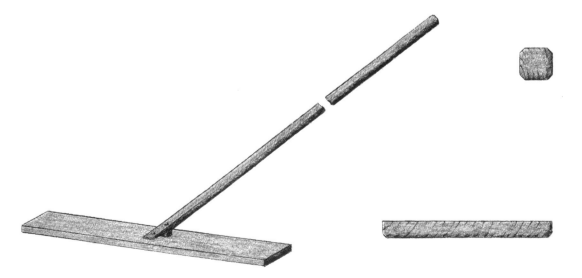

You can make, buy, or rent a bullfloat. Make one with ¾-inch lumber or plywood and a long 4- to 16-foot 2 × 2-inch handle. The blade should be 8 inches across and 36 to 48 inches long—or longer. Wood makes a better bullfloat than metal, even for finishing air-entrained concrete. If the wood doesn't warp and you take proper care of it, your bullfloat should last for years.

Darbies

The darby is best for small projects in which a larger tool would be a bullfloat in a china shop. While you can make your own darby from wood—mahogany is best—a darby costs very little to purchase ready-made. Blade lengths range from 30 inches to 48 inches and more. Larger sizes are harder to work but do a better leveling job. Blade widths taper, head to toe, from 3⅝ inches to about 2¾ inches. The darby's handle provides one or more handholds for controlling it. While metal darbies are available, wooden darbies cost less and do a better job. A metal darby can cause undesirable surface glazing of the concrete.

Small Trowels

To cut concrete away from its forms, you will need either a margin trowel or a pointing trowel. Both do a fine job. The margin trowel should have a 1½-inch-wide blade ground to a rounded end. You'll probably have to do the grinding yourself, since margin trowels don't come that way. The pointing trowel is a small, 4-inch-long version of the larger bricklayer's or mason's trowel. Both of these small trowels have lots of uses in masonry and concrete work.

Edgers

All concrete slabs should be edged. The only proper way to do this is with an edging tool. Made of bronze, stainless steel, or steel, edgers are about 6 inches in length. Their widths vary from 1½ to 4 inches. Two types, both inexpensive, are available, in a variety of edge curvatures. Choose the ½-inch-radius curvature.

One style of edger has up-curved, ski-like front and rear surfaces that allow it to be worked without lifting the leading edge. Another style has a completely flat blade; its leading edge must be raised as it is stroked

Left photo: On smaller slabs, on which a darby will reach all parts for initial finishing, you can get along without a bullfloat. With a blade length of 3 to 4 feet, the darby fills in depressions and cuts off ridges left by strikeoff. Right photo: The ideal edge radius for patios and other outdoor slabs is ½ inch. The leading edge of a flat-bladed edger is raised to keep it from gouging the work surface. (Sakrete photo)

EDGERS

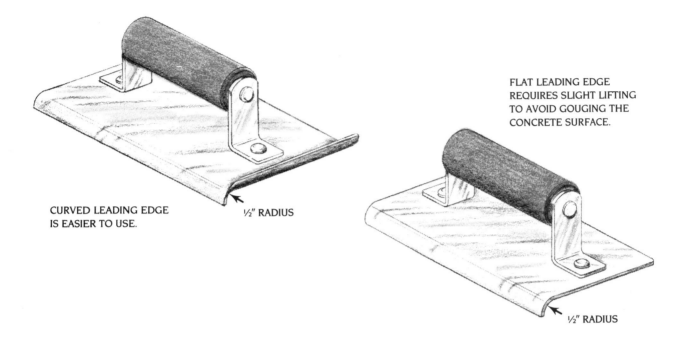

CURVED LEADING EDGE
IS EASIER TO USE.

½" RADIUS

FLAT LEADING EDGE
REQUIRES SLIGHT LIFTING
TO AVOID GOUGING THE
CONCRETE SURFACE.

½" RADIUS

over the concrete surface. Which kind to get? The curved-end edger is easier to work.

Grooving Tools

Groovers are about 6 inches long with 2- to 4½-inch-wide blades. I recommend a groover that makes a ½-inch radius joint (to match the edger's curvature). The edger's bit depth must reach at least one fourth the slab's thickness. Thus, if the slab is 4 inches thick, the groover should have a 1-inch-deep bit (the most popular size). Groovers, like edgers, are available with up-curved or flat ends. Like edging, grooving goes easier with a curved-ended tool.

Avoid grooving tools that make only a shallow groove in concrete rather than a sufficiently deep control joint. If your local building supply outlets don't have a proper deep-bit groover, try a concrete products supplier.

Hand-floats

You need not choose between a wooden and a magnesium hand-float because you will need one of each. Having two hand-floats gives you one to use for hand

Here are the business ends of groovers, good and bad. The good guy on the left is a jointer with 1-inch bit that cuts control joints of adequate depth for a 4-inch-thick slab. The shallow-bit groover on the right can make decorative lines but is not deep enough for control joints. (Roth/Woods project photo)

GROOVER AND JOINTER

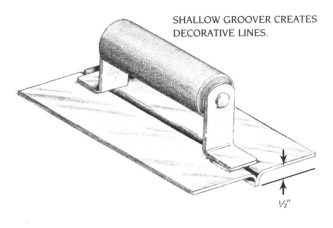

SHALLOW GROOVER CREATES
DECORATIVE LINES.

½"

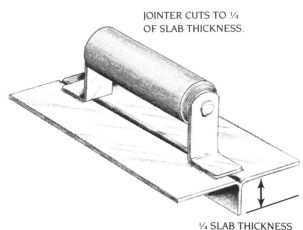

JOINTER CUTS TO ¼
OF SLAB THICKNESS.

¼ SLAB THICKNESS

support when leaning way out over the slab from the edges or working from kneeboards. On air-entrained concrete, always hand-float with a magnesium tool, not a wooden one. On plain concrete, you may use either kind, but the magnesium hand-float is easier to work with. The 16 × 3½-inch magnesium hand-float is a handy size, although other sizes are available.

A new wooden hand-float needs to be used a while before it becomes worn properly, or "broken-in" as the pros say. Whereas a metal float is made with smoothened, curved surfaces.

Steel Trowels

You may decide to steel-trowel and then broom an outdoor slab. Otherwise, you won't need a steel trowel for outdoor concrete finishing. Steel trowels are made

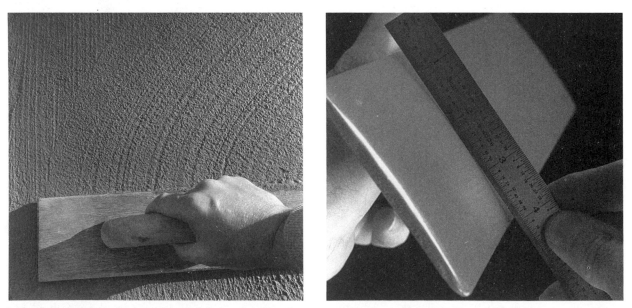

Left photo: The surface texture left by a wooden float provides slip resistance but is difficult to sweep clean. Right photo: A metal hand-float has a slightly convex face with rounded edges and corners to compact the surface yet keep from digging out surface aggregates. It's a must-have tool for outdoor concrete work.

HOME-BUILT FLOAT

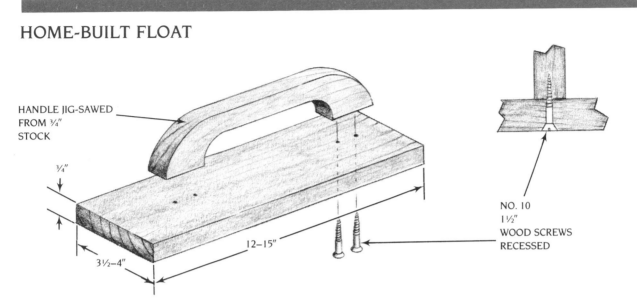

HANDLE JIG-SAWED FROM ¾" STOCK

¾"

12–15"

3½–4"

NO. 10
1½"
WOOD SCREWS
RECESSED

of hard-tempered steel or hardened stainless steel. The best size is 18 × 4¾ inches. A compromise size for both outdoor and indoor work is 14 × 4 inches. You do not need a smaller steel trowel for work on an outdoor slab. Get a high-quality steel trowel with a thick handle attachment that will take your weight as you rest on it while you perform your hand-floating and prior to your troweling.

Kneeboards

You can easily make a pair of kneeboards for getting out onto the slab to hand-float and groove areas you cannot reach from the slab edges. Kneeboards may be as simple as 2-foot-square pieces of ½-inch plywood. Better, they can be made from two pieces of ½-inch plywood measuring 1 × 2 feet by nailing 2 × 2s across the ends. The 2 × 2s serve as handles.

Left photo: Steel trowels are available in an assortment of sizes, but only two sizes should be considered for finishing outdoor slabs: 18 × 4¾-inch (*left*) and 14 × 4-inch. Right photo: A steel-troweled outdoor slab is later given a broomed texture, since troweling leaves it too smooth for a good footing. (Sakrete photo)

If you are alternating floating and troweling while finishing a slab and using the trowel for support, be sure to use a strongly built trowel. Otherwise, its cantilevered handle could snap off. (Roth/Woods photo)

Kneepads

At the same time, you'll want a pair of rubber kneepads. They should be waterproof—that is, made of rubber and not fabric, since fabric might wick water up from the concrete. Strap-on rubber kneepads are readily available at building supply stores.

Texturing Brushes

Almost any broom or brush will work for texturing concrete, but a soft-bristled texturing brush made specifically for concrete-finishing is best. You'll find both slim and fat models. The slim models are less costly and will do fine for texturing.

Texturing Floats

Texturing floats look much like wooden hand-floats. But their soft surface puts a pleasing outdoor texture on concrete as the final step in finishing. Sponge rubber, cork, and canvas- and carpet-faced floats each transmit a unique texture.

Garden Sprayers

The compression-type garden sprayer is used to apply spray-on membrane curing compounds. Plastic and metal models are available.

HOME-BUILT KNEEBOARD

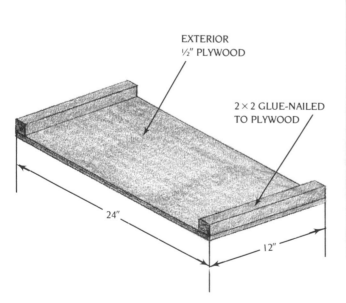

EXTERIOR ½" PLYWOOD

2 × 2 GLUE-NAILED TO PLYWOOD

24"

12"

A garden sprayer makes a superb applicator of curing compound. Spray portions of the slab you cannot reach from the edges by walking out on the concrete after it hardens enough not to show marks.

CHECKLIST OF TOOLS FOR CONCRETE WORK

- Safety goggles
- Safety hat
- Rubber or vinyl work gloves
- Rubber boots
- Hand-tamper
- Garden hose with trigger nozzle
- Fog nozzle for hose
- Short flat-ended shovel
- Small sledgehammer
- Claw hammer
- Measuring tape
- Framing square
- Crosscut saw or
- Circular saw
- Mason's stringline
- Bubble level
- Tube level
- Pail and batch-cans
- Bathroom scale
- Utility knife
- Concrete mixer
- Pneumatic-tired wheelbarrow
- Strikeboard
- Bullfloat or
- Darby
- Margin trowel or
- Pointing trowel
- Edger
- Grooving tool
- Hand-float, wooden
- Hand-float, magnesium
- Steel trowel
- Kneeboards
- Waterproof kneepads
- Texturing broom
- Texturing float
- Garden compression sprayer
- Wire brush

All tools, including a texturing broom, should be washed thoroughly of cement paste. If you start soon enough after work, the spray from a garden hose will do the job. (Roth/Woods project photo)

CARE OF CONCRETE TOOLS

Whether made of wood, metal, or plastic, concrete construction tools should be cleaned immediately after use. If cement paste is allowed to build up and harden, the tools may soon be useless. Put your carpentry tools away before you start concrete work so that they stay dry.

If you keep a pail of water handy, you can rinse off hand-floats, edgers, groovers, and trowels between uses. If you postpone cleaning, you may need the help of a wire brush. Have a wire brush handy anyway to scour off encrusted cement-paste deposits around the tool handles. The faces of hand-finishing tools tend to get scoured during use. A quick rinse is usually all they need.

At the end of a project, you can run water into the wheelbarrow to clean it and other tools together.

Cleaning the Mixer

Of course, a concrete mixer should be thoroughly cleaned after the last batch of concrete has been placed, or whenever you stop work for more than 15 minutes. To clean it, shovel in half a batch of coarse aggregate, add lots of water, and let the drum rotate for several minutes. Spray the inside and outside of the turning drum to remove mortar deposits not reached by the churning ags, spraying each of the mixer blades (backs, too) as they turn. Then dump the drum and give the inside a final hose rinsing. Leave the drum tilted to drain. The dumped aggregate may be used in a subsequent mix.

Keep your mixer clean between batches by placing half the water and half the coarse aggregate for the next batch into the drum immediately after dumping

Left photo: A concrete mixer is cleaned by shoveling a little coarse aggregate into the rotating mixer drum and adding water. The water and aggregate will scour the drum so well that a good rinsing should leave it clean. Right photo: Do the drum-rinse with a garden hose's blast spray, paying close attention to the places where cement paste collects and hardens, such as at bases of blades. While you're at it, spray-clean your other concreting tools, scrape-cleaning them if necessary.

the previous batch. This can mix until you are ready to proportion the balance of the batch.

Preventing Corrosion

Rust on the blades of finishing tools will impair their action. Steel tools, such as edgers and groovers (some are brass), steel trowels, and margin and pointing trowels (unless made of stainless steel), need to be dried rapidly to prevent corrosion of their surfaces. Lay them in the sun or take them inside and dry them. Once dry, spray them with a thin coating of multipurpose aerosol lubricant. Your shovels and wheelbarrow sing out for the same treatment.

Rubber items, including boots and gloves, need a good rinsing.

With the exception of some wooden tools, if you take proper care of your concrete construction tools, they should last a lifetime.

CHAPTER **6**

DOING CONCRETE WORK

Concrete may be the most "user-friendly" patio building material there is. It is a mixture of portland cement, water, and *aggregates* (usually sand and gravel). The portland cement and the water together form a paste that binds or glues the aggregates into a stone-like mass.

In building a concrete slab, many homeowners use one weekend to prepare the ground and get ready. The following weekend, with a little help from friends, they place the concrete. The rest is enjoyment.

Most concrete projects require the building of wooden forms. Forming your patio in small sections, you can break the job down into easy, one-evening steps. You can remove and reuse the wood you use to form the smaller sections. Or, if you use rot-resistant wood, you can leave the forms in place as design elements in the slab. Thus, one of your early decisions is whether to cast the concrete slab all at once or to tackle it in two or more easier-to-handle sections.

Concrete has two states. Freshly mixed, it is said to be in its *plastic* state. Concrete in its *hardened* state is like rock—harder than some rocks. Think of concrete as moldable rock. Wherever you'd like to have rock, place concrete. Concrete paves over mud—gets you out of it. It elevates, steps down, separates, bridges across. Concrete smooths. Concrete creates a patio.

Once a concrete project is formed and readied for placement, it can be completed in about a day. Family and friends supplied with tools often make up such crews. (Roth/Woods project photo)

THE BASICS OF GOOD CONCRETE

The Portland Cement Association (PCA) refers to properly made and used concrete as *quality concrete*. To withstand severe weather and the use of deicers, qual-

A small wooden form with plastic sheet beneath to keep the patio clean makes a great mold for casting concrete stepping stones. Use the form as a guide in striking the surface off flush. (Sakrete photo)

ity concrete should attain 28-day compressive strengths of 4,000 psi (pounds per square inch) and more. (Compressive strength taken at 28 days of age is the accepted measure of the strength of concrete. An age is specified because concrete gains in strength with time.) Creation of quality concrete requires attention to detail. A whole series of steps is involved, from selecting the ingredients to final curing.

The PCA steers concrete users away from the term *pour* when building with concrete. They say that you *place* concrete, you do not pour it. Good concrete cannot be poured into the forms.

If you want your first concrete project to be successful, decide on a quality approach. Quality concrete costs no more than ordinary concrete. In fact, quality concrete is more economical in the long run because of its greater durability.

Follow these rules for quality concrete:

1. Use proper ingredients—portland cement, clean water, plus well-graded, clean aggregates.
2. Proportion the ingredients correctly and mix them thoroughly.
3. Place the mixture into well-made and braced forms.
4. Finish the concrete properly.
5. Moist-cure the concrete for the correct amount of time.

You can choose any of four ways to obtain concrete: (1) order ready mix; (2) proportion and mix the concrete yourself; (3) add water to ready-packaged dry concrete and mix it yourself; or (4) undertake the challenges of haul-it-yourself concrete. If your project is large enough, ready-mixed concrete (fresh concrete from a truck-mixer) may be the right choice. In most cases, it is. But especially if your project is smaller, consider one of the other methods.

MIX-IT-YOURSELF QUALITY CONCRETE

Here's a quick look at the mix-your-own-concrete process. You buy, store, and later proportion and mix the ingredients for concrete. These are: portland cement, concrete sand, and either gravel or crushed stone. Sand is the fine aggregate, and stone is the coarse aggregate.

How much concrete you can make yourself in a workday depends on the size of concrete mixer and the amount of help you have. As a rule, two strong workers using an average-size 3-cubic-foot concrete mixer can proportion, mix, wheel, place, and finish about 2 cubic yards—56 cubic feet—of concrete in a day. The ideal is to have three workers: one feeding the mixer, the second transporting batches to the site, and the third placing and finishing. If the second worker has any spare time, the second can help with placing and finishing.

Dumping a ready-packaged concrete mix into a powered concrete mixer sure beats hand-mixing, especially if you have much to make.

Getting Strength and Durability

For quality concrete, ingredients must have good qualities of their own. And they must be proportioned, mixed, placed, finished, and then cured with quality in mind.

Water is an important ingredient. Water sets off a chemical hardening reaction in portland cement called *hydration*. The water you use should be so clean that it is fit to drink. Around home, no problem. A trigger nozzle attached to the end of a garden hose will provide water control, making it unnecessary to run to the hose bibb every time you need to turn the water on or off—or, worse, to leave the water running. (Later, the trigger nozzle also lets you direct a strong spray into the mixer drum to clean it.)

Cement comes in 94-pound (40 kg in Canada), 1-cubic-foot sacks. The exact-size sacks make for easy proportioning. Though they are plastic-lined, the sacks should be kept dry until used. Buy either Type 1 or Type 2 portland cement. This designation appears on the cement sacks. These two types are sold just about everywhere. You can purchase portland cement at almost any home center, hardware store, or lumber yard. Concrete products suppliers also have it.

Cement Paste. Portland cement combines with water to form what's called *cement paste*. Cement paste is the binder in the concrete mix and imparts strength, durability, and watertightness. There must be enough cement in the mix to make a paste that will surround every particle of coarse and fine aggregate. The cement paste's quality largely determines the quality of the concrete.

Correct proportioning of cement and water in the mix is essential. The amount of water used with cement is called the *water-cement ratio*. The normal water-cement ratio in good concrete is 6 gallons of water per sack of cement. (This widely accepted figure is reflected in the proportioning tables in this chapter.)

Enough water is needed to hydrate (harden) all the cement fully. Only about 3 gallons of water are needed to hydrate an entire sack of cement. But if you used so little water, the mix would be dry and impractical to place and finish. To obtain a plastic cement paste that will surround the aggregates requires twice

CEMENT AND WATER

GALLON JUGS

Photo: Portland cement is marketed in 1-cubic-foot bags that weigh 94 pounds. For home projects, you want either Type 1 or Type 2 cement. Drawing: This 6-gallon per sack ratio provides enough water to hydrate the cement, plus enough additional water to make a workable mix. A ratio with less water wouldn't lubricate the mix sufficiently. A ratio with more water would dilute the cement paste, badly weakening it.

as much water as needed for full hydration, that is, 6 gallons per sack. Adding more water than needed to surround the aggregates weakens the cement paste, making weak concrete. Therefore, the use of water in concrete strikes a compromise between strength and durability on the one hand and workability on the other. (*Workability* is the ease with which concrete can be placed and finished). It's like brewing good coffee —too little water makes it undrinkable; the right amount of water makes it tasty; too much water makes it watery and weak.

Using a home concrete mixer, you will not be mixing a whole sack of cement at once: the mixer drum is not large enough. A one half- or one third-sack capacity is more typical.

Aggregates

The aggregates make up 66 percent to 78 percent of the volume of the finished concrete. The cement paste merely glues the aggregates (ags) together: the ags themselves need to be sound. What you want are concrete aggregates of known performance that are clean, free of earth or organic matter, and well-graded. They should be hard, not flaky. And if the sand or stone cannot stand up to freezing and thawing, concrete made from it cannot do much better.

Sand often contains some silt. Coarse aggregates do, too. While a little silt is okay, too much silt affects the strength of concrete.

Well-graded Aggregate. Well-graded aggregate contains a wide variety of particle sizes. Good concrete sand contains particles ranging from about ¼ inch on down to dust-size. For this reason, fine sand, masonry sand, or sandbox sand should not be used to make concrete. A good coarse aggregate contains particle sizes small enough to overlap the largest ones in the sand up to the largest size ag you want in the mix.

Maximum-Size Coarse Aggregate. The largest-size coarse aggregate you can use in a concrete mix— called *maximum-size coarse aggregate*—is limited by a patio slab's thickness. Too large a maximum size aggregate makes unworkable concrete. By putting a top limit on the size of aggregate of one third the slab's thickness, you'll ensure that the largest stones you use can be worked into place readily. For most patio concrete, the most practical maximum-size coarse aggregate is ¾ inch or 1 inch.

Choose a reputable supplier and order your sand and gravel or crushed stone "for making good concrete." Specify that you want the ¾- or 1-inch maximum-size coarse aggregate.

Too much silt in sand or gravel can weaken your concrete. To test your sand, put a 2-inch sample into a glass jar, add water until the jar is almost full, and shake vigorously. Let the materials settle until the water is clear and measure the thickness of the silt layer covering the sample. If it is less than ³⁄₁₆-inch, the aggregate is clean enough to make good concrete. If the silt layer is thicker, you should wash the ag clean or find another source.

Although sand or gravel in a pickup truck's bed may look like only a partial load, don't be fooled. This quarter-yard loader bucket is all a ½-ton pickup can safely handle.

Below, the table "How Much Typical Building Materials Weigh" will help you estimate how much material you can haul safely. (The table "Handy Metric Equivalents" will help you convert between U.S. Standard and metric units.)

HOW MUCH TYPICAL BUILDING MATERIALS WEIGH

Material	Weight
Water	8.33 lb./gal., 62.4 lb./cu. ft.
Portland cement	94 lb./cu. ft. (bag)
Dry sand	98–115 lb./cu. ft.; 2,650–3,100 lb./cu. yd.
Gravel	95 lb./cu. ft.; 2,560 lb./cu. yd.
Crushed stone	100 lb./cu. ft.; 2,700 lb./cu. yd.
Normal concrete	130–155 lb./cu. ft.; 3,500–4,200 lb./cu. yd.

HANDY METRIC EQUIVALENTS

U.S. Standard Unit	Metric Equivalent
1 inch	25 mm
1 foot	0.3 m
1 pound	0.5 kg
1 cubic foot	0.03 m³
1 gallon	3.8 l
1 cubic yard	0.8 m³
1 square foot	0.09 m²

Proportioning

When you mix your own concrete, you must correctly measure cement, water, sand, and stones into the mixer drum. This is called *proportioning*. Proportioning correctly isn't difficult if you prepare ahead of time.

Handling Cement on the Job

Portland cement is one of the safest materials you can work with. Nevertheless, work sensibly. When you lift sacks of cement, do it properly, using your leg muscles instead of your back. While lifting, your back should be relatively vertical, not bent over.

Cement should be free-flowing. To make the cement usable, any lumps in it should be easily breakable—*friable*—when you squeeze them between a thumb and forefinger.

Handling Ags on the Job

Once on the site, aggregates can be stored as long as necessary, provided they are covered with a tarpaulin or plastic sheet and kept clean. Ideally, piles of fine and coarse aggregate should be positioned so they can be shoveled directly into the concrete mixer. If they are placed on a hard surface, or at least on plastic sheeting, they will be easier to shovel up. A sheet of plywood under them will help.

Most mixer drums swing both ways to allow shoveling into the concrete mixer (called *charging*) from one side and dumping out (called *discharging*) from the opposite side. To minimize the moving of materials, the cement and aggregates are positioned close on one side of the mixer, and the construction site is close on the other side.

Batching

Concrete is mixed a batch at a time. Remember that the size of a batch is limited by the working capacity of the mixing drum.

In batching, special attention must be given to proportioning the cement and water, since the correct water–cement ratio is vital to concrete quality. The tables "Proportioning Concrete by Weight" and "Proportioning Concrete by Volume" show the proportions of ingredients for making quality concrete. These pro-

PROPORTIONING CONCRETE BY WEIGHT
(Air-entrained Concrete)

Maximum-size Coarse Aggregate	Cement (lb.)	Sand (wet, lb.)	Coarse Aggregate* (lb.)	Water (lb.)
⅜ inch	29	53	46	10
½ inch	27	46	55	10
¾ inch	25	42	65	10
1 inch	24	39	70	9

* If crushed stone is used, decrease coarse aggregate by 3 lb. and increase sand by 3 lb.

PROPORTIONING CONCRETE BY VOLUME
(Air-entrained Concrete)

Maximum-size Coarse Aggregate	Cement	Sand (wet)	Coarse Aggregate	Water
⅜ inch	1	2¼	1½	½
½ inch	1	2¼	2	½
¾ inch	1	2¼	2½	½
1 inch	1	2¼	2¾	½

portions produce the ideal water–cement ratio of 6 gallons of water per sack of cement.

The most accurate proportioning is done by weight. In weight-batching, the sum of the separate weights is the total weight of the concrete. Sometimes, though, it's more convenient to proportion by volume. (Shovel-batching is batching by volume.) When you batch by volume, the volume of any batch will be somewhat less than the sum of the separate volumes of ingredients. This is because the smaller particles fit in among the larger particles.

How Much Material?

Before you can order cement, sand, and coarse aggregate, you need to know the size of your patio—its volume. The accompanying chart "How Much Material To Order" is handy for figuring how much concrete smaller projects of four different thicknesses require, based on their area in square feet. To use it, first multiply the patio's length by its width to arrive at its area in square feet. Then find that amount on the left-hand side of the graph. Draw a horizontal line or lay a ruler to the right until it intersects with the slanted

HOW MUCH MATERIAL TO ORDER

Use of this chart is explained in accompanying text.

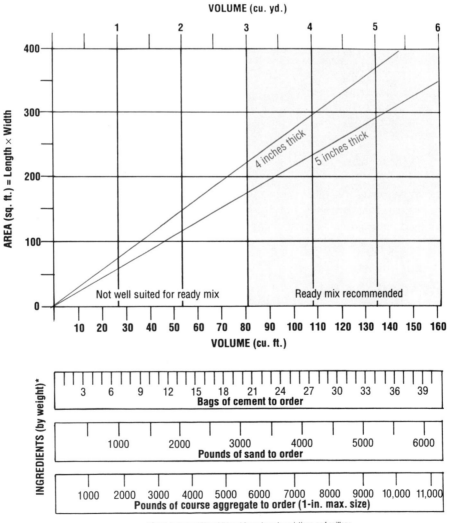

*Graph includes 10% additional for subgrade variations and spillage.

line for your patio slab's thickness, 4 or 5 inches. From that point, go straight up to find the volume of your slab in cubic yards. This is the amount of ready-mixed concrete to order. Go straight down to find the slab's volume in cubic feet. This is the amount of concrete you need to make if you mix your own. (Both figures include 10 percent additional for subgrade variations and spillage.)

For example, suppose a 10 × 35-foot patio slab is being built 4 inches thick. That's an area of 350 square feet. Start on the left of the graph at 350 square feet and then move right (following the dash line) until you meet the 4-inch thickness line. Then go vertically to the cubic-yard scale. You'll hit it at 4.75 cubic yards, 4¾. That's your ready-mix order. If you are mixing your own, move straight down to the cubic-foot scale, which you'll hit at 128.3. That's how many cubic feet of concrete to make.

The tables "Cubic Feet in a Concrete Slab" and "Cubic Meters in a Concrete Slab" do the figuring.

CUBIC FEET IN A CONCRETE SLAB

Area (sq. ft.)	THICKNESS (IN.)	
	4	5
50	17	21
100	33	42
200	67	83
300	100	125
400	133	167
500	167	208

CUBIC METERS IN A CONCRETE SLAB

Area (m²)	THICKNESS (MM)	
	100	130
5	0.50	0.65
10	1.00	1.30
20	2.00	2.60
30	3.00	3.90
40	4.00	5.20
50	5.00	6.50

Continuing down across the ingredients bars below the chart, you can see how much cement, sand, and coarse aggregate to order. For our example, you'd need 33 sacks of cement, 5,000 pounds of sand, and about 9,000 pounds of coarse ag. (If mixing these

quantities concerns you, it should. The size of this project points toward the use of ready mix, not mix-it-yourself. That's why it is well into the "ready-mix recommended" portion of the chart.)

If you use other than 1-inch maximum-size coarse aggregate, the quantities of materials will vary slightly from those shown in the ingredients bars at the bottom of the chart. With smaller maximum-ag sizes, weights of cement and sand will increase a little, while coarse aggregate weights will decrease a little.

To calculate the exact amounts of ingredients to order in the lesser maximum-size coarse ags, find the cubic-foot volume of your project from the foot of the chart. Then multiply the by-weight ingredients figures in the table "Proportioning Concrete by Weight" times the number of cubic feet you need. For example, if you need 30 cubic feet, multiply each by-weight ingredient figure times 30. Using a ½-inch maximum-size coarse aggregate, for example, you'd need 810 pounds of cement (9 sacks), 1,380 pounds of sand, and 1,650 pounds of coarse aggregate. Those are the amounts to order.

If you are working in metric units, figure the slab's volume in cubic meters. Then, in using the table "Proportioning Concrete by Weight," remember that one cubic foot is equal to 0.03 cubic meters. Divide all your cubic-foot weights by 0.03.

If you are proportioning by volume, use the table "Proportioning Concrete by Volume," remembering that the concrete in a batch will end up having less volume than the sum of the volumes of its separate ingredients. So order materials for more volume than is needed.

Follow these rules of thumb for ag ordering:

1. Find how many cubic yards of concrete are needed for the job. Increase it by about 10 percent for waste (the chart does it for you).
2. Order ½ cubic yard of sand for each cubic yard of concrete.
3. Order ¾ cubic yard of coarse aggregate for every cubic yard of concrete.

Figuring Odd-shaped Areas

The areas of slab shapes other than squares or rectangles can be figured by dividing them into regular geometric figures, such as triangles and parts of circles, calculating the areas of the sections, and adding them to get a total.

For example, the slab shown in the drawing "How To Figure the Size of Odd-shaped Projects" is sectioned into three parts: a rectangle, a quarter-circle,

HOW TO ESTIMATE ODD-SHAPED PROJECTS

For an explanation of this diagram, see text beginning on page 153.

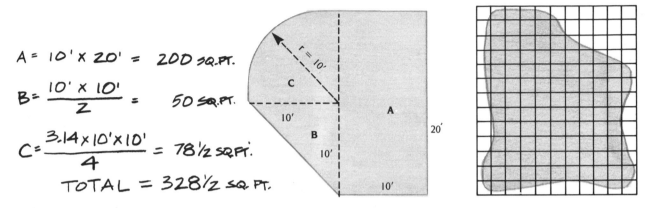

A = 10' × 20' = 200 SQ.FT.

B = $\frac{10' \times 10'}{2}$ = 50 SQ.FT.

C = $\frac{3.14 \times 10' \times 10'}{4}$ = 78½ SQ.FT.

TOTAL = 328½ SQ. FT.

and a triangle. (The triangle is actually half of a 10-foot square.) Rectangle A's area is calculated by multiplying length times width, giving 200 square feet. The formula for figuring the area of a circle is πr^2, and π (pi) equals about 3.14. If C were a full circle, its area would be 3.14 times the radius squared, or 3.14 × 10 × 10. Since C is not a whole circle but one fourth of a circle, you can determine its area by dividing the answer, 314, by 4. This gives 78½ square feet (which you can round down to 78). And triangle B is a right triangle with a 10-foot base and a 10-foot height. The formula for the area of a right triangle is ½ its base times its height, or 10 × ¹⁰½ in the example, which gives 50 square feet. The separate areas add up to 328 square feet.

Truly odd-shaped areas can be estimated by drawing them to scale on graph paper or laying graph paper over a scaled plan and then counting the number of squares and partial squares within the shape. If the squares represent square feet, the simple count of squares will be the answer. If they represent a larger measure, for example, square yards, multiply to arrive at square feet.

START MAKING CONCRETE

Now that you know how much concrete is needed, you can begin making it. Proportion your mix by weight or volume according to one of the tables on proportioning. The tables are based on average materials. If sand

and coarse aggregates did not vary, you could take the figures right from the table and batch your mixer accurately. Trouble is, ags are like people; few of them are average. The sand and stones you are able to buy will likely vary from average in both size and gradation. Thus, your proportions may have to vary, too. To know for sure, you must make what's called a trial mix. It will help determine whether any adjustments in the table quantities are needed for your ags. Nothing need be wasted. A faulty trial mix can be adjusted, remixed, and used in your project. How to make a trial mix is described on page 157.

Here's an efficient and accurate way to batch a half-bag power mixer: Center each cement sack on a 2-foot length of reinforcing bar and then use a utility knife to slice through the bag across its middle and edges. Lifting the rebar, as shown, brings both halves of the sack upright so you can cut apart the paper hinge.

Left photo: While you can get by with only two, it's better to have three batch cans, one (*center*) just for cement, one for coarse ag, and a third for sand and water. Here a margin trowel is being used to add a little cement to achieve a precise weight on the scale under the can. Right photo: Once you've established marks on the batch cans, you no longer need to weigh ingredients. Here cement gets one almost-full pail to the mark; coarse ag will be two full 5-gallon buckets, plus a third to the mark; and sand will be two full pails, plus another to the mark. All marks were established by weighing.

Whether or not you make a trial mix, your first few batches are best proportioned using the by-weight method. The ingredients are weighed out and placed in the mixer drum. This gets concrete-making started on the right foot. Later you can switch to the by-volume method if you wish, counting the number of shovels it takes to achieve the weights already worked out. Don't get careless when shovel-batching—each shovel should contain the same amount.

For by-weight batching, you need a bathroom scale and three pails we'll call *batch-cans*. If you place the scale in a clear plastic sack for protection, it can be sneaked back into the bathroom unscathed. Adjust the scale to read zero with an empty batch-can on it. Then, when you shovel ingredients into the batch-can, you'll be weighing them and not the batch-can. You need at least two batch-cans, one kept dry for batching cement and another for water and aggregates.

Once all weighed-out quantities are settled by the trial mix, you can mark the batch-cans at the proper heights for each ingredient. For example, gravel might be two full batch-cans plus one more filled to the "stone + 2″" mark. Sand might be the same, but using a different "sand + 2″" mark placed at the proper height. Then you no longer need to weigh out subsequent batches. It's a good idea to use separate cans to help avoid mistakes.

Adjusting for Sand's Wetness

Dry sand is rarely available for making concrete. Sand nearly always contains some water, and since the water affects the all-important water–cement ratio, it must be allowed for. (This need only be done for the sand—the coarse aggregate holds too little water to have an effect.)

The table "Proportioning Concrete by Weight" is based on sand of average wetness. To make adjustments, first make the "hand-squeeze" test shown in the photos. Change the amounts in the table as follows.

For very wet sand, which is what you'll find in your sandpile right after a rain, increase the sand requirement shown by the table by 1 pound and decrease the water requirement by 1 pound (a pint is a pound the world around).

For average wet sand, which is what your sandpile will usually have, make no adjustments in the table quantities.

For damp sand, which is what you'll find after lots of sun and little rain, decrease the sand by 1 pound and increase the water by 1 pound.

For dry sand, seldom found except at the surface of a sandpile after lots of drying and no rain, decrease sand by 2 pounds and increase water by 2 pounds. Accurate measuring pays off.

TESTING SAND FOR WATER CONTENT

Before making concrete, test your sand for water content. Pick up a handful and squeeze it; then release. Very wet sand (**1**) forms a cast in your hand and leaves its excess water on your palm. Average wet sand (**2**) forms a cast but leaves no excess water. Neither damp sand (**3**) nor dry sand (**4**) will form a cast; both fall apart when released. Adjust the water requirements of the table "Proportioning Concrete by Weight" (page 151) according to the sand wetness.

If you are volume-batching, there is no need to adjust the proportions shown in the table "Proportioning Concrete by Volume." They are based on average wet sand, but measurement by volume isn't accurate enough to justify correcting for water in sand. Moreover, water in the sand causes an increase in the sand's volume, called *bulking*. The extent of bulking depends on the amount of moisture and the sand's fineness. Dry sand, for example, may bulk as much as 25 percent when wetted. This is another reason why batching by weight is preferable, at least at the start. To get around this if you batch by volume, try to work with average wet sand. If your sand is too dry, you can spray the pile with water and let it stand overnight.

Batching a Mixer

With everything ready, batch your first trial mix, working from the table and making any adjustments necessary for water in the sand. How to batch a concrete mixer properly is demonstrated in the accompanying photos.

Dump mixes into a wheelbarrow with pneumatic tires and haul them to the project site. If you don't have a rubber-tired wheelbarrow, get one, because handling concrete in a hard-wheeled appliance will make the coarse aggregate settle out, rendering the mix unusable. Most do-it-yourself, rubber-tired contractor-type wheelbarrows hold a little more than 1 cubic foot of mix, about the amount you can easily handle. If you will be using just a small amount of concrete—certainly not the output of a concrete mixer—you can carry it to the project in buckets.

Making a Trial Mix. If you want quality concrete, make a trial mix. A trial mix makes it possible to adjust the proportioning tables to your particular aggregates, both fine and coarse. First, batch the trial mix, using the figures in the table for the size batch your mixer will handle. Then dump a little of it into a wheelbarrow. Examine the mix for stiffness—workability—and to see whether it is too wet or too stiff; too gravelly or too sandy; or just right.

It's easy to judge the consistency of your trial mix by comparing it with the three photos showing trial mixes that are, respectively, too sandy, just right, and too gravelly.

Once you've judged the workability of your trial mix by comparing it with the photos, proceed as follows:

If your trial mix is just right, as shown: Write down your figures and proceed with the project. The trial mix indicates that your aggregates are very close to average.

If your trial mix is too wet: To salvage the trial mix, add 3 pounds of dry sand at a time for every cubic foot of concrete you put into the mixer. For example, if you are mixing 3 cubic feet per batch, you'd first add 9 pounds of dry sand. Remix the batch for a minute and retest the trial mix. When you get the trial mix that looks right, record the total weight of sand you had to add. Go ahead and use the corrected trial mix in your project.

In proportioning future batches, reduce the water 1 quart (2 pounds) for each 10 pounds of dry sand you had to add. Maintain the original quantities of cement, sand, and coarse aggregate from the table "Proportioning Concrete by Weight." Suppose, for example, that you had to add 15 pounds of dry sand to get the trial mix right. That's 1½ times 10 pounds, so you'd reduce the water in subsequent batches by 1½ quarts.

If your trial mix is too stiff, as shown: Despite what seems logical, no water should be added. This would only change the water–cement ratio. Instead, to salvage the trial mix, add both cement and water in the proportion 1 quart of water for each 4 pounds of cement. Doing this maintains the water–cement ratio yet makes the trial mix workable by increasing the amount of cement paste.

To adjust the table amounts for your aggregates, cut back on the amount of coarse aggregate in subsequent batches and adjust the figures for your new coarse-ag weight.

Judge the consistency of your trial mix by comparing it to the accompanying three consistency photos.

If your trial mix is too sandy, add coarse aggregate in increments of 3 pounds per cubic foot based on trial-

Use these slump comparisons to make adjustments to your trial mix. When a trowel or shovel back is drawn over the top of the concrete pile, it should produce a closed texture as in the just-right pile (*center*) without much runny cement paste. The too-wet pile (*left*) would let the coarse aggregate settle out during transportation and finishing. The other pile (*right*) is too stiff to be workable.

JUDGING AGGREGATE CONTENT

Also judge the aggregate content of your trial mix. Too-sandy mix (**1**) at right works easily and reproduces fine detail in precast projects but is uneconomical for larger projects. It also shrinks excessively. The gravelly mix (**2**) would prove to be harsh and hard to work. It contains too much coarse aggregate. The just-right mix (**3**) smoothens nicely without an excess of either sand or gravel.

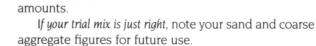

batch size. In the 3 cubic-foot example, 9 pounds of coarse ag would be put in, mixed, then examined. If this doesn't do the trick, add another 3 pounds per cubic foot (another 9 pounds in the example) and try again. Keep at it, if necessary. When the trial mix looks right, use it. Record your new coarse aggregate figure for use in making subsequent batches.

If your trial mix is too gravelly, add some sand to the batch and remix. In subsequent batches cut back on coarse aggregate and increase the sand in equal amounts.

If your trial mix is just right, note your sand and coarse aggregate figures for future use.

Once you have recorded the correct proportions, your concrete mix should not need changing, except, perhaps, to adjust for water variations in the sand.

When you have enough experience at proportioning and mixing concrete, you will be able to judge a

With experience, you can develop an eye for judging concrete in the mixer drum, as Jack Cofran has. The mixing concrete should be uniform in color and drop cleanly from the mixer blades.

mix by watching its behavior in the mixer drum. The proper mix will have a uniform color. It will be neither soupy nor crumbly, but will drop cleanly from the mixer blades. Dump some out and trowel-test the top of the pile to check whether it is correct for use.

Trial-batching a Mixer by Volume. If you do not care to trial-batch using the more accurate by-weight method, you can batch a concrete mixer by volume and get fairly decent results. The following table is based on typical aggregates and 1-inch maximum-size coarse aggregate, making trial batches suitable for most general purposes.

Ingredient	2¼ Cu. ft. Mixer	1⅓ Cu. ft. Mixer
Cement	½ sack	⅓ sack
Water	2½ gal.	1⅔ gal.
Sand	8½ gal.	5½ gal.
Gravel	11 gal.	7½ gal.

Count the shovels of sand and gravel required to get the gallons called for in the table. For later batches, you can count the shovels instead of batching into containers.

Dump out a little of your first trial batch and examine it for workability. If the mix is too wet, add a little sand and coarse aggregate to future batches. If the mix is too stiff, it contains too much sand and coarse aggregate, so reduce the amount of aggregates in the following batches. Never just add more water. You adjust the consistency of the mix by regulating the sand and the coarse aggregate.

Hand-mixing

Small batches of concrete, say for a stepping stone, may be mixed by hand. Work on a clean, flat, hard surface. A sidewalk, driveway, or sheet of plywood will work fine, provided you rinse the surface afterward before any concrete can harden on it.

First, spread the measured out sand evenly and distribute the required cement over the top. Mix the two thoroughly using a short, flat-ended **D**-handled shovel until the color looks uniform. Then spread the mixture evenly again and distribute the measured amount of gravel over the top. Mix again. When all the dry ingredients are blended, scoop out a depression in the center of the pile, like a miniature volcano crater, and add the water a little at a time. Bring the dry ingredients to the water by turning the materials in toward the center on top of the water without letting any water run away. Keep at it until you have workable concrete. You can tell by stroking the shovel flat across the pile. There should be enough cement paste to fill

AT THE MIXER

A concrete mixer should be batched as follows: (**1**) With the drum turning, pour in half the water and half the coarse aggregate. This mixture will help to scour the drum from the previous batch. Then batch the rest of the coarse aggregate and the sand, adding all but the last 10 percent of the water along with these. Next, batch the cement. When these ingredients are a uniform color and texture, add the last of the water and mix everything for at least 2 minutes, longer if necessary to get uniform consistency throughout. If you are using an air-entraining agent, add it to the last water. (**2** & **3**) A less precise but commonly practiced quicker means of batching is by shovelfuls.

You can hand-mix concrete in a plastic tub. Here, a garden hoe serves better than a shovel. Mix dry until all ingredients are blended. Add water in increments, mixing between.

voids between the surface ags yet not so much as to make the mixture runny.

You can also hand-mix in a wheelbarrow or in a plastic or wooden tub.

AIR-ENTRAINED CONCRETE

All outdoor concrete in freezing climates should be air-entrained to prevent surface damage caused by repeated freezing and thawing. Air-entrained concrete is permeated by billions of microscopic air bubbles that act as expansion chambers for freezing water within the hardened concrete. This makes air-entrained concrete highly resistant to winter damage.

Air-entrained concrete is also more workable than plain concrete. Air-entrained concrete acts buttery, resists segregation (separation of ingredients), and is easy to work. Because air-entrained concrete does not *bleed* (conduct excess water to the surface), finishing can move right ahead without waiting for evaporation of bleed water. This is why using air-entrained concrete is a good idea even in a nonfreezing climate.

Air-entraining Agents

When ordering ready-mixed concrete, simply ask for air-entrained concrete. If you mix your own, getting it air-entrained calls for adding an air-entraining agent to the mixing water. The most common agent is an oily, soapy liquid called *vinsol resin*. How much air-entraining agent you need in the mix will depend on the size of mix and the specific air-entraining agent used. Ask the dealer for advice.

You should be able to get some kind of air-entraining agent from a concrete products supplier. If not, try the concrete chemicals firms that produce the agents listed below (addresses in "Preface"). Check each firm's guidelines on how much of the agent to use.

Darex AEA (W. R. Grace and Company). Use ¾ ounce of this vinsol resin agent per sack of cement to get 4 percent to 7 percent entrained air.

Sika Aer (Sika Chemical Company). Use 1 to 2 ounces per sack to get 3 percent to 5 percent entrained air.

MB-VR (Master Builders). This is neutralized vinsol resin. (Try ½ to ¾ ounce per sack.)

Air-Mix (Euclid Chemical Co.). Use ½ to 1 ounce per sack (¾ ounce is average) to get 3 percent to 6 percent entrained air.

In each case, the manufacturers' guidelines hit somewhat below our target air entrainment (see the table on the next page), so use more agent than recommended to achieve better air content.

Very little air-entraining agent will create billions of bubbles. Follow manufacture's instructions. Agent is added to the mixing water, usually about one tablespoon per batch.

For good dispersion, don't just dump the air-entraining agent into the mixer. Instead, add it to the final mixing water before you pour that into the mixing drum.

Only machine-mixing in a concrete mixer is vigorous enough to mix air-entrained concrete. Hand-mixing will not do it, so don't bother adding an air-entraining agent to mix-by-hand batches. An air-entraining agent may be used in a ready-packaged mix as well as in a mix that you proportion.

How Much Air?

The freeze–thaw goal of air-entrained concrete varies, depending on the maximum-size aggregate. Regardless of ag size, the mild-climate goal is 3 percent entrained air.

Maximum-Size Ag	Entrained Air
³⁄₈″	6½–8½%
½″	6½–8½%
¾″	5%–7%
1″	4%–5%

READY-PACKAGED MIXES

For a small project, it is sometimes better to buy a ready-packaged concrete mix than to locate, purchase, and proportion the ingredients yourself. Ready-packaged mixes contain cement, sand, and sometimes gravel. They arrive ready for you to add water, mix, and use. The ready-packageds won't make a mess of your yard and are practical for projects needing up to about ¼ cubic yard. The water may be mixed in by hand or in a concrete mixer. Many brands, especially local ones, tend to be shy about 1 shovel of portland cement per sack. If you think the mix looks harsh or gravelly, you can probably improve it by adding a little portland cement. If you do the job in a mixer, add an air-entraining agent, also.

The ready-packageds come in 60- and 90-pound sacks, with directions on how much water to add. One 90-pound sack makes about 0.67 (⅔) cubic foot of concrete. A 60-pound sack, which is much easier to heft, makes 0.44 cubic foot.

The number of sacks of ready-packaged mix to order varies with the volumes of the sacks. For example, to find how many 90-pound sacks are needed to

READY-PACKAGED CONCRETE

Ready-packaged concrete or gravel mix (*left*) contains portland cement, sand, and gravel. Sand mix contains cement and sand but no gravel. Use concrete mix for projects thicker than 2 inches and sand mix for thin-section slabs and toppings.

provide 8 cubic feet, you'd divide 8 by 0.67 and arrive at 12 sacks. For the number of 60-pound sacks, divide 8 by 0.44; the result is 19 60-pound sacks needed.

Be warned that the dry ingredients in a ready-packaged mix tend to separate in shipping and handling. For this reason, always mix the contents of the whole sack completely before using any part of it. If you just scoop out part of a sack, you may or may not get a good mix.

The ready-packageds come either with a coarse aggregate or without one. Concrete mix, also called *gravel mix*, contains both fine and coarse aggregates. This mix is best for general use in projects thicker than 2 inches. Sand mix, also called *topping mix* or *sand and topping mix*, contains only fine aggregate, no coarse. Use it for projects 2 inches thick or less.

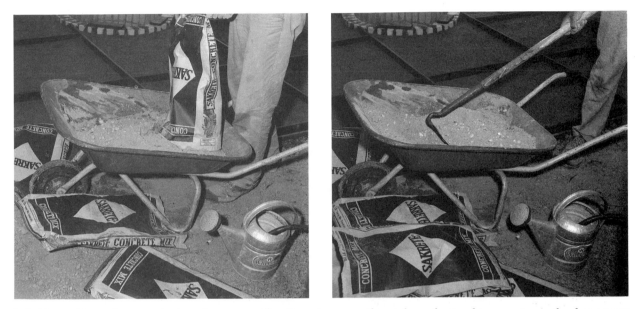

Left photo: To make a project such as a small patio using a ready-packaged mix, dump out a sack of concrete mix and measure out the amount of water called for on the package. Right photo: Mix the ingredients dry first because they may have settled during shipping and storage. (Photographer, Rollyn Puterbaugh; Sakrete photos)

Left photo: Add water a bit at a time. Don't exceed label directions. Right photo: Mix the dampened concrete with a shovel or hoe between water additions until the color is uniform and everything is well blended.

Ready mix is by far the handiest concrete for a project requiring 3 cubic yards or more, though at a price. (Roth/Woods project photo)

Make certain that the mix you get for concrete is not one designed for making mortar. Mortar, *mortar and topping*, and *mortar and stucco* mixes are certain to contain lime or some other plasticizer that weakens concrete. Any lime content relegates a prepackaged mix to brick and block-laying rather than to making good concrete. Be aware, too, that products labeled "fast-setting" are formulated for the patching of concrete, not for making it.

READY-MIXED CONCRETE

Larger projects (those requiring 3 cubic yards—81 cubic feet—of concrete and more) call for ready-mixed concrete. Ready mix is batched from a central weight-batching plant and can be furnished air-entrained to your specifications. It's delivered to you in huge, 7-cubic-yard truck-mixers that unload at your work site. The mix comes ready to use right out of the truck-mixer.

Ordering ready mix is easy. But don't just ask for

"ready mix." Instead, order by specifying: (1) the number of cubic yards needed; (2) where and when delivery is to be made; (3) a 28-day compressive strength of 4,000 psi; (4) a minimum portland cement content of 6 sacks per cubic yard (called a 6-*sack mix*); (5) the desired entrained-air content; (6) either ¾- or 1-inch maximum-size coarse aggregate; and (7) a maximum slump of 6 inches.

Slump is the standard measure of concrete's workability. Concrete with a slump of less than 4 inches is hard to work; concrete with a slump of much more than that tends to be watery and lacks strength and durability in its hardened state. Specifying a minimum strength and minimum cement content ensures that you get a concrete mix that will harden into a sound, durable project.

How Much Ready Mix?

As you may have supposed, the standard unit for ready-mixed concrete is the cubic yard (or cubic meter). Use the chart "How Much Material to Order" (page 152) for figuring how much ready mix to order. It works for orders up to 5½ cubic yards.

For larger projects, here's a simple way to figure how many cubic yards (or cubic meters) to order. First

Base your ready-mix order on the average thickness for your slab. To calculate this, lay a straightedge between the forms and measure from the bottom of the straightedge down to the subgrade. Take measurements throughout all parts of your project and average them to arrive at the average depth. Use the average depth to calculate the slab's cubic-yard volume.

measure the length and width of the project in feet (or meters) and multiply the two figures. This represents the surface area of your project in square feet (or square meters). Multiply this by the slab's thickness in inches (or centimeters). Finally, to get cubic yards (or cubic meters), divide the result by 300 (or 90 for cubic meters). The 300 (or 90) factor allows 10 percent for subgrade variations and waste. Always order a little more than you expect to need; asking the driver to return with a partial load would prove more costly than sending back some leftover concrete.

For example, if you were building a 4-inch-thick concrete patio 20 × 30 feet, you'd multiply 20 and 30 to get 600 square feet, and then multiply times 4 to arrive at 2,400. Dividing 2,400 by 300 gives 8. Order 8 cubic yards. When ordering ready mix, round off your figure to the next-higher quarter cubic yard.

Almost all ready-mix dealers will quote a price for the concrete plus an additional charge for detaining the mixer beyond the normal free-time allowance. A typical dealer allows 5 minutes of mixer unloading time for each cubic yard ordered, then makes an extra charge for each minute of overtime. As you can see, it behooves you not to waste time in getting the ready mix discharged. Orders of less than a full truck-mixer load may cost more per cubic yard. Also, a long haul from the batch plant to your home may cost extra. Some ready-mix dealers may set a higher price on Saturday deliveries; other dealers love them, because contractor business is slow that day.

If more than one truck-mixer will be needed to complete your order, ask that the trucks arrive about an hour apart. This will keep you from being inundated with ready mix. Otherwise, you may get both trucks at once. Staggering may also allow the dealer to assign one truck to your job. Then the same driver goes back to the plant to get your second load. This system may also—if you work fast enough—have the advantage of letting you increase or decrease the amount of the subsequent loads because you will be able to access how far the first loads take you.

It saves work if the truck can chute the mix directly onto the subgrade surface you will have prepared. Most ready-mix chutes can reach about 12 feet back

Here, a 12-foot-long metal extension chute is used to place ready mix from the truck-mixer as close as possible to its final position. Mix is pushed along the chute and into place with flat-end shovels, but it is not actually shoveled. (Roth/Woods project photo)

and swing to the sides. The chute also can be short-ened for close placement. Swing the chute around to deposit concrete wherever you want it. (The maximum permissible distance for concrete to drop from a chute is 3 feet. More than that causes segregation.)

Unless the truck-mixer will be able to back right up to within 12 feet of your forms and dump, ask the dealer about an additional chute. Or, if you will need more chute than the dealer normally provides, you can make your own workable wooden chute by nailing 1 × 6s onto both edges of a 2 × 10 plank. Besides ad-ditional chutes, ready-mix producers may rent you wheelbarrows and major tools for finishing.

Be sure to order your ready mix at least a day before you'll need it. The more notice you can give, the better. If you can, set up forms for an extra project or two so you can make use of any leftover ready mix. Stepping-stones and similar projects are good uses for leftovers.

Planning Ahead

Have a logical plan in mind for concrete placement. And try to be ready when the truck-mixer arrives. Two workers are needed to help place and finish every 3 cubic yards of ready mix. Six cubic yards calls for four workers. Don't count on any help from the truck-mixer driver, whose job is to manage the truck, discharge the concrete, and hose off the equipment afterward with a pressurized water supply on the truck. If the concrete

Most driveways are not thick enough to support a fully loaded ready-mix truck. If the truck must back up your driveway, lay down planks or thick sheets of plywood, as engineer Carl Roth did here, to help distribute the concentrated load of the truck's wheels. (Roth/Woods project photo)

must be wheeled from the truck to the site, have two additional helpers with rubber-tired wheelbarrows. Each cubic yard of concrete will take about 20 wheel-barrow loads.

Because of its weight, keep the ready-mix truck-mixer off sidewalks, driveways, and sewer lines, as well as septic tanks and disposal fields. If you must bring the truck up your driveway, lay planks to spread the weight. And keep in mind that if the driver gets stuck on your property, you may be expected to pay a hefty towing bill. (If access is a problem, or if you anticipate much wheeling of ready mix, you may wish to use a concrete pumping contractor—see upcoming section on pumped concrete.)

Adding Water To Ready Mix

Dealers know that too much water is bad for concrete, and so they sometimes send their mixes out slightly dry. This is fine. So long as you do the job properly, you can add water to ready mix that's too stiff. Begin by adding 1 gallon of water per cubic yard in the mixer. For example, if the load contains 3 cubic yards, have the driver put in 3 gallons of water as a starter. Then the driver should run the drum at mixing speed—fast, not at the slow 1½-rpm agitation speed—for 2 min-

Although all workers won't be busy all the time, you need at least two workers for every 3 cubic yards of ready mix being handled. Those who must walk in the plastic concrete mix should wear rubber boots. (Roth/Woods project photo)

utes or longer. Then run out some mix and check its workability again.

Still too stiff? You can do one more add-mix test procedure, but that's all. Once 2 gallons of additional water has been put into the mixer for each cubic yard

of concrete aboard—6 gallons in our example—you've reached the practical limit. Each gallon of water added to a cubic yard cuts some 150 psi from the concrete's 28-day compressive strength. Durability is reduced, too. So add only enough water to get a workable mix.

Your ready-mix dealer may suggest the use of a concrete additive. Many concrete additives are billed as magic potions to solve all your concrete problems. But it's best to stay away from all additives except an air-entraining agent.

Unless you make other arrangements beforehand, you should be prepared to pay for the ready mix immediately after delivery.

Pumped Concrete

If the truck-mixer cannot back right up to your project, pumped concrete is very often your best solution. An independent concrete pumping contractor works behind the truck-mixer. The contractor brings a small concrete pump to the house and runs its 2- to 3-inch-diameter discharge hose up the driveway, right to a backyard patio site. Ready mix dumped into the pump's hopper is forced through the hose and comes out the end like toothpaste squeezed from a tube.

Pumped concrete can be positioned almost anywhere, as much as 100 feet uphill, 300 feet downhill, or up to 500 feet horizontally around any obstacle, even through an open window or door. Concrete pumping is an almost effortless method for getting concrete mix in place and ready to finish. The pump's

While you are writing a check for the ready-mix delivery, the driver will be cleaning his equipment with pressurized water carried on the truck-mixer.

The combination of ready-mixed concrete and a concrete pumping service gets the mix right where you want it effortlessly for you. The pickup-towed concrete pump works behind the ready-mix truck.

Above photo: Ready-mix dealers favor concrete pumping because they know their truck-mixers will not be hung up on the job. The ready-mix driver's job is to keep the pump's hopper properly full. Right photo: Your task is to handle the discharge end of the hose, placing pumped concrete a bit higher than the form tops to allow for subsequent settling.

hose places every cubic foot of ready mix exactly where it is wanted. With pumping done right, there is no wheeling, no chuting, no shoveling. All that's left to do is the finishing.

A small concrete pump can move some 20 cubic yards of concrete an hour. Pumping is practical only with ready-mixed concrete, however.

Pumping Cost. Naturally, the pumping service costs extra. The pumping contractor usually has a minimum charge that covers pumping a certain number of cubic yards—often 7. Beyond that is a per-yard charge for each cubic yard more than the minimum. The charge includes the pumping and the equipment cleanup, plus reasonable travel to and from the project.

Ready-mix dealers like working with a concrete pumping service because they know their truck-mixer will not be delayed on the job. Concrete pumping can be arranged either through your ready-mix producer or directly with a pumping contractor. Ask your ready-mix dealer, or look in the Yellow Pages under *Concrete Pumping Service*.

How To Order Pumped Concrete. Be sure the ready-mix dealer knows that you plan to use a concrete pump, because a special "grout and pump mix" must be provided at a slight extra cost. It contains ½-inch maximum-size coarse aggregate to slide easily

through the pump and hose. This mix also needs to be made with a particular slump.

Since you want your pumped concrete to be quality concrete, order it as follows (check the details with the pumping contractor): (1) where, when, and how much concrete; (2) 28-day compressive strength of 4,000 psi; (3) minimum of 6 sacks cement per cubic yard; (4) 7 percent to 9 percent entrained air (or 3 percent in a mild climate); (5) ½-inch maximum-size coarse aggregate; and (6) 4- to 6-inch slump.

Who Does What? Pumping contractors expect you to handle the end of the hose. Nonetheless, every one I have ever worked with took over the hose duties if we were underfilling or overfilling our forms. It takes a good eye plus experience to know when the form is full. Too full is better than not full enough. Placement by hose is always begun at the end of the project farthest from the pump, working backward to avoid dragging the hose through the fresh mix. It's nice to have a helper assist with the heavy hose.

Once the job is finished, the pumping contractor will need a spot to dump about a bushel of rinsed-off aggregates. A 6-foot square of plastic sheeting will do. It can be disposed of later. You will be expected to pay the pumping charges on the spot.

Concrete pumping is not a gold watch and a pension. You are placing lots of concrete very quickly, all

Left photo: Haul-it-yourself concrete from a trailer-mixer is one way to get from ¼ to 3 cubic yards. Throwing a lever reverses the mixer drum, discharging concrete down the chute and onto the subgrade. Right photo: With a trailer-mixer, you can dump concrete wherever you need it, across sidewalks and in places big ready-mix trucks can't go. A full-size pickup makes an ideal tow vehicle.

The author's daughter Gail and neighbor Millard Beemer are cleaning a hopper of haul-it-yourself concrete after a disastrous hauling experience. The mix segregated badly on its ride to the author's home. All water rose to the top, pouring out when the discharge door was opened. The remaining layers of ingredients were so stiff they had to be shoveled into the drainage ditch, shown.

of which needs to be finished properly. If you are working alone and trying to finish a large patio by yourself, you may easily fall behind. Avoid problems by having enough help on hand.

HAUL-IT-YOURSELF CONCRETE

Haul-it-yourself is a way of getting as little as ¼ to as much as several cubic yards of concrete for a patio. Haul-it-yourself prices are reasonable compared to having a small amount of ready mix delivered.

Using haul-it-yourself concrete is risky for several reasons. First of all, haul-it-yourself concrete must be properly transported.

Another haul-it-yourself problem: most dealers are not in the concrete business, but some other business. They rarely know enough about how to make quality concrete. Too many haul-it-yourself dealers use volume-batching. Too many add the water according to how the mix looks. To get quality, you'll have to find a haul-it-yourself dealer who is dedicated to quality concrete. Such dealers are extremely rare.

Hopper Hauling. Avoid the use of hopper trailers because they produce segregation of the ingredients. Hopper-hauled concrete is mixed at a central mixing plant, then dumped into the hopper trailer. It receives no more mixing. Once home, you don't yet have concrete; instead you have layers of separate ingredients. The only way to prevent segregation is to start with a concrete slump of only 2 to 3 inches, concrete so stiff you would not want to work with it. For this reason, I advise you to avoid hopper-trailered concrete altogether. Trouble is, this is the method you'll find most often.

The Trailer-mixer Solution. The solution is to use a trailer-mixer. The concrete is batched into a self-powered trailer-mixing machine holding up to 1 cubic yard, which gets mixed on the way home. On arrival at your house, you have nicely mixed concrete. The slump can be a right-on 4 to 6 inches.

A pickup-mounted mixer (you rent both the pickup and the mixer) will also serve well.

Hard Facts on Trailering. A full 1-cubic-yard trailer-mixer scales in at 6,200 pounds. That's more than 3 tons. The concrete alone weighs 3,800 pounds. Any trailer heavier than 3,500 pounds is supposed to be towed with an SAE (Society of Automotive Engineers) Class 3, load-equalizing hitch with 2⅜-inch-diameter hitch ball. Yet the trailer-mixer you will be offered will most likely accept a 2-inch hitch ball (common with Class 2 hitches) and will probably have no load-equalizing equipment. This leaves you with inadequate hitching, right off the bat. The mistaken reasoning is that the hauls are local, involving short trips and slow driving, and that therefore a proper hookup is not essential, as it would be for a high-speed highway haul.

If you accept this faulty rationalization and decide to drive super-carefully and take your chances, in no case should you haul one of these concrete-containing hippos with any but a full-size car or pickup truck. A clamp-on bumper hitch is out; no car bumper is strong enough to handle the load.

Then, too, any trailer that heavy is supposed to have its own brakes. See that your trailer-mixer does, either independently operated surge brakes or electric brakes with the controlling unit in your tow vehicle.

If you decide to take the risk, before you drive off, be sure that the trailer-mixer's taillights and directional signals are properly connected to the tow vehicle and working, and that the safety chains are hooked between vehicle and trailer. Drive slowly and carefully, avoiding fast starts and the need for fast turns and fast stops. With all that weight behind you, an emergency stop will take much, *much* longer than normal.

One worker should be responsible for getting, cleaning, and returning the trailer-mixer. Warning: If the mixer isn't cleaned well enough, the dealer may assess a cleaning charge.

Horse Sense. If you must do any backing, be sure you know how to back a trailer, or else have a helper on hand who does. Steering a trailer backwards requires that you turn the steering wheel opposite to the direction you want the trailer to turn, then correct and follow the trailer around the turn; this takes some practice.

Don't drive over soft ground or septic systems and never let the trailer-mixer down an incline you cannot tow it back up. Stay away from holes in the ground; the trailer-mixer could end up in the hole.

A haul-it-yourself project goes best with three workers, one to handle the mixer—getting, discharging, cleaning, and returning it—and the other two to do the concrete work.

CONCRETE SLAB DESIGN

You want adequate strength in your patio slab to prevent freezing and thawing damage. This calls for correct slab design. Thickness and reinforcement are important considerations.

Slab Thickness

Having sufficient slab thickness is vital whenever you build a patio or other concrete slab around the house. Adequate thickness will give the slab sufficient bending strength. A slab that is too thin could crack under freeze–thaw loads. Although uneconomical, too thick is much better than too thin.

For patios, a minimum thickness of 4 inches is recommended, assuming that quality concrete and proper construction methods are used.

Reinforcing Concrete Slabs

The subject of reinforcement for residential concrete slabs is controversial and has given rise to many mistaken notions. Reinforcement does not really make an on-ground slab any stronger. Reinforcement's main purpose is to keep random shrinkage cracks from spreading.

Crack Containment. The most practical reinforcement for a concrete patio is welded-wire fabric, called *wire mesh*. Reinforcement in concrete does three things: (1) buttresses concrete against tensile ("pull-apart") forces; (2) builds safe load-bearing structures (such as bridges); and (3) holds cracks tightly closed, which is the feature that counts for your outdoor projects. Therefore, wire mesh can take the place of control joints in a slab.

Why might you want to do this? The most likely reason is that cracks that might reflect through paving cannot be tolerated when the slab is being used as a base for mortared-in-place (hard-set) pavers. For most

In two-course reinforced-slab construction, a base course of concrete is struck off 2 inches below the tops of the forms. Welded-wire mesh sheets are laid on top, as shown. Finally, the top course is placed over the mesh for striking off.

other situations, adding an inch of thickness to a slab's design will do more good than wire mesh. The cost is about the same.

Rules for Reinforcing. Wire mesh, the only reinforcement that should be considered for around-the-house use, is marketed according to the spacing and gauge (diameter) of its wires. Common is 6×6-

HOW MESH REINFORCEMENT WORKS

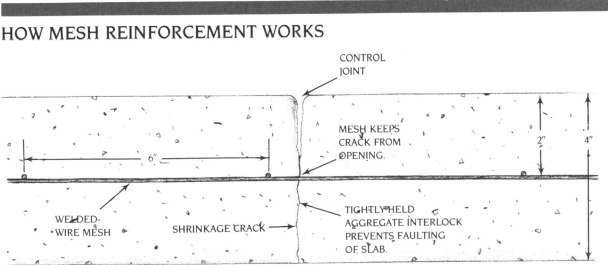

CONTROL JOINT

MESH KEEPS CRACK FROM OPENING.

2"   4"

WELDED-WIRE MESH

SHRINKAGE CRACK

TIGHTLY HELD AGGREGATE INTERLOCK PREVENTS FAULTING OF SLAB.

6"

PLACEMENT OF WELDED-WIRE MESH

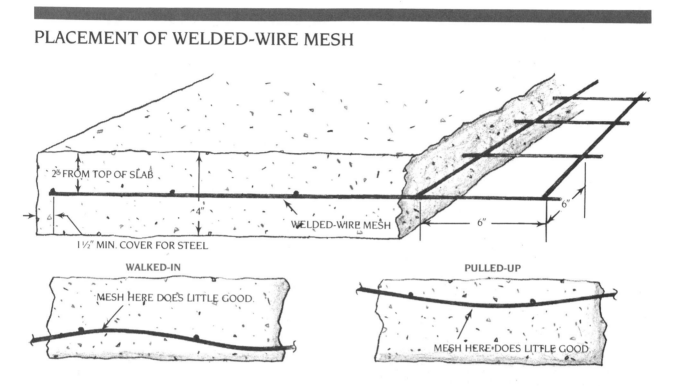

2½" FROM TOP OF SLAB

WELDED-WIRE MESH

1½" MIN. COVER FOR STEEL

4"

6"

6"

6"

WALKED-IN

MESH HERE DOES LITTLE GOOD.

PULLED-UP

MESH HERE DOES LITTLE GOOD.

inch mesh in 6-, 8-, and 10-gauge (the smaller numbers represent the heavier gauges). A 6×6 No. 6/6 wire mesh uses 6-gauge wires running in both directions. The wires in some meshes are heavier in one direction than those in the other direction. Such a mesh is not intended for a home project.

Wire mesh comes in rolls (light gauges) or in 4 × 8-foot flat sheets (heavier gauges). Avoid the rolls, because they're too light to do the required crack-containment job.

How Much Mesh? For successful crack containment, a 4-inch-thick patio slab needs 6×6 No. 6/6 mesh. Anything less will not do the job.

Positioning the Mesh Reinforcement. Wire mesh for crack containment must be 2 inches below the surface of the slab. Arrange for this either by two-course construction or by supporting the mesh at the correct elevation on mesh supports called "chairs" and casting the concrete around it. The chairs are sold for this purpose by concrete products suppliers.

Avoid laying the mesh on the subgrade and trying to pull it up as concrete is placed. That doesn't work and is almost as bad as "walking" the mesh in from the top. Neither method ensures correct mesh positioning. To provide what is called *proper cover* for the steel, no part of the reinforcement should be closer than 1½ inches to any surface of the slab. Proper cover is necessary to keep the mesh from corroding.

Sheets of wire mesh need to overlap by at least

With the supported-mesh method, "chairs"—which are purchased concrete support blocks with tie-wires —are placed beneath the wire mesh to hold it at the desired level.

one whole grid spacing plus 2 inches: therefore, sheets of 6×6 mesh would be overlapped 8 inches on all sides. Wiring the sheets together is not necessary.

One more thing. The crack control that can be added by wire mesh depends on how tightly your concrete bonds to it. For this reason, the steel should be

or a great deal of preparation may be needed to provide uniform support for your slab. If the earth in the area of your project is uniformly dense and well drained, the slab can be cast right on the ground. This is the *subgrade*. But concrete should never be cast on topsoil, sod and other vegetation, wood, or large rocks. All of these must be dug out. Don't build on soft soil, either: dig it out. In any case, dig out enough soil so that the top surface of the finished slab will be about 1 inch above ground level.

It's best to dig exactly to the required depth, thus avoiding any need to backfill. That is, avoid having to refill the area you've dug out with excavated earth or other material. Unexcavated subgrade offers the most uniform support. Grading is usually carried several inches beyond the edge of the slab.

If you must backfill, do it properly. To provide uniform support, backfill must be the same material as the surrounding soil well compacted by tamping. Tamp in layers (called *lifts*) no deeper than 4 inches, tamping one lift before spreading the next lift of fill.

The soil being tamped must be at what is called *optimum moisture content*. This means that it holds just the right amount of water for good compaction. Optimum moisture content is simple to gauge using the same hand-squeeze test you used to find the wetness of your sand. The photo earlier, showing average wet sand, shows the optimum soil condition. If the soil is too dry, sprinkle it with water and wait before tamping. If the soil is too wet, wait for drying.

Concrete is placed around the mesh in a single course to the tops of the forms, with the blocks supporting it 2 inches below the slab's surface.

free of loose rust (light, tight rust is okay), oil, grease, paint, mud, mortar, and other such bond-breakers.

Wire mesh may be cut with a hacksaw (hard work) or with light-duty bolt cutters (much easier). Place concrete carefully to be sure it gets all around, through, and under the mesh.

PREPARING TO BUILD A SLAB

Whether you plan to use haul-it-yourself concrete, ready mix, or concrete you've mixed yourself, you need to prepare the base for it properly. Do this before the day of placing.

Concrete needs uniform support. It should not be placed on ground that is squishy in one spot, hard in another, and muddy or frozen somewhere else. A little

The Subbase

Rather than try to tamp backfilled earth, dig out the loose soil and create a subbase from a compacted granular material—sand, gravel, or crushed stone. Such materials are easier to work than soil. Avoid the use of cinders, because they settle. Whether needed or not for uniform support, sand is a convenient subbase for fine-grading purposes.

If your soil is an expansive clay or other tight, wet soil, do not use it as a base for concrete. To prevent frost-heaving from such soil, dig it out and replace it with a 4- to 6-inch-thick granular subbase. The subbase should be tamped to a uniform density. Try to extend the fill a foot or more beyond the slab edge to avoid undercutting by rain.

For outdoor slabs, plastic sheeting is not needed over the subgrade or subbase. The plastic traps excess water trying to leave the fresh slab, bringing it to the surface as bleed water. On the surface, the bleed water gets in the way of finishing operations. It's better to cast a slab on earth or a porous subbase.

SLOPES AND SUBGRADES

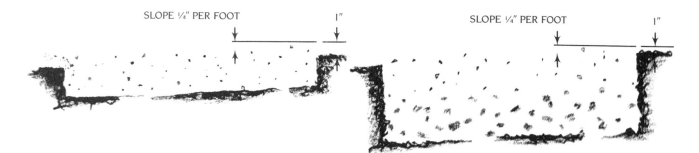

SLAB CAST DIRECTLY ON SUBGRADE   SLAB CAST ON 4'–6' GRANULAR SUBBASE

Backfill should be tamped down firmly. This metal tamper has a 3×3-inch foot welded onto its concrete-filled pipe handle. A home-built tamper is shown on page 134.

Sand is especially good for fine-grading; that is, getting the final surface to the desired slope and elevation. It smoothens and compacts without the effort required for leveling earth.

Besides preparing the earth beneath the slab, the earth around it needs to be graded to carry water away from the slab. The patio surface itself should be sloped to drain, the best slope being ¼ inch per foot (or 1 inch in 10 feet). The bare minimum slope, when a greater slope cannot be provided, is ⅛ inch per foot (or ½ inch in 10 feet). Anything less than that will

You can make a subbase strikeoff tool by notching a board and resting its ear on the form top. The struck-off sand subbase should be tamped before placing concrete on it.

drain water poorly. A handy slope gauge can be made from a long, straight 2 × 4 and a carpenter's level (see accompanying drawing).

The best practice is to slope the subgrade or subbase in the same direction and by the same amount as the slab. The slab itself can then be of uniform thickness.

FORMING SLABS

Concrete slabs are built within wooden forms. Placed exactly at the desired elevation for the slab's surface, the form tops can be used for leveling off the freshly placed concrete. For a patio, 2 × 4-inch forms are used. Forms are held in place by either 1 × 4- or 2 × 2-inch

HOME-BUILT SLOPE GUIDE FOR GRADING

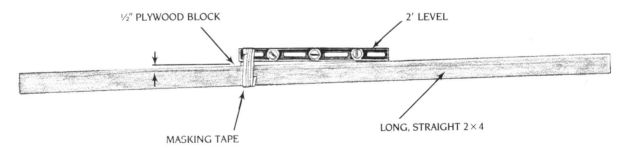

½" PLYWOOD BLOCK

2' LEVEL

MASKING TAPE

LONG, STRAIGHT 2 × 4

DETERMINING SLOPE

½"

2' LEVEL

¼"-PER-FOOT SLOPE MEASURED WITH CARPENTER'S LEVEL

FORM CORNERS

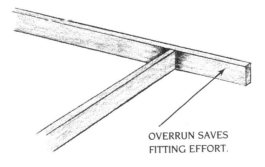

OVERRUN SAVES FITTING EFFORT.

Left photo: To nail forms to 2×2 stakes, use 16d duplex form nails. Their "double head" leaves the top head projecting for easy later pulling with a hammer or prybar. To ensure that your hammering doesn't loosen stakes, back it up with a sledge hammer held in place by your foot. Right photo: Reinforce form joints on the outside by nailing on scraps of 1-inch or 2-inch wood.

wooden stakes driven into the ground just outside the forms. Use 8d nails on 1×4 stakes and 16d duplex nails on 2×2 stakes to attach them to the forms.

A form stake is needed at least every 4 feet along forms, plus one stake at each joint in form lumber. Drive the stakes with a small sledgehammer. Cut stakes off flush with the top of the forms so they cannot become a nuisance.

The tendency is to make slabs the same thickness as the form lumber. But 2×4-inch forms are really only 3½ inches deep. To make a 4-inch slab with 2×4s, you need to stake them half an inch above the subgrade. Then earth backfill is placed beneath them to hold the concrete inside.

Curving Forms

You can cast concrete in curving as well as in straight forms. Curved forms may be built in several ways, but do all nailing with a sledgehammer head for backup, to resist the force of hammering and to keep the nailing from loosening the form stakes.

For long-radius curves, use 1-inch form lumber staked 2 to 3 feet apart, both inside and outside. Double the forms if necessary, nailing the two layers together once they are in place. Or use 2×4 forms with evenly spaced saw kerfs placed close enough together

to permit the desired curve. (The kerfs go on the inside of the curve.)

For tight curves, use ¼- or ⅜-inch plywood with its face grain running vertically, or ¼-inch hardboard. On the tightest curves, a single layer is ample. Stake tightly 1 to 2 feet apart, both inside and outside.

For the tightest curves, use a double layer of ⅛-inch hardboard, staked 8 to 12 inches apart, inside and outside. Once the two layers are nailed to each other, the inside stakes usually may be pulled without affecting the curvature. Or they can be pulled later, once concrete is placed around them.

A strip of sheet metal or flashing material cut with metal snips to the correct form height also makes an easily curved form. If the ends are well nailed, the concrete will help shape it into a smooth curve.

Leaving Forms In

Leave-in forms may be positioned throughout the slab. Forms of 1×4s or 2×4s help section a large slab and create designs; break up a project into easy, one-day placing segments; or form control joints. If you plan to leave any forms in place, choose for these a nonrotting wood such as all-heart redwood, cedar, or cypress. Longest lasting though not the prettiest is

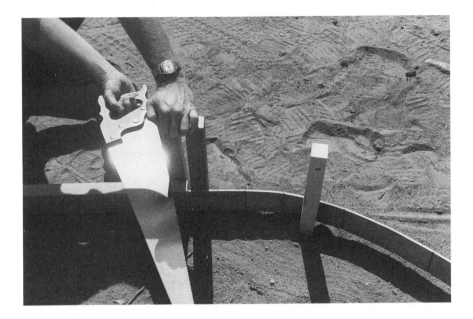

If you saw off the stakes flush with the tops of the forms, they will be out of the way of later finishing operations. To avoid marring the tops of leave-in forms, saw at a slight upward angle.

KERFED AND LAYERED FORMS

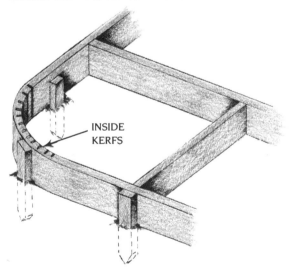

INSIDE KERFS

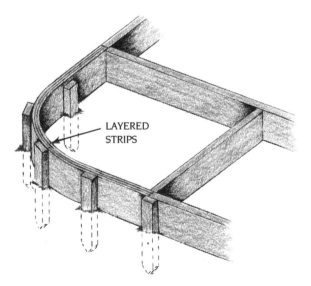

LAYERED STRIPS

pressure-treated wood, treated to Ground-contact rating. Your inside leave-in forms, those with concrete on both sides, will need staking to hold them at the correct elevation. If wood stakes are used, pull these out as concrete placement reaches them or cut them off 2 inches below form tops.

To prevent leave-in forms from settling independently of the slabs they outline, anchor them to the slabs with 16d galvanized nails. Drive a nail every 16 inches midway between the top and bottom of the form, and bend each nail's point slightly. Nails along inside leave-in forms (those that have concrete on both sides) should be driven alternately from opposite sides of the form, 16 inches apart and bent slightly.

Forms must be secure. You should be able to step on them. But no matter how secure, forms should not be used to support concentrated loads such as wheelbarrow ramps. All forms that are to be removed should be oiled with motor oil or form oil for ready separation from the hardened concrete.

HOW TO CURVE FORMS

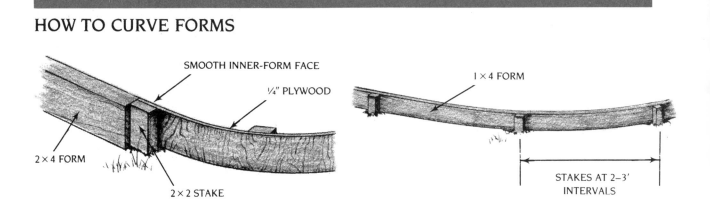

Left: These are suggested wood supports to begin a curve. Right: Use 1-inch lumber for gentle curves.

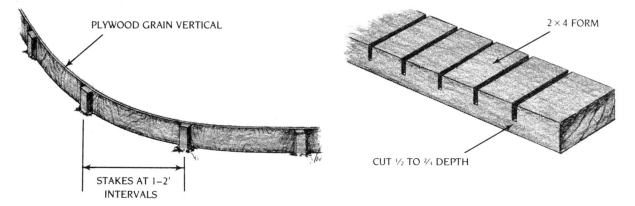

Left: Use ¼-inch plywood or hardboard for short-radius curves. Right: Use saw kerfing to bend 2-inch lumber. Handsaw cuts are so thin they must open on the outside of the form.

LEAVE-IN FORMS

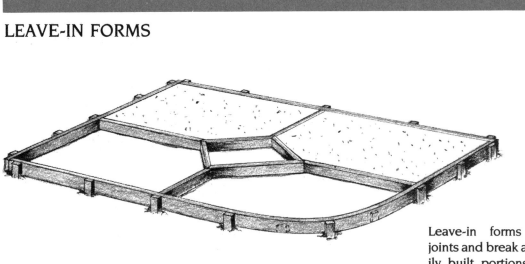

Leave-in forms create control joints and break a project into easily built portions. The diamond-shaped space in the center here will be left open for plantings.

WHEELBARROW RAMP

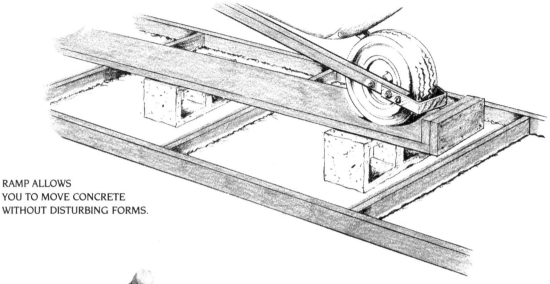

RAMP ALLOWS
YOU TO MOVE CONCRETE
WITHOUT DISTURBING FORMS.

Concrete is placed to fill the slot left by a removed screed board. Once the concrete is "chunked" with a flat-end shovel and finished over, the former screed location will not show.

Temporary Screeds

For very wide projects—those having forms more than 12 feet apart—a temporary intermediate form is needed as a guide in striking off the surface (see photo at left). This temporary form is called a *screed*. A screed is set up and staked into place just like a form. When the concrete has been placed on both sides of the screed and strikeoff has been completed, the screed is pried up and removed. Then a little fresh concrete is placed in the depression left by the screed and chunked with the end of a shovel to join it with the surrounding concrete mix.

JOINTS IN CONCRETE

Joints are very important to a concrete slab. They may be control joints, isolation joints, or construction joints. Each has its particular function.

Control Joints

Control-jointing makes neat, deep, rounded-edged grooves in the slab's surface to give the slab a neat-appearing place to crack as it shrinks on setting. Con-

CONTROL JOINTS

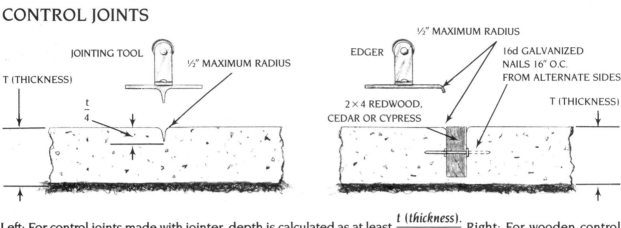

Left: For control joints made with jointer, depth is calculated as at least $\dfrac{t\ (thickness)}{4}$. Right: For wooden control joints, nails alternate 16 inches on centers.

trol joints are needed even if welded-wire mesh has been used within the slab. But do not use them if the slab is to receive bonded-in-place, hard-set pavers.

Leave-in forms may serve as control joints. Otherwise, control joints are tooled into the slab with a jointing tool during finishing.

Control joint depth must be at least one fourth the slab's thickness (labeled $t/4$ in the drawing). If the joint is too shallow, you cannot be certain it will work. A 4-inch-thick slab needs control joints at least 1 inch deep. A true jointing tool with a 1-inch bit is necessary to make them.

Control-joint Spacing. The spacing of control joints is critical. The rule of thumb for the maximum distance between control joints is 30 times a slab's thickness. On a 4-inch-thick patio slab, this means control joints should be located no more than 120 inches (4 × 30 = 120), or 10 feet apart. But when smaller than ¾-inch maximum-size aggregate is used, control joints should be no more than 8 feet apart.

Slabs should be jointed into sections as nearly square as possible. This is because long, narrow sections tend to crack of their own accord. Although a 1:1 aspect ratio (width to length) is ideal, the maximum

Left photo: Control joints in larger projects can be cut. Contractors cut into the hardened surface, within 12 hours of setting, by means of a large water-cooled diamond-blade saw. Right photo: These neatly sawed 1-inch-deep joints are just right for the 4-inch slab. To be effective, sawed joints must be the same minimum depth as formed control joints, which is one-fourth of slab thickness.

CONTROL AND ISOLATION JOINTS

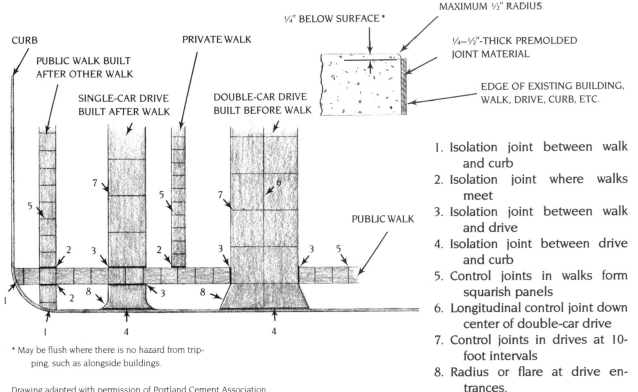

MAXIMUM ½" RADIUS

¼" BELOW SURFACE*

¼–½"-THICK PREMOLDED JOINT MATERIAL

EDGE OF EXISTING BUILDING, WALK, DRIVE, CURB, ETC.

CURB

PUBLIC WALK BUILT AFTER OTHER WALK

PRIVATE WALK

SINGLE-CAR DRIVE BUILT AFTER WALK

DOUBLE-CAR DRIVE BUILT BEFORE WALK

PUBLIC WALK

1. Isolation joint between walk and curb
2. Isolation joint where walks meet
3. Isolation joint between walk and drive
4. Isolation joint between drive and curb
5. Control joints in walks form squarish panels
6. Longitudinal control joint down center of double-car drive
7. Control joints in drives at 10-foot intervals
8. Radius or flare at drive entrances.

* May be flush where there is no hazard from tripping, such as alongside buildings.

Drawing adapted with permission of Portland Cement Association.

aspect ratio for a section should be 1:1½, for example, 6 feet 8 inches by 10 feet. Also, any odd-shaped pieces in a slab should be jointed off to keep them from cracking off haphazardly later on. It's a good idea to measure for all control joints and make marks for them with a felt-tip marker atop the forms.

Isolation Joints

Another kind of joint, called an *isolation joint*, or sometimes an *expansion joint*, is needed to separate your new slab from existing construction around it. A patio must have isolation joints where it meets the house, concrete stoop, walkway, and other existing concrete. Isolation joints are used in addition to control joints.

To make an isolation joint, lay a strip of bituminous-impregnated fiber isolation joint material (see your building-materials dealer) against the existing concrete with its top edge flush with the surface or ¼ inch below it. It may be held in place with hardened concrete nails or construction adhesive. The isolation joint strips are available in ¼- and ½-inch thicknesses with a width of 4 inches, in 8- or 10-foot lengths.

If you have trouble making your impregnated-fiber isolation-joint strips stay in place, use construction adhesive and concrete nails. To avoid chipping the surface, don't nail near the top of a slab.

Construction Joints

A third type of joint, the construction joint, is used only where one day's concreting is finished, to be completed another day.

A construction joint is made using a specially shaped 2 × 4 form fastened across the project where you wish to stop for the day. An angle-ripped wood strip nailed longitudinally along the center of the construction-joint form creates a tapered keyway in the last concrete slab placed in a work session. When work resumes and the form is removed later, the fresh concrete placed for the next slab tongues into the keyway and hardens. This arrangement will transfer loads between the slabs and prevent faulting. The widest portion of the wood strip should be one fourth slab thickness. The angle of ripping for both faces is about 15 degrees.

When finishing, both slabs should be edged along the construction joint to make it look like a control joint (which it also is). But try to avoid construction joints, except where necessary.

PLACING AND FINISHING

Putting concrete between the forms and then surfacing it is called *placing and finishing*. For a quality concrete project, this task must be done correctly. Proper timing of each operation is essential. A common tendency is to overfinish. Another common tendency is to muddle through the job. Before starting, make up your mind to do it properly. If you have ample help, you should not be rushed at any point. Under normal conditions, concrete allows about 1½ hours after mixing to begin the finishing process.

Concreting Safety

Every helper needs to be dressed properly for the job. Concrete is a mild alkali that can eat skin and burn as well as abrade eyes. Do not permit prolonged skin contact with fresh concrete, and keep it out of the eyes. This means that everyone should wear safety goggles while working with plastic concrete. Goggles will also help protect the eyes from blown cement dust. It's a good idea to wear protective clothing. Waterproof work gloves, long pants, and a long-sleeve shirt will help protect the skin. And anyone wading in the fresh concrete should have boots, too. It is a good idea to wear a hard hat (as for any construction).

Concrete tends to absorb moisture and dry out the skin. Moreover, the sand in concrete is abrasive. If skin should come into contact with wet concrete directly or with concrete-soaked clothing, rinse off both skin and clothing well. After washing, a lanolin hand cream will help relieve mild skin irritation and dryness. If you experience severe skin discomfort, see a doctor.

Concrete Placement

Have all your forms securely in place and well braced. They should be oiled to help them strip cleanly later.

CONSTRUCTION JOINTS IN THICK CONCRETE

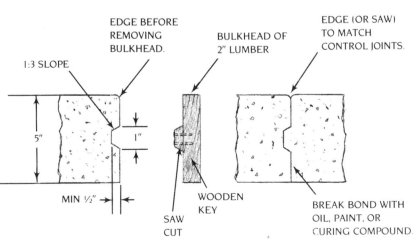

The construction joint is used where work will resume another day. When the form is removed, the tapered keyway leaves a groove that receives a tongue of concrete during placement of the next slab. This mechanical bond helps transfer loads and thus helps prevent faulting.

Left photo: The subgrade should be dampened before placing concrete on it. This prevents a dry subgrade from stealing mix water from the concrete. Nevertheless, there should be no puddles, mud, frozen soil, or wet or soft areas. Right photo: The first batch of concrete should be placed in a corner, full depth and as close to its final position as possible. Avoid dumping and raking or shoveling the concrete into place. Such overworking tends to separate the aggregates and bring water and fine materials to the surface.

All your tools, including a wheelbarrow with rubber tire and access ramps, should be ready. See that your curing materials are on hand, ready to apply.

Just before placement of concrete, the subgrade or subbase should be dampened by spraying it with water from a garden hose. This prevents the subbase from drawing water out of the fresh mix when placed. Avoid creating puddles. A sand subbase should never be really wetted, just dampened; wetting causes sand to bulk up and then shrink on drying, letting the slab settle and encouraging cracks to develop.

Begin concreting by placing the first batch of concrete full-depth against the forms in one corner of the project. Place the concrete as nearly in its final position as you can. This helps to consolidate the mix in place. If the concrete must be moved, push it using a shovel with a flat end. Subsequent batches should be dumped against the earlier ones to help consolidate them.

The less moving of plastic concrete, the better. Spreading may be done by pushing with flat-end shovels or with concrete rakes, which are hoelike tools. But do not use a garden rake or garden hoe on concrete: they cause segregation.

Avoid watering down the mix to make it flow into the forms. If concrete flows, it contains far too much water. Don't let water collect along the forms. Any water that shows up in the corners of forms should be pushed over the sides by filling the forms with concrete beneath the puddle.

Place enough concrete to overfill the forms slightly. This takes a good eye. Overfilled forms that allow for some settlement are better than underfilled forms.

Consolidate the mix further by spading it with a short-handled, flat-end shovel all along the forms. To do this, hold the shovel vertically and plunge it repeatedly into the mix next to the forms. Minimize

Consolidate the mix along the forms by chunking it with a flat-end shovel.

walking in the concrete (although some walking may be unavoidable). To protect your feet when walking in concrete, wear rubber boots. *Never* try it barefooted.

Strikeoff

Strike off the concrete surface across the tops of the forms. This step goes right along with placement, without waiting between.

Strikeoff consolidates the concrete and levels it with the forms. It is done with a long, straight 2×4 strikeboard laid across the forms and see-sawed back and forth. (Handling a strikeoff of more than 6 feet in width is a two-person job.) The strikeboard's ends rest on the forms. With each sawing motion, move the strikeboard forward an inch or two, keeping a little concrete ahead of the strikeboard to fill in low spots. The strikeboard should be about 2 feet longer than the distance between forms.

Strike off twice. On the first pass, cover about 30 inches, tilting the strikeboard forward to make a cutting edge that slices off excess concrete and leaves the surface flush with the tops of the forms. On the second pass, tilt the strikeboard backward so that its leading edge is raised or else use it held straight up.

This helps to even out bumps and ridges left by the first pass.

If a low spot develops beneath the strikeboard, put a shovel of concrete in it and back up and strike off over it. If too much concrete builds up in front of the strikeboard, shovel the excess away, back up a bit, and begin again.

If you are using air-entrained concrete, you'll notice a round, plump roll forming ahead of the strikeboard. This is typical, telling you that the desired air content is there.

Initial Floating

Immediately after strikeoff, you can begin the next prefinishing step, initial floating. For air-entrained concrete, you should begin immediately. The purpose of initial floating is to smooth out the ridges left by the strikeboard, as well as to embed all pieces of aggregate slightly below the surface. Initial floating smooths, shapes, and levels the surface, and brings up a small amount of cement paste for subsequent finishing operations. Try not to overwork the surface at this delicate early stage.

HOW TO STRIKE OFF A SLAB

USING A BULLFLOAT

The bullfloat is a good initial-finishing tool. It can be rented or made according to plans on page 139. In the left-hand photo, concrete-finishing instructor Jerry Woods shows how to first push the bullfloat out over the surface of the slab, holding the handle low to raise the bullfloat's leading edge. In the right-hand photo, Woods pulls the bullfloat back with the handle high to raise the leading edge. Each pass should lap the previous by half. (Roth/Woods project photo)

Hold a darby flat against the surface and work it right to left and back again, adding a slight sawing motion.

Initial floating is done with a special tool, either with a darby or a bullfloat. Which tool you use depends on whether you can reach all parts of the surface without walking on it. If you can reach all parts and working room is limited, use the darby. Otherwise, do the initial floating with a bullfloat. You can make, buy, or rent a bullfloat. The bullfloat is moved across the surface of the concrete, first pushing it, then pulling it. Each time, the leading edge is raised to prevent digging in. No downward force need be exerted. The tool's own weight (whether it is wood or metal) provides enough pressure.

Judging Readiness

Before further finishing, wait for the bleed water to disappear from the slab surface and for the concrete to stiffen somewhat. The length of the waiting period depends on many things. Cool, damp weather tends to extend the waiting period. Under these conditions, your rest break may be several hours. If it is, clean the tools. Wind, sunshine on the slab, and hot, dry weather all tend to shorten the waiting period. Under these conditions, your rest break may be quite brief—or even nonexistent!

Never start the initial hand-floating while the surface is glossy: the water sheen and all bleed water should have left the surface, which should look dull. Avoid the temptation to dust portland cement on the surface to help dry it up. This is a sure way to build in surface problems later on. Test to see whether the concrete is getting properly stiff by putting foot pressure on the surface. Do it in the portion you placed first, which is likely to be the first part to begin stiffening. The boot should leave no more than a ¼-inch depression, which you can smooth over.

Air-entrained concrete does not bleed, and therefore requires very little or no waiting before further finishing. Nevertheless, the lack of bleed water does not mean that air-entrained concrete is setting. Make an impression test to see whether it is properly stiff before you proceed with hand-floating.

Edging

During the waiting period, you can use your time by cutting the slab away from its forms with a margin trowel or pointing trowel. Use the same tool to scrape deposits of cement paste from the tops of the forms.

Even before the slab is ready for floating, you may begin edging it. Edging creates chip-free, contoured edges all around the forms and along any isolation or construction joints. The edger's flat blade also compacts the surface next to the forms where floats and trowels have trouble working. Edging and jointing may start as soon as the concrete is stiff enough to retain the edge. If the edges hold their shape when the tool is run along the forms, you can proceed. You may even be able to get the first edging and jointing out of the way before the slab is ready for floating.

Hold the edger with the curved side against the form and move it back and forth along the edge until a finished edge is produced. All aggregate particles should be covered. Since the concrete is still quite

Left photo: An early finishing step is the cutting of concrete away from its forms. Do this with a margin or pointing trowel, slicing an inch deep between the forms and the slab. This keeps the slab from bonding to its forms, possibly causing edge cracks in the slab when it shrinks. Right photo: Edging is done with a curved-bladed edging tool, holding it against the form and sliding it forward, then backward, raising its leading edge slightly to prevent it from digging into the surface.

Leave-in forms are edged, too. Edge the corners; then continue in the other direction. The marks left by the edger will be removed during hand-floating. If you want the marks in, you must edge again after final floating or troweling.

soft, be careful not to press too firmly, or the edger will leave a depression around the slab that may be tough to remove later.

Two or three rounds of edging may be needed to produce a neat, finished slab edge. The edges need not be perfectly smooth after the first run. The purpose of the first run is to force pieces of coarse aggregate out of the way. Subsequent edgings will smooth more.

Control-jointing

Along with or right after edging, tool-in the control joints (unless you are using leave-in forms as control joints or wire mesh reinforcement with pavers to avoid need for control joints). It helps to have someone work with you to snap lines across the slab between form marks to show where control joints go.

To make a tooled control joint, lay down a guide board—1 × 4 or wider—and then hold the jointing tool against the guide board, pressing down into the surface until the flat part of the tool rests on the slab. Then slide it forward, putting pressure on the rear. Run it back to shape and smooth the joint further. (A single-ended jointer will have to be turned around.) If the concrete is too stiff for easy blade penetration, you

can use a hatchet or axe blade to start the joint. But finish with the jointing tool.

Hand-floating

When the surface is ready, hand-float the slab. (Hand-floating pushes large pieces of aggregate slightly below the surface, smooths off any imperfections and roughness left by initial floating, and consolidates the cement paste at the surface, ready for any subsequent finishing. It leaves an even-textured surface. Floating also removes surface marks left by edging and jointing. (If you want the "framed-picture" marks there, make a final edging and jointing after floating.) Be sure to use a magnesium hand float for floating air-entrained concrete. A magnesium float is easier to move than wood; you will like it on either plain or air-entrained concrete.

To float a slab, hold the hand float flat against the surface and move it with slight sawing movements as you sweep it in broad overlapping arcs. Floating fills in holes as well as cuts off lumps and ridges. Float right over your edges and joints, removing the "picture-frame" marks they leave, and then rerun them.

Kneeboards. If the slab is large, it may be nec-

MAKING CONTROL JOINTS

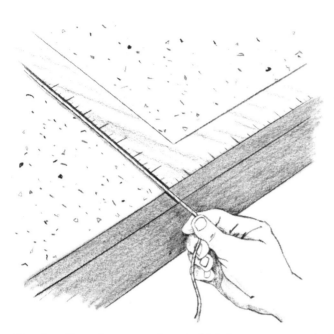

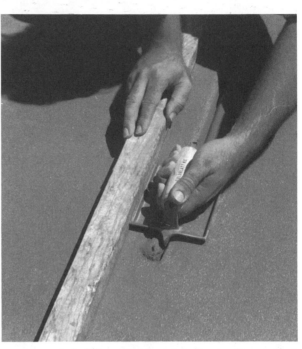

Drawing: To make squared control joints, use a carpenter's square and chalkline. Photo: A jointing tool is worked like an edger, except that you need a guide board, placed half the tool's width from the desired joint. Move the jointing tool forward and backward to cut the joint.

A long 1 × 10 board, offset slightly from the desired control joint, can serve both as a guide for the jointing tool and as your access platform. (Roth/Woods project photo)

FLOATS: WOOD VS. MAGNESIUM

Two types of hand-floats may be applied. The wood float (*left*) may be used on plain concrete, but it tends to tear air-entrained concrete. The magnesium float (*right*) is excellent on either plain or air-entrained concrete. It leaves a gritty surface that is excellent for outdoor purposes.

essary to get onto it for edging, jointing, floating, and subsequent troweling. For this you'll want a pair of kneeboards. With the kneeboards spaced apart, your knees can rest on one kneeboard, your toes on the other. To cushion your knees, as well as protect them from the alkaline concrete, you may want to wear strap-on waterproof kneepads. When using kneeboards, always work from the middle of the slab backwards to the edges to finish over the marks made by the kneeboards.

To change position from kneeboards, climb onto one kneeboard, pick the other up, and drop it at the next location.

If you have two sets of tools, two workers can float at once, one working from kneeboards in the middle of the slab and the other working around the slab edges from outside the forms.

If any pieces of aggregate get in the way of edging, jointing, or floating, either push them down into the surface or pick them out with the corner of a tool. A little extra cement paste can often be scraped from the tops of the forms and used for hole-filling.

A float-finished surface may be exactly what you want for outdoor use, especially if a magnesium float is used. Float-finishing leaves a gritty, nonskid texture that's fairly easy to clean. If you like this, then no further finishing is necessary. Any float marks can be removed by gentle brooming (see the next chapter).

Steel-troweling

The steel-troweled finish is too slippery to make a good outdoor surface unless it is broomed. However, the combination of steel-troweling and brooming (see next chapter) makes a fine patio finish. Steel-troweling should follow hand-floating without any wait in between. Often, both operations are done consecutively in one spot before moving to the next. This way, both the hand float and the steel trowel can be carried with you. Use a large steel trowel measuring about 18 × 4¾ inches, though a midsize 14 × 4-inch trowel is okay. Hold the trowel blade flat against the surface and trowel in broad, sweeping arcs, overlapping about half-way for double coverage. If steel-troweling brings

SUPPORTS DURING FLOATING

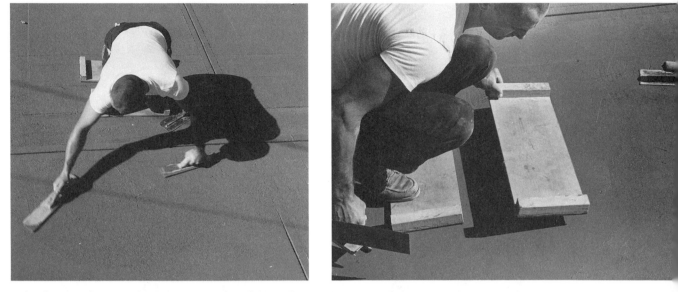

Left photo: When reaching out over the slab to float it from an edge or from kneeboards, you can support yourself with your other hand on an extra float. Later, float over the depression the second float caused. Right photo: Kneeboards are easy to make. A pair of kneeboards lets you move onto the slab for floating, jointing, and troweling. (Roth/Woods project photos)

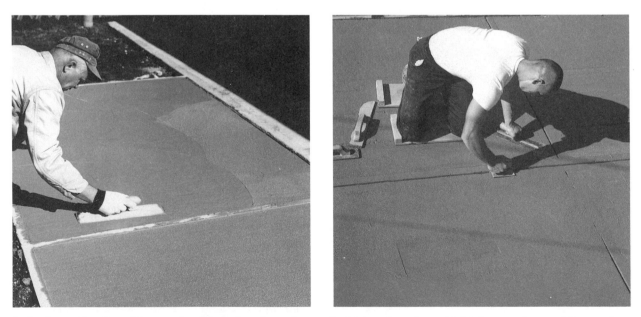

Left photo: Smaller slabs can be floated and steel-troweled from the edges. Hold the steel trowel flat against the surface. Angling it creates ripples that can never be troweled out (Cement and Concrete Association photo). Right photo: Floating and troweling over previously tooled edges and joints partially fills them, so you will want to rerun them. You won't need a guide board for jointer reruns because the tool will follow the groove. (Roth/Woods project photo)

water and fine materials to the surface, wait for the concrete to gain additional stiffness.

One steel-troweling is all that outdoor concrete should receive. Follow by texturing with a stiff broom.

Cleaning Up

With water, clean the trowels, floats, edgers, jointers, strikeboard, screed boards, wheelbarrow, concrete mixer, and other tools. Hard deposits may need wire brushing. Don't forget to scrape off the tops of leave-in forms. During washup, brush the materials into a pile, letting the water flow away. When the water has drained, the pile of solids can be shoveled into a barrel and disposed of. It's best to do this before the pile hardens.

Concrete Finishing in a Nutshell

- Strike off as you place
- Wait for bleed water to disappear
- Darby or bullfloat
- Cut slab away from its forms
- Do first edging and control-jointing
- Make ¼-inch indentation test for stiffening
- Hand-float
- Rerun edges and joints if necessary
- Steel-trowel if desired
- Rerun edges and joints if necessary
- Give textured finish if desired
- Clean up
- Moist-cure

MOIST-CURING

No step is more important to making quality concrete than moist-curing. Concrete gains most of its strength during the first few days of hardening—soon after you place it—yet it keeps on getting harder, stronger, and more durable for many years. Once concrete dries out, though, the hardening process slows greatly. So to make your concrete as strong and durable as possible, keep it damp for seven days after construction. This is called *moist-curing*.

Think of it this way: if you spend a lot of money for the ready mix to make a patio but fail to cure it, you're getting less than half your money's worth.

Any system that keeps the slab moist for a seven-day period will allow it to cure. Surface-curing methods include continuous sprinkling, covering with plastic sheeting weighted down around the edges, covering with clean sand kept wet, and curing using a curing compound. Waiting for several days to strip the forms helps, too. In any case, partial drying during the curing period should be avoided.

A fine method of curing a patio slab is with a spray-on membrane curing compound, available either in wax-base or resin-base (both effective). If you use a curing compound on a patio slab that is to receive hard-set pavers later, be sure to use a resin-base compound, which leaves no gummy residue. Wax-base curing compounds fail on this score.

Application of curing compound goes easiest with

CONCRETE CURING TIMES

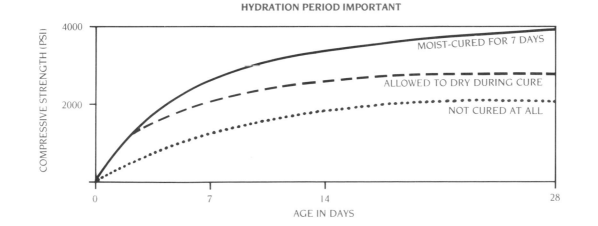

HYDRATION PERIOD IMPORTANT

MOIST-CURED FOR 7 DAYS

ALLOWED TO DRY DURING CURE

NOT CURED AT ALL

COMPRESSIVE STRENGTH (PSI)

4000

2000

0   7   14   28

AGE IN DAYS

APPLYING CURING COMPOUND

Left photo: Spray-curing is one of the easiest methods of curing. It employs membrane curing compound, poured into a compression-type garden sprayer and applied evenly over the entire slab. Right photo: You can also apply curing compound with a roller, but this takes longer on a large project. Apply compound like paint. Cleanup is usually with water.

a pump-up garden compression sprayer. Start spraying within 15 to 30 minutes after the final finishing—no more. No standing water should be on the surface. Cleanup of the sprayer is usually with water.

Spray-on membrane curing compounds are available from concrete products dealers. The compound should be marked ASTM C156 and C309, indicating that it meets U.S. national standards. Look for those numbers on the label. Some curing compounds should be diluted before use. Be sure to follow the label directions.

The Drying Out Period
Concrete that will be exposed to freezing and thawing or to deicing chemicals needs to cure, then dry out, for at least four weeks before a heavy frost hits. This applies to air-entrained concrete as well. For this reason, you may wish to avoid applying a curing compound late in the year. If so, use another method that gets air-drying started sooner.

HOT- AND COLD-WEATHER CONCRETING

On a hot, dry, breezy day, concrete can harden too quickly for you to finish it. Sunshine on the slab greatly increases the risk. The concrete surface can stiffen so fast that if you haven't floated it completely within minutes, you're out of luck. On a cold day, on the other hand, it can take into the night for the concrete to stiffen enough to be ready for final finishing. And subsequent cold weather may subject the slab to too-early freezing. Plan ahead to avoid such problems.

Hot-weather Concreting
If the temperature is likely to go to 85 degrees F-plus (30 degrees C), postpone the project until a better day.

That's the safest approach. (Be sure to give a ready-mix dealer as much notice as you can.) Another option is to start concrete placement at dawn. Then you can be well into the finishing process before the hottest part of the day. Another strategy is to delay starting until late afternoon, which delays finishing into the cooler evening hours. If you decide to go ahead as planned, at least have an extra helper or two with tools on hand to move the finishing along rapidly. Here are other aids for hot-weather concrete work.

- Dampen the subgrade and forms well before you start.
- Ask your ready-mix producer about putting crushed ice into the mix as part of the mixing water to cool it—at extra cost, of course. (If the producer suggests adding a retarder, say no, thanks.)
- Put up windbreaks and sunshades.
- Lay a temporary covering such as a plastic sheet over the slab, uncovering only the part you're working on. Or apply a light fog spray to keep the surface cool and prevent rapid evaporation of mix water.

Cold-weather Concreting

The most successful cold-weather concrete advice is to wait for warmer weather. Weather too cold for fresh concrete is also too cold for pleasant working. Never place concrete on frozen ground. Settling and damage are sure to result when the ground later thaws.

Concrete's strength-gain is slowed by cold temperatures. For example, concrete cured at 33 degrees F (1 degree C) has only two thirds the strength of concrete cured at 72 degrees F (22 degrees C). In any case, make sure the slab's temperature does not fall below 50 degrees F (22 degrees C).

Chemical Deicers. Using chemical deicers on concrete that has not had a chance to dry out can cause damage. Air-entrained concrete resists deicer damage. If your concrete is not air-entrained, the extent of damage is likely to depend on the chemical applied, its concentration, and the frequency of application.

The least-harmful deicers are sodium chloride (halite, table salt, or rock salt), calcium chloride, and urea. From every standpoint except cost, urea is the best deicer. It has no harmful effect on concrete and neither hurts vegetation nor corrodes reinforcing steel.

You should avoid using ammonium nitrate and ammonium sulfate. While these are beneficial to plants, they are murder on concrete.

All deicers act by lowering the freezing point of water on the surface of the slab. How much the freezing point is lowered depends on the concentration of deicer. Some generate heat when applied, which helps them to melt ice and snow. Snow accumulations deeper than 2 inches should be removed, because deicers cannot handle much snow.

If you can do so safely, avoid using any deicers during the slab's first winter. Instead of applying a chemical deicer, spread dry sand on ice to make the slab slip-resistant. If a deicer must be used the first year, apply a clear concrete sealer to the dry slab surface. Follow label directions.

Final Note

Making, placing, and curing quality concrete may seem to take more effort than following the usual "pour-a-slab" methods we've all used at one time or another, and perhaps it does. But I can tell you that watching your project survive where so many others fail makes it well worth the extra care.

In cold, damp weather, concrete can take a long time to stiffen. This may keep you working into the night, which is okay as long as the slab's temperature stays above 50 degrees F.

CHAPTER **7**

MAKING CONCRETE LOOK GREAT

Most concrete is plain and gray. Why? Because regular Type 2 portland cement is plain and gray. Besides, ordinary finishing leaves concrete with no design or pattern. Yet concrete is a versatile material and need be neither plain nor gray. Instead, it can be made in an unlimited number of colors and surface textures, traditional or contemporary. If you build concrete plain and gray, it should be because you *want* it that way.

Textures may be finished in, tooled in, or incised as the final part of the finishing process. The accompanying table lists some of the more popular concrete textures.

Colors can be imparted by any of four methods: integral one-course coloring, integral two-course coloring, dry-shake coloring, or painting.

HOW TO MAKE TEXTURED FINISHES

Concrete finishing designs may be grouped as textured finishes, tooled-in patterns, and surface-exposure finishes. Since pattern-stamping and surface exposure are invariably combined with concrete coloring, they will be covered later in this chapter.

Remember that whatever textured finish is chosen, an outdoor slab needs to be both walkable and cleanable. It should also drain well.

The concrete finishes covered here require only a beginner's skill. One nice thing about most textured treatments is they call for little more effort than finishing a plain, once-troweled concrete slab. A few finishes, such as pattern-stamping, involve additional work, but they are well worth the extra effort.

Any texturing of a slab will improve its slip-resistance. On the negative side, increased slip-resistance

Textured Finishes and Surface Designs

Textured Finishes
Floated
Swirled
Broomed
Stippled
Burlap-drag
Rock-salt

Tooled-in Patterns
Leaf imprint
Tin-can
Cookie-cutter
Geometric
Tooled flagstone
Impressed
Pattern-stamped

Surface Exposure
Exposed-aggregate
Rustic terrazzo

The patio pattern shows colored-concrete sections that had been formed-off. This chapter will show you how to do many color and texture variations based on this concept. (Portland Cement Association photo)

To make it feel cooler, this patio was given a beige color through the dry-shake coloring process described on pages 208–211.

brings increased sweep-resistance. The hardest-to-sweep surface is exposed-aggregate.

Floated Patterns

Considerable visual interest can be added to floated finishes by pattern-floating—moving the float (wooden or magnesium) in patterns during the final floating. If you use a wooden float, choose only a broken-in float. Magnesium floats do not need breaking-in. The patterns may be swirls, uniform overlapping arcs (loose or tight), or lapped-over zigzags or twists. To produce these effects, hold the float flat on the surface. Try a few different patterns and see which you and your family like best.

Pattern-floating is done during the second hand-floating, after the initial floating in the normal manner. The second floating should, of course, be the final one. Pattern-floating can begin when all surface shine from the first hand-floating is gone and the surface appears dull. The appearance can be controlled by timing, that is, by how long you wait for additional stiffening after the surface water disappears. The softer the concrete, the more pronounced the patterning. The stiffer it is, the more subtle the patterning.

The coarsest textures are made by wooden or tex-ture-faced floats. Magnesium floats will produce what is known as medium textures.

Swirled Finishes

A swirled finish produces a fine, nonslip matte surface. The true swirled finish is done with a steel trowel, which produces a smoother texture than either a wooden or a metal float. Wait for the surface shine to disappear after the first steel-troweling and for the concrete to develop enough stiffness to give the appearance you like. Experiment on the first-placed section of slab.

To make swirls, hold a broken-in steel trowel—not a new one—flat on the surface and move it in semicircular or fanlike motions, always with the trowel pointed in the same direction. As you progress to fresh parts of the slab, the semicircles will overlap, creating the swirled effect. The diameter of the semi-circles described with the trowel determines the effect. For the best overall effect, work across the slab and back again, lapping the previous pass part-way. Keep going from one side to the other. Swirls may be arranged in rows or staggered, whichever effect you prefer.

On wide slabs, you will have to work from knee-boards, so plan your progress to swirl over the knee-

Left photo: Wiggling the broom as you pull it toward you produces an attractive wavy texture. The pattern is affected by the amount of side-to-side broom movement. Be sure to pattern consistently throughout the slab (Portland Cement Association photo). Right photo: A sponge float produces a coarse, sandpaperlike texture. This tool also removes the marks left by hand-floating.

Left photo: Large overlapping swirls made with a float or trowel produce this effect. Adjust the arc for desired effect. Right photo: A stiff-bristled broom makes a coarse-grained texture on this just-floated slab. Giving the concrete more time to stiffen would yield less texture. (Portland Cement Association photos)

board marks left by previous passes. If the edges of the trowel dig in, the trowel is not sufficiently broken-in for successful swirling.

Broomed Finishes

Simply brooming a once-troweled surface lightly with a soft-bristled concrete-texturing brush (*not* a stiff garage-cleaning broom) will cut surface gloss. Do this immediately after troweling, or a bit later, when it produces just the desired effect. The surface should not be wet when brushed.

The full-fledged broomed finish goes one step beyond steel troweling and has a more pronounced effect than simple reduced-gloss finishing. It is done not only to increase slip-resistance but to impart an interesting pattern. The texture achieved depends on the stiffness of the concrete and the stiffness of the broom used. Early brooming with a stiff broom produces a coarse texture. Late brooming with a soft broom produces a fine texture as for reduced-gloss finishing. Downward pressure applied to the end of the broom also has an effect: obviously, the more pressure, the more texture.

After the slab has been hand-floated or steel-troweled, experiment on the first-placed portion. Start as soon as the shine leaves the surface, noting the effect.

A soft-bristled broom etches a fine-grained texture into this just-floated slab. Waiting longer for surface stiffening would produce an even finer texture. (Roth/ Woods project photo)

Too rough? Wait a bit and try again. Too smooth? Apply pressure to the broom and get going before the increasing stiffness of the concrete decides the texture for you. Or switch to a stiffer broom.

For a softer finish, and to keep the bristles from collecting cement paste, the broom is normally wetted and shaken once or twice to rid it of excess water before each stroke. A wheelbarrow filled with water

Left photo: A thicker, many-bristled texturing brush requires fewer passes to texture the surface of a slab. Note here how Jerry Woods' brooming removes marks left by earlier floating and troweling (Roth/Woods project photo). Right photo: A skinny concrete-texturing broom has 2¼-inch bristles. It creates surfaces that are fine-textured (Portland Cement Association photo).

will serve as a water container. If you don't like the damp-bristles effect, try brooming dry.

Most brooming is done either pushing or pulling the broom—but not both, because the two methods create different textures.

You may choose among many ways of working the broom, each creating a particular effect. Broom transversely, longitudinally, or diagonally; make straight lines, curved lines, or wavy lines; try zigzags, crisscrosses (done checkerboard-style with sectioned-off smaller slabs).

Of course, it's important to impart uniform and consistent textures to the project. Better not to texture at all than to end up with a variety of textures in the same project.

Rock-salt Finishes

In nonfreezing climates, the rock-salt finish is popular, especially for sidewalks. In freezing climates, the water that collects in the holes left by the rock salt freezes and breaks up the surface. Hence, the rock-salt finish should not be used on concrete subject to freezing.

Pockmarked texture (*left and right slabs*) is created by spreading rock salt over the surface, then troweling it in. Later washout leaves the pockmarks.

To make a rock-salt finish, cast rock salt over the soft surface just before hand-floating. Keep in mind that where a chunk of rock salt gets impressed, there will be a hole in the finished slab. Spread the rock salt sparingly, with perhaps several pieces of rock salt per square yard, or profusely with several chunks per square foot. Push the pieces into the surface by hand-floating. Get them flush with but not below the surface. Steel-troweling, brooming, or whatever else you wish to do to texture the concrete must be done without disturbing the rock salt. Cure as usual.

The first rain will dissolve the rock salt, leaving interesting pockmarks over your slab. Your friends will ask how you did it. Tell them it took lots of skill.

TOOLED-IN TREATMENTS

By pushing or troweling patterned objects into the soft concrete surface, you can make incised designs. The most common choice is leaf imprints, but other possibilities abound. Wooden house-number cutouts can be used. Or family members' names may be spelled out. Tin cans of various sizes are another common incised treatment, and cookie cutters make interesting designs. The accompanying photos show several techniques you can employ to incise patterns into your concrete.

A word of advice: a little incising goes a long way. Incising is easy to overdo. Think about it. An entire patio of tin-can circles may not be what you want. Just an edging might be preferable. Test your idea, if you like, on an existing patio by dipping the incising tools in carpenter's powdered chalk and imprinting with them. The chalk prints, unlike incised concrete, may easily be rinsed away with a garden hose.

Tooled-in Flagstone Effects

Tooled-in flagstone patterns are more natural-looking. The flagstone effect may be created on the solid slab by tooling in "joints." These remain as grooves in the surface of the slab, separating the "flagstones."

Begin tooling right after bullfloating or darbying, when the surface water has evaporated. Don't wait until the surface gets too stiff: it must be soft so that the coarse aggregate at the surface will move aside for the tool. Score in random flagstone designs with a

Left photo: Leaves (one tree leaf under the trowel and barely visible here) can be troweled into a slab's surface, then peeled away, leaving fossil-like impressions. The narrow end of a trowel embeds the leaves flush with the surface (Portland Cement Association photo). Right photo: You can make patterns to impress into soft concrete, thus customizing a slab. With a knife, you can cut the pattern from roofing paper. During hand-floating, embed your pattern, using a metal float or trowel to make the cutout flush with the surface. After the concrete has set, remove the cutout. (Sakrete photo)

MAKING A RANDOM FLAGSTONE PATTERN

Left photo: To make a random flagstone pattern, first score the floated surface while it is still soft, using an S-shaped length of copper tubing. Try to make the "stones" look as much like real flagstones as possible. Right photo: Hand-floating and troweling will clean up the burred edges where you scored the surface. The flagstone effect is most convincing if the slab is colored by the dry-shake method, discussed on pages 208–211. (Portland Cement Association photos)

Left photo: You can clean up the scores with a large paint brush. Then moist-cure the slab, as for any concrete. Right photo: The finished sidewalk looks much like random flagstone. Note the straight control joint.

shaped ½ × 18-inch or ¾ × 18-inch copper tubing. Try to shape the edges to look as much like natural flagstone edges as possible. The tool will leave the edges of the grooves burred, but that's okay.

Do no more until the surface is ready for its normal hand-floating. Float the surface, then run the grooves again with your S-shaped tool to smooth them further. Finally, when ready, trowel carefully. Follow up with a light brushing to remove the burrs. The joints may be touched up with a dampened paint brush.

MAKING COLORED CONCRETE

Coloring concrete reduces the glare from direct sun on a slab. It works wonderfully with air-entrained concrete. The most lasting and most satisfactory way to color a concrete slab is to add a color pigment to the concrete mix. Using concrete color pigments, you can make a slab any color or shade you wish. The colored concrete may be placed in one course or two courses.

For one-course coloring, an integral color pigment is added to the concrete mix and the resulting colored concrete is placed full-depth in the slab. The one-course method puts color all the way through a slab. But this method requires lots of color pigment. It's not economical, especially for the lighter, brighter colors. Enter two-course coloring. Two-course coloring puts the color only in the top portion of a slab and is the more economical way to get color. The two-course method is to place a plain gray slab base and then top it with a thin integrally colored course. Most of the slab—the base course—is plain gray. While the two-course method requires more effort, it economizes greatly on coloring pigment.

Still less costly is dry-shake coloring. A color-pigment mixture is dusted onto the slab's surface during finishing and is floated in. Only ¼ inch or so deep, the color layer is on the surface, where it shows. Dry-shake coloring is effective for many purposes.

Concrete Color Pigments

Color pigments are fine powders meant for use in concrete and mortar. Most are either natural or synthetic mineral oxides. Organic pigments are not used in concrete, because they weaken it. Neither are food colors, fabric dyes, or paint pigments.

You can get suitable concrete color pigments in 1-, 5-, and 50-pound bags from a concrete products or terrazzo supplies dealer. The pigments generally are not expensive: blue and green are exceptions, costing more than earth colors such as brown and red.

Avoid the following color pigments: Prussian blue (it disappears in time), chrome green (a mixture of chrome yellow and Prussian blue; it fades), chrome yellow (it fades), and bone black (its soluble salts leave a powdery whitish dust on the surface). Don't confuse chrome green with green chromium oxide, which is a fine concrete-coloring pigment.

THREE WAYS TO COLOR CONCRETE

ONE-COURSE INTEGRALLY COLORED

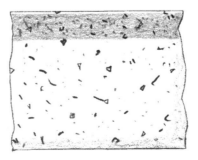

TWO-COURSE INTEGRALLY COLORED

DRY-SHAKE COLORED

Color pigment comes in 1-, 5-, and 50-pound bags. For approximate coloring, you can volume-batch it into the mixer, as here with a can. But the most accurate color-batching is by weight.

Carbon black and wettable lampblack, while hard to handle, are okay. The table "Concrete Coloring Pigments" shows the pigments and suggested amounts. Be aware, though, that black is the toughest color to make and maintain. Often, a blue-black color results. When the slab becomes damp, soluble salts in the black concrete bleed out, causing a whitish haze called *efflorescence* to stand out on the dark surface. Although treatment with dilute muriatic acid will remove it, the efflorescence may reappear again and again. It's best to be satisfied with a dark gray slab that looks black when wet rather than to aim for jet black when dry.

How Much Pigment?   Color pigments should be proportioned by weight. This is the only certain way of getting uniformity of color, batch to batch. The amount of pigment added to a concrete mix is calculated as a percentage of the weight of cement in the mix. The usual proportions are from 1 to 10 percent color pigment by weight of cement. Never use more than this, because too much pigment can weaken the concrete. For example, for each 94-pound bag of cement, you'd want to use at most 9.4 pounds of color pigment. Some pigments, particularly black, are more potent than others, and less of them is needed.

White Cement.   Using plain gray portland cement with colored concrete grays the colors. For dark gray, dark brown, and black concrete, this is no problem. But for clean pastels, white portland cement must be used. White cement is sold by the same dealers who carry the coloring pigments. It costs about

CONCRETE COLORING PIGMENTS

Desired Color	Commercial Name of Pigment	QUANTITY TO TRY (% BY WGT. OF CEMENT)		
		Pastel*	Light Shade	Medium Color
White	No pigment. White portland cement, white sand			
Black, blue-black, gray	Black iron oxide	—	1	2
	Carbon black and wettable lampblack	—	½	1
	Black manganese oxide	—	1	2
Brown to reddish brown	Metallic brown oxide	1½	5	10
Brownish red, dull brick red	Red iron oxide	1½	5	10
Bright red, vermilion	Mineral turkey red	1½	5	10
Pink	Red iron oxide	½		
Red sandstone, purplish red	Indian red	1½	5	10
Buffs, yellow, cream	Yellow ochre	1½	5	10
	Yellow oxide	1	2	4
Green	Chromium oxide green	1½	5	10
	Greenish-blue ultramarine	2	6	—
Blue	Ultramarine blue	1½	5	10

* Use white portland cement.

twice what you'll pay for normal gray portland cement. Proportioning and everything else is the same for white portland cement as for regular cement.

White cement mixed with normally beige-colored and brown sand makes varying shades of cream, yellow, and buff. If a true white or a light-pastel concrete is wanted, white silica sand should be used instead of ordinary sand to avoid the beige and brown undertones. Silica sand, which looks like table salt, can be found at concrete products suppliers and at many lumber yards.

Using Pigments. For integrally colored concrete, color pigments are added to the concrete mix in the mixer drum along with the aggregates and cement. The pigments can also be used in hand-mixed concrete or added to a ready-packaged mix. Maintaining exact proportions of cement, color pigment, and water is essential. Because the quantities are minute, a postal scale or baby scale is handy for pigment proportioning.

How much color pigment to use depends on whether you are working with a natural pigment or a synthetic pigment (ask your dealer). With a natural pigment, as a good starting point, if you are after pleasing pastels, use the equivalent of 1½ percent coloring pigment in white cement (except for ultramarine pigment, which generally requires 2 percent); for more color, try 5 percent; for fully saturated colors, use 7 percent. With a synthetic pigment, for pastel colors, try ½ to 1 percent pigment with white cement, and twice that with gray cement; for richer hues—which cannot be obtained with natural pigments—try 4 to 10 percent synthetic pigment in gray cement.

As with artists' paints, pigments of varying colors may be combined to produce custom colors. For example, to get a yellowish green, mix green chromium oxide with a small amount of yellow oxide. But you must test to know what color you'll get.

Color-testing Samples. Because mixing a full batch is wasteful for color-testing, mix small test batches in a coffee can, using an old screwdriver as a mixing tool.

Suppose you wonder what a 7-percent color mix would look like. Using a postal scale, weigh out half an ounce of the desirable color pigment and add it to 7 ounces of cement (0.5 is very close to 7 percent of 7). Since sand has some effect on a pastel color, it should be used in such a test. Try 2¼ times as much sand as cement, or 15¾ ounces of sand in our example. Coarse aggregate has so little effect on color that it may be omitted from the tests. Mix in just enough water for workability, then put the test mix into a mold and strike it off.

This 1-inch length of PVC plastic drainage pipe was slit up one side with a saw. It makes an excellent form for color test samples. The pipe is peeled off the hardened sample for reuse.

I've found that a great way to cast color samples is in 1-inch-long cutoffs of 3- or 4-inch PVC plastic pipes, with each mold split vertically by sawing for easy peel-away from the hardened sample.

Colors should be judged when dry. If one-day-hardened samples are fast-dried in an ordinary oven —not a microwave—set at 250 degrees F (120 degrees C), in a few hours they should be ready for color comparisons. (Such fast-drying is an awful thing to do to quality concrete, but these are just samples.)

The table "Proportioning of Color Samples" gives guidelines for the amounts of pigment, cement, and sand to use in your sample. You can work with any scale (such as a postal scale) that will accurately weigh amounts as small as half an ounce. To try a 7-percent-yellow color in white portland cement to see what it

PROPORTIONING OF COLOR SAMPLES

Percent Pigment (by wgt.)	Pigment	Cement	Sand
		AMOUNTS TO USE	
½	½ oz.	6 lb. 4 oz.	14 lb. 1 oz.
1	½ oz.	3 lb. 2 oz.	7 lb.
1½	½ oz.	2 lb. 1 oz.	4 lb. 11 oz.
5	½ oz.	10 oz.	1 lb. 6 oz.
7	½ oz.	7 oz.	1 lb.
10	1 oz.	10 oz.	1 lb. 6 oz.

looks like, find 7-percent pigment in the first column, then go across to the weights of pigment, cement, and sand for the 7-percent sample. Using figures from the table, you'd weigh out ½ ounce of yellow pigment, 7 ounces of white portland cement, and 1 pound of sand. Mix dry, add water, mix again, and then mold a 7-percent-yellow sample. It's that simple.

Proportioning a Colored Batch. Once you have a colored sample you like, the amount of color pigment you used to make it can be scaled up and applied to your trial-batch quantities from the previous chapter. For example, if you like the effect of 1½-percent pigment and your trial batch calls for 54 pounds of cement, you'd add just 0.81 pounds of color pigment—in other words, 13 ounces of color pigment per batch (1.5/100 × 54 × 16 = 12.96).

The table "Weight of Pigment Per Cubic Foot of Concrete" shows another way to do this. Look up your desired percent of pigment in the first column—1½ percent in the example. Then find the pounds of cement per cubic foot of concrete you are using from the table "Proportioning Concrete by Weight" in the previous chapter. (It depends on the maximum-size coarse aggregate you are using in your trial batch.) Let's say it's 27 pounds. Find 1½ percent in the first column of the table and read across under 27 pounds of cement per cubic foot. The table indicates that you would use 6.5 ounces of color pigment in each 27 pounds of cement to get 1½ percent pigment. Then simply multiply 6.5 ounces by the size of your batch in cubic feet and you have the weight of color pigment (in ounces) to put in the mixer drum. Say that your mixer batch size is 2½ cubic feet. Multiplying 6.5 by 2.5 gives 16.25 ounces of pigment per batch, or 1 pound ¼ ounce.

If the percentage of pigment you desire falls between two figures in the first column of the table, choose the 1-percent pigment weight figure and multiply it by the actual percent. For example, if you're looking for a 4-percent color pigment content, look up 1 percent and multiply by 4.

Color-batching a Mixer. When you mix your own colored concrete, batching the mixer or hand-mixing goes a bit differently than it does for plain concrete. The color pigment and cement should always be blended dry before any water is added. The reason for this is that the color pigment coats each particle of cement, rather than dyeing the mix. Therefore, dry-mixing of cement and pigment ensures thorough coating.

First, batch the portland cement. Then batch the color pigment. Add the coarse aggregate and sand, mixing all these ingredients dry until uniformly colored. Finally, add the water. The amount of water in colored concrete must be carefully controlled. Too much wetness makes a lighter color.

For complete blending of the color pigment, be sure to mix batches of colored concrete longer than the usual 2 minutes after adding the final ingredient.

Color-finishing. Finishing colored concrete is not much different from finishing uncolored concrete. During color-finishing, try not to trowel the surface too much, because this blotches the color. If a metal hand-float should make "burn marks" on the surface of a light-colored slab, switch to a wooden float.

Special Curing. Adequate curing is as vital to colored concrete as it is to plain. Avoid curing colored concrete with plastic sheets, because any air bubbles trapped underneath can spot the color, *permanently*. Use a curing compound. You can also cure colored concrete with a 2-inch layer of *clean*, nonstaining sand, kept wet. If you *must* use a plastic curing sheet, weigh it down evenly with a full layer of sand. Continuous wetting of the slab with a soaker hose is okay, too.

WEIGHT OF PIGMENT PER CUBIC FOOT OF CONCRETE

Desired Pigment (% by wgt.)	PIGMENT WITH CEMENT CONTENT*			
	29	27	25	24
½	2.3 oz.	2.2 oz.	2 oz.	1.9 oz.
1	4.6 oz.	4.3 oz.	4 oz.	3.8 oz.
1½	7 oz.	6.5 oz.	6 oz.	5.8 oz.
5	1 lb. 7 oz.	1 lb. 6 oz.	1 lb. 4 oz.	1 lb. 3 oz.
7	2 lb. 8 oz.	1 lb. 14 oz.	1 lb. 12 oz.	1 lb. 11 oz.
10	2 lb. 14 oz.	2 lb. 11 oz.	2 lb. 8 oz.	2 lb. 6 oz.

* Refer to the table on page 151 ("Proportioning Concrete by Weight")

Pre-weighed concrete coloring pigments can be purchased in 1-pound bags. Depending on color objective, one bag in each mixer batch might be just right.

Two-course Integral Coloring

Once mixed, integrally colored concrete may be cast full-depth (one-course method) in a slab, or used as a colored topping (two-course method). Only a lightly colored slab made with gray portland cement is economical for a full-depth slab. Cost rules out one-course construction for the clean pastel colors that call for the use of white portland cement. One-course construction should also be ruled out for rich, saturated colors of anything but the lowest-cost color pigments. The cost of the color pigment for a two-course project will be less than one fourth that required for a one-course slab.

Two-course construction consists of a plain gray concrete base struck off ½ to 1 inch below the tops of the forms and a colored topping course placed over the base and struck off flush with the forms. If properly constructed, the topping course becomes one with the base course.

The costlier the colored topping, the thinner you'll want to make it. If the topping is to be made with rich colors using white portland cement, aim for the minimum ½-inch thickness.

Total slab thickness is the sum of the two course thicknesses. For example, a 3-inch base course and a 1-inch topping course make a 4-inch-thick slab for thickness-design purposes. If a coarse aggregate is

used in the topping, pieces of aggregate will be left sticking up out of it. For this reason, any coarse aggregate used in topping concrete should have a small maximum size.

If control joints are to be eliminated, welded-wire mesh reinforcing should be used in the base slab. Otherwise, control joints must be formed in the base slab and then duplicated exactly above them in the topping.

Two-course construction may either be carried right through from beginning to end, which we'll call *same-day topping*, or split over two work sessions, with the base course cast at one time and the topping course bonded to it later. We'll call that *bonded topping*, though with either method the topping course must bond tightly to the base slab. Whichever method you choose, ready-mixed concrete may be used for the base course. Unless your ready-mix dealer can furnish the colored topping economically, which is not likely, you will need to proportion and mix that yourself.

Same-day Topping. Casting base and topping courses the same day is best. To do a two-course project all the same day, first place the base course of plain air-entrained concrete in the usual manner. Nail a template board onto the bottom of the strikeboard to strike the base off the desired distance below the tops of the forms.

To calculate how much topping concrete is needed, use the upper portion of the chart "Quantities for Sand-mix Topping." Multiply the slab's length times its width to find its square-foot area and locate this figure at the left of the chart. Suppose, for example, the slab area is 300 square feet. Lay a ruler horizontally at that level and read across where the ruler crosses the slanting line showing the thickness you've chosen for your concrete topping. Suppose, for our example, that it's ¾ inch thick. Then move straight down from the slanting line until the ruler intersects the volume scale and read the topping volume in cubic feet. In the example, it is very close to 20.6 cubic feet. Since this figure allows 10 percent for waste, this is the amount of topping concrete to mix.

The lower portion of the graph is for ordering ready-packaged sand-mix topping.

If you are using a topping mix containing a coarse aggregate, use the table "Proportioning Concrete by Weight" from the previous chapter to calculate the weights of ingredients. Since the table gives the weights of the materials for making 1 cubic foot of quality concrete, you can simply multiply each ingredient's figure by the number of cubic feet you need. In our example, using ⅜-inch maximum-size coarse aggregate, you would order 597 pounds (7 bags) of ce-

SAME-DAY COLOR TOPPING

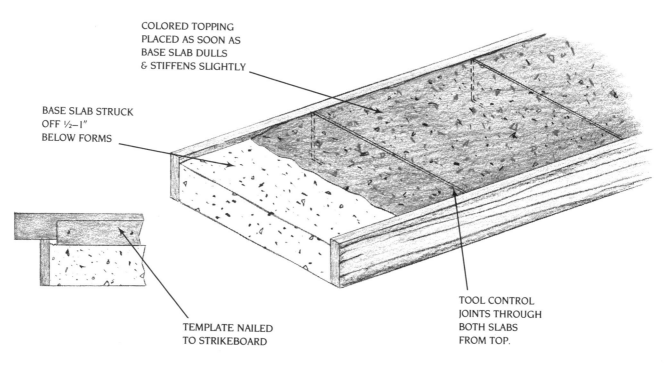

COLORED TOPPING
PLACED AS SOON AS
BASE SLAB DULLS
& STIFFENS SLIGHTLY

BASE SLAB STRUCK
OFF ½–1″
BELOW FORMS

TEMPLATE NAILED
TO STRIKEBOARD

TOOL CONTROL
JOINTS THROUGH
BOTH SLABS
FROM TOP.

QUANTITIES FOR SAND-MIX TOPPING

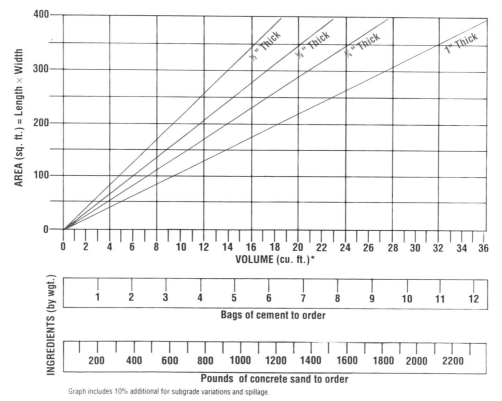

Graph includes 10% additional for subgrade variations and spillage.

BONDED COLOR TOPPING

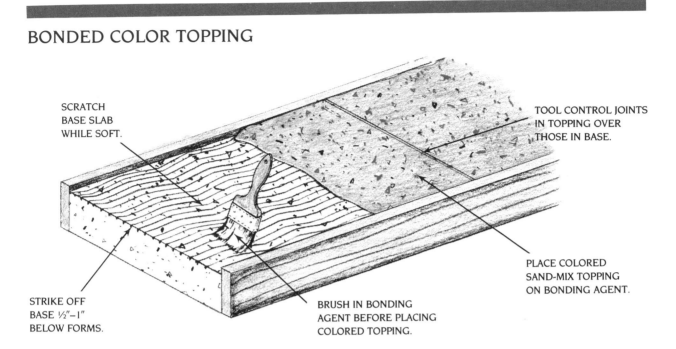

SCRATCH BASE SLAB WHILE SOFT.

TOOL CONTROL JOINTS IN TOPPING OVER THOSE IN BASE.

PLACE COLORED SAND-MIX TOPPING ON BONDING AGENT.

STRIKE OFF BASE ½"–1" BELOW FORMS.

BRUSH IN BONDING AGENT BEFORE PLACING COLORED TOPPING.

ment; 1,100 pounds of sand; and 950 pounds of coarse ag (rounding off).

Once the base course is placed and struck off, do no more until it stiffens and the surface water leaves. No bullfloating, no darbying, and no hand-floating should be done. Do no edging or control-jointing, either. Use the time you have to remove any gray cement paste that has been spilled onto the form tops so that it cannot end up as a gray splotch on your colored topping.

When the base course has lost its sheen, place the topping over it, striking the topping off across the forms. Now bullfloat or darby, edge, joint, and hand-float the topping, as usual. And give it any texturing you want. These operations are no different from those done on a plain slab. When edging and jointing, take special care not to bring any gray cement paste up into the colored topping.

Bonded Topping. If for some reason you cannot place the base and topping courses the same day, they can be tackled separately, so long as they are bonded together. To make a bonded topping (which can be done any time, not necessarily the next day), place and strike off the base course as described for a same-day topping.

Unlike same-day topping, either control joints or wire mesh reinforcement are a necessity to manage shrinkage cracking in the base course. Leave-in wooden forms serve quite well as control jointing. Do no other finishing on the base course. Once the water has left the surface and it has stiffened slightly, scratch the surface all over, including around the edges. A good tool for this is a folded scrap of metal lath or chicken wire. (For handling the wire, you may want to wear heavy work gloves.) Portions of the slab that cannot be reached from the edges can be scratched by nailing the wire to a stick. The rougher you get the surface, the easier time the topping course will have bonding to it.

Cure the base course as usual, avoiding the use of membrane curing compounds, which could interfere with the bond. Instead, plastic sheeting can be used for curing. Keep the base concrete clean. If the slab gets dirty or muddy, it will have to be hosed off to ensure a good bond.

Bonded Topping Mix. The topping course may be placed any time later, no hurry. This is the nice thing about bonded toppings. When you are ready to place the topping, treat it as a separate slab. To calculate how much topping concrete you need, use the chart "Quantities for Sand-mix Topping." A bonded-topping mix cannot be made with any coarse aggregate. It must be sand-mix concrete only, since the topping is less than 2 inches thick and your cured base leaves no soft surface for coarse ags to retreat into. Colored sand-mix concrete contains cement, color pigment, concrete sand, and water, but no coarse aggregate. You can buy a ready-packaged sand mix, which will be made with normal gray portland cement, or mix your own with gray or white cement.

Here is a good by-weight mix for proportioning 1 cubic foot of colored sand-mix topping: portland ce-

A folded length of chicken wire or metal lath can be used to score the soft surface of the base slab in order to help the topping course bond to it.

ment (white or gray), 32 pounds; color pigment as desired, up to 3 pounds 3 ounces; concrete sand, 66 pounds; water, 11 pounds. The lower portion of the chart "Quantities for Sand-mix Topping" will help you figure how much of each ingredient is needed. Suppose the graph shows that 25 cubic feet of topping mix is needed. Reading down from 25 cubic feet on the graph shows that 800 pounds (9 bags) of cement and 1,650 pounds of concrete sand is needed. Since 10 percent for waste is included in the graph, these are the quantities to order.

When proportioning batches, be sure to adjust for water in your sand (to judge sand's wetness, see the photos on page 156). While it is best to proportion all of the ingredients in colored concrete by weight, a good by-volume sand mix is 1 part cement to 2¼ parts concrete sand.

Besides its color, the topping course may contain a good-looking aggregate specifically meant for exposure. Even with aggregate to expose, the two-course method is the same. (The use of small, attractive exposed aggregates is covered later in this chapter.)

Bonding Agents.   The surface of the base course needs a bonding agent to prepare it to accept the topping so that the two will act as a monolithic (one-piece) slab. The best bonding agent is a portland ce-

ment-and-water slurry. Add water to cement and mix it to a thick-cream consistency. Dampen but do not wet the base slab (there should be no standing water), then brush the slurry onto the slab with a scrub brush, a large paintbrush, or a wallpaper brush. Neatness doesn't count, except that you'll want to keep the slurry off the form tops, where it might get onto the topping. Thorough, brushed-in coverage *does* count.

Vinyl concrete bonders are available, and I have used them with success in a nonfreezing climate. Nevertheless, the bonding agent I feel most confident in is portland cement slurry. The use of a vinyl product seems chancier. Be sure that whichever bonder you get is suited to outdoor use. Get a reputable brand and use it according to label instructions. Sometimes, for additional bonding, a little bonding agent may be added to the topping concrete's mixing water. Since this could affect the resulting color, if the color is critical, be sure to test.

Dry-shake Coloring

The dry-shake or dust-on coloring method puts the color only in the top ⅛ to ¼ inch of the slab. This can make colored concrete easily affordable. It also permits you to color uncolored ready-mixed concrete. With dry-shake coloring, you don't have to mix your own concrete or even have a concrete mixer.

A disadvantage of dry-shake coloring: bright colors are not practical because of the gray concrete you are coloring. Still, it produces good tile reds, browns, buffs, and grays.

Plan on doing only about half the dry-shake project you'd tackle without the additional coloring steps. Not that dry-shake is difficult; it just takes time.

How To Dry-shake.   Concrete for dry-shake coloring is preferably air-entrained. A dust-on mixture of portland cement, fine sand, and color pigment is purchased or made up and applied to the surface of the slab during finishing.

Place the slab, strike it off flush with the tops of the forms, and bullfloat or darby as usual. As soon as the water sheen has left the surface, give the slab a preliminary hand-floating, edging, and jointing, using a magnesium, but not a wooden, hand-float. This brings up·moisture to combine with the dust-on mixture. The floating also removes peaks and valleys that might impair an even coloring.

Immediately apply the dust-on mixture. Because the edges of a slab often stiffen first, you may wish to sprinkle around the edges first, then do the center. During application, let the dust-on mix sift out between your fingers, trying for an even spread right up

BONDING AGENTS

Left photo: Portland cement-water slurry makes the best bonding agent. Mixed to thick-cream consistency, it is brushed onto the dampened surface. Right photo: Before the slurry dries white, the topping concrete must be placed over it. The slurry will tightly bond the topping to its base slab.

Left photo: Vinyl concrete bonder may be used instead of portland cement slurry, though the slurry is preferable. Bonder is rolled on like paint and allowed to become tacky before the topping is placed on it. With some brands, the bonder may be allowed to dry before you top it. Right photo: Topping concrete, here a troweled-on white-cement topping (placed without forms to resurface an old slab), is spread over a vinyl bonder. Putting a little bonding agent into the topping's mixing water added flexibility and helped increase the bond.

FINISHING BONDED TOPPING

Left photo: Providing a colorful resurface, this topping is smoothed with a steel trowel. A later broom-texturing removed the trowel marks. Right photo: It's a good idea to give bonded topping courses the tap-test. When the surface is completely cured, tap lightly all over with a screwdriver handle. Hollow-sounding taps indicate inadequate bond with the base course.

HOW TO DRY-SHAKE COLOR

Left photo: Dry-shake coloring is the easiest and most economical means of coloring a slab as you build it. The dust-on mixture is sifted through the fingers onto the surface in an even layer. Right photo: Then hand-float the coloring into the surface. Best for this is the metal float shown. A second, lighter dust-on application followed by another floating completes the coloring process.

to the edges. If too much dust-on mixture is applied in one spot, nonuniform coloring may result. Also, the surface may later peel in that area. Aim for applying two thirds of the required dust-on material during the first spread.

As soon as the dust-on mixture absorbs water and becomes damp, begin floating it into the surface. Thorough and uniform floating is the goal. Then, without waiting, apply the rest of the dust-on mixture evenly and float edge, and joint it in the same way. Avoid any temptation to add water to the surface. This could cause surface scaling later.

Follow the final floating with steel-troweling and finish by brushing, if you like these effects. Cure thoroughly with spray-on curing compound or a layer of clean, wet sand.

You can purchase the dust-on mixture in 100-pound bags in the desired color. One reputable manufacturer with wide distribution is Master Builders, which makes *Colorcron* dust-on mix. Generally, if you buy the dust-on, you can look at color samples that will be quite close to the results you'll get. Most concrete products suppliers should be able to furnish a dust-on mix. Figure on about 30 pounds of dust-on mix for each 100 square feet of surface.

If you cannot find a commercial dust-on product, you can make your own. Use the same color pigments that are used for making colored concrete. Proceed as follows: combine 2 parts white portland cement; 1 part color pigment of the desired color; and 2 parts fine, dry sand (mortar sand), the drier the better. Mix dry until color-streaking disappears. Mix-your-own batches will take about 6 pounds of color pigment per 100 square feet.

To avoid color variations, make enough dust-on mix at once to do the entire project. If there is any water in your sand, don't make the mixture much ahead of use, or it may cake.

PATTERN-STAMPING SLABS

Pattern-stamping is a surface-incising process on a grand scale. It gives the rustic, handmade appearance of brick, tile, adobe, or cobblestone without giving up the advantages of concrete slab construction. Tools called *stamp pads* are impressed into the soft surface to create pattern lines of the joints between "pavers." For cost, pattern-stamping beats most other slab-beautifying treatments.

Pattern-stamping and pumped concrete go well together. Both require a mix without any large particles. Although reinforcement may be used in a pattern-stamped slab, it need not be.

A concrete slab with stamped-hexagonal tile pattern has its grooves grouted with mortar to enhance the "pavers" effect. Nonlinear patterns are the easiest to create.

Left photo: This cobblestone pattern with grouted joints looks like the real thing. The pattern has straight lines in one direction only. Right photo: This random-cobble pattern-stamped design was done by Bomanite professionals. It forms a patio for a rammed-earth house built by Earth Resources Technology in northern California. The grooves have been lightly grouted for effect.

Stamp Pads

To do pattern-stamping, you will need a pair of stamp pads. The most readily available ones are Brickform plastic pads, offered in four patterns: brick, hexagon tile, 8-inch-square paver, and cobble. Need we say that both of your pads should be the same pattern? If local concrete products suppliers don't have the pads, try Goldblatt Tool Co. (listed in this book's "Preface"), which sells Brickform pads by telephone and mail. Along with the pads come two chisel-like hand tools, wide and narrow.

The stamp pads are the only special tools you'll need, except a 3- or 4-pound dead-blow hammer to set pads. Don't try to set pads with an ordinary hammer. It will overstress the pads. A Stanley Compocast Soft Face dead-blow hammer works just fine.

Pattern-stamping Concrete Mix

A cement-rich concrete mix for a pattern-stamped patio must be special-ordered from a ready-mix producer. The maximum-sized coarse aggregate should be ¼ inch. Tell the dealer what you are doing with the concrete and that you want the mix to contain enough fine materials and the right aggregate gradation to

Tough, reinforced-plastic stamp pads are available in various patterns. The top of the pad (*left*) has handles for positioning the pad on the slab. Its bottom (*right*) contains inch-deep grooving blades. A dead-blow hammer (*foreground*) is needed to set the pads properly into the concrete.

STAMP-PAD PATTERNS

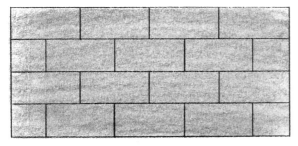

BRICK

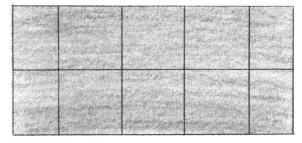

SQUARE TILE

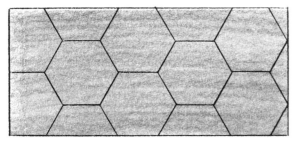

HEXAGONAL TILE

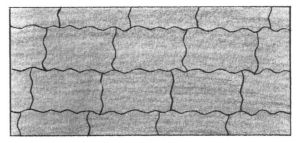

COBBLESTONE

make a workable, easily finished pattern-stamped slab. You will have to pay extra for such a mix. Specify 7½ percent entrained-air content, plus or minus 1 percent, for a freezing climate. Use 3 percent in a non-freezing climate.

Project Size

Cut down on the size of the project you will take on in one day, because the stamping operation will hold up progress. It must be completed before the surface stiffens so much that the stamp pads will not mark it. As a rule of thumb, you can handle about 100 square feet of slab per person stamping. Don't tackle more than 300 or 400 square feet of slab in one day, no matter how much help you have. It's better to divide the project into smaller segments, doing them on different days. If the weather is hot and dry, and the sun will be shining on your slab, cut those amounts in half, or the surface will surely stiffen before your stamping is completed.

Now I'm going to make an exception to my no-additives-in-concrete rule. Since you'll need all the help you can get, it's nice to be able to use an additive to take some of the pressure off the stamping opera-

This patio pattern-stamping crew comprises (*left to right*) ready-mix driver Jack Rechnitzer; concrete pump operator Larry Van Laar; homeowners Doug and Leanna Day; and stamper Bob Hunt. The crew found that they needed three stampers for a 400-square-foot patio project—the most that should be attempted in a day.

tion. Ask your ready-mix dealer to add a *water-reducing retarder* to the mix, plus a small amount of *superplasticizer*. This combination, which will cost a bit extra, produces a high-slump condition and makes the concrete stay workable for two to three hours. (If your ready-mix producer has any questions about what you need, refer him or her to National Ready Mixed Concrete Association Publication 158.)

Forming for Pattern-Stamping

Forming a slab properly for pattern-stamping is a little different from forming a regular slab. The forms should be arranged to accommodate multiples of your stamp-pad size. If using the Brickform pads, this means multiples of 1 × 2 feet. On top of that, you'll need an additional allowance for what's called *float*. Float comes about when the stamp pads move slightly as they are impressed into the soft surface. A common float allowance is ⅟₁₆ inch per foot. Therefore, a 12-foot-wide patio slab would be formed 12 feet ¾ inches wide. This is the inside measurement between the forms or between the isolation joint at the house foundation and the outer form.

Control joints are best handled by leave-in forms. If you impress the stamp pads their full 1-inch depth,

you can dispense with other control joints: the pattern creates its own control joints.

To cut down on an appearance problem called *straight-line irregularity*, try to arrange the pattern so that its long lines run *across* the primary line of sight. Straight-line irregularity occurs when the stamping gets off course and you have to make a course correction to get back on line. Like a ship's wake after a course correction, your straight-line irregularity will show a noticeable bend. The cobblestone pattern, which has far fewer straight lines, minimizes straight-line irregularity.

How to Pattern-stamp

To do your own pattern-stamping, place, strike off, bullfloat or darby, edge, joint, and hand-float your concrete. Color the surface using the dry-shake method. Work quickly with dry-shake coloring, since you must begin stamping as soon as the surface is right for it.

Test a stamp pad on the surface. If you can stand on the pad without sinking its frame down to the surface, the concrete is ready for stamping. I've had no trouble with a pad sinking too low. They have always

FORM ALLOWANCE FOR STAMPING FLOAT (SEE TEXT ABOVE.)

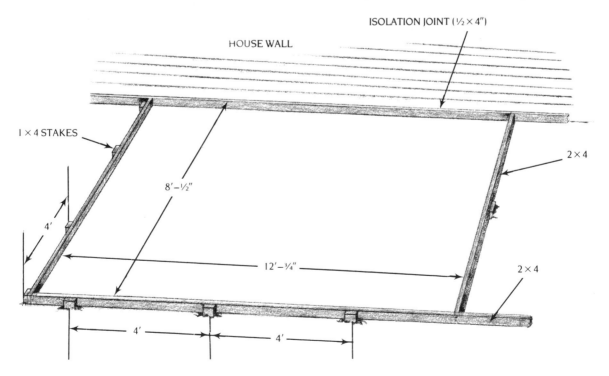

ISOLATION JOINT (½ × 4")

HOUSE WALL

1 × 4 STAKES

8′–½"

4′

2 × 4

12′–¾"

2 × 4

4′

4′

required pounding to set them properly, at about half-depth.

Start stamping by getting the first pad aligned with the house wall or other master line. (It can be helpful to make a dry run with the pads on the subbase a day or two beforehand.) The open side of the pad's pattern should go against the master line or edge. Take some care, because the other pads will all align with the first one. Then place the second pad against the first and lower it onto the surface with its edges aligned. You may have to stand on the first pad while doing this.

Now the pads are ready to be impressed into the surface. Grooves should be about ½ inch deep, which often requires pounding the pads in with the dead-blow hammer. To discourage float, pound first in the center of the pad, then at other places. Don't pound over an unsupported edge of the pad because you might break it off.

Once both pads have been set, stand on the second one and lift the first one out. The Brickform pads are lightweight and have lifting handles for this purpose. Move the pad to the other side of the second pad, align, and lower it onto the surface. Then set it. Stand on it while moving the second pad to the next location. Keep going until the whole first row has been stamped.

Then begin row 2, aligning its first pad with the last pad of row 1. The patterns interface on all four sides, so you can take off in any direction. Turn-arounds are done by ranking the pads rather than filing them. However, always keep them facing the way they were when you began. Row 3, row 4, and so on are done the same way until the whole slab has been stamped. An occasional hosing of the pads by an assistant standing by will help you do a cleaner job.

The pattern can be carried around a corner by hand-tooling a miter line at a 45-degree angle and patterning up to it from both directions.

While one person stamps, another can be hand-tooling lines around the edges, where the pads may not quite reach the form. The hand tools work best if dunked in a pail of water now and then.

Should your project not work out in even stamp pads and part of the last row of pads reaches past the form, use this pro's trick for patterning right up to the form. Position all pads for the last row, lapping them over the form and pushing on them enough to get an indication of the pattern. Then use the hand tool to deepen the impressions to normal depth. It will look fine. Remember that it is better to leave a slightly oversize row of units (bricks, tiles, whatever) at the slab's edge than to tool in a narrow row. Anything much less than half a unit will look odd.

You may choose between two methods of stamping: standing on the stamp pads or working from knee-boards. I have tried both and found that working from

HOW TO USE STAMP PADS (CONTINUES ON NEXT PAGE.)

Left photo: Stamp pads are positioned and set into the concrete by pounding with a dead-blow hammer. Standing on the pad being pounded helps to set it. Right photo: The first pad is lifted out and placed next to the just-set pad. Having two stamp pads provides a place to stand while repositioning the second pad.

STAMPING (CONTINUED)

Left photo: The stamp pads are aligned on the concrete surface before being set. The pads interface on all four sides. Right photo: A new row is begun as shown. Careful alignment of the pads with a master line, here the house wall edge, is needed to avoid straight-line irregularity. Here, stamping had progressed inward from the patio edge to the house wall and now goes back out again.

Pattern grooves around the edges can be extended or deepened using this plastic hand tool. The tool can be positioned to match shapes in the stamp pads.

Left photo: You gain better control over stamp-pad alignment if you work from kneeboards instead of atop the pads themselves. However, this requires that you float-out impressions left by the kneeboards before stamping there. Right photo: As Bob Hunt demonstrates, working from kneeboards requires that pad-setting be done entirely by dead-blow hammer, with no help from your own weight.

kneeboards is slower and more difficult because your weight is not helping to set the pads; nevertheless, it does a better job. The marks left by kneeboards must be floated over before stamping.

The completed pattern-stamped slab should be cured as usual, using any method suited to curing of dry-shake colored concrete.

Mortaring Joints

For a touch of realism, the pattern lines may be filled with mortar. If you are planning to mortar the joints, it's best to set the stamp pads their full blade depth to make the mortar lines in the finished slab that much wider. Avoid a spray-on curing compound: it would spoil the mortar's bond. Use another method of curing instead.

Joint-mortaring should begin soon as you can walk on the slab without scuffing it. Make a batch of mortar using a ready-packaged mortar mix, adding water and mixing as directed on the label to a thick-paste consistency. The mortar may be colored if you wish, using an integral coloring pigment. Use a pointing trowel or

If they are shallow, you can leave grooves open; if deep, grout them. Grout as soon as the concrete sets enough to walk on it without scuffing. Dampen the slab and trowel-on a thick-paste mortar. Brush off any slop-over before the grout sets hard.

margin trowel to pack the mortar into the grooves, leveling it slightly below the surface. Wipe off excess mortar with a damp cloth or sponge.

While the largest size of stone for exposure is usually 2 inches, 3- to 6-inch smooth cobblestones were placed in the surface of this plain-gray concrete slab. The stones were hand-placed with their flattest side up. (Portland Cement Association photo)

MAKING EXPOSED-AGGREGATE SLABS

Concrete made with its cement paste at the surface brushed away to expose attractive coarse aggregates is the most beautiful concrete of all. This is called *exposed-aggregate concrete*. Making exposed-aggregate concrete requires little more work than finishing an ordinary concrete slab. Exposed-ag almost cries out for color in the *matrix*—the mortar between the aggregates. When attractive stone and a colored-concrete matrix are combined, concrete shows to its best advantage.

The minimum slope for good drainage in an exposed-ag slab is ¼ inch per foot; more slope is better.

Aggregates for exposure can be any size up to 2 inches in diameter. They may be purchased from a concrete products or terrazzo supplies dealer. The table "Common Commercial Aggregates for Exposure" shows the range of possibilities. Some ags, both imported and domestic, are incredibly beautiful. Whatever aggregate is used, it should qualify as a good concrete aggregate. Soft, porous ags won't last outdoors, no matter how great they look.

Crushed stone used for exposure requires more work, since it tends to "stack" during ag-spreading. Also, it often presents sharp edges.

The aggregates in an exposed-ag slab get there in either of two ways: by tamping them into a just-finished slab or by mixing them in the concrete. Which to choose? The tamp-in method concentrates all the pretty ags at the surface to look best; the mix-in method is much less effort. Tamp-in is best used for the larger aggregates (from ¾ to 2 inches). For the smaller ones, it's better to mix them into a topping course, colored or plain. Just as with two-course colored concrete, the topping may be placed over the base slab the same day or else bonded to it later.

The construction details are much the same as for casting a colored topping. Therefore, only things specific to the exposed-aggregate process will be discussed below. Dry-shake coloring is not a suitable technique for an exposed-ag slab, because its color doesn't penetrate deep enough.

COMMON COMMERCIAL AGGREGATES FOR EXPOSURE

Aggregate	Size	Color Range	Availability
Pebbles	¼"–2"	White, red, orange, buff, black	West, Southwest
Marble	½"–2"	White, red, buff, yellow, black	All areas
Marble chips	⅛"–⅜"	White, red, buff, yellow, black	All areas
Granite	¾"–2"	Red, gray, buff, dark blue, black	Midwest, West
Quartz	½"–2"	White, pink, gray, clear	East, West, South, Midwest

METHODS OF MAKING AN EXPOSED-AG SLAB

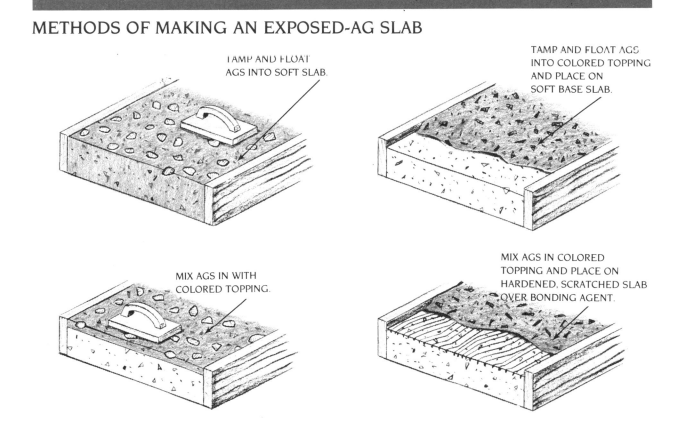

TAMP AND FLOAT AGS INTO SOFT SLAB.

TAMP AND FLOAT AGS INTO COLORED TOPPING AND PLACE ON SOFT BASE SLAB.

MIX AGS IN WITH COLORED TOPPING.

MIX AGS IN COLORED TOPPING AND PLACE ON HARDENED, SCRATCHED SLAB OVER BONDING AGENT.

Tamping-in

To use the tamping method of making exposed-ag concrete, one helper is needed for each 50 square feet. The section-a-day method is highly recommended. You'll need clean aggregates for exposure at about the following rates:

Ag Size	Lb./Sq. ft.
⅜-inch	3
2-inch	6

Have the aggregate selected for exposure stockpiled, protected from the ground yet handy on the day of casting. All ags needn't be the same size, but may be. The tinier the aggregate, the smoother the slab's surface will be. When choosing your ags, remember that larger ags make the surface harder to walk on, especially in high heels. It will be harder to sweep clean, too.

The slab's concrete mix should be somewhat short of coarse aggregate, since you will be adding more ags at the surface. With this exception, the proportions for quality concrete apply. If you are mixing your own

The author made this two-course exposed-aggregate patio by striking off the plain base concrete 1 inch below the tops of the forms and placing colored sand-mix concrete directly on top while the previously placed base was still soft enough to accept ags.

concrete, try for a mix in between the normal mix and the sandy mix in the photos on page 158. Slump should be the normal 6-inch maximum, but not less than 2 inches. To allow for the volume of ags being added by tamp-in, strikeoff should be ⅛ to ⁷⁄₁₆ inch below the desired finished grade. Allow as follows:

Ag Size (Inches)	Allowance (Inches)
⅜ to ⅝	⅛ inch
½ to ¾	³⁄₁₆ inch
¾ to 1	¼ inch
1 to 1¼	⁵⁄₁₆ inch
1¼ to 2	⁷⁄₁₆ inch

Place, strike off, and bullfloat or darby the slab as usual. Control-jointing is needed, too, but edging is not. Begin ag-spreading, called *seeding*, immediately. If the ags sink out of sight, allow more time for stiffening before seeding any further. Use a flat-ended shovel to cast an even spread of dampened but not wet aggregate. If you want a tight exposed-ag pattern, fill the surface one-ag deep with aggregate placed tightly together. Pick out any flat, slivery pieces, as well as stacked-up ones. If you prefer a more open effect, be more skimpy in seeding. In any case, make your spread even over the entire slab. If the ags are large, arrange them by hand. Fill in any bare spots. Give special attention to edges and especially to corners. These may call for a bit of handwork.

Embedding Aggregates. Aggregate embedding goes best with a darby or the narrow edge of a short 2 × 4, as shown in accompanying photos. A hand-float will do it, too. Whichever tool you choose, avoid creating bumps and birdbaths. End by floating over the ags with a metal float so that all pieces are fully embedded. Mortar should surround each stone. Don't overfloat, or pieces may sink below the surface. The ideal is to have a ¹⁄₁₆-inch layer of cement paste over each stone. Although the normal look is like a slab just floated, gaps not filled with mortar may crop up between pieces of aggregate. This is all right as long as they are only surface gaps. Any stone that isn't surrounded by cement paste is sure to pop out later. Enough mortar for gap-filling can usually be scraped from the tops of the forms.

Exposing the Aggregates

Now comes the fun part—exposing the pretty stones. Wait while the surface concrete stiffens to the point that it can be brushed without forcing out any pieces of aggregate—typically about 2 hours, but be sure to keep checking throughout that 2-hour period. One way to gauge readiness is to press a thumb into the surface. If a slight thumbprint remains, conditions are right for ag exposure. A worker on kneeboards should leave no impression on the slab.

Left photo: Bullfloating over the seeded surface should embed aggregates about ¹⁄₁₆ inch beneath it, with cement paste surrounding each particle. At this point the slab should look like a normal one would after floating. Right photo: The exposed-aggregate concrete combined with plain-gray and leave-in wood forms creates an extraordinary patio. To add further interest, the plain sections were given a directional broom-texturing. (Portland Cement Association photo)

Left photo: The 1- to 1½-inch select stones in the author's own patio were spread, tamped-in (*above*), and later exposed by means of brooming. Leave-in forms allowed creation of a square or two as convenient. Right photo: As the surface stiffens, a straight 2 × 4 used on edge makes a good tamping tool. During tamping, you should avoid creating birdbaths in the surface.

Aggregate exposure is a matter of timing. By pressing a finger into the surface, you can tell whether the surface is hard enough to keep the aggregates from being brushed out. In this test, you should be able to make an impression, yet the surface should hold your print.

Aggregate exposure may be done while walking on the slab. Wear rubber boots and safety goggles, because you could get spattered with cement paste.

Exposure is done with a stiff, plastic-bristled broom, such as a garage broom. Use the broom to sweep cement paste lightly from the surface to show the upper part of the aggregates just beneath. If many pieces brush out, give the surface more time to stiffen before further brushing. While brushing, use a fine spray from a garden hose to wash the brushed-off mortar away. This is a good job for a helper. Brushing and flushing proceed together.

Do the brushing and flushing in several passes, with delays between to let the surface stiffen further. Later brushings and flushings can be more vigorous. You may quit when the flush water runs off clear.

The depth of exposure is up to you. The deeper you expose, the more rustic the effect—and the greater the chance of aggregate brushout. The usual exposure is the top one eighth to one third of the ags, allowing them to show but keeping them locked firmly in the concrete matrix. Any pieces exposed beyond the halfway point may well get knocked out later. You should be as consistent as you can about exposure depth in all portions of the slab. The final result

Exposed-ag concrete with varied depths of exposure and varied ag sizes has slightly exposed small aggregate in the large squares and heavily exposed large aggregate in the 6-inch-wide joints.

should be a slab evenly exposed all over and without a cement film on the ags.

When all ag exposure is finished, go on to curing. Plastic sheeting, water-ponding, or continuous wetting of a burlap covering are best. Avoid the use of membrane curing compound on exposed-ag concrete.

Should any aggregates pop out after the project is completed, cement them back in with an outdoor epoxy glue. Avoid the 5-minute epoxies; choose one that takes weathering. The pieces will be as firm as though cement paste were still bonding them.

Acid Wash
If the cured and dried surface looks dull or whitish, some cement paste is probably still clinging to it. Ordinary washing won't take it off, but a muriatic acid solution will, brightening both ags and matrix. Wait at least two weeks, longer if possible, before giving the acid wash.

Wear rubber gloves, rubber boots, safety goggles, waterproof kneepads, and old clothes when you apply the wash. Pour 1 part muriatic acid (about 8 percent hydrochloric acid) into 5 parts of water in a plastic pail. *Never* pour the water into the acid. Dampen the surface; then work the solution in with a scrub brush. Bubbling indicates that the acid is doing its job. When the bubbling stops, the acid has changed into a salt solution. Rinse off the reacted residue thoroughly, leaving no trace of acid. Test with litmus paper.

Two-course Exposed Aggregates
The best-looking exposed-ag is made using the two-course method. That way, you can employ ready mix for an easy-to-do base slab and choose any aggregate you like for seeding into the colored sand-mix topping. Use either the same-day topping method or the bonded topping method (using small aggregates only), just as described in the section on two-course concrete color.

Same-day topping is less work. Furthermore, it is accommodating to large aggregates, since the base slab will be soft enough to accept any pieces pushed down into it. To make it easier to embed larger topping ags, the base course is best made with ¾-inch maximum-size coarse aggregate.

Mix the topping, using sand-mix concrete of the desired color. Place it on the base course before the base stiffens much, striking it off across the tops of the forms. Let the topping stiffen slightly, then seed, tamp in, and expose the aggregate as explained above. If any gray cement paste works its way up to a colored concrete surface, tamping is being done too early. Give the base slab more time to stiffen.

When exposure has been completed, cure the slab as for colored concrete.

Rustic Terrazzo. One variation of the two-course method creates a surface called *rustic terrazzo*. Rustic terrazzo is unground terrazzo. Its aggregates are exposed by brushing and flushing instead of by grinding (the procedure used for true terrazzo). Rustic terrazzo makes a marvelous outdoor slab.

Rustic terrazzo is made with colored marble chips or other quite small ags in the topping mix, just as true terrazzo is. One, two, or several kinds of colored aggregates may be combined in any proportions for multicolored effects, as they are in terrazzo. The combination of a clear, bright-colored matrix and colorful exposed ags is art come to concrete.

Rustic terrazzo is made in two courses, like two-

HOW TO DO RUSTIC TERRAZZO

Left photo: Portland cement-water slurry is made by wetting the hardened base slab, dusting on enough cement to form a heavy cream-consistency paste, and brushing it onto the base slab as a bonding agent. Right photo: After that, select aggregate (here stored in an old white-cement sack) is shoveled into the concrete mixer and made into terrazzo topping.

Left photo: The rustic terrazzo topping is placed on the base slab. Chuck Kearns sectioned off his patio into 2-foot squares. That way, the cast-in-place rustic terrazzo pavers needed to be only 2 inches thick. Right photo: The topping course is struck off across the forms, using a short strikeboard. Kearns made some squares with dark-brown and some with light-beige topping matrix, all with pea gravel as exposed aggregate. The darker matrix shown delineated Kearns' outer patio edges. (Photo sequence continues, next page.)

RUSTIC TERRAZZO (CONTINUED)

Above left: Continuing from previous page, the lighter-colored topping is spread evenly with a pointed trowel before being struck off flush with the forms. Above right: After strikeoff, the trowel is used to smooth the surface. Note the notched ends on Kearns' strikeboard. Turned over, the strikeboard had earlier been used for striking off base concrete ½ inch below the forms. At right: When the time is right, the surface mortar is brushed away from the pea gravel aggregate. Although the colored mortar runs across the finished squares, it can easily be flushed away cleanly with water, leaving the pea gravel aggregates shining brightly. Kearns used pumped-in-place ready mix for his base slab as shown on page 235. He used the two-course bonded method for the exposed-ag surface, shown on page 219.

course colored concrete. Rather than seed the colorful aggregate onto the surface, though, mix the ags into the ⅝-inch-thick colored concrete topping. Normally, the ags are ⅜ inch and smaller. Marble chips are used for true terrazzo because they are colorful yet soft enough to be ground easily. For rustic terrazzo you aren't limited to soft aggregates. Quartz, crushed tile, crushed brick, and river-washed gravel may all be used. In fact, you can go with any aggregate that's suitable for concrete-making and not larger than about half the thickness of the topping course. Two or more different ags may be combined in one rustic terrazzo patio.

The table on the next page shows the mix design for making 1 cubic foot of rustic terrazzo topping. Notice that it contains no sand or coarse aggregate, just white cement, coloring pigment, and ag chips. Use just enough water to make the mix workable.

Rustic Terrazzo Mix
1 part white portland cement
Color pigment (desired amount)
2 parts aggregate chips

To avoid having to put control joints in both base slab and topping, leave-in forms are recommended. They should divide the project into 6 × 6-foot or smaller sections.

Handle topping placement just as you would for a two-course colored slab. Either same-day or a bonded topping is suitable to rustic terrazzo. Place, strike off, and bullfloat or darby the terrazzo topping. But do not edge or hand-float.

Clear Sealer

Run water on your finished exposed-aggregate project. Notice the brightened colors. You can have that look all the time if you apply a clear, nonyellowing sealer to the surface. What's more, a concrete sealer helps to keep concrete from staining. And any stain that does turn up is easier to remove if the surface has been sealed. (These coatings are also good for preventing deicer damage.)

Both glossy and satin sealer finishes are available. The glossy ones make the surface actually look wet and may not be what you want outdoors. In any case, the nonyellowing quality is important. Follow application directions on the label.

CHAPTER 8

BUILDING A PATIO

In the United States, patios got their start in California and New Mexico, the idea having been introduced by Spanish settlers. Now they are popular coast-to-coast.

Size your patio as large as you can afford. About 20 square feet of patio space serves one person comfortably. That is, a 300-square-foot patio allows you to entertain some 15 people in style. On the other hand, a patio of only 12 × 12 feet can make a pleasant setting for outdoor living. One size guide is to design your patio larger than the largest room in the house.

A few technical requirements affect how you build a patio. Drainage is a primary concern. For the patio to drain well, its surface needs to be at least 1 inch above the surrounding ground. For good surface drainage, the patio should slope away from the house by at least ⅛ inch per foot. In addition, where it meets the house, a patio should be 1 to 3 inches below the house floor—6 inches below is·okay, too. The idea is to keep rain and snow out of the house.

If an adequate drainage slope away from the house cannot be arranged, the patio can slope to a grated central drain with a drain pipe leading away to a good draining spot.

PATIO MATERIALS

While most patios are concrete, you should at least consider the other patio materials.

Brick

The most adaptable paver choice, brick is suited to almost any patio use. Brick patio pavers are easy to lay soft-set, or they may be placed in mortar as hard-set pavers. I recommend soft-set brick for patios (see the next chapter).

Brick is available in many colors, shapes, textures, and sizes. What's more, you can lay brick in any of a variety of bond patterns. You can choose among new, used, or salvaged brick, though the latter has become so popular that it can cost more than new brick. Common brick is most used for patios in nonfreezing climates. Vari-colored brick may be used to highlight traffic patterns, make designs, or add interest or accents. To see what's available, visit a masonry supplies dealer.

The drawbacks of brick include cost and the fact that weeds tend to grow up through a soft-set brick patio. The surface may not stay as even and smooth as when it was installed, especially in regions where frost heave is common. The only way to prevent this is to hard-set the brick.

Tile

Tile patios are made using kiln-fired quarry tile or patio pavers. These may be smooth or heavily textured, but are always earth-colored and warm-looking. They are tough enough to withstand lots of traffic and resist staining. They are also easily cleaned. Tile is best hard-set either on a concrete slab or on the ground in a bedding of mortar.

Ceramic tile may be used, but the smooth-glazed ceramics are too slippery to risk outdoors.

Adobe

Adobe pavers, which are not fired but should contain enough portland cement or asphalt stabilizer to make them weather-resistant, may be used to make a rustic-

With plantings, fencing, and furniture, as shown, a patio can provide the sense of a private space. Benches and retaining walls can also afford privacy.

Left photo: This patio has a curved outer edge with matching slat bench, curving protrusion on the right-hand side, angled leave-in wood forms, and textured concrete. Right photo: This patio contains less than 150 square feet, yet provides a goodly amount of space. (Portland Cement Association photos)

Hard-set tile makes an excellent patio. Additional features here include planters, benches, firepit, and fiberglass screening. (Filon Division, Vistron Corp. photo)

looking patio. "'Dobies,'' as they're called, are usually set directly on the subgrade or in sand, with 1-inch open joints that may be filled with mortar or sand or else left open for plantings. Adobe pavers may be difficult to find outside of the U.S. Southwest and Mexico. They tend to crumble if hard-set.

Flagstone

Flagstone may be sandstone or limestone, according to where you live. Relatively expensive, flags create a rustic, softly colored patio. Their irregular shapes impart texture to the setting. If you prefer to minimize their irregularity, combine flagstone with other, more regular-shaped materials, such as brick or concrete. Be careful, though; flagstone is noted for being hard to combine tastefully with other materials.

To keep them from breaking up in a harsh freeze/thaw climate, flagstones are best hard-set in mortar. Soft-set flagstones work well in a mild climate, and in such a climate may even be placed directly on the subgrade.

The chief drawback to flagstone will become apparent the minute you try to balance a chair or table on their uneven surface. For the same reason, flags

make a poor patio for children to play on. Moreover, properly matching the irregular shapes of the flags takes considerable care.

One thing to check before you proceed with flags is whether enough material is available in the color you want to do the whole job. Sometimes flagstone is tough to find in quantity.

Wood

As a patio material (rather than a deck material), wood goes either in or on the ground. Cutoffs of pressure-treated Ground-contact wood may be used as pavers, laid right on the ground with the grain running vertically. Or they may be embedded in sand or gravel. It is a good idea to soak each piece in more wood preservative before laying it. Even so, with the end grains exposed to the ground below and to weathering above, any wood—pressure-treated or not—will eventually rot and need replacement.

Sliced-up telephone poles, tree trunks, or railroad ties make great wood pavers. Or you can buy pressure-treated modular 3 × 3- or 4 × 4-foot wood squares that are made up into "tiles" designed to be laid in a sand bed as deck squares.

Loose Materials

Loose materials such as stone and gravel represent the low end of patio paving. They're best used for temporary low-cost surfacing. A stone surface can be awful to walk on in high heels, and weeds grow among the stones with abandon. Laying the stones on plastic sheeting or 15-pound asphalt-impregnated roofing felt works until the weeds find holes to grow up through.

You can get stone in natural rounded shapes ("pea gravel") or in angular, rough shapes left by rock crushers. The latter type is usually called *crushed stone*. Rounded stone looks much better but may not be available. Crushed stone works best with a wood edging to keep it from spreading. Crushed brick may be used instead of stone. Perhaps the best use of stone is as filler between pavers that are set some distance apart.

A loose-stone patio needs lots of maintenance to keep it free of debris. (This is done with a rake.) The stones may also catch soil or work down into the mud beneath, requiring more stone on top.

Chips of wood may also be used for a patio. You may purchase these in bags, but they need frequent replenishment. They do, however, provide a soft surface with minimal likelihood of causing injury if someone falls. It's best to use wood chips where they're contained by a gridwork of pressure-treated wood.

Concrete

Concrete block pavers make wonderful patios. The new interlocking pavers are even used for city paving throughout the downtown area of Montreal, Quebec, where they are exposed to severe weathering. Concrete-block paving appears frequently in this book. It is often called "patio block."

Concrete patio blocks that you buy or precast yourself and lay in sand can make a wonderful patio. Most are 1½ or 2 inches thick. They may be colored, textured, or plain.

PATIO CONSTRUCTION

I would like to be able to tell you that building a patio is easy work. On the contrary, it can be very hard work, though the result is well worth the effort. The more your existing yard must be renovated to accommodate the patio, the more work it will take. And the larger

This large patio leaves islands for trees and other plantings, and it visually opens up the backyard. (Portland Cement Association photo)

the patio, the more work needed to build it. If electricity or plumbing runs are needed under any patio, you must plan ahead for these.

Building Permits

Getting a building permit with its attendant official inspections is almost a universal requirement for patio-building. This may or may not involve submitting scale drawings of the project. A quick call to your local building department will answer that question.

Drainage

The water that runs off your patio must drain somewhere. It may drain into natural runoff courses (*swales*), creeks, drainage ditches, or a low spot in your own yard where it can percolate into the ground. Do not cause it to drain onto a neighboring property (unless the runoff presently drains there). The best patio drainage sheets water off the patio to one side or end. One good way to handle runoff water is to put in a planting area along the low edge of the patio and let the runoff water your plants.

Another solution is to put in subsurface pipes and

run the water to a dry well or seepage trench. A patio that has walls on all sides needs this kind of drainage. For example, a patio may be sloped toward one corner away from the house, and a drain grate with a drainage tile line be placed there. The patio floor should slope ⅛ inch per foot toward the drains. Because of the work they require, however, subsurface drains should be avoided if at all possible.

In freeze/thaw climates, the subsurface pipes, to work in winter, must run below the frost line. The easiest kind of drain lines to work with are plastic sewer and drain pipes. Use solid-wall pipes for carrying water away and perforated pipes for seeping it into the ground. The twin rows of holes in perforated pipes should be placed facedown. Laying them on gravel in a trench and then backfilling over them with more gravel before finishing the backfill with soil greatly increases the amount of water that can percolate into the ground. Plastic pipes can be cut with a fine-

toothed saw and be solvent-welded to fittings with a compatible solvent cement. Plastic pipes come in three materials: PVC, styrene, and ABS (acrylonitrile-butadiene-styrene). Other drainage pipe choices (harder to work with) are: clay tile, concrete tile, pitch-fiber (bituminous) pipe, and cast-iron pipe.

The first step in building any patio is to mark off and excavate the site. This means removing the topsoil (which is better suited to plants than to serving as a patio subgrade). Digging out also gives you the opportunity to place the patio surface at the desired elevation.

Site Layout

Start laying out a patio site with stringlines and batter boards. Mason's line is best to use, because you can pull it very tight without breaking it. Here, we will use a rectangular patio as our example, and the house wall will serve as one edge of the patio. To establish the patio's other edges, set up batter boards just outside the patio area. *Batter boards* are right-angled, horizontal 1 × 4s nailed to three vertical stakes, which may be 2 × 2s, 1 × 4s, or 2 × 4s driven into the ground with a sledgehammer. The boards form their right angle beyond the outer corners of the patio.

Also drive two stakes next to the house wall. The inside edges of these should go at the edges of the patio. Hang a line level on a strong string and stretch it between a house stake and the corresponding batter board. Before nailing that batter board to its stake, have someone help you level the string. Do the same with the other house stake at the other corner of the patio and its batter boards. These stringlines outline two patio edges.

The third stringline is stretched on the level between batter boards parallel to the house wall. It should be equidistant from the house wall at the ends.

Now, square up the two edge stringlines with the house wall, using a carpenter's framing square. When you have the stringlines squared with the house, saw out kerfs in the batter boards to hold the stringlines in the correct position.

As a check, measure the diagonals of the stringlines. The diagonals should be about equal. If they aren't, adjust the strings.

To ensure proper drainage, the patio subgrade should be graded to slope slightly away from the house. As shown on page 175, a ½-inch shimmed 2-foot level taped to a straight 2 × 4 can help you establish the desired slope of ¼ inch per foot.

Excavation

The stringlines represent the outer edges of the patio, though not its surface elevation or grade. With a bit more calculation, you are ready to dig out the topsoil and excavate. Figure out how thick your patio will be,

LAYING OUT A PATIO

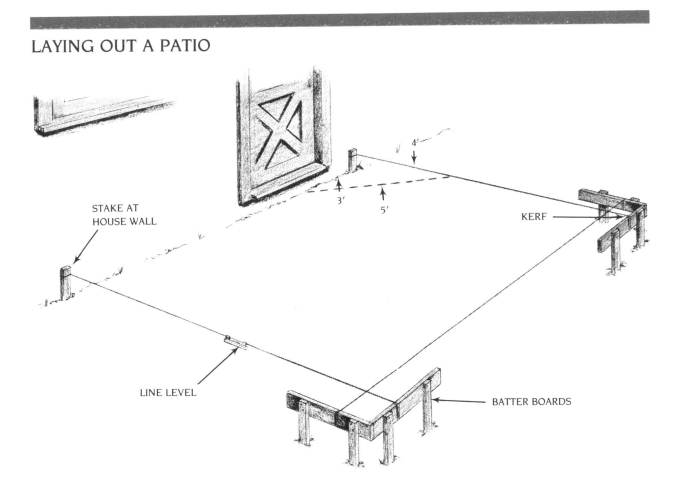

STAKE AT
HOUSE WALL

3'

4'

5'

KERF

LINE LEVEL

BATTER BOARDS

Left photo: Before installing any patio forms, Chuck Kearns uses a rented tractor's rear scraper to level the subgrade. Right photo: He fine-grades with a garden rake.

Left photo: Author's son Doug drives form stakes for a concrete patio. Right photo: Forms to be left in after the concrete hardens need to be tied to the slab. This can be done by driving 16d hot-dip galvanized nails through the forms 16 inches apart. While not necessary, bending each nail, as shown, helps it hold. The nails lastingly link the form and the slab, keeping the two from settling separately or pulling apart.

bottom to top. With a concrete patio, this is easy—a 4-inch slab is 4 inches thick. If a gravel drainage layer is needed because of poorly drained soil, its thickness is added. For other kinds of paving, total the thickness of the subbase; a mortar layer, if any; and the thickness of the pavers themselves.

Next, calculate the elevation of the surface of the patio, remembering that it should be at least an inch below the house and an inch above the surrounding grade. How far below the stringlines is this? Add that distance to the thickness of the patio. This is the distance you must dig out below the stringlines at the house wall.

For example, suppose the patio is to be 4 inches thick without any subbase, and its surface is to reach exactly 1 inch below the house floor. And suppose that the stringlines measure 5½ inches above the house floor. This makes the patio surface 6½ inches below the stringlines at the house. So, 4 + 6½ = 10½ inches from the stringline down to the bottom of the dug-out area. And suppose further that the patio is to be 20 feet wide. Now, since your excavation must slope for drainage at least ⅛ inch per foot, its outer edge will be $\frac{20}{8}$, or 2½ inches, lower than its house edge. Thus, the far edge will be dug out 10½ + 2½, or 13 inches, below the stringline. Simple? It really is.

Sloping the Forms. Set the side forms for a concrete or edged-paver patio by measuring down from the stringlines (for our example, 6½ inches at the house and 6½ + 2½ = 9 inches at the outer edge). This will make the forms slope away from the house just enough for good drainage. Once they're in, you can check the forms for correct slope with a 2-foot carpenter's level by placing a ¼-inch drill bit under the low end of the level atop a sloping board. The level should read level, indicating the form has ⅛-inch-per-foot slope for drainage.

The form board that runs parallel to the house wall at the outer patio edge is usually installed level. Thus, in our example, its lower edge would be 10½ inches below its stringline all the way across. Sight along your stringlines occasionally to make sure the lines don't sag. If they do, pull them tighter, before any sag can be transferred to the forms and thus to the patio surface.

Once you have the edges of the patio area dug out to proper depth, you can install the forms and use them to help determine how deep to dig through the middle of the patio. This can be done by stretching a taut stringline across the form tops and measuring the patio's thickness down from it. If the patio is to be 4 inches thick and every string-to-dirt measurement

Left photo: Chuck Kearns builds a gridwork of 1 × 2 heart redwood and lays it on the already-sloped subgrade. Because the gridwork creates small 30-inch-square slabs, Kearns reduced slab thickness from the usual 4-inch requirement to only 2 inches, creating what might be termed cast-in-place patio blocks. Right photo: Kearns does his fine-grading with sand and a notched-board template that levels the sand even with the bottoms of the forms that are not already in contact with the subgrade. He will leave other forms spaced ½ inch above the subgrade to form 2-inch-thick slabs.

comes up 4 inches, your digging is done. But if an area is only 3½ inches from string down to soil, you have more digging to do in that area. Likewise, if you have an area that's 5 inches from string to soil, you've dug too deep in that area. Either backfill it or plan to order enough additional concrete to fill it in.

For easy subgrading, make a wooden template that rides the forms and hangs down exactly 4 inches. It can be used to fine-grade a sand subbase or to indicate high spots in an earth subgrade. It should be moved along like a straightedge for striking off concrete but need not be seesawed.

Backfilling

When you dig, try to excavate cleanly to the desired depth so that no backfilling is needed. If backfilling becomes necessary, use sand, since backfilling with soil calls for rock-solid compaction. Sand, too, must be compacted, but sand takes much less tamping than backfilled earth does. If concrete is placed on uncompacted fill—sand or earth—it will not receive uniform support and will surely crack eventually. Pavers placed on uncompacted fill will settle.

Shovel the topsoil into a wheelbarrow and use it for plantings around your property. Use any excavated undersoil as raw fill for low spots around your property, covering it with topsoil.

Ready-Mix Backfill. For a concrete patio, my brother Stu proposes a theory that backfilling with concrete is cheaper and much easier than using anything else as backfill. If you subscribe to this idea, here's a good way to figure your ready-mixed concrete order. When you finish excavating, measure down from the string stretched between form tops every couple of feet or so, and record the measurements on a sheet of paper. Move the string about 2 feet along the forms and take another series of measurements. Keep going until you have a depth measurement for every square yard or so of the patio. If you've done a perfect job of digging, every measurement will be almost the same. If not, they may vary quite a bit. Make sure (digging out farther as necessary) that no measurement is less than the minimum required thickness for patio concrete—4 inches, usually. Now, add up all the separate measurements (including new replacements where you've dug farther) and divide the total by the number of measurements.

Suppose, for example, that you have 74 measurements varying from 4 inches to as much as 5¾ inches and totaling 318 inches. Dividing 318 by 74 gives an

Left photo: You can make easy-driving, metal form stakes by drilling nail holes through ½-inch reinforcing bars. Here the top of the form is lined up with a stringline before the stake is nailed (Photographer, Rollyn Puterbaugh; Sakrete photo). Right photo: Where the yet-to-be-placed patio slab will abut this concrete pier, ½-inch-thick isolation-joint material (dark panels shown) separates the pier from the eventual slab.

Left photo: You can level a sand subbase to the desired elevation using a template made by notching a 1 × 6 so that exactly 4 inches extends downward. Pulled around the forms, as shown, it strikes off the sand to a uniform depth. Once subbase elevations are achieved near the forms, it's easier to grade the rest to match. Right photo: Dampen the subbase before placing any concrete on it. The fine spray from a garden-hose nozzle serves well. Dampening keeps a dry subbase from drawing water out of the plastic concrete.

Because his patio was inaccessible to a ready-mix truck, Chuck Kearns decided to use a concrete pumping service with a 3-inch hose to carry mix in through the garage in the background. Chuck, at left, holds a remote switch to stop and start the concrete pump, which is in front of the garage. Each grid is slightly overfilled with pumped concrete, which emanates from the hose like ketchup from a squeeze bottle.

Left photo: Doug Day tools a control joint aligned with the edge of a concrete door stoop (out of photo) he left in place because it was thought to be attached to the house slab foundation. A pair of 2 × 4s guide Doug's jointer while providing a platform for working on the soft slab. Right photo: For floating, Doug's brother-in-law Chris Kania moves about on kneeboards. The hot sun shining directly on the concrete brought on its initial set so quickly that two finishers were needed, one working around the edges and Chris in the middle.

Left photo: To keep concentrated loads off the forms, you can lay concrete blocks on the subgrade to support a sturdy plank (Sakrete photo) . Right photo: A ½ × 4-inch strip of isolation-joint material is often sold as "expansion joint." You can use concrete nails to attach it to the house foundation, thereby isolating the new slab from the foundation. The material cuts easily with a handsaw. Here, author's son Doug had tacked up newspapers to protect his stucco wall from concrete splashes.

average depth of close to 4.3 inches. So, instead of fine-grading with sand to get a uniform 4-inch depth, order enough ready mix to build a 4.3-inch-thick concrete patio. A side benefit of taking careful thickness measurements is that you needn't add 10 percent to the total volume of the project for subgrade and spillage errors. You've got the subgrade figured *exactly*. You need to add only 5 percent, solely for spillage. On a 20 × 30-foot, 4.3-inch-thick patio, the figuring would go like this: 4.3/12 × 20 × 30 = 215 cubic feet; 215/27 = 7.96 cubic yards; 7.96 + 5% = 8.36, or 8.4 cubic yards of ready-mixed concrete to be ordered.

CONCRETE PATIO DETAILS

If the soil beneath your patio is well drained and not soft or mucky, the concrete may be placed directly on the ground. Soft spots should be dug out and replaced with sand or gravel, tamped. In the case of clay soil that drains poorly, dig out enough so that you can place a 4- or 6-inch layer of compacted sand, gravel, or crushed stone over it as a subbase for your slab. In any case, plastic sheeting is not needed beneath a concrete slab outdoors.

Next to the house, a driveway, and other existing construction, ½ × 4-inch isolation joint material should be installed to separate the patio from the in-place construction. The columns for a patio cover need not have any special footings; they can rest directly on the patio surface.

Openings may be left in your patio for planters, trees, pool, and so on. Just form around the openings, placing the openings where control joints will go.

Curves may be formed as described in Chapter 6. Unless the slab is to be covered by hard-set pavers, it needs no mesh reinforcement. The 4-inch-thick patio slab should have control joints at 10-foot intervals, maximum, as shown on the next page. Any odd-shaped sections should be jointed to divide them into approximately square slabs.

FORMING AND JOINTING A CONCRETE PATIO

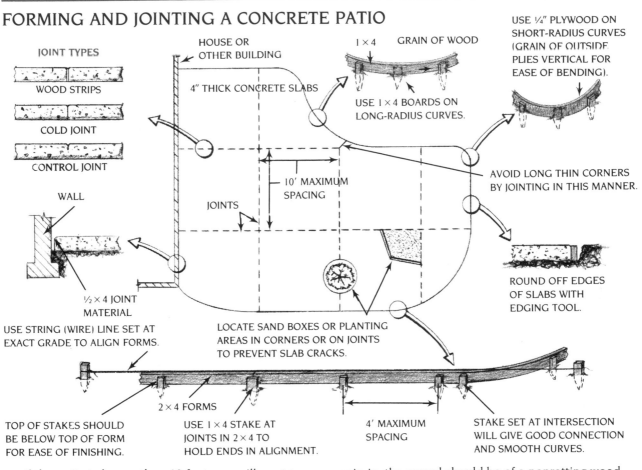

JOINT TYPES

WOOD STRIPS

COLD JOINT

CONTROL JOINT

WALL

½ × 4 JOINT MATERIAL

USE STRING (WIRE) LINE SET AT EXACT GRADE TO ALIGN FORMS.

HOUSE OR OTHER BUILDING

4" THICK CONCRETE SLABS

JOINTS

10' MAXIMUM SPACING

1 × 4   GRAIN OF WOOD

USE 1 × 4 BOARDS ON LONG-RADIUS CURVES.

USE ¼" PLYWOOD ON SHORT-RADIUS CURVES (GRAIN OF OUTSIDE PLIES VERTICAL FOR EASE OF BENDING).

AVOID LONG THIN CORNERS BY JOINTING IN THIS MANNER.

ROUND OFF EDGES OF SLABS WITH EDGING TOOL.

LOCATE SAND BOXES OR PLANTING AREAS IN CORNERS OR ON JOINTS TO PREVENT SLAB CRACKS.

TOP OF STAKES SHOULD BE BELOW TOP OF FORM FOR EASE OF FINISHING.

2 × 4 FORMS

USE 1 × 4 STAKE AT JOINTS IN 2 × 4 TO HOLD ENDS IN ALIGNMENT.

4' MAXIMUM SPACING

STAKE SET AT INTERSECTION WILL GIVE GOOD CONNECTION AND SMOOTH CURVES.

If the patio is longer than 10 feet, you will want to place an intermediate screed to make it easier to strike off. The screed may be left in the patio, or it may be removed while the concrete is still plastic and fresh concrete put in its place and finished over. If it is to remain in, the screed should be of a nonrotting wood, and 16d weather-resistant nails should be installed every 16 inches on alternating sides to tie it to the adjacent slabs.

Texture or color your concrete patio slab.

CHAPTER **9**

USING PAVERS

Pavers—flat units laid on a base, subbase, or on the ground as paving—may be grouped in two categories: *soft-set pavers* and *hard-set pavers*. Either kind may be used in building a patio. Use soft-set pavers to reduce expense and to lessen installation work. Use hard-set pavers for a high-quality, low-maintenance, loadbearing slab.

Soft-set pavers may be almost any weather-resistant material, ranging from whole brick or specially designed half-thick brick to flagstone, ceramic tile, and decorative blocks.

SOFT-SET PAVING

For paving to be set more or less loosely on a subbase or on the ground, a number of types of low-cost pavers may be used.

Types of Soft-set Pavers

Brick is probably the most popular soft-set paver. It is available in some 40 shapes and sizes from basic rectangles to squares and hexagons. In a freeze/thaw climate, you must use brick rated for paving—brick *pavers*. Porous common brick intended for building walls will break up if left in contact with freezing ground.

Slate in variegated colors is available in squares, rectangles, and other shapes.

Flagstone is not a specific kind of stone. The word may be applied to any nearly flat stone suitable for *flagging*—flat placement with edges aligned as much

The author poses by a soft-set brick patio laid in herringbone pattern. Fine, dry sand is swept into the joints to set the bricks. A curving cast-in-place concrete curb keeps the brick from separating. The pattern and the curbing required angled cutting of edge bricks, as shown on page 247.

Right photo: Joints for these cast-in-place concrete pavers are filled with soil planted to grass. As with all movable pavers, such a project can be done a little at a time (Portland Cement Association photo). Photo below: Soft-set pavers work well, even for large patios. Interlocking concrete masonry block paves 19,000 square feet around this graceful 1887 residence. Originated in Europe, pavers like this link together and will withstand severe weather without degrading (National Concrete Masonry Association photo).

This rather formal look was achieved with tile pavers bordered by slabs of marble, both types hard-set.

as possible with surrounding flags to create a surface.

Cutoff ends of redwood and pressure-treated woods (which must be treated to a rating of 0.40 Ground-contact or greater) are often used as pavers.

Precast concrete pavers are also suited to the soft-set method. You may precast your own pavers, or buy them ready-made. A wide variety is available. Shapes may be interlocking or simply flat squares, rectangles, or other patterns. Sometimes precast concrete pavers are called "patio blocks."

For soft-setting, avoid materials such as thin tiles that break easily and crumbly sandstone. Soft-set materials need to be at least 1½ inches thick and highly weather-resistant.

Preparation

Getting a surface ready to accept soft-set pavers is fairly simple. As is always the case, grading needs to be sloped away from the house at least ⅛ inch per foot. You don't need to be ultra-precise in grading because beneath soft-set paving, the ground retains its capacity to percolate water. Sometimes, a good

Keyhole-shaped concrete masonry pavers are designed to interlock neatly, forming attractive patterns. (Portland Cement Association photo)

You can cast your own concrete pavers with take-apart forms. Half-lapped at the corners, they stay together without fasteners, yet once the paver has cured, the 2 × 2 forms are disassembled. (Sakrete photo)

raking of the area is all the grading required. Other times, you may find it necessary to dig from 6 to 8 inches below the expected top level of the project. This space will be occupied by a layer of gravel, then of sand, and finally of the pavers themselves.

Layout and Grading

Your long-term satisfaction with your soft-set paved patio, sidewalk, or other project depends on sensible procedures in layout. Start by laying out the paving design with stakes at its corners. Tie mason's line to those stakes to provide an overall outline. Level the mason's line at the finished height of the pavers at the highest side, that is, the side nearest the house.

Now, drive stakes at 5-foot intervals. If the paved area will be quite large, the intervals may be 10 feet. At the building side of the plot, mark the first stake at the height of the finished pavers. Then go along the other outline stakes and mark the grade. If stakes are at 5-foot intervals, mark ½ inch lower at each stake; if at 10-foot intervals, 1 full inch lower at every stake.

SOFT-SET BRICK PAVING

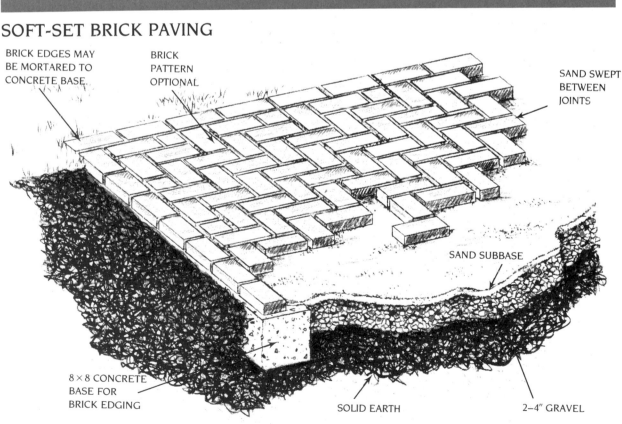

BRICK EDGES MAY BE MORTARED TO CONCRETE BASE.

BRICK PATTERN OPTIONAL

SAND SWEPT BETWEEN JOINTS

SAND SUBBASE

8 × 8 CONCRETE BASE FOR BRICK EDGING

SOLID EARTH

2–4" GRAVEL

STEPS IN LAYOUT

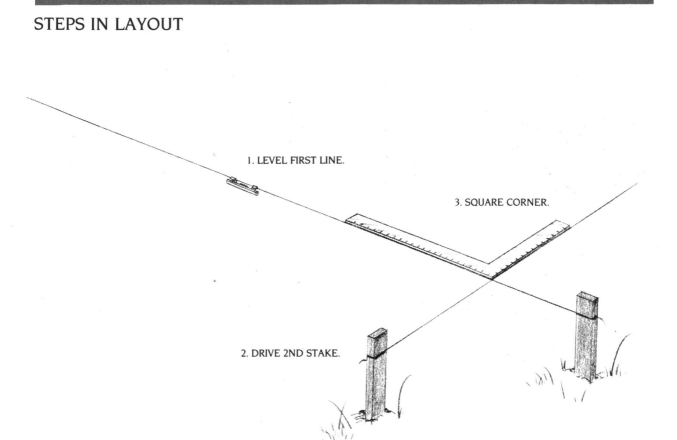

1. LEVEL FIRST LINE.

3. SQUARE CORNER.

2. DRIVE 2ND STAKE.

Excavation is next. You need to excavate to a depth at least equal to the thickness of the pavers you are using plus 2 inches for a sand subbase. When digging, whether by hand or machine, remove as little soil as possible. Try just to achieve the depth of your subbase at each point. Disturbed soil recompacted under the subbase makes a poor subgrade. To keep the subgrade as even and solid as possible, it is better to fill low spots with coarse sand. Now, place the sand subbase, unless you're laying large stone such as flagstone.

If you have good drainage from the area, large flagstones may be installed directly on a solid soil subgrade. If drainage is mediocre to poor, then a sand subbase is required. Flagstone may even be cut directly into the sod, leaving strips of sod at the stone edges. Simply lay the stone down and mark around it with an old screwdriver or similar tool. Then use a spade to lift out the sod to the depth of the stone. Finally, set the stone in place.

Excavate to a depth at least equal to the thickness of your pavers, plus 2 inches for a sand subbase. Avoid digging deeper than necessary.

SOFT-SET EDGING STYLES

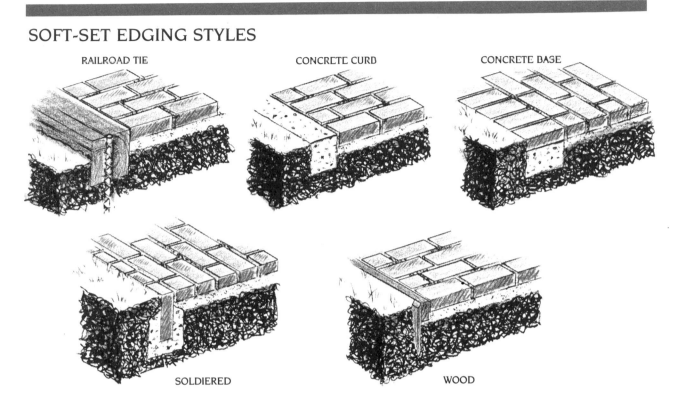

RAILROAD TIE CONCRETE CURB CONCRETE BASE

SOLDIERED WOOD

If drainage is likely to be a problem, such as with a heavy clay soil, the sand subbase should be laid on a layer of gravel. Usually, 2 to 4 inches of gravel will improve subbase drainage enough to cure such problems. Thus, allowing for 2 inches of gravel, 2 inches of tamped sand, and a 2-inch-thick paver, you will have to dig down some 6 inches. With a 4-inch gravel layer, the amount of sand may be cut to only 1 inch, so the paver plus sand plus gravel total would then be 7 inches. If the patio is to be higher than surrounding ground, you may dig shallower. An inch above grade is a good call.

Edging

An edging is advisable with soft-set pavers, both to allow a height increase and to hold the pavers in position. Though the height is up to you, the edging is usually level with the pavers. The edging may consist of landscape timbers, railroad ties, or nonrotting wood from 2×4s on up. All 2-by lumber should be placed on edge. Pressure-treated wood stakes must be at least 18 (to 24) inches long to hold the edging. Drive them until their tops are 1 or 2 inches below the top of the edging frame. Then bevel the tops (a reciprocating saw is great for this) and cover them with soil to hide them. Wood edgings also may be held with ⅜-

Soft-set paving, such as these bricks, complements other surfaces, including this ground cover, redwood edging, and cast-in-place concrete.

HOW TO EDGE WITH TIMBERS

Above left: Check the height from a stringline. Above right: Adjust the height and slope with sand.

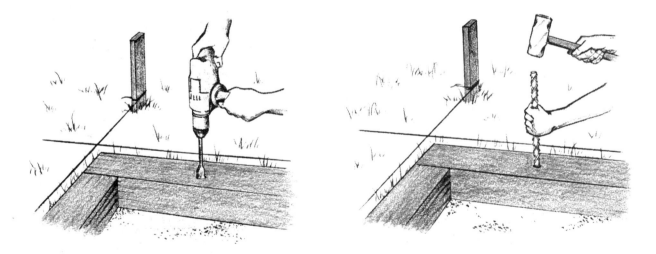

Above left: Drill tight-fitting holes for the rebar anchors. Above right: Drive the rebars.

or ½-inch rebars driven into the ground through holes drilled in the wood. Rod length should be 24 inches. Rod staking should be at 4-foot intervals.

Brick edgings, best-looking with brick pavers, may be set on end in a shallow trench backfilled to hold them. But if the sand subbase is more than 2 inches deep, this method does not work. A better brick edging method involves the laying of a small mortar footing about 12 to 18 inches below the patio surface and setting the brick into it.

Cast-in-place concrete edgings are made by placing concrete in a trench 8 to 12 inches deep. Plywood at least ⅜-inch thick will serve as a form for the edging. Stake the forms at 2-foot intervals with the tops at grade and leveled across. Place and finish the concrete; then strip the forms. If you use redwood forms, they are rot-resistant and so may be left in place. But be sure to drive 16d galvanized nails through the leave-in forms at 16-inch intervals to hold them in place once the concrete edging hardens.

Redwood or pressure-treated wood may be laid on edge as leave-in dividers within the pattern of pavers. Installing these is very much like installing edging of the same material, but staking is unnecessary.

Subbase

Once the edging is ready, you need to place the gravel drainage layer, if any, and the sand subbase. Do this by pouring them in place from a truck, wheelbarrow, or bags. Before dumping sand for the subbase, mark the level it must reach on the edging. Do this on each side by holding a paver level with the edging at one end, marking under it, doing the same at the other end, and then snapping a chalkline between the two marks.

Rake the sand as level as possible and then come back over it with the rake held upside down to smooth it. Tamp, then give it a final leveling off.

For small spaces—anything up to 6 or 8 feet wide —select a 2 × 4 straightedge and cut it to a width that reaches the outside of the edging. Next, notch each end of the 2 × 4 so it has a center drop ½ inch less than the depth of your pavers. Run this notched 2 × 4 —a sort of strikeoff tool—along the edging to give a final leveling to the sand subbase. An extra ½ inch or so of sand allows the pavers to sit above the edging by that much. This allows for later settling, plus any tamping and wiggling of the pavers that you do while setting them.

HARD-SET BRICK PAVING

BRICK PATTERN OPTIONAL

½" MORTAR LEVELING BED

4" CONCRETE

4" GRAVEL

WIRE MESH

2 × 4 STAKE AND FORM

Here is a cross-sectional view of elements required for hard-set brick paving (adapted from a drawing by the Brick Institute of America).

SMOOTHING THE SUBBASE

LEVELED SUBBASE

NOTCHED STRAIGHTEDGE

2 × 4 GUIDE

Use a notched-board template to smooth the subbase to the desired depth.

Preliminary Paver Layout

In the process of planning your project, you will have chosen a particular paver pattern and figured the number of pavers required. Some paver cutting is usually needed, but cutting can be minimized by careful layout once the edging is in place.

Begin by laying out the first row, close to the edging, starting at one side with a full paver. Use pieces of scrap plywood or hardboard of the thickness you plan for the sand-filled joints as spacers to separate the pavers. The smallest practical joint size is about ¼ inch, but you may have as much as ½ inch. Slate and similar large flagstones look good with joints upwards of an inch wide. Small variations in flagstone joints may help you avoid cutting.

Continue to the other side to see what amount of paver cutting would be required there. If you are very lucky—or measured both pavers and edging layout with exceptional care—full pavers will fit snugly across.

Depending on your pattern and the size and general layout of your project, you may only need to pre-lay that single row of pavers. Most designs, though, require laying several rows. And you will, in any case, want to lay a leg to form an **L** along the edging, even in a perfectly square or rectangular pattern. That leg will give you the paver cuts needed for courses in both directions. To reduce cutting, and to eliminate tiny chips of paver, move intermediate pavers so that you get at least half a paver on each end of each row. Some adjustment is also possible in the joint sizes, but this should be kept to little more than ⅛ inch per joint, which is not a great deal of help in a small project.

For more complex patterns—octagons, diamonds, ovals, and so on—you may find it best to lay out the entire pattern, shifting paver lines as necessary to get the arrangement requiring the fewest cuts. Again, try for at least half a paver at edgings, though you may find that some very complex patterns are impossible to work that way. In these cases, the ⅛ inch or so adjustment possible on each joint may become more

BRICK PAVING PATTERNS

useful than it usually is with rectangular projects, in which too much of a paver shift will throw another line totally off.

For rectangular and square patterns, a good solution is to leave one or more edging boards loose enough to be shifted slightly to accommodate full pavers. The time it takes to secure the loose edging is likely to be less than would otherwise be spent in cutting a whole row of pavers. This trick will result in a better-looking job, too.

For more complex patterns, edging should go in solidly, first. Then the pavers are settled in, as you cut them to fit as necessary.

Cutting the Pavers

Cutting of pavers is fairly simple, but you may spoil a few before you get the hang of it. Use a mason's hammer and a brick chisel (a small chisel with a wide blade). Work with the paver in sand or on a flat surface. Wearing safety goggles and work gloves, first score the paver lightly all around where you want it

To cut a brick or concrete paver, place it on a flat surface (or on sand) and score it all around with a brick chisel and mason's hammer. Then a few sharp blows to the chisel will make a clean break along the score. (Work gloves are recommended.)

cut. You can use the chisel edge or very light taps with the sharp peen on the mason's hammer to make the score. Then cut, placing the brick chisel in the score mark and tapping it with the mason's hammer until the paver breaks. Chip away uneven edges with the hammer's peen end.

Some kinds of pavers may not cut well using the above procedure. For these—primarily glazed pavers and some types of slate and granite—you will need an abrasive rod for a hacksaw, or else an abrasive blade for a circular saw. I don't recommend cutting pavers with a power tool, but if you do, you *must* wear safety goggles—preferably a face shield—*and* a dust mask. Be prepared to avoid injury should the blade be twisted in the cut and shatter explosively.

Laying Pavers

Now you are ready to lay the pavers in their permanent positions. Each goes down with a slight twist and enough pressure to settle it into the sand. The process can be performed very rapidly, since no mortar is involved.

Keep spaces between pavers as regular as you can. Interlocking pavers will set their own joint spacing. For the others, cut a good supply of ¼- or ⅜-inch plywood or hardboard spacing gauges, making them an inch taller than the paver thickness and one third to one half the length of the pavers. For laying rectangular pavers, also cut a supply of gauges about an inch less than the pavers' short-end dimensions. Use the gauges to control paver spacing, pulling them out just before checking the run of pavers with a straightedge. This is the primary reason those spacers are cut an inch taller than the pavers are deep.

Plastic pans that rest on the ground may be purchased to control spacing of brick pavers. Self-draining, they remain in place beneath the patio. Going by the name of Patio Pal, they're marketed by Argee (address in "Preface").

Sand-jointing

Now comes the finale. Spread sand over the entire surface of the project with a shovel, scattering it reasonably evenly. Then use a stiff broom to sweep the surface, working the sand into the joints. If the project is so large that you can't reach in from the edges, do your best not to dislodge any pavers as you walk on them. Walk flat-footed. Pick up most of the excess sand with a shovel, but don't be at all finicky about leaving plenty of sand behind.

Finally, set a garden hose to a light mist and spray

LAYING SOFT-SET PAVERS

Left photo: Interlocking keyhole concrete pavers are laid together on a smoothed sand subbase. The paver is then wiggled to settle it firmly into the sand. Right photo: Final edge spacers are driven in to complete the interlocking design and hold it all together. (Portland Cement Association photos)

You can reduce the need for cutting if you lay edging bricks after all others. Right photo: This mortarless method allows you to build a brick patio without the skill and effort required for brick laid in mortar. (Brick Association of North Carolina photos)

These pavers are home-cast concrete and are soft-set in sand. (Sakrete photo)

With hard-set pavers, you don't have to bother with grass growing between joints.

the whole surface. This will flush the remaining sand into the joints while compacting the sand already there.

The project may be used right away. In five or six weeks, check for extreme settling of sand in the joints. If settling is obvious (and it usually is), spread more sand near the joint lines, sweep it in, and moisten again. Repeat this process at intervals until there is no further settling.

HARD-SET PAVING

Hard-set pavers act more like a concrete surface than soft-set pavers do. Once you've properly laid hard-set pavers, they are there to stay. The permanence of hard-set pavers makes it a good idea to spend plenty

Stone-textured precast concrete pavers—called "Pennine Paving" in England, where they are manufactured—
are soft-set in this large garden terrace. (Cement and Concrete Association photo)

Hard-set pavers wear well and, under a shady roof in summer, stay comfortably cool to bare feet.

These hard-set herringbone-patterned brick pavers have long-lasting, sand-swept mortar joints.

of time deciding on materials, general layout, project placement, and the paver pattern you will lay.

The Concrete Base

Hard-set pavers are laid on a base slab of concrete and then embedded into either mortar or adhesive, or into the concrete itself. Whether or not mortar is used, the concrete base, or *pad*, will always be there. Install the concrete base just as for any other concrete project, with one major difference—don't worry about a finished look, for the pavers will hide the concrete surface. In this instance the concrete is employed only for stability.

A concrete base keeps frost heave from becoming a problem. A 4-inch-thick concrete slab is the minimum for frost-heave protection. If soil drainage is poor, build the slab over a 4- to 6-inch layer of gravel or crushed stone. To prevent shrinkage cracks from reflecting up through pavers bonded to it and cracking them, the concrete base also should contain adequate wire mesh reinforcement set midway in the slab. Chapter 6 tells how to proceed.

In milder climates, where frost heave is not a problem, some kinds of hard-set pavers may be laid and set without a slab. Flagstone tends to work reasonably

CONCRETE BASES FOR PAVERS

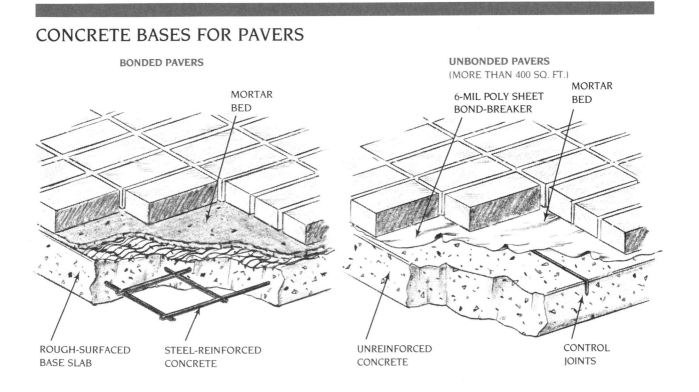

BONDED PAVERS

MORTAR BED

ROUGH-SURFACED BASE SLAB

STEEL-REINFORCED CONCRETE

UNBONDED PAVERS
(MORE THAN 400 SQ. FT.)

6-MIL POLY SHEET BOND-BREAKER

MORTAR BED

UNREINFORCED CONCRETE

CONTROL JOINTS

well used this way. The use of mortar in the joints still qualifies the design as hard-set.

Because water cannot penetrate a hard-set patio to percolate into the ground, the patio must be properly sloped away from the house to drain (¼ inch per foot).

A concrete pad for hard-set pavers is planned, graded, formed, and placed using the same techniques as for a solid concrete slab. The major difference comes in the elevation. To establish your elevation correctly, keep in mind that you must deduct the depth of the pavers plus that of any mortar beneath them from the finished depth of the concrete. Most standard-sized pavers are 2¼ inches thick, and a typical mortar bed will be ½ inch thick; thus, the typical slab must be planned, graded, and placed so that the top surface is 2¾ inches below the desired level of the finished project. If the pavers and mortar bed will vary from this formula, plan accordingly. Pavers such as stone, slate, and tile have different thicknesses. Plan for them after you have the material on hand and after you've determined accurately the depth of the mortar bed and paver together. In the discussion that follows, we will take brick as our model hard paver.

Unbonded Base Slab. In hard-set brick construction, some base slab reinforcement may be dispensed with. For projects of more than 400 square feet, build control joints into the 4-inch-thick base slab instead of reinforcing it. Before laying the brick pavers, place a bond-break between the slab and the mortar-set brick. The bond-break is needed because the rigid hard-set brick paving and the rigid concrete base have different thermal and moisture movement. A bond cannot be allowed to occur between them. A bond-break is simply a layer of 15-pound asphalt-saturated roofing felt or 6-mil polyethylene plastic sheet placed between the base slab and the hard-setting mortar bed to keep them from bonding together. A very thin layer of sand will work, too.

Control joints in the unbonded base and top surfaces need not be aligned over one another, *provided that the bond-break method is used.* If a bond-break is not used, control joints in the base and paving need to be aligned, one directly above another.

For hard-set brick projects of less than 400 square feet, the differential movements are so small that the brick paver layer may be bonded to its concrete base just as in most hard-set paving. Then the base slab should be suitably reinforced to hold shrinkage cracks tightly together.

Once you've placed the base slab, you'll need only to rough-float the surface. If you instead want to bond the pavers to the base, it's a good idea to scratch the

Left photo: In this two-on-two brick pattern, mortar was troweled into the joints and smoothed flush with the brick surface. Right photo: Proper grading allows rain runoff in desired directions. Though it is not apparent in the photo, this patio had several different slopes.

surface all over to roughen it for a better bond. It isn't necessary to cure the concrete before setting your pavers, but you should allow it at least 24 hours to harden sufficiently.

Brick in Mortar

Pavers may be laid in mortar in a number of ways. The standard method is to lay a mortar bed from ⅜ to 1 inch thick (a ½-inch bed is the usual thickness). Brick pavers are then "buttered" on the sides and ends with more mortar and laid in the bed.

Another technique is to lay the pavers in a mortar bed placed on the base slab and sift in a dry-mix of sand and cement between the pavers. (The proportions for this dry-mix are given below.) Then mist the pavement down with water to set the sifted mixture hard. The obvious reasons for using this dry-mix method are greater speed, economy of materials, and less general mess.

Mortar-making. The use of ready-packaged mortar mix saves a great deal of hassle. This comes in 60-pound bags and requires mixing in only enough water to bring it to the consistency of a fairly wet mud. The rule of thumb for mixing mortar is the opposite of that for concrete. You want mortar to be as wet as possible, so long as it's thick enough that the units set into it don't sink too low. The extra water ensures a good bond with pavers. Package directions are reasonably explicit on premixes. Use a wheelbarrow or a mortar box to mix the mortar with water. A garden hoe is a good mixing tool.

If you prefer to proportion your own mortar, a Type M portland cement-lime mixture is best. To make it, use 1 part Type 2 portland cement to ¼ part lime and 3 parts clean mortar sand. This mix is suitable for both standard and dry-mix applications. Start with small quantities because the mix sets fairly quickly. The rule of thumb is to mix no more than you will use in half an hour. The problem is to figure how much you will actually use in that time. The least wasteful method is to start with a gallon or two of mortar, and increase the amount from there as you gain proficiency.

Consider adding color pigments to mortar, because the dark colors tend to look cleaner after the paving has seen some use. For this, just use standard concrete color pigments.

Preparation

Depending somewhat on the edging material, it is usually simpler and easier to lay the edging first, leveling it carefully, and then use that edging as a guide for paver-laying. You will also want a mason's line for

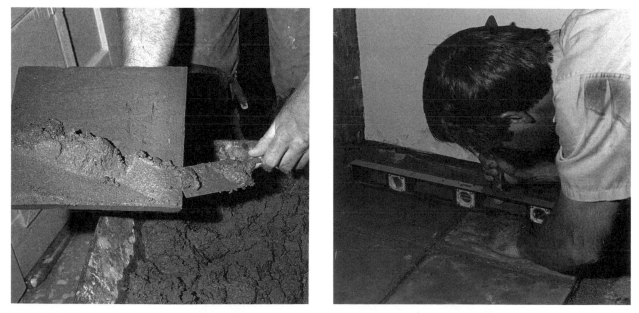

Left photo: Thin 12 × 12-inch Mexican tiles are buttered with mortar on the bottom. The base slab is mortared generously with a margin trowel. The tiles are then lowered into the mortar and tapped with the trowel handle (right photo) until they reach the desired elevation.

You can make your own elaborate pavers of 1½-inch-thick concrete. The mold, above, was made of 2 × 6 lumber with semicircles saber-sawed out, then cut in half and repositioned. A fairly dry mix of sand-mix concrete goes in. Just lift the form off for reuse when the paver has hardened sufficiently.

leveling, as well as a carpenter's level to check with every now and then. Of course, it is imperative to maintain the proper slope away from the house. The simplest way to do this is to use a 2-foot carpenter's level with a tapered shim at one end that is double the amount of per-foot pitch. For example, for a ¼-inch-per-foot pitch, the shim should be ½ inch thick. Tape it onto one end of the level with masking tape. In checking pitch, the shim is placed away from the house. To check unpitched areas, flip the level over so the shim is on top, out of the way.

Next, lay the mortar. Use a good mason's 10-inch trowel with a width of about 4½ inches (exclusive of handle).

It pays to make a dry run, laying down brick in the pattern you intend to use, including the desired joint spacing. The dry run ensures that you won't wind up with a tiny piece of paver at the opposite edge of the patio. Shifting the entire row half a paver will usually get rid of those tiny pieces. Cut a hard-set paver just as described and illustrated earlier for soft-set pavers.

Laying Pavers

Brick—even brick rated for paving—is porous and absorbs water readily. If you are using brick pavers, hose down the pile of brick before use. Also hose down the mortar bed area to be covered in your working session. Let the wetted bricks air-dry on the surface before laying them. The reason is simple: if the bricks are laid when dry, they will rapidly suck all the moisture from the mortar, long before the mortar has time to bond to them properly. The result is a weak bond. Brick is the only paver you should wet down in this manner.

Work with the mortar on a 2 × 2-foot plywood mortarboard. Cut the mortar off and place it with the trowel. Bedding mortar should be laid only in an area you are sure you can cover in 30 minutes. If you have practiced setting the brick down, and have everything cut and at hand, start with a 3-foot-square area, covering it with mortar thicker than the ultimately desired ½-inch bedding.

If you have already laid the edging, work from one side to the other, that is, assuming you have carefully laid out the brick dry and made the necessary adjustments and cuts. Where you've *not* laid the edging, you will be smarter to start from the center of the patio and work toward both edges.

Depending on the type of bond, butter the first few bricks with mortar on all sides that butt against the edging or other bricks. If you are starting from an edge, you'll find it simpler to lay in a bed of mortar alongside the edging, instead of buttering the brick being laid in. After that, you need only butter the adjacent edges. Shove the last brick firmly against the one already placed, and butt gently. Use the handle of your trowel to tap the brick into place as needed, and then to tap the brick into the mortar bed. If that isn't enough to settle the brick properly, use a wooden or rubber mallet to force the recalcitrant brick into place.

Slice off the excess mortar with the side of your trowel as you go along, returning it to the mortar board. Mortar cut off like this can be reused so long as it maintains its consistency. If the mortar starts to dry out, retemper it by adding water and remixing with the trowel. Discard any mortar older than 2½ hours.

Continue checking the level as you proceed. After you've covered a large area, you can lay a long, straight 2 × 4 over the area and place the level on it to check for flatness and proper slope. Keep a running check on mortar-joint width, too, but don't worry too much about minor variations. The pavers themselves won't always be perfect, and neither will you. So a bit of extra mortar will seldom show up—if it is really a *bit* and not a large slug. Pull out and reset any brick that is too far off, so long as the mortar is still plastic. If the mortar has lost its plasticity, scrape it off and apply fresh mortar.

Filling Joints

If you choose the dry-mix joint-mortaring method, your dry run can also be your final run. Once the bricks are in place, mix the mortar dry and then gently broom it into the brick joints. Check again to ensure that no bricks got upset or edged too far out of place while you were applying the dry mortar mix. Now, with garden hose, spray a light mist over the entire patio surface to dampen the mortar and begin its setting process. Don't apply so much water that you wash cement out of the mortar mix.

Let the patio dry. Then check the joints to see that there are no holes. There will probably be some: fill them with more dry-mix mortar and apply a little water from a plant-misting sprayer to harden it.

Experts generally agree that flush joints are best for this type of construction, because the flush surface helps keep water from standing and doesn't collect debris that would make the patio hard to sweep or hose clean.

At the end of each day's work, clean up as much excess mortar as you can. After you've finished the entire job, you can remove the worst mortar stains on the brick with a mixture of muriatic acid and water (add 1 part commercial-strength muriatic acid to 10 parts water). Pour the acid into the water, rather than

Plastic forms can be purchased for home-casting of concrete pavers. This form has a textured interior surface that creates nonskid top surfaces on pavers.

Interlocking metal forms from R. L. Spillman frame a home-built aggregate-transfer paver. Made upside down, the paver's attractive ags are hand-placed into a soft ½-inch layer of sand. Then colored sand-mix concrete is shoveled in over the ags. Finished ag-transfer units look like exposed aggregate, but needed no brushing or flushing. They emerge finished from the form.

the reverse. Wear heavy rubber gloves and eye protection, and keep body parts well covered with old clothing. Then do your very best not to splash the liquid around. Because muriatic acid is caustic, you may prefer to work with a somewhat milder concrete etching compound, such as United Gilsonite Laboratories' Drylok Etch. Follow the label directions.

Hard-set Stone

Stone, like brick, is suited to several methods of hard-set installation. The basic courses of grading, placing, reinforcing, and finishing the slab are the same as for brick, as is the dry-run method.

Factory-cut stone may be laid in a mortar bed, like brick. But instead of buttering mortar into the stone

Dressed-stone pavers are so regular they can be laid in brick patterns.

joints, use the grout-dribbling technique, with a grout bag. With stone, pouring the mortar into the joints is preferable to buttering because the stone is harder and less porous than brick, and any excess mortar left on the stone surface comes off far more easily.

Random-sized flagstone is set in a similar manner, but the mortar is mixed to a thick-mud consistency because the joints are wider.

Because of depth variations, it is nearly impossible to lay irregular flagstone using any of the above paver-layout methods. For a small project, you can sometimes set the flagstone directly into the concrete before it sets. The major problem with this is the setting time of the concrete versus the laying time of the flagstone. If you don't finish setting the stone in time, the entire job is spoiled.

For flagstone, sand-mix concrete is used as mortar, rather than a more workable mortar. The Building Stone Institute recommends the mortar-grout technique for hard-set flagstone, in both cold and warm climates. Climate determines whether or not a concrete base slab is placed between the gravel and the grouted flagstone. If frost may be expected, place the slab.

In a mild climate, dig to a depth of 6 inches (make this 10 inches if a base slab is required to prevent frost heave). Install the edging. Mix grout of one part portland cement and three parts clean mortar sand. No lime is used. (Ready-packaged sand-mix concrete

may be used.) Spread the grout to the depth of the thickest flagstone sections, no more than several inches. Begin laying flags in one corner, using an attractive mix of large and small ones interspersed, trying to keep gaps to about ½ inch. But don't be upset if some joints reach an inch or more. As you place each stone, press it firmly into the grout bed. Pound it down with a rubber mallet or 4 × 4, leveling it as much as possible. If you are laying dressed-stone pavers, be sure to stagger the joints attractively.

Bonding Stone Pavers. Now, you must make sure the flags will stay where you've put them. Starting in one corner of the project, turn up each stone and spread a portland cement-and-water slurry onto the underside of the flagstone. Then lay each paver back into place, giving it a couple light raps with the trowel handle. The cement slurry will bond the stone firmly to its base. Let it set overnight before mortaring the joints.

Jointing. The richer mortar for jointing stone is 1 part portland cement to 2 parts sand, applied with a pointing trowel and smoothed with a jointing tool. Finally, go over the project with a damp sponge, wiping off any excess mortar from the stone faces.

Hard-set Tile

Tile makes an excellent hard-set surface, highly attractive and very durable. Tile for outdoor use generally falls into two categories: patio tile and quarry tile. Either is suitable for a patio. Patio tile comes in brick-red and earth tones, and has irregularities in shape and texture that tend to look very informal. Quarry tile is more regular in shape and so lends a more precise, formal look. Medium-sized quarry tile is quite attractive, but the large 12 × 12-inch tiles seem to be more popular outdoors.·

Ask your tile dealer what method of setting is recommended for the tile you choose. Mortar-setting with a vinyl bonding agent in the mortar mix resists weathering. Some tiles should be laid over an exterior-type tile adhesive applied with a notched trowel. With larger tile you may wish to avoid adhesives, instead going for the somewhat simpler method of spreading a mortar bed in a manner similar to the one I described for mortared brick pavers, beginning on page 253. But with the much-larger tile, you need to apply mortar both to the back of the tile and to the base slab. To prevent air pockets from forming, peak up the mortar in the center of the tile so the center touches first, driving out any air.

Tile Patterns. Tiles are usually laid in formal, regular patterns with aligned joints. Do a dry run to

Tiles are smooth, formal, and elegant. The slimmer tiles need a rigid concrete base for support and may be set in mortar or adhesive.

Photo left: Although adobe pavers are fine for soft-setting, don't try to hard-set them because they are likely to crumble. Photo right: These precast concrete rectangles are soft-set, their joints filled with soil instead of sand. Such joints require mowing, however.

be sure you get things right. Lay the tiles with ⅜- to ½-inch joints; the larger the tile, the wider the joint allowed. Joints are easily smoothed or tooled with a ½-inch hardwood dowel. Do this when the mortar is thumbprint hard.

With tiles laid in adhesive, spread no more adhesive than you can cover with tile in half an hour. A 3- or 4-foot square is enough at first. Many dealers sell joint-spacers for tile that are exceptionally handy. Some tile pavers are self-spacing. In most cases, spacers should not remain in place when the joints are grouted. You can also use pieces of scrap plywood of the right thickness and then remove them before doing the jointing.

Other Pavers

Slate, decorative masonry block, and precast concrete block—just about anything else that will survive weathering—may be used for hard-set pavers. Avoid using adobe, however. Apply the basic techniques above to whatever material you select.

Hard-set Edging

Edging is not essential with hard-set pavers. Tile, however, is vulnerable to cracking if field tiles are used on the edges. Depending on the style of tile, you may be able to locate "bullnose" (rounded-edge) tiles for a finished edging. Or a nonrotting wood edging will hide the raw concrete base slab. Place the edging flush with or slightly below the paver surface.

If some concrete shows, cover the sides of the slab with the same materials used on the surface. Tile or thin stone is easily set onto the concrete sides with adhesive. Brick, on the other hand, is too thick to apply in that manner. Brick must be laid into a small footing beside the slab. Place the footing at the same time you place the slab. Then apply the brick vertically.

Care and Maintenance

One of the great attractions of hard-set pavers is their general durability under rough use. Those who wish their pavers to retain a shiny, new look can give them a coat of clear, nonyellowing sealer every few years.

One of the major reasons for building with hard-set pavers is not to have to worry about upkeep. So forget about care and maintenance, because it really is almost never needed. Sit back and enjoy.

CHAPTER 10

BUILDING DECK AND PATIO COVERS

Because outdoor rooms are designed to take the sun, a roof for a patio or deck may seem at first like a raincoat for the bathroom shower. Yet when the summer sun beats down on an area most of the day, the use of that area may be limited to overcast or cooler days. A desire for shade is probably the most common reason for building a full or partial cover over a deck or patio. A cover can also provide shelter from rain, as well as a feeling of protection.

Covers may not be needed for north-facing decks and patios. But for south-facing areas, a partial cover for shade may be desirable. When the deck or patio faces east, the sun will strike during the cooler morning hours, a better time to enjoy it. Location on the west side of a house means that a patio or deck will get the hottest, meanest sun of all.

In a region that gets heavy rainfall, a water-shedding cover may be a real benefit. In northern climates, you need to allow for snow load.

PLANNING THE COVER

Though forethought for sun and rain are crucial, you should also take your house's style into account. A stately mansion will look bizarre with a modern roof jutting out, while a plain clapboard ranch house would look strange with an ornate appendage.

Patio or deck shape may well dictate design. Square and rectangular decks and patios are easy to roof, partially or wholly, since most roofs are built in those shapes. An oval or other odd shape is far harder to roof with style.

You have additional decisions to make. Do you wish partial shade? Full shade? Translucent shade? You may elect to build a gridwork of 2×4s and other timbers over the area, allowing sunshine to infiltrate but not hammer down fully. And this may be supplemented by fully covered areas.

Materials

The materials will depend on the same concerns as the kind of cover you decide upon.

Patio and deck covers seldom employ shingles, because the covers are almost always flat or shed-style, without enough slope for a shingled roof. Perforated aluminum panels, burlap, thin-sheet plastic, window screening, hardware cloth, and other materials have all been used. In most cases, such materials are not practical because they are either too flimsy or too expensive. A good number are ugly. The table "Deck or Patio Cover Methods" presents the merits and drawbacks of the more practical choices.

If rain is no concern, wood slats and louvers or lattice panels are suitable. Such covers will keep out as much sun as desired and will still soften the rain. The wood may be arranged "eggcrate"-fashion (see illustration on page 262). Vines may be trained to grow over a relatively open roof for natural shading.

Translucent fiberglass and plastic panels provide

This wood-slat patio cover built by the author and his son Doug has anchors cast into the patio slab for support. At the house wall, a 2×6 ledger board is lag-screwed to the wall for support but extends beyond the house for additional shading. The rafter ends are decoratively angle-cut.

an airy feel, while also fending off excess sun and rain. These are attached to a light wood frame. Most panel manufacturers offer complete plans and even kits. These lightweight panels differ in strength. For example, acrylic plastic is not as strong as fiberglass, which is really fiberglass-reinforced plastic (FRP). Fiberglass is the preferred panel when strength is a factor, and thus is used where snowfalls are heavier. In most cases, patio or deck covers are made of fiberglass that is corrugated, which provides extra strength. All panels are shatter-resistant and easy to clean with a garden hose. A number of color choices are offered, including

DECK AND PATIO COVER METHODS

Method	Materials	Benefits	Drawbacks	Cost
Solid wood	Plywood covered by shingles or roll roofing.	Provides rain- and snow-proofing.	Requires full-strength structure; allows no solar penetration.	Moderate to high
Wooden slats, louvers, grids	Nonrotting 1 × 2s flat, 2 × 2s, 2 × 4s flat, or ready-made lattice panels.	Provides shade; softens rain; permits lightweight structure; may be covered with shade cloth.	Offers no rainproofing; may create zebralike or diamond-shaped light patterns beneath.	Low
Bamboo and reed	Rolled strips of woven wood over a light wooden frame.	Makes soft light patterns.	Not durable, lasting only a couple of seasons.	Low
Plastic panels	Flat or corrugated acrylic or FRP sheets installed over a frame.	Provides rain- and snow-proofing; lets some light through; permits lightweight structure.	Tends to trap heat beneath; can't be walked on; may discolor or fade; needs 3-in-12 pitch.	Moderate
Shade cloth	Screenlike plastic material, usually colored green and laid over a light wood frame.	Durable; provides shade without making light patterns below; may be taken down for winter storage; softens rain; available in degrees of shade; may be rolled back.	Needs wood-frame supports; subject to wind damage; can't be walked on.	Moderate
Canvas, Dacron	10.10 army duck, other canvas, or Dacron over a wood frame.	May be opened or closed as desired; permits lightweight structure.	Needs wood or pipe supports; not totally DIY; subject to wind damage; shouldn't be walked on.	Moderate to high

EGGCRATE COVER

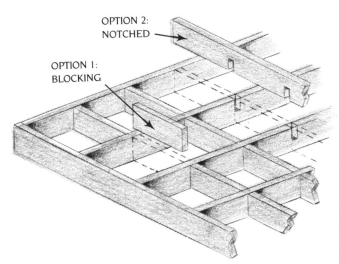

OPTION 2: NOTCHED

OPTION 1: BLOCKING

An eggcrate patio cover can be built of 1 × 6 lumber notched for overlapping. The cover in the photo has a varied mosaic of rectangles. (Drawing adapted from California Redwood Association literature)

Left photo: Translucent corrugated fiberglass panels fastened to a light wood frame provide rain protection as well as shade, while letting through soft light (Filon Division, Vistron Corporation photo). Photo right: This fold-out canvas patio cover is fitted to brackets that open over the patio like an awning (Inter Trade Inc. photo).

uncolored translucent. The darker colors let through much less light. Colors may also affect both the deck or patio atmosphere and the light inside your house.

The translucent panels let light and heat in, but they don't allow much heat to rise through them. While this is fine in cooler climates, this tendency may make you regret your choice in very hot climes, especially hot and humid climes. If you live in an area where muggy weather is frequent, select darker colors to keep out solar heat. Roof slopes for plastic panels should have at least 3-in-12 pitch (3 inches down for each 12 inches of horizontal distance).

Do not use glass for patio and deck roofing, unless it is mesh-reinforced safety glass—and that's expensive. Ordinary window glass is far too dangerous for horizontal overhead use. Besides, glass is so much more costly and hard to work with than the plastics that it simply isn't a sensible choice.

Roof Fabrics.   Cotton canvas is widely used. An even better canvas is Dacron, but Dacron is quite costly and may be hard to find unless you live in a region where marine goods are sold. (Dacron is widely used in top-grade sailmaking.) Cotton canvas is relatively inexpensive and holds up to the elements sur-

prisingly well. Wind damage can be minimized by making sure the canvas is laid tightly.

Canvas thickness is measured in weight, which may range from 7 to 15 ounces per square yard. You will also find a wide range of colors, which are dyed by several different methods. Without going into the relative merits of different weights, dyes, and colors, it is enough to say that the type of canvas most commonly used for patio roofs (and awnings, for that matter) is 10.10-ounce army duck. This doesn't mean your patio or deck cover has to look like an army tent, though that's where the name originated. Army duck refers to specially woven and chemically treated material designed for outdoor use. It is—or should be—treated to avoid mildew and fungus. In spite of its name, army duck is available in a wide range of colors, including plain off-white and uncolored pearl gray. The gray is not very attractive, but the off-white is quite nice, because it lets a little sunlight through and reflects heat, as well.

For colored canvas, you'll find painted canvas is best. The modern acrylic paints adhere much better and longer than the oil-based paint used decades ago. Dyed canvas sounds good, but it tends to fade and is quite expensive. It will also stretch and allow puddles to form, although it is fine for vertical applications. If you like whites and pastels, you may wish to pay extra for vinyl-coated canvas, which is sun-fast and sheds dirt better than plain canvas.

Properly designed and installed, a canvas roof can look quite elegant. On the other hand, if it is put up without much thought or care, it will look rough and sloppy. One of the prime advantages of canvas is that it may be rolled up and stored. This feature makes it ideal for a small patio or deck on which you would like to have a cover in some seasons but would like openness in others.

Remember, however, that working with canvas is not a typical do-it-yourself skill. Canvas requires cutting and sewing, a problem for those of us who have difficulty sewing a button on a shirt. Men's liberation notwithstanding, most men will have a few problems here. Whoever does the sewing will want to use a No. 13 sailmaker's needle and heavy Dacron thread. If extensive sewing is involved, it would be best to use a machine—but the machines that can penetrate several layers of 10.10 canvas are heavy-duty commercial machines, not the typical home sewing machines. It may be wise to check the cost of having an awning dealer sew the canvas for you, though that is likely to push the price up considerably.

Canvas of good quality is not cheap, but can be relatively inexpensive if you plan well and minimize waste. To reduce waste, check with the local suppliers to determine standard sizes of canvas and then base your cover design on those sizes. Using standard sizes is always cheaper than custom-fitting. By means of a grommet tool, you can install grommets for tying the canvas to a framework.

Outdoor plastic shade cloth makes an excellent sunscreen when laid over light framing supports. It provides cooling as well as protection from ultraviolet rays. Made much like window screening, plastic shade cloth comes in green, white, or black—in saran, polyethylene, or polypropylene, respectively. A choice of weaves is available, giving from less than 30 percent to more than 90 percent shade. This allows you to enjoy the amount of solar protection you want. Shade cloth, whether stapled, tied, or laced to supports, should be installed loosely to prevent shrinkage from straining it.

Woven bamboo and reed make fine sunshades. Laid over a light framework, they don't give the harsh, regular light patterns of slats and lattice panels. You buy the material in a roll and lay it over the cover frame. Long life is not a bamboo or reed trait, so plan on periodic replacement.

STRUCTURAL DESIGN

Before starting a cover, even for an existing deck or patio, check with the local building department to find out whether a building permit is needed and what setbacks from property lines are required.

Structural framing is a crucial topic, no matter what the cover is. Poor design and execution can mess up your roof, *and* cause injuries. How deeply you need to get into design depends on the type of patio roof you've chosen. Screen-style roofs present less cause for worry than solid ones. Since wind, snow, and rain pass through screen-style roofs, these roofs generally need to support no more than themselves.

It's smart to build your patio or deck cover to withstand any force of nature that might arise. Snow and other loads are recorded at your local building-department office. Even if snow is not an issue, a solid roof must be strong enough to allow someone to climb on it for painting and repairs. Wind stress, no matter where you live, can occasionally become brutal. Your roof must be designed to withstand the worst.

Standard Structural Design
The suggestions here apply to most types of roofs and fulfill the requirements of most building codes. Again, you must check locally for special wind and snow-load requirements. If you find nothing to the contrary in your local codes, these suggestions will suffice for most parts of North America. You may be tempted to skimp a little, but skimping is unwise. Skimping saves little money up front and can cause big problems later.

Read this entire section before you draw up cover plans. Consider such factors as joist and beam spans versus dimensions before you dig your first posthole. You don't want to find out, for example, that the posts won't support the beams and that the footings must be dug all over again. If at all possible, keep lumber sizes standard, using 2×4, 4×4, and 4×6 material, as required. Ordering special lengths and sizes increases lumber costs greatly.

Again, be sure your plans adhere to local building codes and are based on sound engineering. A falling beam, or even a 2×4, could be fatal. Safety goggles and a hard hat are *essential* when working with materials overhead.

COVER STRUCTURE

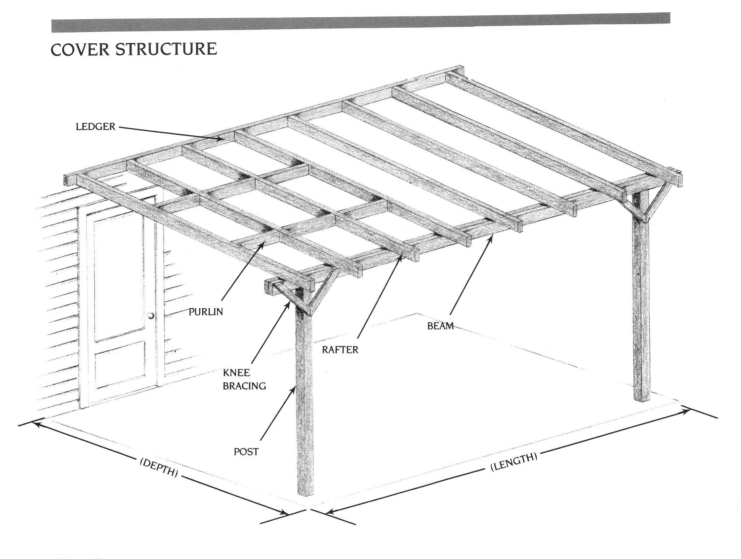

LEDGER

PURLIN

KNEE BRACING

POST

RAFTER

BEAM

(DEPTH)

(LENGTH)

Footings

Most patios and decks have an adequate foundation to build upon. But if you don't already have an adequate foundation, you'll need to create concrete footings for posts. The footings should be twice the diameter of the posts (that's 8 inches in diameter for a 4 × 4 post). And they should extend below the frost line. (Frost-line figures for your area are available from your local building-inspection office.) If frost is not a problem in your locale, you'll still need footings. They must be just as wide as standard, but can likely be placed only 12 inches deep. If a concrete patio is of cast-in-place concrete at least 4 inches thick, posts usually may be directly connected to the slab using post anchors that support the post bottom up off the concrete. But check with your building department.

If you deck-mount the posts, you'll need galvanized steel post anchors to prevent excessive movement and to help hold the posts plumb. Various brands of wood-to-wood post anchors are available.

Standard post anchors for concrete footings consist of three pieces, with the largest fitting over an anchor bolt. An included washer is placed over the bolt, and the nut is threaded on.

Posts

For most deck or patio covers, 4 × 4 posts will provide adequate support. The post-height table in Chapter 2 will serve as a guide as to maximum post lengths. Choose only redwood, red cedar, cypress, post (black) locust, or pressure-treated lumber. In a very few cases, with an extremely high or heavy deck or patio cover, you might need to use 6 × 6 posts. For a massive effect, heavier posts can always be used. Posts can also be decorated with trim boards.

POST FOOTINGS

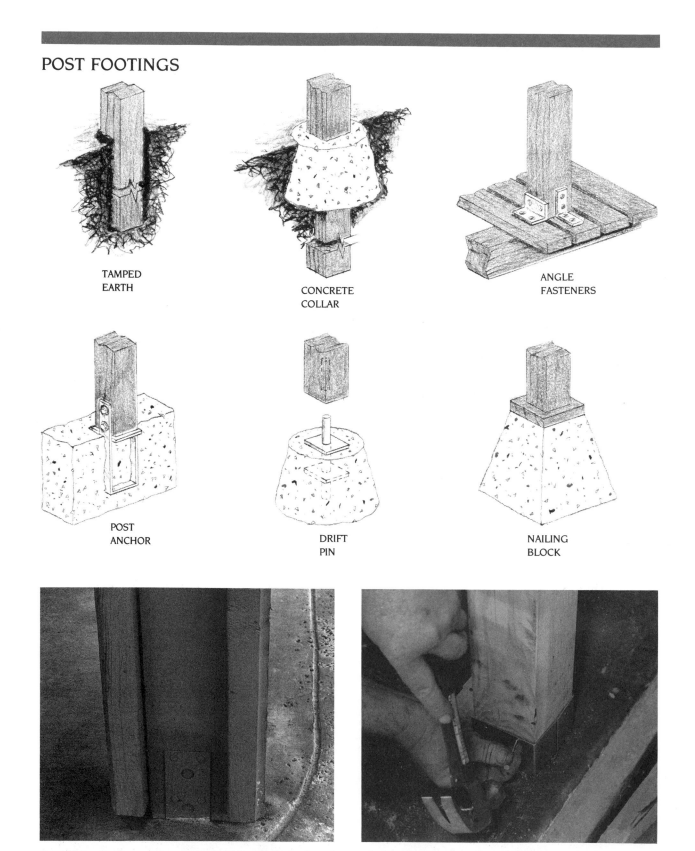

TAMPED
EARTH

CONCRETE
COLLAR

ANGLE
FASTENERS

POST
ANCHOR

DRIFT
PIN

NAILING
BLOCK

Posts for a deck or patio cover must be anchored, in these photos to a concrete slab. The best post anchors hold wood posts slightly up off the concrete to prevent rot. These anchors were nailed to the posts.

POST-AND-BEAM CONNECTIONS

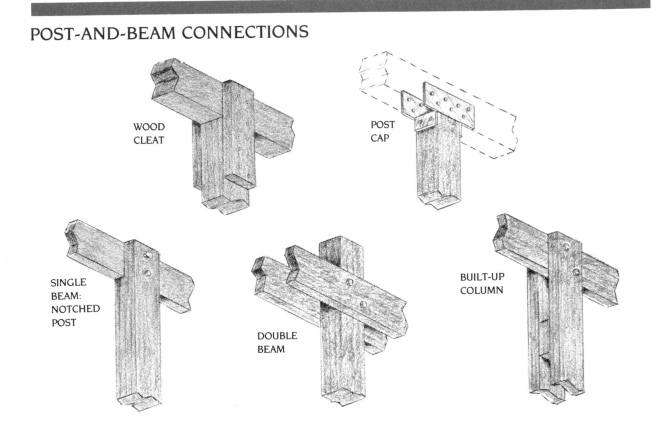

WOOD CLEAT

POST CAP

SINGLE BEAM: NOTCHED POST

DOUBLE BEAM

BUILT-UP COLUMN

Beams

Beam size is determined by the wood species, span, and spacing, as well as by the load the beams must support. The beam-span tables in Chapter 2 are your guide. As a general rule, you'll find it safe, though perhaps a bit overbuilt and costly, to use a 4-by beam depth in inches corresponding to the length of the span in feet. That is, for supports 6 feet apart, you would use 4×6 beams. For posts 8 feet apart, use 4×8 beams, and so on.

Rafters

Rafters are the framing members between roof beams. They correspond to the joists in a deck floor. If your posts and beams are strong enough, rafter size is simple to figure. Use 2×4s for spans up to 8 feet in length with centers up to 16 inches apart. For centers of more than 16 inches, use 2×6s. When the span is from 8 to 12 feet, use 2×6s unless the spacing is more than 16 inches. Then go to 2×8s. For 12- to 16-foot spans, use

2×8s on 16-inch centers, and 2×10s for wider-spaced centers to 32 inches.

Ledgers

In many cases, the back, or high, edge of your deck or patio cover will be connected to a house wall. If the house structure is sturdy, the wall should have enough strength to support the roof with no additional bracing. On shingle or clapboard, simply attach a ledger board of the same size as the rafters, using $\frac{3}{8} \times 5$-inch weather-resistant lag screws and washers. Use one lag screw at every wall stud. You may need to use a stud finder to locate the house-wall studs. When you find one, the others should be 16 inches on centers.

For brick or masonry, drill properly sized holes at least 2 inches into the masonry—preferably into the mortar joints—and install $\frac{3}{8}$-inch lead-shield or wedge-bolt anchors to fit. Use $\frac{3}{8}$-inch lag bolts through the header and into the anchors. The lag bolts should be $3\frac{1}{2}$ inches, spaced at least every 16 inches.

Joist hangers offer the easiest and best way to attach rafters to the ledger. You may also wish to nail

Photo left: Nailed-on 2 × 6 boards add some strength to these 4 × 4 cover posts, though the 2 × 6s are essentially decorative. Photo right: The supports for a deck or patio cover need not be wood. Galvanized pipes can serve the purpose. Here, pipe flanges are screwed to rails and directly over supporting posts. (Western Wood Products Association photo)

a support strip (using a 2 × 2 strip for 2 × 6 ledger, a 2 × 4 for 2 × 8 ledger, and so on) along the bottom of the ledger. Notch the bottom of the rafters to fit over the support strip, and toenail each rafter to both the ledger and the support strip.

Other Supports

For the typical deck or patio cover roof, exterior plywood sheathing (APA-rated for the rafter spacing) is nailed directly to the rafters. Then the roofing materials themselves are laid. Other roofs, however, may require intermediate structural members called *purlins*. Plastic or fiberglass panels come in lengths of 8 feet and more, usually with a 2-foot exposure in width. Since all panel edges must be supported, purlins are installed where the panels overlap at the ends. At the

edges they must overlap above rafters. The purlins are not technically a part of the structure, but they are necessary to hold up the ends of the sheets and to act as cross-panel nailing strips.

TYPICAL CONSTRUCTION

As always, draw a detailed plan before starting the project. Have the plans approved by the local building department, if required. The fewer surprises as you proceed, the better the job will go.

Posts are attached to footings by one of the methods I've already described. As you position each post, construct temporary angle-braces for support until the beams and other cross-members can be installed. Plumb each with a level and secure it.

The beams used in deck or patio cover construction can be quite heavy indeed. If so, you'll need a strong friend or two to help erect them safely. You can use various types of hoists, but usually a helper with a pair of sturdy stepladders is cheaper and easier. A helper also lets you install material without first needing to secure one end, go to another end, unlatch, move, resecure, and so on.

Once the posts and beams are up, make sure all are plumb and level. Posts *must* be plumb. Beams *must* be level. Move or remove any bracing, temporarily, to make adjustments. Then rebrace until the rafters are nailed tight.

Pitched roofs require notched rafters that fit tightly over the beams and snugly against the ledger on the house. Any of a number of accepted methods may be used to create such rafters. Carpenters use a framing square to mark angle cuts. But the easiest method, least prone to error for the do-it-yourselfer, is to create one rafter first, by trial and error, and then use it as a template for the others.

To create rafters, lay the lumber for one rafter across the beam and against the house ledger. At the house end, lay a piece of wood against the house wall and along the side of the rafter. Draw a line on the rafter piece along the front of the scrap wood, to get the correct cut-off angle. Make that cut, and put the rafter back in place against the house and over the beam. Use the same wood scrap to draw angles where the rafter hits the beam. Cut out the notch to fit along those lines. Replace the rafter and check carefully for fit. Make any recuts carefully, and recheck the rafter in place. Once the fit is exact, cut the remaining rafters by laying the first one on all the others as a template.

Rafter material will be 2-by. If you are using the template method, you might feel uncertain about your ability to cut the first rafter correctly the first time, thereby wasting costly lumber. In that case, make your template from a straight, cheap 1-by board of the same width and length as the rafter material.

Once the rafters are in place, and if bracing is needed, lay in the purlins. Roofs built with plywood

RAFTER–LEDGER CONNECTION

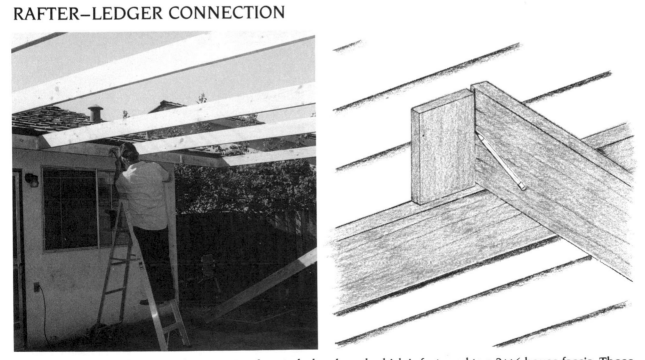

Photo: Bob Hunt is fastening this cover's rafters to ledger board, which is fastened to a 2 × 6 house fascia. These 2 × 8 rafters are being installed in joist hangers 4 feet apart and will receive 4 × 8-foot redwood lattice panels. Drawing: Here's how you can mark the rafters for cutting.

decking do not need purlins and can be braced at panel ends with Plyclips (ask your dealer for them). If you are building with fiberglass, plastic, or lattice panels, you'll need purlins. For plastic panels, purlins are installed according to the manufacturer's instructions, but they must be flush with the top of the rafters. Purlins may be of lighter stock than other members—2 × 2s, for example. The braces are not intended to increase overall structural integrity. Instead they are intended to support the roofing. But since nailing roofing into lightweight purlins can be a bouncy chore, you may prefer to use 2 × 4 braces after all.

After completing the framing, you can remove the post angle-bracing. If the frame seems wobbly, you may need knee braces or some plywood gussets between posts and beam.

Of course, deck or patio covering framing does not have to be wood. Structural steel, wrought iron, or pipe may be used. For a canvas roof, ¾-inch threaded galvanized water pipe makes a dandy frame. After you have your plans drawn up, a comprehensive hardware or plumbing dealer can cut and thread the pipe to your specifications. Or you can rent the pipe-cutting tools. Awning dealers carry the fittings and other attachments you will need. The dealer may even be willing to draw up plans for you.

Follow the manufacturer's instructions for installing framing types other than wood.

Bob Hunt aligns a rafter to its mark and is about to install a tiedown strap to secure it.

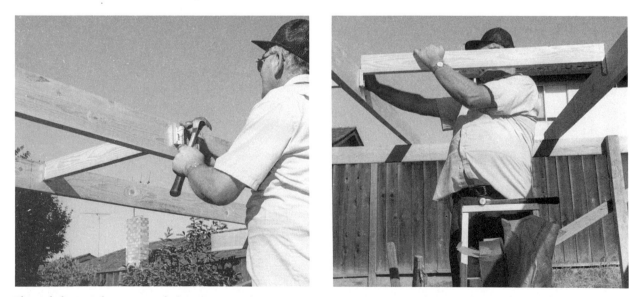

Photo left: At 8-foot intervals between each pair of rafters, 2 × 4 purlins will support the ends of lattice panels. Bob is nailing purlin hangers. Photo right: A 2 × 4 purlin is installed between two hangers. Hangers are much stronger and better than toenailing the purlins at each end.

INSTALLING THE ROOF

If you plan to paint or stain your framing, the best time to do it is before putting it up. Be sure that any corrugated plastic or fiberglass panels that require special closure strips have them; these are manufactured to match the configuration of the panels to the framing. Most FRP panels should overlap about 2 inches, or one corrugation, at the sides, and about 4 inches top-over-bottom where the panel ends meet. Allow at least a 2-inch overhang at all edges. Apply the manufacturer-recommended elastomeric (rubber-like) sealant at overlaps.

Most plastic-panel manufacturers offer their own aluminum deformed-shank nails, with soft neoprene washers under the heads. All plastic panels should be predrilled with a ⅛-inch or ⁵⁄₃₂-inch bit to avoid crack-ing and crazing (minute cracks). Drive nails every 12 inches along the framing. For a waterproof roof, apply sealant all along the top of the frame before laying the panels. With corrugated materials, always nail on the crowns, never in the valleys, unless a cut section forces you to nail at an edge.

If you have to cut a panel (plastic, fiberglass-reinforced, or aluminum), use a fine-toothed carbide-tipped blade in a circular saw. (You can cut fiberglass and other plastics with a standard blade, but this causes rapid blade wear. Carbide-tipped blades are best.) Eye protection and a dust mask are mandatory; face protection is recommended.

Louvered, wood screen, and other kinds of patio and deck roofs require varied installation methods. Limited space here prevents me from covering all the possibilities. Yet the basic carpentry skills covered throughout this book, care in the design phase, and careful measuring and cutting are all you'll really need. With attention to detail, your roof should be attractive and long-lasting.

Above: Galvanized nails are driven every 6 inches to hold the lattice panels to the framework. Author's son Doug (on roof) distributed his weight onto temporary rafter-to-rafter boards. Below: High contrast in this photo exaggerates the spotty lighting, which is scarcely noticeable to Leanna Day and friends.

Redwood lattice panels are hoisted onto the cover roof for installation between rafters. Panel ends will be centered on 2 × 4 purlins for all-around support.

CHAPTER 11

FENCE DESIGN AND CONSTRUCTION

A well designed and properly installed fence adds a pleasing accent to a house. It can also provide privacy, containment, and security.

The wood species used for fences are the same as those for general outdoor carpentry. For their longevity in outdoor conditions, the best choices are redwood and cedar, and species used for pressure-treated lumber. When using a pressure-treated wood, make sure the treatment level corresponds to the wood's intended use. For example, treatment should be "In-ground" for posts, "Ground-contact" for use within 6 inches of the ground, or "Weather-exposure" for aboveground uses.

Also, remember to build the fence with rust-resistant hardware. Hot-dipped galvanized or aluminum nails are a necessity. So are plated bolts, screws, hinges, and other hardware.

FENCE-PLANNING PRELIMINARIES

As with all other outdoor construction projects, take your time at the design stage and again at the layout stage. That can save you time and money during construction.

A book chapter can't adequately cover every fence variant for residential use, let alone for farm and other areas. Yet the types and methods I discuss here present enough options to allow you to design a pleasing and durable fence for your own needs.

Fences should be styled to complement house and outbuilding styles. A high picket fence with lots of fancy filigree work isn't appropriate for a small ranch house on a tiny lot. A simple privacy fence with vertical boards, possibly with spaced uprights between the posts to allow wind flow-through, would look much better.

An axiom of design is that simple additions frequently go well with complex house designs, while ornate additions almost never go well with simpler house designs.

Attractive fencing may be costly or relatively inexpensive. Yet no durable fencing is cheap. The style is up to you, within the limits of local building codes.

Codes and Fences

As always with large projects, it pays to check with the local building department about fence permits, codes, and zoning ordinances. These will cover such factors as allowable height and required setback from boundary lines. Even rural areas tend to have fence setback restrictions. Among other things, building codes ensure that your fence is either on or inside your property lines. Many urban and suburban areas restrict fence heights, though usually well within the limits of common sense. For example, 6 feet appears to be a common height restriction for residential fencing. If you want to go higher, you can try asking for a variance —maybe first consulting your neighbors.

Above: Taller palisade fences, shown in the backyard, provide good privacy but would look less neighborly in the front yard. There, shorter pickets are used (Photographer, Gordon N. Converse; Walpole Woodworkers photo). Left: Half-round pickets in this stockade fence dip lower at the gate, making the gate look inviting and allowing users to see over (Walpole Woodworkers photo).

Find out whether a building permit is needed to construct a fence. If so, make sure all drawings of your fence layout, both plot and structural drawings, meet applicable codes for material, setback, burial depth of posts, and fence height. Check on any other restrictions. Some very strict codes even set out fence color and maintenance requirements.

To keep children out, codes almost always require a nonclimbable fence around an "attractive nuisance," such as a swimming pool.

Building permits at least imply inspection of the project, whether during or after it is erected. If inspection is necessary, be sure to coordinate with the building inspector. In case the inspector insists on a visual

Left photo: This diagonal screen divider looks massive. Construction common redwood was used, with construction heart posts (Photographer, Ernest Braun; California Redwood Association photo). Right photo: This well-detailed fence employs doubled 2 × 4 posts and curving rails that support fine vertical boards. Plantings at the base fill the gap for privacy.

Left photo: Lattice and plantings can provide good privacy, while looking more like decoration than a barrier (Photographer, John Fulker; Council of Forest Industries of British Columbia photo). Right photo: A post-and-rail fence will complement many house designs (Walpole Woodworkers photo).

check of post burial depth in relation to height, it's wise not to fill postholes until after inspection.

Before you build the fence, consult your neighbors. If approached properly, they may even agree to share in the cost and maintenance of the fence, since the fence benefits both parties. In return for cooperation, they will surely want a say in what the fence looks like. If you come to an agreement, write it up and have all parties sign it. Then have it recorded against the real-estate deeds. Once that is done, the agreement becomes legally binding on all parties, even new owners. As a bonus, having an agreement allows you to place the fence directly on the property line. Be sure you have an accurate survey of the property line before you fence.

If your neighbors are uncooperative, you may want to consider abandoning the fence idea. If you go ahead despite the neighbors, avoid putting any parts of the fence on your neighbor's property. Stay at least an inch on your side of the property line. In fact, some codes require this. Code may even require the fence owner to leave enough space on the neighbor's side so that you won't need to trespass when maintaining the fence.

In the interests of neighborliness, you'll probably want to build a fence that looks good on both sides. Or else you could turn the good side toward your neighbors. After all, you'd want them to do the same.

Another factor: the law of *adverse possession* in many areas eventually may award every bit of property on the other side of your fence to your neighbors. Often, a time period is specified, such as 5 years, after which they can legally claim the land on their side of the fence. Because of this, fences have a way of becoming property lines. For this reason, you don't want to build much inside your property line.

BOARD FENCES

Board fences consist of a structure and a facing. The board-fence structure is wonderfully adaptable because a myriad of facings may be installed.

The construction principles for a wood fence are basically the same, whatever the facing. Posts, usually 4 × 4s or round pressure-treated posts called *peeler cores*, are set securely into the ground. The posts are spaced to allow for panel lengths of from 4 to 8 feet (usually). The panels are 2 × 4 horizontal rails reaching between the posts. One rail is at the top, often nailed to the top of the posts. The other rail runs between two posts and butts up to them. This rail is attached to the posts, often by toenailing, and supported by a wooden block. Better, it may be held with metal hardware. The facing is attached to the rails on one side, on both sides, or in the middle.

Sometimes the rails are dadoed (slotted) to hold the boards. Then the upper slot is twice as deep as the lower slot. A board is inserted into the upper slot as far up as it will go, so that the lower edge can be slipped into the lower slot.

The facings on board fences should be above-

The smooth side of this one-sided board fence faces the house. Cutting board tops level with post tops allows a continuous, decorative top rail that also protects board ends from the elements.

A turret top adds an airy touch. The true, structural top rails are attached a foot below the perceived top rail. The structural rails also help weatherproof board ends.

ground so they won't rot. If it is necessary to keep chickens and children from crawling under the fence, a 1×8 or 1×10 *ground board* (page 279) may be installed along the bottom of the fence. Because the ground board is buried several inches below ground, the ground board must be of very rot-resistant wood.

Both board-and-board and board-and-batten fences (page 278) employ vertical boards, but of different widths (the battens are narrow strips of wood). These fences make excellent privacy screens, windscreens, and sunscreens. The boards and battens are nailed, alternately, to both sides of 2×4 rails. For plain board fences, boards may simply be nailed to one side of the rails, and battens may be added.

Some board fences are two-sided, designed to look equally good to both neighbors. These may employ boards on opposite sides, alternating boards, or alternating panels. Another approach is the "Good Neighbor" fence, with two-sided boards held between dadoes in the top and bottom rails.

Board fences are often pierced to provide frameworks for planters and similar things.

Picket Fences. Most fence pickets are 1×3s, although pickets may be anywhere from 1 to 4 inches wide if made of 1-inch stock. Or 2×2s may be used. Narrow stock may prove costly because so many pickets will be needed. To make pickets with a saber saw, clamp several pickets together with the top one

Author poses with son Doug's "good-neighbor" fence, which looks identical on both sides. It was cooperatively built and paid for by Doug and his neighbors.

FENCE DESIGNS (CONTINUES ON NEXT PAGE)

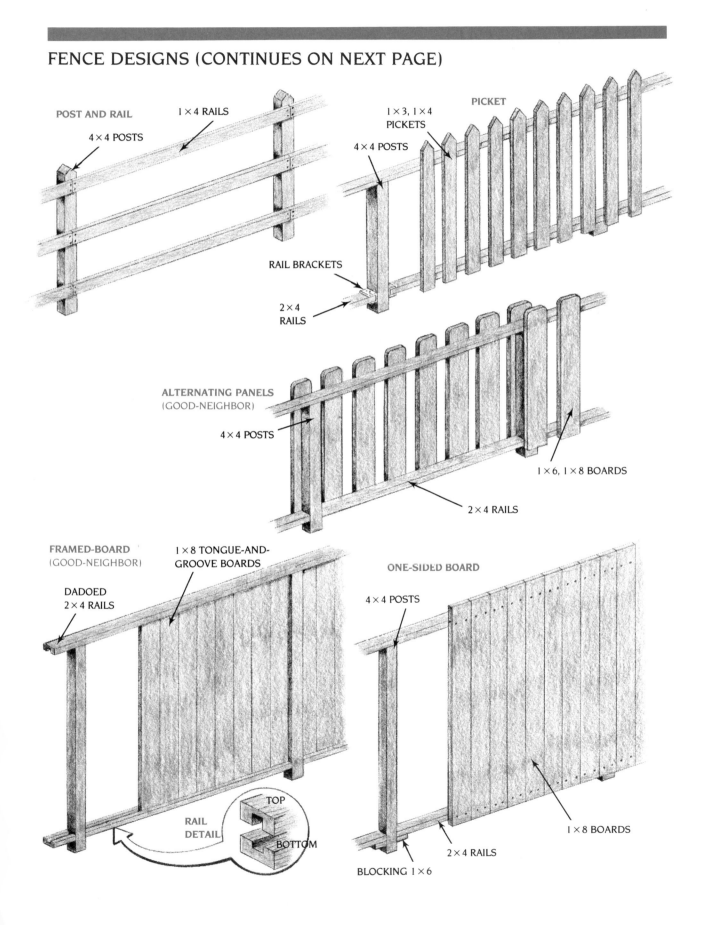

POST AND RAIL

1 × 4 RAILS

4 × 4 POSTS

PICKET

1 × 3, 1 × 4 PICKETS

4 × 4 POSTS

RAIL BRACKETS

2 × 4 RAILS

ALTERNATING PANELS
(GOOD-NEIGHBOR)

4 × 4 POSTS

1 × 6, 1 × 8 BOARDS

2 × 4 RAILS

FRAMED-BOARD
(GOOD-NEIGHBOR)

1 × 8 TONGUE-AND-GROOVE BOARDS

DADOED
2 × 4 RAILS

RAIL
DETAIL

TOP

BOTTOM

ONE-SIDED BOARD

4 × 4 POSTS

1 × 8 BOARDS

2 × 4 RAILS

BLOCKING 1 × 6

FENCE DESIGNS (CONTINUED)

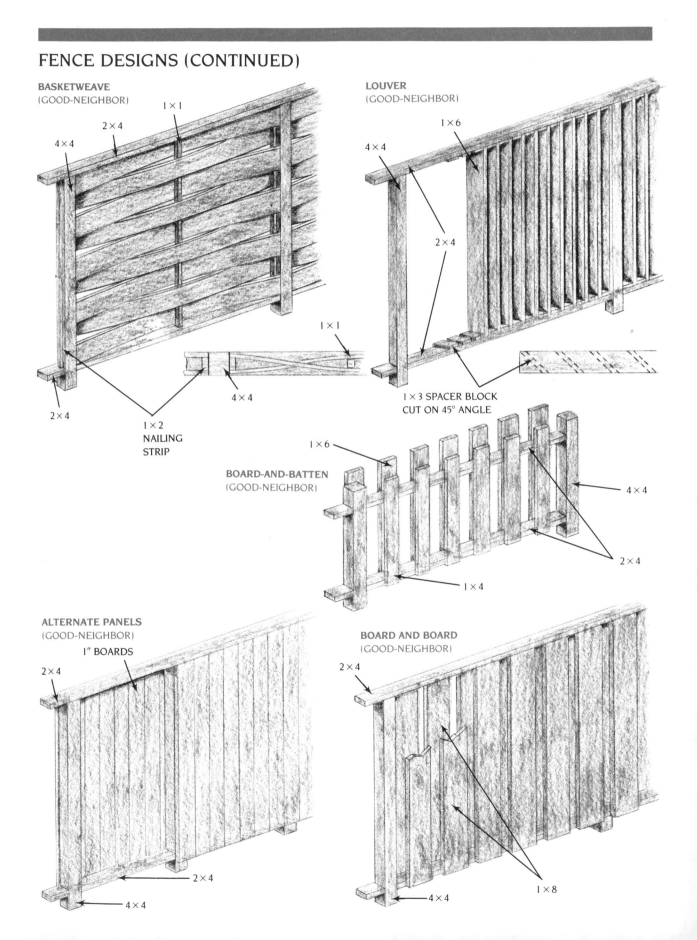

BASKETWEAVE
(GOOD-NEIGHBOR)

4 × 4

2 × 4

1 × 1

2 × 4

1 × 2 NAILING STRIP

4 × 4

LOUVER
(GOOD-NEIGHBOR)

4 × 4

1 × 6

2 × 4

1 × 1

1 × 3 SPACER BLOCK CUT ON 45° ANGLE

BOARD-AND-BATTEN
(GOOD-NEIGHBOR)

1 × 6

4 × 4

2 × 4

1 × 4

ALTERNATE PANELS
(GOOD-NEIGHBOR)

1″ BOARDS

2 × 4

2 × 4

4 × 4

BOARD AND BOARD
(GOOD-NEIGHBOR)

2 × 4

1 × 8

4 × 4

WAYS OF ATTACHING RAILS TO POSTS

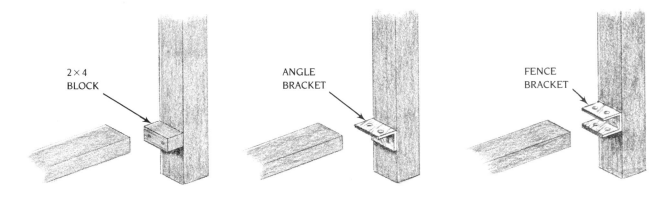

2 × 4
BLOCK

ANGLE
BRACKET

FENCE
BRACKET

GROUND-BOARD ATTACHMENT

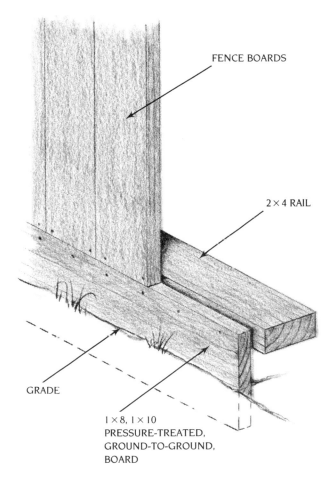

FENCE BOARDS

2 × 4 RAIL

GRADE

1 × 8, 1 × 10
PRESSURE-TREATED,
GROUND-TO-GROUND,
BOARD

marked for cutting, and saw away. Save the top one as a master for marking succeeding tops.

Although a less attractive option to most people, a snow fence is technically a picket fence. (Highway departments use them to control snow drifting.) They usually come painted red, but you can repaint them. The pickets are all held spaced by wires. The ends of snow-fence pickets are squared off. If you want some other shape, you'll have to work tediously on each with a saber saw.

Louvered Fences.   Louvered fences are a handsome variation on board-fence construction. Use smaller uprights spaced in dados cut at an angle across the 2 × 4 rails. The angle may be anywhere from 90 degrees to 15 degrees. Smaller angles give greater privacy.

Trellis Fences.   These are formed of lattice, also called "trellis board." You can buy bargain-priced factory-made lattice panels and U- or H-moldings from building materials dealers. Or the entire fence may be built of 1 × 4 material, again on 4 × 4 posts and 2 × 4 rails. Cut or groove posts and rails to hold the lattice units in place. Preassembled lattice panels come in two widths, 2 × 8 and 4 × 8 feet. It is far less complex to run factory-made lattice.

Other fence parts, too, are available now with a lot of the work already done. Naturally, precut wood costs more.

Basketweave Fences.   A basketweave fence starts with basic 2 × 4 posts, with 2 × 4 upper and lower rails, and requires a firmly set structural member at least 1 inch square at the center of each panel. Then boards, either 1 × 4 or 1 × 6, are woven (bent) against

Left photo: A board fence combined with slump-block columns provides privacy, security, windbreak, and shade. Right photo: Boarded panels alternate on this two-sided "good-neighbor" fence, giving builder and neighbor essentially equal views. The fence posts were set in concrete, formed a few inches aboveground in bottomless plastic pots like those shown on page 115.

PICKET FENCES

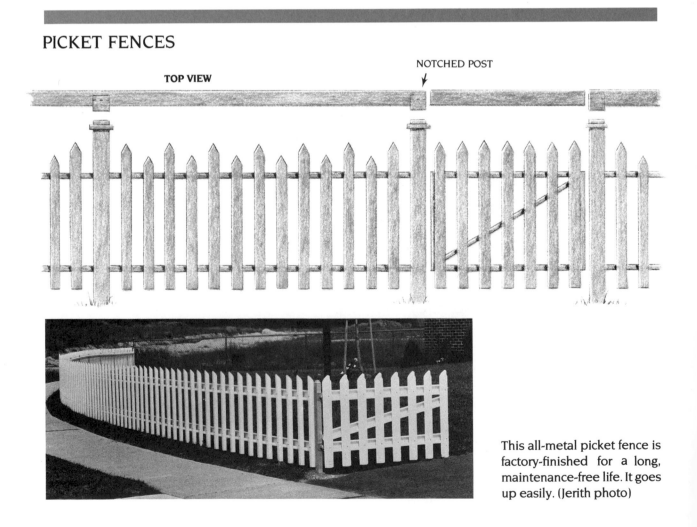

This all-metal picket fence is factory-finished for a long, maintenance-free life. It goes up easily. (Jerith photo)

READY-MADE POSTS AND PICKETS

You can buy posts and boards topped in various styles, such as gothic, tapered, and dog-eared.

HOW TO MAKE A LOUVERED FENCE

Louvered fences allow see-through from one angle and privacy from the complementary angle.

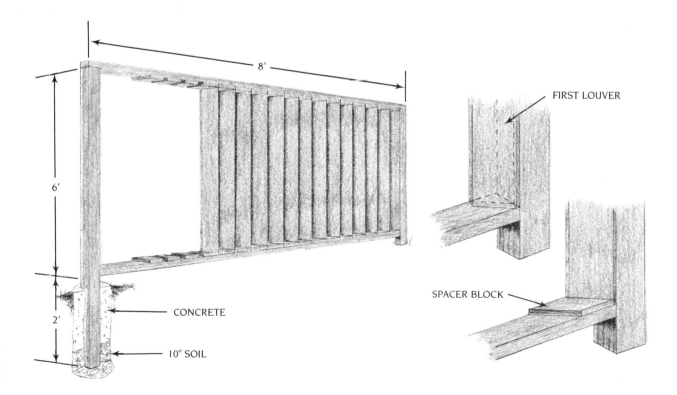

PREASSEMBLED LATTICE

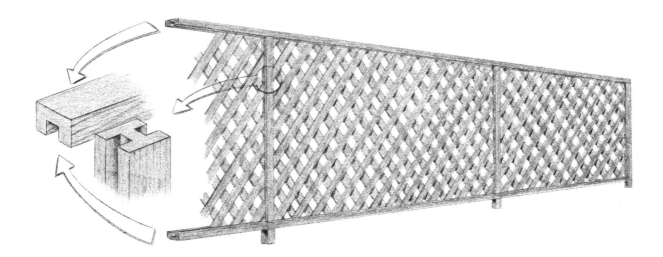

Preassembled lattice panels fit neatly into dadoed top and bottom rails.

Left photo: A basketweave fence made of thin wood boards offers privacy, yet it avoids the "billboard" look of a plain-panel fence (Edward D. Dionne photo). Right photo: This basketweave is metal. The woven "boards" slip into slots in the posts (Jerith photo).

this central member and fitted into grooves in the posts. Basketweaving variations abound; the weave may be made using different lumber sizes or set at different angles.

Plywood-panel Fences.   APA 303 plywood siding panels, and other exterior-grade plywood patterns, make good-looking, solid fencing. See the varieties of exterior-grade plywood at your lumber yard. One-sided APA 303 Texture 1–11 plywood paneling comes in many thicknesses and patterns, including V-grooves on varying centers. Remember that wind impact on the unperforated panels is going to be high, so the fence posts may need to be sized to 6×6 or larger to keep them from snapping off during a fierce storm.

Split-rail fences have been around since colonial times. Though wasteful of wood, they eliminate the need for postholes—a boon in rocky terrain. Most are made of durable black locust. (Charles R. Self photo)

sets of doubled posts at a time, a rail is placed between the doubled posts of two sets. The rail ends rest atop the ends of the rails already placed on either side. The posts are tied off at the tops with heavy aluminum wire. It's best to use treated or rot-resistant lumber for the posts and for the bottom rails.

Wire fencing, not surprisingly, has different applications and is installed differently from wood fencing. It is seldom used as decorative fence, however, and is less useful for screening—whether for wind or privacy. Types of wire fencing include chain-link, "chicken-wire" or poultry netting, wire-mesh and barbed wire fences, and plain wire fences that are electrified. If you want a wire fence, it's best to follow the instructions supplied by the manufacturer.

Concrete-block fences may be laid in mortar. But the easier way is to purchase special column-block and panel-block that ties into the columns. The block columns rest on cast-in-place concrete footings and have slots for the panel-block. If you decide to build a concrete masonry fence, get information from a local concrete products dealer on what fence units are available and how to erect them.

You can also find fiberglass fence columns with fiberglass panels to match. But the cost is usually higher than for the wood fencing it tries to simulate.

RAIL FENCES

Post-and-rail fencing abounds in suburban and rural areas, both for its good looks and for its low cost. Home-built zigzag, or snake, fencing is popular in the southern United States, where land is less at a premium than in some other parts of the nation and where lumber is relatively inexpensive. Stacked post-and-rail fencing is also popular in those areas.

Both zigzag and stacked post-and-rail fences are often made with rot-resistant lumber such as locust. But they eventually require replacement. Zigzag fences are easy to erect because they simply sit on top of the ground, with rails laid in a zigzag pattern to provide support for each other. The pattern is essential to keep the rails from toppling over. The real work occurs in the cutting of trees and the splitting of rails.

Stacked post-and-rail fences are built between sets of doubled posts set in the ground. Working with three

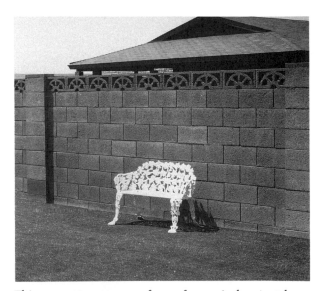

This concrete masonry fence for an indoor/outdoor-carpeted patio features slotted column blocks that accept panel blocks. The slotting makes building easier. (Ozite Corporation photo)

FENCE DESIGN

Basics of design apply to nearly all types of fences. Post size and depth must be sufficient to support the panels. Corner posts must be 25 percent larger than line posts. Posts must be buried to a sufficient depth to support the panels and their own weight over a long period of time.

Panel length depends largely on the weight of the material in the panel. The recommended maximum panel length for wood fence is 8 feet. Heavier wood panels should be shorter—6- or 7-footers. And even with the sturdiest post-and-rail fences, rails should not éxceed 10 feet.

Panels with internal bracing may be used to a greater width—for example, nominal 1-inch or lighter material used inside 2 × 4 or other framing.

Once the design and materials sizes are decided, you'll need to gather some nonstandard tools, that is, nonstandard for general carpentry, but useful in fence- and deck-building. These include certain spades and shovels, posthole diggers, and a wheelbarrow.

As a rule of thumb, line posts are buried to about one half of the fence height. That means a 6-foot-high fence will need at least 9-foot posts, with 3 feet placed below ground.

Most corner posts should be about 25 percent larger in cross-section than the other posts for good rigidity. Again, that isn't always practical, either for design reasons or because of the post sizes available. For example, 4 × 4 posts would call for 5 × 5 posts at corners. The readily available sizes, are 4 × 4 and 6 × 6.

Gate posts, too, require larger sizes. For a heavy gate that will be used a lot, the gate post could be at least 6 × 6 and buried deeper. On the other hand, posts for most fences 3 feet high or less may be 2 × 4s.

LAYING OUT A FENCE

First locate one corner and drive a small stake there. You will already have determined the general direction and length of all fence lines. If the line goes off in a right angle, tasks are simplified. Run mason's line from the top of the original stake, which we'll call Stake 1, to Stake 2. Do the same from Stake 1 in the other direction to Stake 3. Check for square with a carpenter's framing square.

If you are not using right angles, siting corners may be considerably more difficult—or easier, depending on the sight lines of the terrain. If you simply wish to go off at "about that angle" to a second location, there is little need to fuss. Peg the first corner by driving a small stake into the ground. Then draw the mason's line tight from there to the site for the second corner. Peg this, too. Consider how the fence will look relative to your site plan, fence measurements, fence design, and other factors. If all still looks good, aim for the next corner.

If sight lines must pass over rises in the ground

HOW TO USE BATTENS DURING LAYOUT

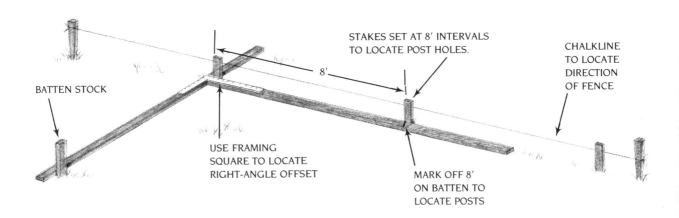

BATTEN STOCK

USE FRAMING SQUARE TO LOCATE RIGHT-ANGLE OFFSET

STAKES SET AT 8' INTERVALS TO LOCATE POST HOLES.

8'

MARK OFF 8' ON BATTEN TO LOCATE POSTS

CHALKLINE TO LOCATE DIRECTION OF FENCE

that you cannot see over, you'll need a helper with a tall pole that you can see from your location. Remember, when erecting a fence, fence panels should remain horizontal, not slope with the terrain. Instead, they are *stepped* up and down a slope.

Start stakes at the spotted corners and run mason's line from stake to stake. Spot the panel corners on the mason's line with tape or small fabric flags. Drive stakes where the fence posts will go, and then go back and measure the distances one more time. This will help you avoid having to redig and backfill out-of-place postholes, an annoying business at best.

In terrain with huge subsurface boulders, you may be wise to dig just one posthole ahead of post placement. This is so because a boulder may prevent your digging a hole deep enough and so require that you dig at a shorter panel distance there.

SETTING POSTS

Posthole diameters should be 2½ to 3 times the size of the post, whether square or round. For example, the typical 4 × 4 post would need a hole just less than 12 inches in diameter.

Digging Postholes

Postholes are never excavated to a diameter less than 6 inches, and are often 10 or 12 inches in diameter. They should be at least 6 inches deeper than the portion of the post to be buried, to allow for a gravel subbase and possibly a cap on the subbase. Postholes should also extend below the frost line for your area to prevent frost-heaving. If you intend to use underground cross-braces, the hole will need to be large enough to accept them. Generally, postholes a foot in diameter will be sufficient for almost any kind of fence, including the gate posts.

Digging postholes, the hardest part of any fence construction job, is made easier by use of a rented power auger. A power auger becomes practical when more than a dozen postholes need to be made. Follow the rental agency's instructions for operating the machine.

Most manual posthole diggers have clamshell-shaped diggers with long wooden handles that move in and out to open and close the diggers. Wear work gloves when digging, and hold your hands at different levels on the digger handles so you don't rap your knuckles when the handles are brought together to

Power posthole augers make quick work of digging. If you have many holes to dig, such rental equipment is worthwhile. (American Rental Association photo)

release a load of soil. A piece of tape around the digger handles at the appropriate depth will show you when the hole is finished. Splay the hole out a bit wider toward the bottom. The bigger base will make room for more gravel and give better drainage beneath the post. Leave the upper posthole walls narrow.

Once the posthole is finished, put its post on the ground near it. Gather any gravel, below-ground cleats, and other materials you plan to use at each posthole site.

You can choose among several methods of post-setting. With good soil, no frost heave to consider, and a fence 3 feet tall or less, backfilling postholes with soil or a mix of soil and gravel is suitable. Slope fill up toward the posts aboveground, to help drain water away from the post.

You can set a post on 6 inches or more of gravel with a flat stone or concrete cap on top, and then fill around the post with tamped gravel. Gravel-setting is the fastest, most convenient, and least costly method of adding extra holding power to fence posts.

HOW TO USE A POSTHOLE DIGGER

THRUST
DOWN.

OPEN
HANDLES.

LIFT
DIRT.

BREAK UP ROCK
OR HARDPAN.

THREE WAYS TO SET POSTS

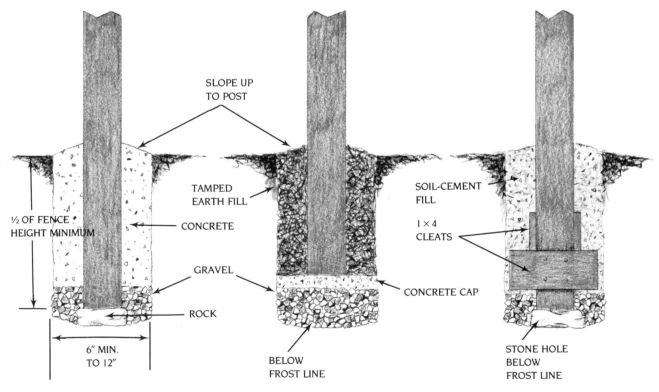

SLOPE UP
TO POST

½ OF FENCE
HEIGHT MINIMUM

CONCRETE

GRAVEL

ROCK

6" MIN.
TO 12"

TAMPED
EARTH FILL

CONCRETE CAP

BELOW
FROST LINE

SOIL-CEMENT
FILL

1 × 4
CLEATS

STONE HOLE
BELOW
FROST LINE

Setting Posts in Concrete

For the strongest post-setting, use concrete. When setting posts in concrete, place the concrete *after* the post has been set on 6 inches or more of gravel for drainage. Using a 90-pound bag of ready-packaged concrete mix in each hole is a good way to ensure that the posts stay put. You need not mix the concrete with water. Just dump it into the post hole dry and tamp it well. Plumbing the post is quite easy while you are tamping. Just tamp harder on the side the post leans toward. It will straighten right up. If the concrete doesn't extend above grade, you can backfill over it with soil. If rain seems some time away, sprinkle the surface with water, which will percolate down into the dry concrete to harden it.

If posts are set in plastic concrete rather than dry-tamped, brace them to the ground, using slanted supports such as 1 × 4s tack-nailed to the post and to nearby stakes. Position the braces at right angles to each other to hold the post plumb until the concrete sets. Give posts a few days to set before proceeding.

Soil-cement Backfill

Soil-cement—dirt dug from the posthole and mixed with portland cement—is an excellent, low-cost material for setting fences posts solidly. To make it, mix about 1 part portland cement with 4 or 5 parts soil having optimum moisture content. Soil at optimum moisture content, when squeezed in the hand, forms a tight cast that does not fall apart when released (see page 156). Tamp the soil-cement mixture into the hole around the fence post, plumbing the post as you go. Once the soil-cement sets, the post will never move.

The simplest, though not least costly, method of giving a fence post more holding power is to nail a rot-resistant wood cross-member 6 inches to a foot above the bottom of the post, using aluminum or galvanized nails. The larger and wider the cross-member, the greater holding power it will provide.

If posts are not to be set in gravel, concrete, or soil-cement, but the ground is relatively soft, add at least 1 foot to post burial depth, and use another method to increase holding power.

HOW TO PLUMB A FENCE POST

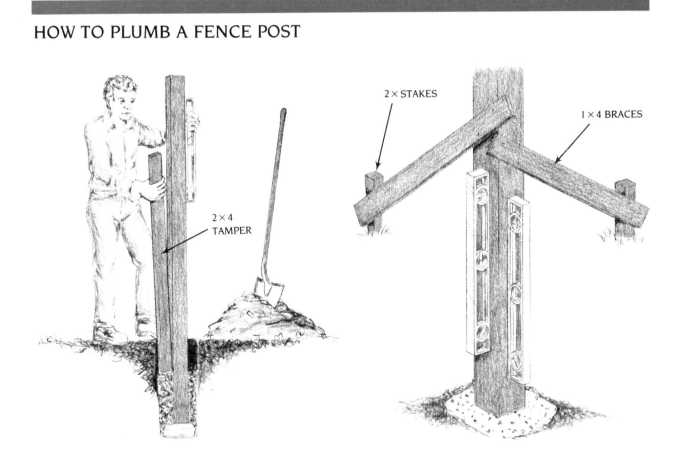

2 × 4 TAMPER

2 × STAKES

1 × 4 BRACES

Gate posts may be set with several cross-cleats instead of a single cross-cleat. Nail three or four different cross-members onto the post at varying angles, placing two about 6 inches from the bottom of the post and one or more 6 inches above that point.

All posts need to be plumb from all directions—north-south and east-west. But checking two adjacent sides will do it. Check plumb with a carpenter's level held vertically. Or a strap-on post level, such as the Empire No. 720 Polycast, may be used for leveling.

More on Posts

A wood-panel fence may be built in one of two ways: in the air and on the ground. Try in-the-air building first; if you think you'd do better building on the ground, switch.

If you are erecting a post-and-rail fence, do *not* set the line posts solidly at the beginning. You'll need some play to insert the rails. The line posts are plumbed and tamped only after the rails are in place. But the line posts for a board or other panel fence, or for a wire fence, may be plumbed and firmed into place immediately.

FENCES ON HILLS

ON GENTLE SLOPES, PANELS SLOPE.

ON STEEP SLOPES, PANELS ARE LEVEL AND STEPPED.

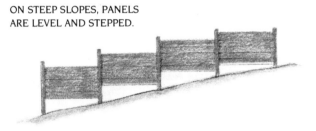

HOW TO LAY OUT A FENCE

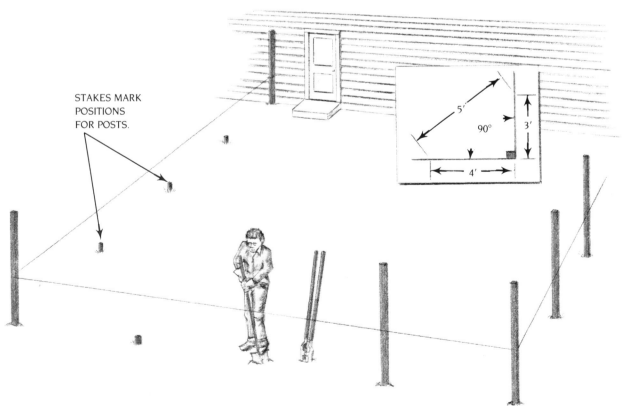

STAKES MARK POSITIONS FOR POSTS.

FENCE JOINTS

The basic fence-building joint is the butt joint, with support from formed-metal fasteners. Or weather-resistant nails or screws may be used. Almost any fence can be built using such joints, but design interest and strength can often be increased with the use of other joint styles.

Most post-and-rail fences have the rail ends set as tenons into mortises in the posts. Generally, more precise mortise-and-tenon joinery is not really suitable for outdoor construction, because it's too time-consuming. Post-and-rail mortise-and-tenon joints are simple, fairly rough examples of the type.

Dadoed joints—cross-grain slots—are often used to construct fence panels and to join boards to posts. Dadoed designs are easy to produce with simple tools. A router and straight bit, for instance, make it a simple matter to construct redwood or cedar slat fences. Simply mark out the dadoes to take the ends of the slats and cut the required dadoes.

The groove, or with-the-grain dado, is used for a great many fence styles as well. It is probably best indicated by the **H**- and **U**-moldings now available.

Miter joints, often used atop posts, are butt joints cut at a bias, or angle. Simple butted or notched joints may be used instead.

Butt joints used without any support other than a couple of angled toenails joining rails to posts are best supported from underneath with blocks. The blocks may be plain cut-off sections of the rail or may be shaped to provide some decoration.

POST-TOP PROTECTION

If post tops are not covered by boards forming a railing, some other form of protection from weathering is needed. Otherwise, rainwater can penetrate into the end grain of exposed post tops. As weathering progresses, the cracks widen, and still more rainwater gets in, even with rot-resistant wood. Then freeze/thaw cycles widen the cracks even more. It takes only a few such vicious cycles to split a fence post down the middle.

The simplest method of making sure that water runs off the tops of posts is to cut them off on a slant.

You can mortise split-cedar fence posts for rails using a large post-auger and wood chisel. Usually, each post is set and its rails installed from the previous post before digging begins for the next posthole.

Many precut fence posts are now furnished this way. Others have formed tops that provide for water runoff.

Where cuts or designs are not feasible, a post cap may be used, instead. The cap may be made the same size as the post top and simply fastened in place. If it is treated as a design element, it may be any size and shape that suits, as long as it exposes more side grain than end grain to rain and snow. Shaped metal caps are also available.

GATES

One thing about a fence is virtually certain: the first failure will be at or next to a gate. Therefore, gate design needs additional care. Gates may follow the basic construction of the fence itself, but they will always require extra bracing.

Gate planning starts with a thought to width, including the width of the gate swing. Should the gate open more than 90 degrees? Most do, and today's hinges allow that. Does the gate need to be 3 feet wide or 6 feet wide? Does it need to accommodate any vehicles, and, if so, what size?

It makes little sense to size a gate too small. Virtually all gates eventually need to admit such items as wheelbarrows and riding lawnmowers at the very least. The *minimum* gate width for an average fence is

FENCE JOINTS

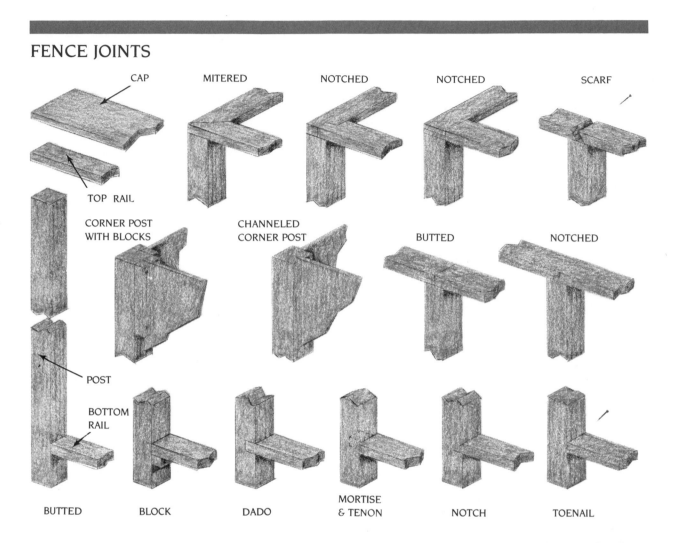

CAP

MITERED   NOTCHED   NOTCHED   SCARF

TOP RAIL

CORNER POST
WITH BLOCKS

CHANNELED
CORNER POST

BUTTED   NOTCHED

POST

BOTTOM
RAIL

BUTTED   BLOCK   DADO   MORTISE & TENON   NOTCH   TOENAIL

Left photo: When the rails are butt-jointed to the posts, support them with 2 × 4 blocking (Charles R. Self photo). Right photo: The tops of fence posts are particularly susceptible to weathering. For 4 × 4 posts, you can buy metal caps, secured by a single rust-resistant nail.

Sturdy gates can be attractive too. They lend substance to the setting. (Photographer, John Fulker, Council of Forest Industries of British Columbia)

probably 42 inches. This width will allow wheelbarrows, most riding lawnmowers and lawn tractors, and wheelchairs to go through. Vehicle gates need to be a minimum of 8 feet wide even in these days of compact cars and minivans.

Gate styles are limited, though they may appear to vary widely. The gate is a door, and as such takes a square or rectangular frame. Decoration and support alter the appearance and make the gate match or complement the fence style. You can buy heavy gate hardware to meet all needs.

The gates themselves should be framed on all four sides, and should have at least one diagonal cross-brace for those sized 4 feet and under. Gates more than 4 feet wide need double cross-cleats forming an X.

For stability, wooden gates are best assembled with weatherproof screws rather than nails.

Gate posts are best set in concrete. Even so, it does not one bit of harm to put cross-cleats at the lower ends of gate posts so that the concrete will have even more to grip.

Your wood fence and gate may be left unfinished or stained with a semitransparent or solid-color stain. Stain is generally the longest-lasting, most maintenance-free finish. Though you can also paint a fence, knowing you'll have to paint again someday.

HOW TO CONSTRUCT A GATE

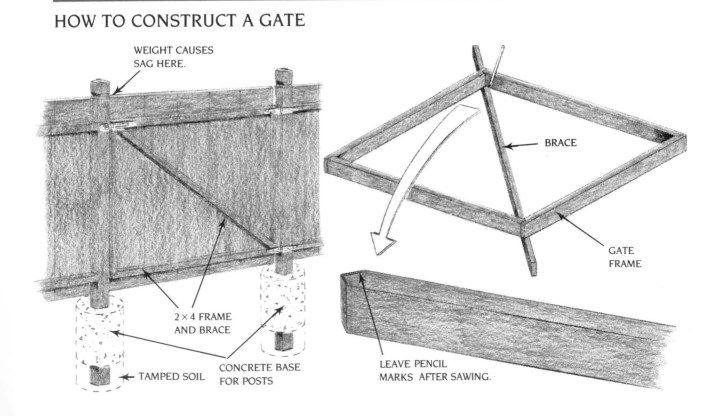

WEIGHT CAUSES SAG HERE.

2 × 4 FRAME AND BRACE

CONCRETE BASE FOR POSTS

TAMPED SOIL

BRACE

GATE FRAME

LEAVE PENCIL MARKS AFTER SAWING.

INDEX

Abrasives, finishes, 67, 68
Access, planning considerations, 10
Acid wash, 222
Actual size. See Nominal/actual size
Adhesives
    described, 60
    information sources for, vii
Adobe, patio construction, 226, 228
Adverse possession law, fencing, 275
Aggregates
    concrete work, 150–151
    exposed-aggregate slabs, 218–225
A-grade plywood, described, 26
Air-entrained concrete, 161–162
Aluminum oxide paper, 68
American Optical Corporation, vii
American Plywood Association, vii
Appearance-grade plywood, 27
Appearance planning, preliminary
    plans, 18
Argee Corporation, vii
Ash
    lumber selection chart, 23
    structural design considerations,
        36
Asphalt shingle, pier construction,
    46–47
Attached versus freestanding
    styles, 7, 9

Backfill and backfilling
    fence post setting, 287–288
    patio construction, 233–236
Ball-peen hammer, described, 75
Balusters
    design details, 51
    railing construction, 128–130
Bamboo covers, described, 264
Basic carpentry. See Carpentry
Basketweave fences, 279, 282

Batching, concrete work, 151–152,
    154–155
Batching a mixer
    colored concrete, 204
    concrete work, 157–159, 160
Bathroom scale, concrete work, 136
Batter boards, construction layout,
    112, 113
Beams
    cover construction, 269
    deck structure, 35
    design details, 44–46
    setting of, 114–116
    structural design, 38–40
Birch, lumber selection chart, 23
Bits, electric drills, 91–92
Bleaches, finishes, 67
Board fences, described, 275–283
Board foot/lineal foot, lumber,
    21–22, 23
Board grade, lumber grade stan-
    dards, 25
Bonded topping technique,
    described, 207–208
Boots, concrete work, 132–133
Box nails, described, 52
Bracing
    cover construction, 269–270
    lateral bracing, design details, 47
Brick(s)
    information sources for, vii
    patio construction, 226
Brick Association of North
    Carolina, vii
Brick edging, soft–set paving, 244
Brick in mortar, hard–set paving, 253
Broomed finishes, concrete, 197–198
Brushes, texturing brushes, 144
Building codes and permits
    fencing, 272–273, 275
    joist placement, 117

patio construction, 229
planning
    preliminary considerations,
        10, 12
    preliminary plans, 14
    working plan, 18–19
post siting and setting, 114
railings, 47, 130, 131
stairs, 123–124
structural design, 37, 43
Bullfloats
    described, 139–140
    use of, 185
Burke Company, vii
Butt joints, fencing, 289

Calculations
    concrete work
        mix-it-yourself quality concrete,
            152–154
        ready-mixed concrete, 164–166
    structural design, redwood
        deck, 43
California Redwood Association, vii,
    43, 64
Cantilevered beams, 40, 41
Cantilevered joists, 38, 39
Canvas covers, 262, 263–264
Carpenter's level, described, 82
Carpenter's square, described, 81
Carpentry, 20–70. See also Construc-
    tion; Cover construction
    clean-up, 69
    decay resistance, 29–33
        lumber selection and, 30–31
        overview of, 29
        pressure-treated wood, 31–32
        wood preservatives and, 32–33
    deck structure, 33–36
        deck parts, 35–36
        general rules in, 33–34

span considerations, 34
design details, 43–51
  beams, 44–46
  joists, 44
  lateral bracing, 47
  ledger boards, 43–44
  piers, 46–47
  planking, 47, 48, 49, 50
  railings, 47, 51, 52
fasteners, 52–64
  construction adhesives, 60
  framing anchors, 61–64
  large fasteners, 60–61
  nails, 52–55
  screws, 55–60
finishes, 64–68
lumber, 20–25
  board foot/lineal foot, 21–22, 23
  defects, 20–21
  edge-grain boards, design
    details, 43
  grading, 22–25
  nominal/actual size, 21
  selection guides, 21, 22–23
  structural design considera-
    tions, 36–43
measurements, 20
ordering wood, 33
plywood, 25–28. See also Plywood
  grades of, 26–27
  overview of, 25–26
  thicknesses of, 27
  types of, 26
  working with, 28
safety precautions, 68–69, 70
structural design, 36–43
  beams, 38–40
  calculations for redwood deck,
    43
  planks, 36–38
  posts, 40–43
Carpentry tools, 71–106
  care and maintenance of, 104–106
  circular saw, 96–98
  concrete work with, 134–135
  cordless tools, 93–95
  hand tools, 73–84
    chalklines, 83
    hacksaws, 76
    hammers, 74–75
    handsaws, 75–76
    holding tools, 83–84
    inventory for, 73–74
    levels, 81–83
    measuring tapes, 77–79
    miter boxes, 76
    planes, 83
    screwdrivers, 76–77
    squares, 79–81
  personal protective gear, 71–73
  portable power tools, 85–93

electric drill, 89–93
electric shock, 86–87
extension cords, 87–88
ground-fault protection, 85–86
safety rules, 88–89
reciprocating saw, 102, 103–104
saber saws, 98–103
Carriage bolts, described, 60–61, 62
Casing nails, described, 52, 54
Cast-in-place concrete edging,
  pavers, soft-set paving, 244
C-grade plywood, described, 27
Chalklines
  concrete work, 135
  described, 83
Chemical deicers, concrete work, 193
Childproofing
  design details, 52
  fencing, 273
  railings, 130, 131
Circular saw
  concrete work, 135
  described, 96–98
Clamps, described, 83
Claw hammer. See Hammers
Cleanup. See also Maintenance
  carpentry, 69
  concrete work, 191
Clear finishes, 67
Clear sealer, exposed-aggregate
  slabs, 225
Codes. See Building codes and permits
Cold weather, concrete work and, 193
Color, concrete finishes, 201–211
Computer-aided design, preliminary
  plans, 15
Concentrated loads, deck structure,
  34, 43
Concrete-block fencing, 283
Concrete chemicals, information
  sources for, vii
Concrete construction tools, 132–146
  basic requirements, 132–137
  care and maintenance of, 145–146
  checklist for, 145
  forms and accessories, informa-
    tion sources for, vii
  placing and finishing tools,
    137–144
Concrete finishes and finishing,
  194–225
  colors, 201–211
  exposed-aggregate slabs, 218–225
  pattern-stamping slabs, 211–218
  textured finishes, 194–199
  tooled-in treatments, 199–201
Concrete forms, 147
  concrete slab forming, 175–179
  information sources for, vii
  lumber selection chart, 22

plywood selection chart, 27
Concrete mixer
  cleaning of, 145–146
  described, 132, 136–137
Concrete work, 147–193
  air-entrained concrete, 161–162
  basics of, 147–148
  cleanup, 191
  fence post setting, 287
  haul-it-yourself concrete, 169–170
  information sources for, vii
  joints, 179–182
  mix-it-yourself quality concrete,
    148–161
    aggregates for, 150–151
    batching, 151–152, 154–155
    batching a mixer, 157–159, 160
    hand-mixing, 159, 161
    on-the-job handling of, 151
    proportioning, 151, 154–155
    quantity calculations, 152–154
    sand wetness adjustments,
      155–156
    strength and durability require-
      ments, 149–150
  moist-curing, 191–192
  patio construction, 229, 236–237
  pavers, hard-set paving, 251–253
  placing and finishing, 182–191
  ready-mixed concrete, 164–169
  ready-packaged mixes, 162–164
  safety, 182
  slab design, 170–173
  slab forming, 175–179
  slab preparation, 173–175
  temperature and, 192–193
Construction, 107–131. See also
  Carpentry; Cover
  construction
  beam setting, 114–116
  final inspection, 131
  joist placement, 116–118
  layout, 107–113
    ledger board fastening, 107,
      111–112
    overview of, 107–111
    sides and ends, 112–113
  plank laying, 118–123
  post siting and setting, 114
  railings, 127–131
  stairs, 123–127
Construction adhesives. See
  Adhesives
Construction joints, concrete work,
  182
Construction Products Division, W.
  R. Grace and Company, vii
Control-jointing, concrete work,
  179–181, 187
Cordless tools
  charging of, 94

Cordless tools (*Continued*)
  drills, 93–94
  safety rules for, 94
Corrosion
  concrete construction tools, 146
  nails, 52
  screws, 55, 57
Costs
  planning, 10–12
  pumped concrete, 168
  tax considerations, 9–10
Cover construction, 260–271. *See also*
    Carpentry; Construction
  materials for, 260–264
  planning, 260
  roof installation, 271
  structural design, 264–268
  typical example, 268–270
Curing
  concrete colors, 204
  moist-curing, concrete work,
    191–192
Curving forms, concrete slab form-
    ing, 176, 177–178
Cutting
  of pavers, soft-set paving, 247
  of plywood, 28
Cypress
  decay resistance and, 31
  lumber selection chart, 21, 22

Dadoed joints, fencing, 289
Darbies, described, 140
Dead load, deck structure, 33
Decay resistance, 29–33
  lumber selection and, 30–31
  overview of, 29
  pressure-treated wood, 31–32
  wood preservatives and, 32–33
Deck adhesives. *See* Adhesives
Deck construction. *See* Carpentry;
    Construction
Deck covers. *See* Cover construction
Decking, plywood selection chart
    for, 27
Deck paint, finishes, 67
Deck planning (decks and patios). *See*
    Planning
Deck-rail panels, plywood selection
    chart for, 27
Decks
  lumber selection chart, 22, 23
  planning of. *See* Planning (decks
    and patios)
Defects, carpentry, lumber, 20–21
Deicers, concrete work, 193
Detail plans, planning, 19
Dewey and Almy Chemical Division,
    W. R. Grace and Company, vii
Direct Safety Company, vii

Double-headed nails, described, 54
Douglas fir
  lumber selection chart, 21, 22
  structural design considerations,
    36, 40, 41
Draftsman, professional
  detail plans, 19
  preliminary plans, 13–14
Drainage
  patio construction, 229–230
  soft-set paving, 242–243
Drilling
  pilot holes, 55–57
  plank laying, 120–121
Drills. *See* Electric drill
Dry-shake coloring technique,
    described, 208–211
Drywall screws, described, 57, 59
Dust mask, pressure-treated
    woods, 32

Easements, preliminary plans, 15
Edge-grain board, selection of, 43
Edgers, described, 140–141
Edging
  concrete work, 186–187
  hard-set paving, 259
  soft-set paving, 243–245
Electric drill
  accessories for, 91–93
  cordless, 93–95
  described, 89–91
Electric shock, first aid for, 86–87
Elevation
  layout, 107, 111
  planning, 9
  working plan, 18–19
Empire Level Manufacturing
    Company, vii, 114
Euclid Chemical Company, vii, 161
Excavation
  patio construction, 230–233
  pavers, soft-set paving, 242
Expansion joints, concrete work, 181.
    See also Joints
Exposed-aggregate slabs, concrete
    finishing, 218–225
Extension cords, portable power
    tools, 87–88
Exterior-type plywood, plywood
    selection, 26, 27
Eye and face protection, 71–72. *See
    also* Personal protective gear

Fabric covers, described, 262,
    263–264
Fasteners, 52–64
  construction adhesives, 60
  cover construction, 265–267

framing anchors, 61–64
large fasteners, 60–61
nails, 52–55
screws, 55–60
Fence panels, plywood selection
    chart for, 27
Fence posts
  protection of tops, 289
  setting of, 285–288
Fencing, 272–291
  board fences, 275–282
    basketweave fences, 279, 282
    louvered fences, 279
    overview of, 275–276
    picket fences, 276–279
    trellis fences, 279
  building codes and permits,
    272–273, 275
  design basics, 284
  gates, 289, 291
  joints, 289, 290
  layout, 284–285
  lumber selection chart, 22, 23
  planning preliminaries, 272–275
  post setting, 285–288
  post-top protection, 289
  privacy and, 11–12
  rail fences, 283
Fiberglass covers, 260–263
Fiberglass fencing, 283
Finishes and finishing, 64–68
  abrasives, 68
  bleaches, 67
  clear finishes, 67
  deck paint, 67
  plywood and, 28
  pressure-treated woods, 32
  roof, cover construction, 271
  stains, 64, 65, 66–67
  summary table of, 65
  wood preservatives, 33, 64
Finishing nails, described, 52
Fire extinguishers, 73
First aid, electric shock, 86–87
Flagstone, patio construction, 228
Flagstone effects, tooled-in concrete
    finishes, 199–201
Flint paper, abrasives, 68
Floated patterns, concrete finishes,
    196
Floating, concrete work, 184–185
Floats, texturing floats, described,
    144
Foot and hand protection, 73. *See
    also* Personal protective gear
Footings
  cover construction, 265
  deck structure and, 35
  post siting and setting, pier
    method, 114, 115
  structural design and, 38, 41–43

Forms. *See* Concrete forms
Framing anchors
　construction, beam setting, 114–116
　described, 61–64
　structural design and, 38
Framing members, deck structure, 33
Framing square
　concrete work, 134
　described, 81
Freestanding versus attached styles, 7, 9
Frost line, footings and, 35
Fungi, wood decay and, 29
Furniture
　lumber selection chart, 22, 23
　plywood selection chart, 27

Galvanized nails, described, 52
Garden grade redwood, 30, 31
Garden hose, concrete work, 134
Garden sprayers, described, 144
Gates, described, 289, 291
Gibson-Homans Company, vii
Gloves. *See also* Personal protective gear
　concrete work, 132
　personal protective gear, 73
Goldblatt Tool Company, vii
Grade standards
　lumber, 22–25
　plywood, 26–27
　redwood, decay resistance, 30, 31
Grading, pavers, soft-set paving, 241–243
Graph paper, preliminary plans, 14–15
Gravel, patio construction, 229
Grooving tools, described, 141
Ground board, fencing, 276
Ground-Contact lumber, described, 32
Ground-fault circuit-interrupters, 86
Ground-fault protection, 85–86

Hacksaws, described, 76
Hammer(s)
　concrete work, 135
　described, 74–75
Hammer-drills, described, 91
Hand and foot protection, 73. *See also* Personal protective gear
Hand-drilling hammer, described, 75
Hand-floats and hand-floating
　concrete work, 187–189
　described, 141–142
Hand-mixing, concrete work, 159, 161
Hand plane. *See* Planes
Handsaws, described, 75

Hand-tamper, described, 133–134
Hand tools. *See* Carpentry tools: hand tools
Hardwoods
　grade standards, 24
　selection guides, 23
Haul-it-yourself concrete, 169–170
Hazardous wastes
　finishes, 67
　pressure-treated woods, 32
Headers, cover construction, 267–268
Headgear
　concrete work, 132
　personal protective gear, 72
Hearing protection, 72
Heartwood, decay resistance and, 29, 30
Hemlock
　lumber selection chart, 21, 22
　structural design considerations, 36
Hillyard Chemical Company, vii
Holding tools, described, 83–84
Hoses, concrete work, 134
Hot tubs, structural design and, 43
Hot weather, concrete work and, 192–193

Improved sidings, plywood grades, 27
Interior-type plywood, plywood selection, 26
Isolation joints, concrete work, 181

Joints
　concrete work, 179–182
　fencing, 289
　pattern-stamping slabs and, 217–218
　pavers
　　hard-set paving, 255–256
　　soft-set paving, 247–249
Joist(s)
　construction, placement of, 116–118
　cover construction, 267–268
　design details, 44
　structural design, 37–38, 39
Joist hangers, described, 63, 64
Kerfs, concrete slab forming, 176, 177–178
Kneeboards
　described, 143–144
　use of, 187, 189
Kneepads, described, 144
Knives, concrete work, 136

Ladders, safety precautions, 68–69
Lag screws, described, 60
Landscaping, preliminary plans, 15

Larch, structural design considerations, 36
Large fasteners, described, 60–61
Lateral bracing, design details, 47
Law of adverse possession, fencing, 275
Layout
　fencing, 284–285
　pavers, 241–243
Layout tools, preliminary plans, 14
Ledger board
　attachment of, 61
　construction, fastening, 107, 111–112
　described, 35
　design details, 43–44
　structural design and, 38
Level(s) (tool)
　concrete work, 135
　described, 81–83
Levels (elevations). *See* Elevation; Multilevel design
Lifestyle factors, preliminary planning considerations, 5, 7
Lineal foot. *See* Board foot/lineal foot
Line level, described, 82
Live load, deck structure, 33
Live oak, lumber selection chart, 23
Loadbearing capacity
　deck structure, 33–34
　structural design, 41–43
Location of project, preliminary planning considerations, 10–12
Log oil, wood preservatives, 64
Lot topography
　fencing and, 288
　planning considerations, 11–12
Louvered fences, described, 279
Lubrication, screws and, 57, 59
Lumber. *See* Carpentry: lumber

Machine bolt, 61
Maintenance. *See also* Cleanup
Maintenance (*continued*)
　carpentry tools, 104–106
　concrete construction tools, 145–146
　hard-set paving, 259
Maple, lumber selection chart, 23
Marshalltown Trowel Company, vii
Mash hammer, described, 75
Masonry, ledger board attachment, 61
Master Builders, vii, 161
Measurements, carpentry basics, 20
Measuring tapes
　concrete work, 135
　described, 77–79

Metal forms, information sources for, vii
Mine Safety Appliances Company, vii
Miter boxes, described, 76
Miter joints, fencing, 289
Moist-curing, concrete work, 191–192
Moisture content, lumber grade standards, 25
Mortaring joints, pattern-stamping slabs and, 217–218
Multilevel design
  deck and patio planning, 5
  privacy and, 11–12

Nail(s), described, 52–55
Nail pulling, hammers and, 74
Nail shanks, described, 54–55
Neighbors, fencing and, 275
Nominal/actual size, carpentry, lumber, 21
Norway pine, lumber selection chart, 22
Nozzles, concrete work, 134

Oak, lumber selection chart, 23
Ordering wood, advice on, 33
Oriented-strand board (OSB), described, 27
Outdoor furniture, plywood selection chart for, 27
Outdoor plastic shade cloth covers, described, 264

Packaged deck plans, preliminary plans, 13
Pails, concrete work, 135–136
Paint, deck paint, finishes, 67. See also Finishes and finishing
Panel-grade plywood, described, 27
Patio construction, 226–237
  backfilling, 233–236
  building permits, 229
  concrete patio details, 236–237
  drainage, 229–230
  excavation, 230–233
  materials, 226–229
  planning for. See Planning (decks and patios)
  site layout, 230
Patio covers. See Cover construction
Patterns, plank laying, 118–123
Pattern-stamping slabs, concrete finishing, 211–218
Pavers, 238–259
  concrete, patio construction, 229
  hard-set paving, 249–259
    brick in mortar, 253
    care and maintenance, 259
    concrete base, 251–253
    hard-set edging, 259

hard-set stone, 256–257
hard-set tile, 257–258
joint filling, 255–256
paver laying, 255
preparation, 253–255
soft-set paving, 238–249
  edging, 243–245
  layout and grading, 241–243
  paver cutting, 247
  paver laying, 247
  preliminary layout, 246–247
  preparation for, 240–241
  sand-jointing, 247–249
  subbase, 245
  types of, 238–240
wood, patio construction, 228
Peeler core, fencing, 275
Permits. See Building codes and permits
Personal protective gear, 71–73
  carpentry, 69
  concrete work, 132, 182
  cover construction, 264
  eye and face protection, 71–72
  fire extinguishers, 73
  hand and foot protection, 73
  headgear, 72
  hearing protection, 72
  information sources for, vii
  power tool safety, 88–89
  pressure-treated woods, 32
  respiratory protection, 72–73
Phillips head screws
  power screwdriving, 57, 59
  screwdriver selection and, 77
Picket fences, described, 276–279
Picnic tables, plywood selection chart for, 27
Pier(s), design details, 46–47
Pier method, post siting and setting, 114, 115
Pilot holes
  nails, 55, 56
  plank laying, 120–121
  screws, 55–57, 58
Pitched roofs, cover construction, 269
Planes, described, 83
Plank(s) and planking
  construction, laying of, 118–123
  deck structure and, 35
  design details, 47, 48, 49, 50
  structural design, 36–38
Planning
  cover construction, 260
  fencing, 272–275
  gates, 289
  stairs, 124
Planning (decks and patios), 3–19
  detail plans, 19
  overview of, 3–5

preliminary considerations, 5–12
  freestanding versus attached styles, 7, 9
  lifestyle factors, 5, 7
  location of project, 10–12
  location regulations, 10, 12
  space and shape, 7
  tax effects, 9–10
preliminary plans, 12–18
  appearance planning, 18
  examples of, 16–17
  packaged deck plans, 13
  professional draftsman for, 13–14
  self-drawn plans, 14–15
  site plan, 12–13
  "walking" the project, 15, 18
  working plan, 18–19
Plastic covers, described, 260–263
Plastic forms, information sources for, vii
Plastic shade cloth covers, described, 264
Plotting, preliminary planning considerations, 14–15
Plumbing (carpentry), 39, 46
  corner posts, 113, 114
  cover construction, 269
  fencing, 288
Plywood. See also Carpentry: plywood
  cover construction, 268
  information sources for, vii
Ponderosa pine, lumber selection chart, 21
Poplar, lumber selection chart, 21, 23
Portable power tools. See Carpentry tools: portable power tools
Portland Cement Association, vi, vii, 147
Post(s)
  cover construction, 265–267, 268–269
  deck structure and, 35
  fasteners and, 62
  lumber selection chart, 22, 23
  plumbing of, 113
  siting and setting of, 114
  structural design, 40–43
Post anchors, 63
Post-and-rail fencing
  described, 283
  joints, 289
Posthole digging, described, 285
Post setting, fencing, 285–288
Post-to-beam connections, design details, 44–46
Power screwdriving, described, 57–60
Power tools. See Carpentry tools: portable power tools
Preco Company, vii

Preliminary plans. *See* Planning (decks and patios): preliminary plans

Preservatives. *See* Wood preservatives

Pressure-treated wood, decay resistance and, 31–32

Privacy, preliminary planning considerations, 11–12

Professional draftsman. *See* Draftsman

Project location. *See* Location of project

Property lines
preliminary plans, 14–15
survey, for fencing, 275

Proportioning, concrete work, 151, 154–155

Protective gear. *See* Personal protective gear

Pumped concrete
described, 167–169
pattern-stamping and, 211

Purlins, cover construction, 270

Quality concrete, described, 147–148

Quantity calculations
mix-it-yourself concrete, 152–154
ready-mixed concrete, 164–166

R. L. Spillman Company, vii

Rafters, cover construction, 267, 269

Rail fences, described, 283

Railing posts, fasteners and, 62

Railings
construction of, 127–131
deck structure and, 35–36
design details, 47, 51, 52

Rail panels, plywood selection chart for, 27

Ready-mixed concrete, 164–169

Ready-packaged concrete mixes, 162–164

Reciprocating saw, described, 102, 103–104

Red cedar
decay resistance and, 30
lumber selection chart, 21, 22

Red oak, lumber selection chart, 23

Redwood
advantages of, 115
decay resistance and, 30, 31
information sources for, vii
lumber selection chart, 21, 22
pavers, soft-set paving, 245
structural design calculations for, 43
structural design considerations, 36, 38, 40

wood preservatives, 64

Reed covers, described, 264

Reinforced concrete slabs, described, 171–173

Respiratory protection, 72–73

Rexford Chemical Products, Inc., vii

Robertson head screws
power screwdriving, 57, 59
screwdriver selection and, 77

Rock–salt finishes, concrete finishes, 198–199

Roof, cover construction, 271

Roofer's square, described, 81

Rubber gloves, concrete work, 132

Rustic terrazzo, exposed-aggregate slabs, 222–225

Saber saws, described, 98–103

Safety goggles
concrete work, 132
described, 71–72
pressure-treated woods, 32

Safety precautions. *See also* Personal protective gear
carpentry, 68–69, 70
concrete work, 182
cordless tools, 93–95
finishes, 67
portable power tools, 88–89
pressure-treated woods, 32

Sanding, plywood and, 28

Sanding pads, electric drills, 91

Sand-jointing, soft-set paving, 247–249

Sandpaper, abrasives, 68

Sand wetness adjustments, concrete work, 155–156

Sapwood, decay resistance and, 29, 30

Sawhorses, described, 83

Saws
circular saw, 96–98
concrete work, 135
hacksaws, described, 76
handsaws, described, 75–76
reciprocating saw, 102, 103–104
saber saws, 98–103

Scale, preliminary plans, 14

Scale (bathroom scale), concrete work, 136

Screeds, concrete work, 179

Screening, privacy and, 12

Screw(s)
described, 55–60
screwdriver selection and, 76–77

Screwdriver, described, 76–77

Sealer, exposed-aggregate slabs, 225

Self-drawn plans, preliminary plans, 14–15

Shade cloth covers, described, 264

Shape and space considerations,

preliminary planning considerations, 7

Sheet-metal screws, described, 57, 60

Shoes, personal protective gear, 73

Sides and ends, construction layout, 112–113

Sika Chemical Company, vii, 161

Site layout, patio construction, 230

Site plan, preliminary plans, 12–13

Size
deck and patio planning, 5, 7
span considerations, deck structure, 34

Slab design, 170–173

Slab forming, 175–179

Slab preparation, 173–175

Sledgehammer
concrete work, 134
described, 75

Slump, concrete work, 164

Soft pine, structural design considerations, 36

Soft-set paving. *See* Pavers: soft-set paving

Softwoods
grade standards, 24
plywood selection, 26, 27
selection guides, 22–23

Soil(s)
loadbearing capacity, deck structure, 33–34
structural design and, 41–43

Soil-cement backfill, fence post setting, 287–288

Solvents
deck paints, 67
respiratory protection, 72–73

Southern pine, structural design considerations, 36

Space and shape considerations, preliminary considerations, 7

Span considerations
deck structure, 34
structural design and, 36–40

Spas, structural design and, 43

Splitting reduction
drill techniques for, 93
nails and, 55
screws and, 57, 59

Spruce
lumber selection chart, 22
structural design considerations, 36

Squares, described, 79–81

Stains, finishes, 64, 65, 66–67

Stair construction, 123–127
basics of, 123–124
layout, 124–126
planning of, 124
stringer support, 126–127

Stair treads, framing anchors for, 64
Staking
    construction layout, 112
    soft-set paving, 241
Stamp pads, described, 212
Steel trowels and troweling
    concrete work, 189–191
    described, 142–143
Steel wool, abrasives, 68
Stone
    hard-set paving, 256–257
    patio construction, 229
Storage units, plywood selection
    chart for, 27
Strength, span considerations, deck
    structure, 34
Strength and durability require-
    ments, concrete work,
    149–150
Strikeboards, described, 139
Strikeoff, concrete work, 184
Stringers
    layout of, 125–126
    supports for, 126–127
Stringlines, concrete work, 135
Stripping wheel, electric drills, 91, 93
Structural design, 36–43
    beams, 38–40
    calculations for redwood deck, 43
    planks, 36–38
    posts, 40–43
Subbase, soft-set paving, 245
Swirled finishes, concrete finishes,
    196–197

Tampers, described, 133–134
Tape measures. See Measuring tapes
Tax effects, preliminary planning
    considerations, 9–10
Temporary screeds, concrete work,
    179
Terrain See Lot topography
Terrazzo, rustic terrazzo, 222–225
Textured finishes, concrete, 194–199
Texturing brushes, described, 144
Texturing floats, described, 144
Thompson's Water Seal, vii

Thoro System Products, Inc., vii
Tile
    hard-set paving, 257–258
    patio construction, 226
Tool belt, 84
Tool board, 84
Tooled-in treatments, concrete fin-
    ishes, 199–201
Tools. See Carpentry tools; Concrete
    construction tools
Topography. See Lot topography
Torpedo level, described, 82
Trellis fences, described, 279
Trowels
    small trowels, 140
    steel trowels, 142–143
Try square, described, 79, 81
T-strap, 63
Turpentine, finishes, 67
Two-course integral coloring tech-
    nique, described, 205–208

Uniformly distributed loads, deck
    structure, 34
United Gilsonite Laboratories, vii
Utility knife, concrete work, 136

Variable-speed drills, 93–94
Views, preliminary planning consid-
    erations, 11–12
Vises, described, 83–84

W. R. Grace and Company, vii, 161
W. R. Meadows, Inc., vii
"Walking" the project, preliminary
    plans, 15, 18
Walks
    deck and patio planning, 9
    lumber selection chart, 22
Waste disposal
    finishes, 67
    pressure-treated woods, 32
Waste minimization
    ordering wood, 33
    plywood working and, 28
Water-repellent preservatives. See
    Wood preservatives

Water tube level, described, 82
Weather Exposure lumber,
    described, 32
Western cedar, structural design con-
    siderations, 36
Western larch, lumber selection
    chart, 21, 22
Western pine, structural design con-
    siderations, 36
Western red cedar. See Red cedar
Western spruce, lumber selection
    chart, 21
Western Wood Products Association,
    vii
Wheelbarrow, described, 137
Wheelbarrow ramp, concrete work,
    179
White cedar, lumber selection
    chart, 22
White fir
    lumber selection chart, 22
    structural design considerations,
    36
White oak, lumber selection chart, 23
White pine, lumber selection chart,
    21, 23
Willson Safety Products, vii
Winds, joist placement, 117–118
Wire-brush wheels, electric drills,
    91, 93
Wire nails, described, 52
Wood. See also Carpentry: lumber;
    Plywood
    information sources for, vii
    patio construction, 228
Wood covers, described, 260
Wood preservatives
    decay resistance and, 32–33
    finishes, 64
Woodworking. See Carpentry
Working plan, described, 18–19

Yellow pine, lumber selection
    chart, 23

Zinc-coated nails, described, 52
Zinc-plated drywall screws, 57